CHILDREN
MOVING:
A REFLECTIVE
APPROACH TO TEACHING
PHYSICAL EDUCATION

Mayfield Publishing Company

CHILDREN MOVING:

A REFLECTIVE APPROACH TO TEACHING PHYSICAL EDUCATION

GEORGE GRAHAM

SHIRLEY ANN HOLT/HALE

TIM McEWEN

MELISSA PARKER

Credits

PAGE i *Rhymes and Reasons* by John Denver. © Copyright 1969, 1970 Cherry Lane Music Co. International Copyright Secured. All Rights Reserved. Used by Permission.

PAGES 6, 60 From *Ribbin', Jivin' and Playin' The Dozens* by Herbert L. Foster. Copyright 1974 by Ballinger Publishing Company.

PAGE 9 From *Teachers Make A Difference* by Thomas L. Good, Bruce J. Biddle, and Jere E. Brophy. Copyright © 1975 by Holt, Rinehart and Winston. Reprinted by permission of Holt, Rinehart and Winston.

PAGE 14 From "Schema Theory: Implications for Movement Education" by Richard Schmidt, *Motor Skills: Theory Into Practice*, 1977, Vol. 2, No. 1.

PAGE 26 From "Professional preparation of the elementary school physical education teacher" by Margie R. Hanson. *Quest*, Monograph XVIII, Spring Issue, June, 1972.

PAGES 26, 30, 51 Reprinted by permission of Schocken Books Inc. from *On Teaching* by Herbert Kohl. Copyright © 1976 by Herbert Kohl.

PAGE 38 From *Freedom and Beyond* by John Holt. Copyright © 1972 by John Holt. By permission of the publisher, E. P. Dutton.

PAGE 38 Reprinted from *Born to Win* by Muriel James and Dorothy Jungeward. Copyright © 1973 by Addison-Wesley Publishing Company, Reading, MA.

PAGES 40, 82 From "Quiet Individualizing: What One Teacher Did." In D. Hellison (Ed.), *Personalized learning in physical education*. Washington, D.C.: American Alliance for Health, Physical Education, and Recreation, 1976.

PAGE 42 From *The Inner Game of Tennis* by W. Timothy Gallwey. Copyright © 1979 by Random House, Inc. Reprinted by permission of the publisher.

PAGE 46 From "Teacher behavior" by L. F. Locke and D. Lambdin. In D. Hellison (Ed.), *Personalized learning in physical education*. Washington, D.C.: American Alliance for Health, Physical Education, and Recreation, 1976.

PAGES 60, 63, 107 From *The Naked Children* by Daniel Fader. Copyright © 1971 by Daniel Fader. Reprinted by permission of the publisher, Macmillan Publishing Co., Inc.

PAGE 66 From *Developing Teaching Skills in Physical Education* by Daryl Siedentop. Copyright © 1976 by Houghton Mifflin Co.

PAGES 67, 117 From *The Lives of Children* by George Dennison. Copyright © 1970 by Random House, Inc. Reprinted by permission of the publisher.

PAGE 70 From *Teaching Gymnastics* by E. Mauldon and J. Layson. Copyright © 1965 by MacDonald and Evans. Reprinted by permission of the publisher.

PAGE 79 From *Self Concept and School Achievement* by W. Purkey. Copyright © 1970. Reprinted by permission of Prentice-Hall, Inc.

PAGE 80 From "Evaluation of Processes and Products" by Rosemary McGee in *Physical Education for Children*, edited by Bette Logsdon. Copyright © 1977 by Lea and Febiger, Inc.

PAGE 87 From *Society and the Adolescent Self-Image* by Morris Rosenberg (Princeton University Press, 1965; Princeton Paperback, 1968). Reprinted by permission of Princeton University Press.

PAGE 90 From "Observing Teaching Systematically" by John Cheffers. *Quest*, Monograph 28, Summer Issue, 1977.

PAGE 137 From "The Awful Beginning" by James A. Smith. *Today's Education* April, 1972.

PAGE 139 From "Educational gymnastics is for everyone" by A. Boucher. *Journal of Physical Education and Recreation*, September 1978.

PAGE 141 From "The Little Gymnast" by Dan Zadra. Published in *Young Athlete Magazine*, June 1976, page 8.

Library of Congress Catalog Card Number: 79-91832
International Standard Book Number: 0-87484-467-3

Manufactured in the United States of America
Mayfield Publishing Company
285 Hamilton Avenue, Palo Alto, California 94301

This book was set in Palatino and Helvetica by Computer Typesetting Services and was printed and bound by Von Hoffmann Press. Sponsoring editor was C. Lansing Hays, Maggie Cutler supervised editing, and Carol Talpers was manuscript editor. Art supervision and book and cover design by Nancy Sears. Mary Burkhardt prepared the children's figure drawings, Judi McCarty of Innographics prepared the technical artwork, and David Dwinell was photographer. The book was dummied by Mary Michael McTeague. Michelle Hogan supervised production. Children's artwork was supplied by students in the authors' classes.

CONTENTS

PREFACE / xi

ACKNOWLEDGMENTS / xv

SECTION 1 OVERVIEW / 3

CHAPTER 1   **REFLECTIVE TEACHING** / 5

The Need for Reflective Teaching / 6
Implications of the Reflective Teaching
   Concept / 12
Summary / 12

CHAPTER 2   **TEACHING BY SKILL THEMES** / 13

Characteristics of Themes / 13
Support in the Literature / 14
Skill Themes and Movement Concepts / 15
Context Variation / 19
Summary / 19

SECTION 2 TEACHING SKILLS / 23

CHAPTER 3   **PLANNING / 25**

Reflective Planning / 25
Effective Planning / 27
Lesson Design / 36
Making Planning Enjoyable / 37
Summary / 38

CHAPTER 4   **CLASS, GROUP, AND INDIVIDUAL INSTRUCTION / 40**

Viewpoint / 41
Organizational Patterns for Instruction / 42
Mainstreaming / 49
Selecting a Form of Organization / 50
The Teacher's Role / 51
Summary / 52

CHAPTER 5   **ESTABLISHING A LEARNING ENVIRONMENT / 53**

Fostering Appropriate Attitudes / 54
Listening Skills / 54
Safety / 55
Influence of the Presence of Disabled
    Children / 55
Learning Environment Versus Recess / 57
Summary / 58

CHAPTER 6   **DISCIPLINE / 59**

Helping Individual Children / 60
Class Discipline / 66
Corporal Punishment / 67
Discipline and Teaching / 67
Summary / 68

CHAPTER 7   **OBSERVING, ANALYZING, AND PRESCRIBING / 70**

The Process of Observation / 71
Learning to Observe Effectively / 75
Summary / 78

CHAPTER 8   **EVALUATING STUDENT PROGRESS / 79**

Summative and Formative Evaluation / 79
Evaluation Techniques / 80
Uses of Evaluation / 86
Evaluation in the Real World / 89
Summary / 89

CHAPTER 9   **ASSESSING YOUR TEACHING PERFORMANCE / 90**

Unassisted Assessment Techniques / 92
Student-Assisted Assessment / 92
Peer-Assisted Assessment / 95
Combining Assessment Techniques / 100
A Support Group / 101
Summary / 101

SECTION 3   PROGRAM CONTENT / 105

CHAPTER 10   **DETERMINING GENERIC LEVELS OF SKILL PROFICIENCY / 107**

Levels of Skill Proficiency / 108
Task-Specific Levels / 110
Developmental Stages of Motor Skills / 111
Using Skill Levels in Teaching / 111
Summary / 111

CHAPTER 11   **TEACHING GAMES / 113**

Game Experiences / 113
Game Lesson Designs / 117
Which Game Design Is Best? / 121
A Final Thought / 121
Summary / 121

CHAPTER 12   **TEACHING DANCE / 123**

Purpose of Dance in Elementary School / 123
Dance Forms / 125
The Content of Expressive Dance / 126
Dance Experiences / 128
Dance-Making / 132

The Process of Teaching Dance / 133
A Final Thought / 136
Summary / 138

CHAPTER 13   TEACHING GYMNASTICS / 139

Purpose of Gymnastics / 140
Content of Educational Gymnastics / 141
The Process of Teaching Educational
    Gymnastics / 146
A Final Thought / 148
Summary / 148

SECTION 4 MOVEMENT CONCEPT AND SKILL THEME DEVELOPMENT / 151

CHAPTER 14   TEACHING SPACE AWARENESS / 153

Developing the Concept of Self-Space / 154
Developing the Concept of General Space / 156
Developing the Concept of Directions / 159
Developing the Concept of Levels / 161
Developing the Concept of Pathways / 164
Developing the Concept of Extensions in
    Space / 168
Applying the Concept of Space Awareness / 169

CHAPTER 15   TEACHING EFFORT CONCEPTS / 172

Developing the Concept of Rate of
    Movement / 173
Developing the Concept of Weight / 177
Developing the Concept of Flow / 180
Applying the Effort Concepts / 183

CHAPTER 16   TEACHING RELATIONSHIPS / 185

Developing the Concept of Relationships / 185
Developing the Concept of the Relationships of
    Body Parts / 187
Developing the Concept of Relationships with
    Objects / 193

Developing the Concept of Relationships with People / 201
Applying the Concept of Relationships / 209

CHAPTER 17 **TRAVELING / 211**

Travel Patterns / 211
Levels of Skill Proficiency / 217

CHAPTER 18 **CHASING, FLEEING, AND DODGING / 239**

Chasing / 239
Fleeing / 240
Dodging / 242
Levels of Skill Proficiency / 242

CHAPTER 19 **JUMPING AND LANDING / 257**

Fundamental Jumping Patterns / 257
Vertical and Horizontal Jumping / 258
Levels of Skill Proficiency / 258

CHAPTER 20 **ROLLING / 286**

Levels of Skill Proficiency / 291

CHAPTER 21 **BALANCING / 309**

Static and Dynamic Balance / 309
Levels of Skill Proficiency / 311

CHAPTER 22 **WEIGHT TRANSFER / 330**

Levels of Skill Proficiency / 330

CHAPTER 23 **KICKING AND PUNTING / 342**

Levels of Kicking Skill Proficiency / 342
Levels of Punting Skill Proficiency / 356

CHAPTER 24 **THROWING AND CATCHING / 367**

Levels of Throwing Skill Proficiency / 367
Levels of Catching Skill Proficiency / 375

CHAPTER 25 **VOLLEYING AND DRIBBLING / 400**

Levels of Volleying Skill Proficiency / 400
Levels of Dribbling Skill Proficiency / 416

CHAPTER 26   STRIKING WITH RACKETS AND
                  PADDLES / 429

                  Levels of Skill Proficiency / 429

CHAPTER 27   STRIKING WITH LONG-HANDLED
                  IMPLEMENTS / 445

                  Levels of Skill Proficiency / 454

SECTION 5 DREAMS / 477

CHAPTER 28   PHYSICAL EDUCATION FOR TOMORROW'S
                  CHILDREN / 479

APPENDIX 1   APPROACHING DANCE THROUGH MUSIC:
                  A LIST OF SOURCES / 485

APPENDIX 2   PARTNER STUNTS / 489

INDEX / 495

PREFACE

We are teachers of children first. And writers second. As teachers we have worked in suburban, small town, private, and inner-city schools. We have taught on playgrounds and fields, in classrooms, gymnasiums and hallways, and in rooms that seemed no larger than closets. We have worked with children from three to twelve, black and white, rich and poor. Some of them loved physical education. Others hated it. A few were ambivalent. We have worked for administrators who were cooperative and helpful, and for some who were indifferent. We have known hostile, apathetic, eager, and supportive parents.

In this text we share information, about children and about teaching physical education, that we believe will be useful to other teachers. Whenever possible we combine discussion of theory with illustrations from our teaching experiences. We avoid discussing the cognitive, affective, and physical dimensions of learning as separate entities, because those dimensions are not separate in teaching situations. Anecdotes are included, to help others learn from our mistakes and to demonstrate that teaching is not an exact science.

The book is divided into five sections. Section One is an overview of the ideas that guide our teaching. Chapter One acquaints the reader with our philosophy of physical education and provides a definition of reflective teaching. Chapter Two describes how we structure the curriculum to present an alternative to teaching based on grade levels.

Teaching skills are the focus of Section Two. This entire section emphasizes the need to know how to teach. The purpose of Section Two is to describe, with examples, the teaching skills that we have found to be prerequisites to successful teaching. Preactive skills (those used prior to teaching), active skills (those used while working with children), and postactive skills (those used after the lesson has been concluded) are discussed in these chapters.

This is a book about children and about the teaching process in the real world. It is not about homogeneous classes of children or about perfect or predictable situations—there are none. We stress teaching skills as much as content in an effort to help teachers achieve increased effectiveness. You may find less theory and more application than you expect. For those readers who are particularly interested in theory, we have cited additional sources.

We do not assume that all the children in a class are equally skillful or equally developed physically. They are not. A reflective teacher observes the children as individuals, as well as the class as a whole. And so we have included observation techniques and hundreds of ideas about what to look for when observing. The reflective teacher also takes into consideration such factors as class size and available equipment and facilities. And so we talk about teaching the class as a whole, in groups, and as individuals, and we provide development ideas for each of these. And we include instructions for some easy-to-make and fun-to-use equipment.

The content of teaching is examined in Section Three. The first chapter in this section describes a system for assessing the physical abilities of the children in order to provide tasks that match their skill levels. These assessments are used in the selection of appropriate physical education activities. The remaining chapters in this section discuss the teaching of games, dance, and gymnastics as related to the development of skill themes.

Section Four contains the teaching content of the book. The first three chapters describe how we teach the movement concepts of space awareness, effort, and relationships. The next eleven chapters describe the development of skill themes. In each of the skill theme chapters, numerous tasks—presented under Ideas for Development—are arranged in a sequence based on the children's levels of proficiency. Guides for the observation of each task are also provided.

The ideas for development of each movement skill are divided into four levels: precontrol, control, utilization, and proficiency. The ideas within each level are presented in a progression that is intended to help the children acquire proficiency in each skill. Many of the ideas for development are expandable. They can be used with children who are at various skill levels.

In the final section we talk about the way things would be for students and teachers of physical education, if we could have our way

Topics that are vitally important to teachers—such as ways to meet the needs of individual students, discipline, mainstreaming, safety, and creating interesting lessons—are discussed in this book. Individual insights, gained during years of teaching experience, and ideas to enhance teacher success are sprinkled throughout the text. We hope these will help the reader feel more comfortable in the struggle to become a successful teacher.

We have tried to write a text that is philosophically consistent. The activities suggested in Section Four are in accordance with the philosophy expressed in the first three sections. Teaching is presented as an ongoing developmental process that can be as exciting as it is challenging. We hope that by sharing our experiences we can help others to enrich the lives of children.

The four authors share the teaching philosophy on which this book is based. We all consider ourselves to be reflective teachers. We want physical education to be an enjoyable experience for all youngsters. And we want the children in our classes to learn movement skills that will enhance their lives—as children now, and as adults in the years to come.

Our philosophy has evolved during our teaching careers, as have our teaching skills. And both will continue to develop as long as we teach. We hope that, by sharing with you our beliefs and our ways of teaching, we are encouraging you to think about the teaching process and so to develop your own philosophy and techniques—and as much pleasure in your work as we have in ours.

ACKNOWLEDGMENTS

We wish to express our appreciation to the children of the following elementary schools: Christ the King in Atlanta, Georgia; Codwell in Houston, Texas; Barnett Shoals, Gaines, and Oglethorpe in Athens, Georgia; and Linden in Oak Ridge, Tennessee. Not only did these children help us with certain aspects of the book but, more importantly, they also taught us the meaning of reflective teaching.

To those administrators and friends who supported our efforts through their encouragement and cooperation, especially Estelle Farmer, Daphne Hall, Sister Jean Liston, Daisy Mathis, Fran O'Meara, Robert Smallridge and Ida Lou Stephens, we offer special thanks.

L. David Dwinell labored under less than ideal circumstances to provide us with a wealth of perceptive and varied photographs. Mary Burkhardt translated a series of cold, impersonal sketches into the warm reality that represents the world of children. We thank you both for your sensitivity to children as you helped make the book come to life.

We are grateful to the following individuals who reviewed the manuscript in its various stages, providing us with thorough, insightful and useful analyses: Dolly Lambdin, University of Texas; John Fowler, University of Colorado; Betty Keough, Illinois State University; Corlee Munson, University of Oregon; Glenn Norris, Montana State University; Marie Riley, University of North Carolina-Greensboro: Robert Pestolesi, California State University-Long Beach; Anne Scarborough, San Jose State University; and Betty Jane Wilheim, San Diego State University.

A special thank-you is extended to the staff at Mayfield Publishing Company for their humanistic professionalism. C. Lansing Hays, we thank you for your confidence in the project throughout. Carol Talpers, we thank you for your painstaking, exact editing of such a complex manuscript.

Our three typists did excellent work with patience and understanding even under the pressure of deadlines—thanks to Linda Kobel, Beverly Kozlowski, and Judy Mitchell.

Finally, and most especially, we want to express our appreciation to our families, who supplied the hope and support that enabled this dream to come true.

CHILDREN MOVING:

A REFLECTIVE APPROACH TO TEACHING PHYSICAL EDUCATION

RHYMES AND REASONS

John Denver

So you speak to me of sadness and the coming of the winter,
Fear that is within you now that seems to never end,
And the dreams that have escaped you
                    and the hope that you've forgotten,
And you tell me that you need me now,
                    and you want to be my friend.
And you wonder where we're going,
                    where's the rhyme and where's the reason,
And it's you cannot accept it is here
We must begin to seek the wisdom of the children
And the graceful way of flowers in the wind.

For the children and the flowers are my sisters and my brothers,
Their laughter and their loveliness would clear a cloudy day
Like the music of the mountains and the colors of the rainbow
They're a promise of the future and a blessing for today.

Tho the cities start to crumble and the towers fall around us,
The sun is slowly fading and it's colder than the sea.
It is written from the desert to the mountains they shall lead us
By the hand and by the heart they will comfort you and me.
In their innocence and trusting they will teach us to be free.

For the children and the flowers are my sisters and my brothers,
Their laughter and their loveliness would clear a cloudy day
And the song that I am singing is a prayer to non-believers,
Come and stand beside us, we can find a better way.

SECTION 1
OVERVIEW

In the first two chapters, we describe key aspects of the reflective approach. The first chapter, Reflective Teaching, describes critical variables that significantly influence one's success as a teacher. Rather than presenting a single approach that is intended to succeed for every teacher in every school, we focus on trying to reach every child by matching the physical education program to the environmental characteristics of a particular school. We have termed this approach reflective teaching.

The second chapter, Teaching by Themes, describes an alternative to the usual organization of the physical education curriculum into games, dance, and gymnastics. Skill themes transcend each of these areas and provide an appropriate focus for the teacher. These themes also differentiate between the actual movements (skill themes) and the various qualities (concepts) that characterize movements.

CHAPTER 1
REFLECTIVE TEACHING

**The good teacher must relate his teaching to the world
of his students as it is, not as he would like it to be.**
HERBERT FOSTER

In any physical education class you will find children who are there
because they must be, not because they want to be. And you will find
some who are eager to become skillful enough to participate in varsity
athletics. We are determined to foster the development and enthusiasm
of all the children in our classes. We want all of them to experience
success and pleasure and a sense of competence.

No two children are exactly alike. There are obvious physical differences and more subtle personality and individual differences. What
is exciting to one child is boring to another. Some youngsters are able
to accomplish a great deal on their own. Other children require almost
constant monitoring if they are to accomplish anything. For each child
who delights in the challenge and camaraderie of a team game, another
will prefer the challenge and satisfaction of individual activities.

Children are different, and so are the schools they attend. Some
school buildings have open designs. Others are divided into permanent classrooms. Administrators can be strict, stultifying, or supportive.
Fellow teachers can be cooperative or competitive, helpful or obstruc-
tive. Gymnasiums, plentiful physical education equipment, adequate
field space, and small class sizes are basic necessities in some elementary schools; others view such facilities as frills. Parents are concerned,
meddlesome, apathetic, helpful, or unavailable.

And how is a teacher to succeed amidst this diversity? We have no
magical answers. But we are convinced that a linear approach* to

---

*Dwight Allen defined *linear thinking* as searching for the answer to a problem by
investigating a single solution without considering feasible alternatives (Allen, 1975).

teaching is not effective. And so we have developed the concept of reflective teaching. The successful teacher who achieves professional satisfaction employs a variety of teaching skills that interact effectively with the particular teaching environment. We have termed this type of teaching "reflective."

The concept of reflective teaching is not new. Indeed, it seems likely that reflective teaching has been practiced since the beginning of formal education. Nor are we attempting to add another term to an already cumbersome educational jargon. What we are trying to convey is the concept that effective* teaching is situational rather than generic. A teacher who succeeds in suburbia may fail in the ghetto, unless the techniques and skills used are adapted to the specific educational environment. Too many teachers start their careers with standard pedagogical skills but without adequate understanding of the influence of the circumstances in which these skills are to be used. For a number of teachers the attempt to transplant predesigned programs of education without considering the ecology of a given school has been disastrous for both the children and the teacher.

As used in this book, the term *reflective teaching* does not refer to any particular methodology or style of teaching. Rather, it refers to the many teaching skills employed by individuals who are respected as master teachers. The reflective teacher is one who can design and implement an educational program that is congruent with the idiosyncrasies of a particular school situation.

Invariant teaching, unlike reflective teaching, is characterized by the use of one approach in all teaching situations (see Table 1.1). For many years educational researchers have tried to determine which pedagogical skills are used by a successful teacher. We are far from establishing a definition based on research. However, the terms *reflective teaching* and *invariant teaching* have helped us to more clearly define and better understand *some* of the components that seem to collectively constitute "good" and "bad" teaching.

THE NEED FOR REFLECTIVE TEACHING

The casual observer who visits a number of classes or schools may not be conscious of the differences in teaching environments. However an experienced teacher is often aware of those differences and can describe how they influence students, teachers, and teaching (Locke, 1975). Each teaching environment is composed of a variety of factors, as illustrated by Figure 1.1.

Our conversations with teachers, as well as our own experiences, have revealed that the same few characteristics seem to substantially influence what are generally referred to as "good" or "bad" teaching situations. Five of the variables—socioeconomic status of the children, size of the classes, the teacher's education and experience, equipment and facilities, and discipline—are most commonly mentioned by teachers to illustrate the need for reflective teaching. These variables are discussed below.

Some inner-city youngsters often test their teachers according to rules governing their street corner behavior rather than by their teachers' middle class rules and expectations. This testing by street corner rules happens to teachers and administrators in inner-city schools every day. And most of the teachers and administrators neither realize nor understand what is happening. Indeed, until you actually experience this testing—when all your middle-class niceties do not count a damn and you wonder why this kid is doing that to you because you are not as prejudiced as the others and you really want to help blacks—it will be hard, if not impossible, for you to understand what I am talking about.

HERBERT FOSTER
Ribbin', Jivin' and Playin' the Dozens

*The terms *successful teaching* and *effective teaching* are used throughout the book to indicate that, as a consequence of the teaching process, the outcome (product) of a given educational experience has resulted in the sought after multivariate (physical, affective, and cognitive) effects.

Table 1.1 Components of reflective teaching and invariant teaching

VARIABLE	THE REFLECTIVE TEACHER	THE INVARIANT TEACHER
Planning	Adjusts lesson plans to differences between classes and children	Uses the same plan for each primary grade and the same plan for each intermediate grade
Progression within and between lessons	Bases progression on such factors as: (1) rate and extent of improvement of the children; (2) physical skill needs of the children; (3) children's interest in a particular topic or activity	Bases progression on such factors as: (1) six-week units; (2) amount of material to be covered in a semester or year; and (3) a predetermined formula for progression
Methodology	Varies the methodology according to such factors as: (1) kinds of children in the class; (2) purpose of the lesson; and (3) ability of the children to accept responsibility	Employs the same methodology with all classes and hopes that the children will eventually fulfill the teacher's expectations
Curriculum	Designs curriculum for each unique class of children after examining the children to determine their abilities and needs	Utilizes predetermined curricular content without considering such factors as children's ability, community influences, or children's interests
Equipment and facilities	Modifies activities and lessons to available equipment and facilities	Teaches activities and lessons that use available equipment and facilities
Discipline	Attempts to understand management problems, and then seeks the causes, modifying teaching procedure accordingly	Assumes that the children are misbehaving and resorts to punitive measures to modify individual and class behavior
Evaluation	Regularly evaluates the children, and seeks evaluative information about his/her teaching from children and colleagues	Evaluates sporadically, and often bases evaluation on whether children liked the lesson, how long they remained interested, and how well they behaved

Socioeconomic Status of Children The behavioral characteristics of children of low socioeconomic status (SES) and those of middle-high SES are different. Elementary school teachers are aware of these differences. But many teacher education institutions prepare teachers as if children from the inner city were just like children from suburbia. They are not.

For many years elementary school teachers have recognized differences between the learning styles of low SES children and those of middle-high SES children. Recent research on teaching effectiveness has demonstrated these differences. One research summary, for example, pointed out that low SES children succeed better (based on achievement scores) when a direct (teacher-dominated) style of teaching is employed. Middle SES students seem to achieve more when teachers use a less direct pattern of instructional interaction (Rosenshine, 1976).

We are not aware of any studies that have demonstrated a relationship between SES and achievement in physical education. But our experiences in elementary schools are consistent with research data indicating that in middle-high SES schools teaching styles are less direct than in low SES schools (Chapter Four). The socioeconomic status of the children within a school or class has an obvious impact on the teacher that seems to demand reflec-

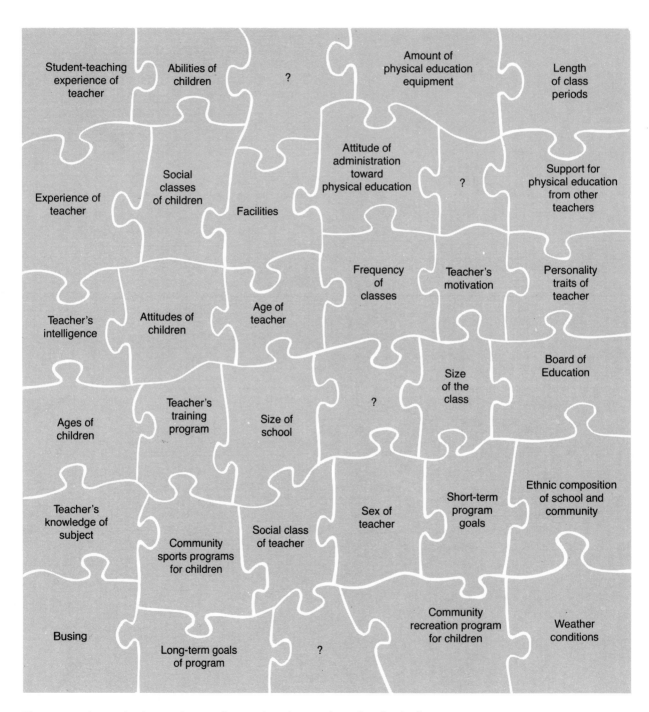

Figure 1.1   Interacting factors that contribute to the unique ecology of each school

There is reason to believe that indirect teaching may be as much an effect as a cause of student behavior. It is much easier to be "indirect" in a classroom full of bright, well-motivated students than it is in a classroom populated by disadvantaged students who find school difficult and are not particularly interested in its curriculum. In the latter type of classroom, teachers are virtually forced to be more direct.

THOMAS GOOD, BRUCE BIDDLE, AND JERE BROPHY
Teachers Make a Difference

tive teaching. And yet socioeconomic status is but one of many variables.

Class Size Another variable—one that is particularly important to the physical education teacher—is class size. Physical education classes are historically the largest classes in a school. One does not need much teaching experience to realize that the number of students within a given class, other variables excluded, dictates in a significant way what a teacher can accomplish. Lessons that are possible with twenty-five children are difficult, if not impossible, with one hundred children.

If a teacher is to do more than provide directions to a mass of children, she or he must have opportunities to observe and analyze, and to provide

At the heart of complexity in the gym is numbers. That the teacher is one and the learners are many is a fact of life which shapes every aspect of the teacher's experience. What many outsiders fail to appreciate is that an average class contains a lot of kids for one person to handle even if there were no intent to teach anything. This failure particularly is true of parents who often feel qualified as experts on child management because they deal more or less successfully with their own children in groups rarely exceeding three or four.

LARRY LOCKE
"The Ecology of the Gymnasium: What the Tourist Never Sees."

feedback to children. The logistical problems of providing individual instruction for each child in a class of fifty children who meet for half an hour are overwhelming. The educational literature provides support for this viewpoint. As Good, Biddle, and Brophy (1975, p. 70) wrote, "The more successful teachers did more tutorial teaching. They spoke to the class as a whole in order to provide structure and give general direction, but most of their actual instruction was given in small groups or to individuals." Class size can determine the teaching approach that a given teacher can use to foster a successful educational experience.

Experience Roland Barth, in *Open Education and the American School* (1972), described his attempt to transplant a program of open education into what had been a traditional school. Barth was aided by a group of apparently enthusiastic teachers who were committed to the concept of open education but had little experience. Reflecting on the results of the unsuccessful experiment, Barth (1972, pp. 143–144) offered the following insight:

> Successful teachers in informal classrooms
> have often taught several years in traditional
> classes. They are experienced teachers who have
> turned to informal methods when they found
> the transmission-of-knowledge model inadequate. These teachers are fully capable of
> running a class like a Marine drill sergeant if
> need be. They don't want to do this, and rarely
> need to; but they know, parents know, and
> the children know that strength and confidence
> underlie their permissiveness and kindness.
> In such classrooms a child can experiment as the
> agent of his own learning, just as he can explore being naughty—with the confidence that
> a strong authority figure is there to back him
> up in case things go awry.

As Barth suggests, experienced teachers often possess teaching skills that permit them to function effectively in a variety of circumstances—to teach reflectively.

Facilities and Equipment   A fourth variable usually mentioned by teachers who are discussing the quality of a physical education teaching situation is the adequacy of the facilities and equipment within a particular school. Established programs of physical education are often characterized by adequate equipment supplies and a reasonable solution to the utilization of indoor space during inclement weather. Fledgling programs of physical education are frequently characterized by a dearth of physical education equipment. In some schools, physical education classes are forced to use classrooms, cafeterias, or even hallways on rainy days.

Some teachers are masters of improvisation. Others are unable to function without adequate facilities and equipment. The teaching skills acquired during student teaching, when equipment and facilities were ideal, often must be adapted to less desirable conditions. You may find that there is only one ball per class, instead of one ball per pupil. You may find yourself, on a rainy afternoon, teaching in a classroom instead of on a playground. Different environments call for different teaching skills.

Discipline   Another variable that contributes to the need for reflective teaching is generally referred to as "discipline"—the process of dealing with children who behave in ways that are unacceptable to a teacher. The ability to effectively discipline children is one of the major concerns in education today, among parents as well as teachers.

The ability to manage a class of children effectively is also one of the few teaching skills that educators agree is a prerequisite to successful teaching. A teacher must be able to create and maintain an appropriate environment if children are to learn.

*Facilities influence the type of
physical education activities that can
be implemented*

Some teachers are able to maintain desirable student behavior by simply glancing occasionally at certain children within a class. Other teachers spend most of their time trying to maintain order. We believe that specific teaching skills can be effectively employed to create and sustain an appropriate environment.

Unfortunately, many textbooks—and many teachers—seem to underplay the role of discipline.

These texts and teachers seem to assume that a "good" teacher does not have discipline problems (Siedentop, 1976).

Our experience suggests otherwise. During a teaching career, a teacher encounters many kinds of classes. Some will test the teacher's ability to maintain appropriate behavior. Others are cooperative. Successful teachers are able to work effectively with both types of classes.

IMPLICATIONS OF THE REFLECTIVE TEACHING CONCEPT

Although many variables interact to create the idiosyncrasies of a particular teaching situation, the five variables discussed above seem to be the most common concerns of elementary school physical education teachers. These are the factors that are most important in determining the environment in which a teacher works—how a teacher adapts basic methods and skills to achieve success in a particular environment.

A reflective teacher assumes that each class is capable of achieving the desired goals. Such a teacher is not content to let the environment limit the progress achieved. Instead, the reflective teacher elicits the most satisfactory educational experience possible from each situation.

SUMMARY

The reflective teacher assesses the ecology of the teaching environment in an attempt to understand the variables that will determine the most effective physical education program for a particular situation. Then the teacher plans the teaching process that will be most effective.

The characteristics of each class are considered. So, too, are the abilities of the individual students. A reflective teacher does not expect all children to respond in the same way or to achieve the same level of skill. A reflective teacher engages in a continual process of observation and analysis. This process facilitates revision of expectations and adaptation of all of the components of the program, so that the effectiveness of the teaching program is constantly being improved. The reflective approach to teaching requires constant, accurate monitoring by the teacher as he or she attempts to design and implement a physical education program for a given school.

REFERENCES

Allen, D. The future of education—Where do we go from here? *Journal of Teacher Education* 26 (1975): 41–45.

Barth, R. *Open education and the American school.* New York: Agathon Press, 1972.

Dunkin, M. J., & Biddle, B. J. *The study of teaching.* New York: Holt, Rinehart and Winston, 1974.

Foster, Herbert L. *Ribbin', jivin', and playin' the dozens: The unrecognized dilemma of inner-city schools.* Cambridge, Mass.: Ballinger, 1974.

Good, T. L., Biddle, B. J., & Brophy, J. E. *Teachers make a difference.* New York: Holt, Rinehart and Winston, 1975.

Locke, L. F. The ecology of the gymnasium: What the tourist never sees. *Southern Association of Physical Education for College Women Proceedings,* Spring 1975.

Rosenshine, B. Recent research on teaching behaviors and student achievement. *Journal of Teacher Education* 27 (1976): 61–64.

Siedentop, D. *Developing teaching skills in physical education.* Boston: Houghton Mifflin, 1976.

CHAPTER 2
TEACHING BY SKILL THEMES

A physical education program for children which begins
with an organized sport is analogous to a language arts program beginning with a Shakespearean sonnet.
IRIS WELSH

Typically, children who are learning to read are taught to recognize
letters, then parts of words, then complete words, and finally sentences. Children who are studying mathematics learn to solve problems after they have grasped the basic functions of numbers and signs.
When a child is learning to play a musical instrument, he or she studies
the scale before attempting a song. In physical education, however,
children frequently are taught games, dances, or complex gymnastic
stunts before they are able to perform the necessary skills. Too often
children know the rules for a game or the formation of a dance but do
not have the skills needed for successful and enjoyable participation.
As an alternative to teaching children how to participate in various
activities, we have chosen to focus on the development of the skills
necessary to function effectively in a variety of situations. We refer to
this approach as teaching by skill themes.

CHARACTERISTICS OF THEMES

In music, a theme reoccurs in different parts of a song, sometimes in
exactly the same way, at other times in a slightly different form. *The
Random House Dictionary of the English Language* defines a theme as "a
short melodic subject from which variations are developed." In physical education, various movements can be thought of as a theme.

By revisiting a movement—sometimes in the same context as before,
sometimes in a slightly different context, and sometimes in a radically
different context—we provide children with variations of a skill theme.
These variations lead to proficiency as well as diversity. Jumping can

be presented as jumping from an object—a box or a table—and landing softly. This movement can be revisited with a slight variation—jumping from an object and landing facing in a different direction from the take-off position. Jumping for distance or leaping in synchronization with the leap of a partner would be radically different, and yet the theme would still be jumping.

Some movements, such as jumping, traveling, and balancing, can be focused on in games, gymnastics, and dance. Other movements, such as throwing and dribbling, are primarily utilized in only one of these three areas. Whenever possible, we point out to students the similarities in movements used in different contexts. This is done to enhance their cognitive understanding of the principles that underlie successful performance of a movement. We are not certain that this influences skill performance (transfer of learning), but it does not seem to have any adverse effects.

The instructor who teaches by themes can focus on helping children to become skillful movers. They will have plenty of opportunities as they grow older to learn games, dances, and gymnastic activities. But first they must learn the basic skills needed for successful participation in these activities.

Essentially, the notion is that these elements are learned in early life through the various activities performed (such as jumping, throwing, striking, and the like), and then when a new act is to be learned in later life, the student can piece together these elements in a more efficient way to achieve the new motor goal. The assumption is that by jumping over objects of various sizes, shapes, heights, etcetera, the student will have more effective "elements" for the performance of the next jumping tasks (e.g., the running long jump in high school).

RICHARD SCHMIDT
"Schema Theory: Implications for Movement Education"

Many adults choose not to play tennis or swim or dance. They do not enjoy these activities because they do not possess the skills needed to participate successfully. An unskilled adult, attempting to learn a complex set of dance steps, may be embarrassed and frustrated. So, too, will the adult who is trying to learn to play tennis but cannot even hit the ball into the opponent's court.

The instructor who teaches by themes and focuses on basic skills can also involve children in games, dance, and gymnastics. The primary goal, however, is to provide children with opportunities to utilize skills in appropriate contexts. The theme being studied determines the activity to be taught and not vice versa.

SUPPORT IN THE LITERATURE
Teaching by themes is not a novel idea. It is utilized in approaches described in other elementary school physical education textbooks (Logsdon et al., 1977; Stanley, 1969; Kirchner, Cunningham and Warrell, 1978; Krueger and Krueger, 1977).

Support for teaching by themes can be found in the research literature. In describing a concept he calls "schema theory," Schmidt (1977) presents the results of studies that suggest that "a variety of movement experiences produces an increased capacity to move." Schema theory suggests that teaching by themes is an efficient way to enhance transfer of basic movements, or movement elements, to more complex movements utilized later in life.

Not all studies of schema theory substantiate the positive implications we describe. Our experience, however, suggests that teaching by themes is an effective way to help children to become skillful movers. We have found that, when utilizing skill themes, we are able to focus on providing children with appropriate movement experiences. When instructors use game, gymnastic, and dance units, children learn how to do the activity but do not necessarily improve their skills. The purpose of physical education in elementary school is to help children learn to become skillful movers. The individual who is a skillful mover can play a sport far more successfully than can the individual who knows a great deal about playing the sport but lacks the necessary skills. Teaching by themes emphasizes the acquisition of appropriate skills.

SKILL THEMES AND MOVEMENT CONCEPTS

We use the terms *skill themes* and *movement concepts* to differentiate between the movements (skill themes) and the ideas (movement concepts) used to modify or enrich the range and effectiveness of skill employment. Skills themes are the major focus of our teaching (Table 2.1). Movement concepts are usually subthemes (Table 2.2).*

The curricular interaction between skill themes and movement concepts can be represented schematically by five concentric circles (Figure 2.1). The two inner circles represent the skill themes; the three outermost circles represent the movement concepts.

The innermost circle includes the general categories of skill themes: manipulative, nonmanipulative,

---

*The major source for this explanation of skill themes and movement concepts is Sheila Stanley's *Physical Education: A Movement Orientation* (1969).

and locomotor skills. The next circle contains a breakdown of the skills in each category. Manipulative skills include throwing, catching, collecting, kicking, punting, striking with rackets and long-handled implements, and dribbling and volleying balls or other objects. Nonmanipulative skills include turning and twisting, rolling, balancing, weight transfer, jumping and landing, and stretching and curling. Traveling movements such as walking, running, hopping, skipping, galloping, chasing, fleeing, and dodging are the locomotor skill themes.

The outermost circle includes the three categories of movement concepts: space awareness (where the body moves), effort* (how the body moves), and relationships. The fourth circle from the center subdivides each of the three movement concept categories. Space awareness is subdivided into location, directions, levels, pathways, and extensions. Effort is subdivided into time, force, and flow, and relationships is subdivided into the categories of body parts, objects, and people.

The movement concepts are subdivided even further in the third circle from the center. The

---

*Some movement analysis frameworks include the concept of space (direct and flexible) as a quality of movement. In our teaching, however, we use this concept so infrequently that we have chosen not to include it in our discussion of the qualities of movement.

Table 2.1   Skill themes

LOCOMOTOR SKILLS	NONMANIPULATIVE SKILLS	MANIPULATIVE SKILLS
Walking	Turning	Throwing
Running	Twisting	Catching and collecting
Hopping	Rolling	Kicking
Skipping	Balancing	Punting
Galloping	Transferring weight	Dribbling
Chasing, fleeing, and dodging	Jumping and landing	Volleying
	Stretching	Striking with rackets
	Curling	Striking with long-handled implements

Table 2.2   Movement concepts

SPACE AWARENESS (WHERE THE BODY MOVES)		EFFORT (HOW THE BODY MOVES)		RELATIONSHIPS
Location:	Self-space and general space	Time:	Fast / slow Sudden / sustained	Of body parts: Round (curved)
Directions:	Up / down Forward / backward Right / left	Force:	Strong / light	Narrow Wide Twisted
		Flow:	Bound / free	Symmetrical / nonsymmetrical
Levels:	Low / middle / high			With objects and / or people:
Pathways:	Straight / curved Zig-zag			Over / under On / off Near / far
Extensions:	Large / small Far / near			In front / behind Along / through Meeting / parting Surrounding Around Alongside Leading / following Mirroring / matching Unison / contrast
				With people: Alone in a mass Solo Partners Groups Between groups

teaching concepts that we utilize, primarily as subthemes to enhance skill acquisition, are contained in this circle.

In Figure 2.1, the two inner circles representing the skill themes are stationary. The three outer circles are connected to each other but are able to rotate around the two inner circles. This rotation illustrates the idea that the same movement concept can be utilized to enhance the development of different skills. The concept of levels in space, for example, is useful for refining such skills as catching, striking, volleying, and balancing. The concept of fast and slow can be applied to the study of such skills as traveling, rolling, dribbling, weight trans-

A PRACTICAL APPROACH TO UNDERSTANDING THE INTERACTION OF SKILL THEMES AND MOVEMENT CONCEPTS

Mount the wheel (Figure 2.1) on a piece of cardboard (a manila folder works well). Cut the wheel between the second and third circles, and glue the outer three circles onto a second piece of cardboard. The two inner circles are attached to the second piece of cardboard by a clasp that allows the inner circles to rotate. This provides a way to explore the interaction between skill themes and movement concepts. If you mount the wheel on poster board, you can illustrate the framework to your classes.

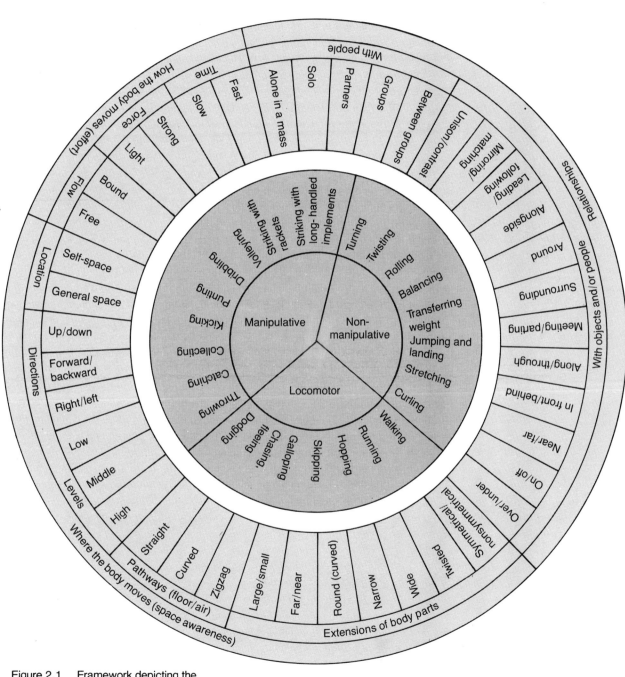

Figure 2.1   Framework depicting the interaction of movement concepts and skill themes

fer, and dodging. At times, some concepts serve as subthemes for other concepts. For example, fast or slow may modify pathways, and forward and backward may be used to modify over and under.

The distinction between skill themes and movement concepts can be clarified by a reference to grammar. Skill themes are always verbs—they are movements that can be performed. Movement concepts are always modifiers—they describe how a skill is to be performed. This distinction also should clarify how movement concepts are employed to embellish, enhance, or expand the quality of a

The framework can be enlarged to help children understand movement concepts and skill themes

movement. A verb by itself—strike, travel, roll—is typically less interesting than when it is modified by an adverb—strike hard, travel jerkily, roll smoothly. Skills can stand by themselves. You can roll or gallop or jump, but you cannot slow or high or under. Concepts modify skills.

CONTEXT VARIATION

Initially movement concepts are taught as themes. The children study the vocabulary that is used to describe movement, and they learn to execute movements that express an understanding of each of the movement concepts (Chapters Fourteen, Fifteen, and Sixteen). After the children have learned this movement vocabulary, the movement concepts are taught as subthemes that foster the acquisition of particular skills.

When teaching a skill, we present the children with experiences that progress from simple to complex. The experiences are generally made more difficult by combining the skill with appropriate concepts. Skills are combined to increase the challenge of a task. We change the context in which the skill is practiced by focusing on different concepts or different combinations of skills.

Each skill theme (Section Four) is represented by a spiral that indicates the progression from simple to complex. This progression is facilitated by variations of the contexts in which a skill is practiced to make it increasingly more challenging (Figure 2.2). The spiral is a graphic reminder that the same context (task) may be revisited and that, when appropriate, the context can be varied to provide the learner with a more difficult challenge.

The concepts of faster or slower, for example, can be used to increase the challenge of a task. But the use of the concept depends on the skill theme being studied. The context variation for the skill theme of rolling or of transferring weight can be made more difficult by challenging the children to move more slowly. But with a skill like dribbling, which is easier to perform at a slower rate, the challenge "dribble faster" increases the complexity of the task.

In short, there is no standard formula that can be used as a guide for varying the contexts in which all skill themes are studied. Each skill theme is different. The spirals illustrate the progression from simple tasks to complex tasks for the skill themes.

The spirals are not intended to suggest the length of time to be spent studying a particular theme. In reflective teaching, the context is varied when appropriate for a particular class or child (see Chapter One).

Finally, the spiral represents a progression from the precontrol level up to the proficiency level (see Chapter Ten). When the context of a movement is varied, many children will regress to a previous level. This does not mean that children will drop from the utilization level or proficiency level to a precontrol level each time the context of a task is varied. But the teacher can expect to observe a variation in skill performance each time the context of a task is varied.

Skill progressions are represented in each chapter by a spiral (Section Four). The order in which the context variations are listed represents a progression from simple to complex, from less challenging to more challenging tasks. These progressions are based on our knowledge of the pertinent literature and on years of teaching experience. But you may find that a different ordering of the context variations is more appropriate for a particular teaching situation. Each child, each class, each teaching environment differs from all others, and the reflective teacher adapts to these differences.

SUMMARY
Teaching by themes represents an alternative to teaching games, gymnastics, and dance. The focus, when teaching by themes, is on the acquisition of specific skills and the use of those skills in a variety of contexts, rather than, for example, on the skills needed to play a particular game. Some skills are studied in games, dance, and gymnastics contexts while others may be studied in only one or another of these contexts.

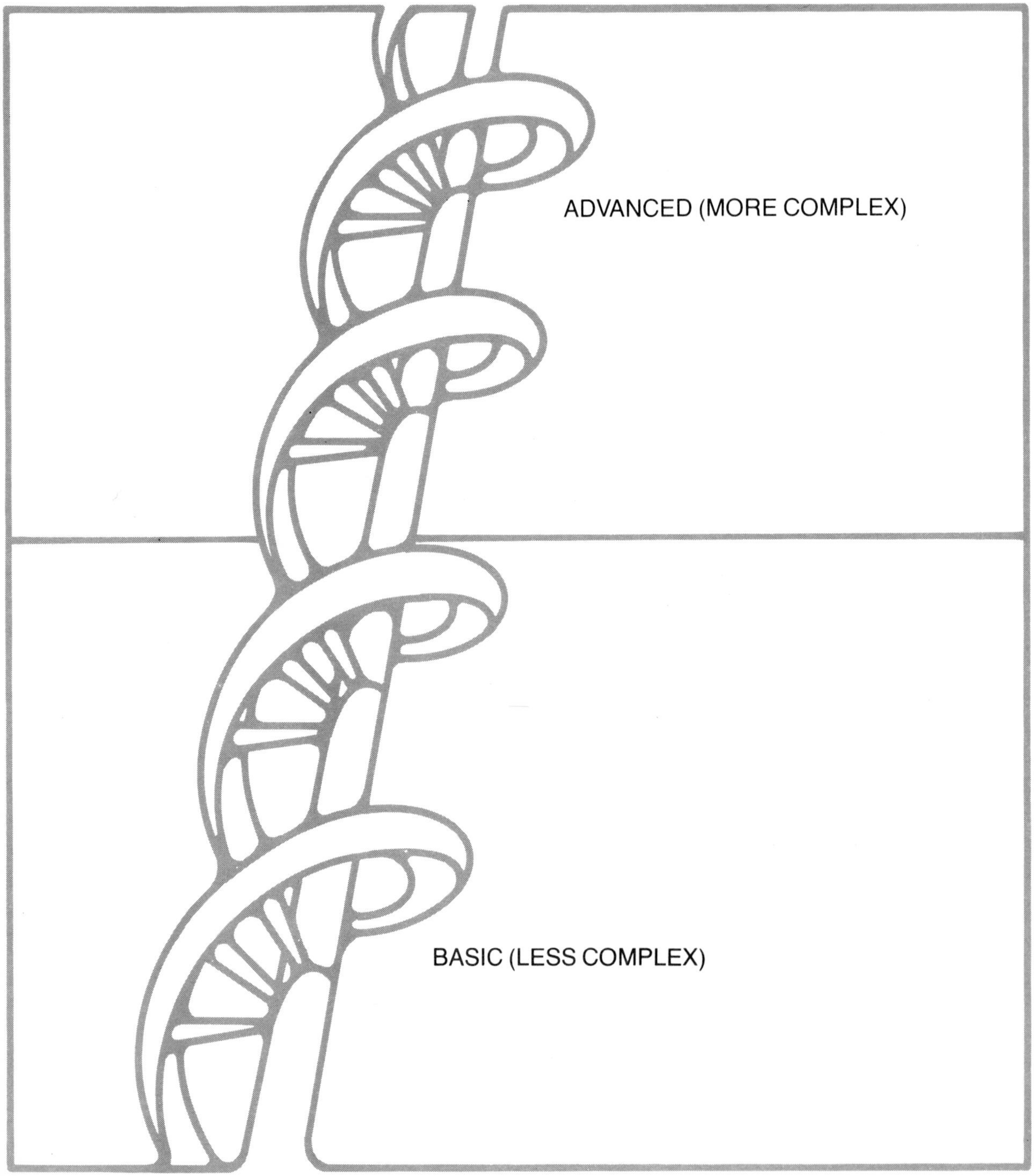

ADVANCED (MORE COMPLEX)

BASIC (LESS COMPLEX)

The research literature describes a concept called *schema theory*. This theory suggests that the individual who learns a variety of skills early in life has an enhanced ability to become proficient in later years. In other words, teaching by themes appears to enhance transfer of learning.

Movement concepts are used to develop the range and efficiency of skill employment. Once children have acquired a functional understanding of a concept—such as the ability to travel in different directions or the ability to differentiate between fast and slow movements—concepts are utilized as subthemes to increase the range and repertoire of their movement abilities.

A teaching progression for skill themes can be represented graphically by a spiral that depicts the contextual variations in which a particular skill theme can be studied. The spiral is a visual reminder that each task is revisited to enhance skill acquisition and retention, and that skills are best learned when presented in a progression from basic to advanced.

REFERENCES

Kirchner, G., Cunningham, J., & Warrell, E. *Introduction to movement education*. Dubuque, Ia.: William C. Brown, 1978.

Krueger, H. & Krueger, J. M. *Movement education in physical education*. Dubuque, Ia.: William C. Brown, 1977.

Logsdon, B. J. et al. *Physical education for children: A focus on the teaching process*. Philadelphia: Lea & Febiger, 1977.

Schmidt, R. A. "Schema theory: Implications for movement education." *Motor Skills: Theory Into Practice* 2 (1977): 36–48.

Stanley, Sheila. *Physical education: A movement orientation*. Toronto: McGraw-Hill, 1969.

Figure 2.2   Progression spiral used to illustrate the contextual variations in which skill themes can be studied

SECTION 2
TEACHING
SKILLS

The successful teacher must know not only what to teach but also how to teach. This section focuses on the teaching skills that we believe are needed by successful teachers of physical education.

The first two chapters, Planning (Chapter Three) and Class, Group, and Individual Instruction (Chapter Four) discuss lesson planning skills. A poorly planned or inappropriately organized lesson often will fail, regardless of a teacher's ability to interact with children.

The next three chapters—Establishing a Learning Environment (Chapter Five), Discipline (Chapter Six), and Observing, Analyzing, and Prescribing (Chapter Seven)—discuss skills that are used in the instruction process. Most of these involve direct interaction with children. Chapter Five includes ideas for differentiating between physical education class as a learning experience and as recess. Practical ideas on discipline are contained in Chapter Six. Approaches for working with individual children and with entire classes are explained, and specific examples from actual teaching situations are included. Chapter Seven focuses on the process of teaching physical education and includes a discussion of the use of teacher feedback.

The final two chapters in this section, Evaluating Student Progress (Chapter Eight) and Assessing Your Teaching Performance (Chapter Nine), are devoted to postactive teaching skills. Behavior is observed and data are collected during a lesson. Assessment or evaluation—of both student and teacher—is conducted after a lesson, or a teaching day, has ended.

CHAPTER 3
PLANNING

"Will you please tell me which way I ought to go from here?"
"That depends a good deal on where you want to get to," said the Cat.
"I don't care much where," said Alice.
"Then it doesn't matter which way you go," said the Cat.
LEWIS CARROLL

Planning may be one of the least enjoyable aspects of teaching. And yet it is essential. Failure to plan appropriately can lead to lessons that are disastrous. Dangles, flip-flops, and an excessive amount of time spent on management characterize the lessons of the teacher who has not planned effectively.

Inappropriate planning can also have long-term implications. One of the important tasks of physical education in elementary school is to provide a variety of learning experiences that give children a broad foundation of movement abilities. Children who are skillful in only a few activities, typically games, may be the products of programs characterized by inefficient planning. The instructor who does not plan is likely to teach only what she or he knows well and the children enjoy. This often results in an unbalanced program over the years.

Because planning is typically done during the teacher's own time rather than during school time, the temptations to avoid planning are strong. It can be much pleasanter to watch television, go to a ball game, or just go to bed early. But planning, even though you may think of it as being as onerous as homework, is necessary.

REFLECTIVE PLANNING

The reflective planner considers many factors when trying to devise the best lessons possible under the circumstances. Planning cannot be reduced to an exact formula. But some factors will always influence the effectiveness of a lesson. Each factor is important, and all interact to determine the teaching environment for which the reflective teacher

Teachers, not properly prepared, turned to elementary game books and exercise charts, or called upon their knowledge of athletics to design programs for children. As a result, many new local guides, even today, reflect programs of simple circle and low organized games, a few singing games, miscellaneous rhythmical activities, calisthenic programs familiar to every serviceman, watered-down secondary sports programs, and the inevitable relays with long waiting lines.

Such stereotyped programs spell the potential demise of elementary physical education. Limited programs make it appear that any aide or para-professional who has a short course or reads a book can perform the task. Parents, principals, and superintendents recall these kinds of programs as part of their childhood experiences, observe them in their own schools, and on that basis often reject the need for well-prepared teachers and for physical education in the curriculum.

MARGIE HANSON,
"Professional Preparation of the Elementary School Physical Education Teacher"

must plan. When planning, we consider class size, frequency of class meetings, available equipment and facilities, personal characteristics of the children, and their skill levels and interests.

Class size often determines the amount and types of information that can be presented. It is fairly safe

One way of discovering what age youngster to begin working with is to visit a lot of schools. Try to find teachers you like and respect, and spend a few days working alongside them. Don't visit for an hour or two. It is important to stay all day (or if you have time, all week) to get a sense of the flow of time and energy working with that age person involves. Of course, your rhythm as a teacher might be different, but it is important to have a sense of what it is like to be with young people all day before becoming a teacher.

HERBERT KOHL,
On Teaching

to assume, for example, that a class of fifteen children will accomplish significantly more in a year's time than a class of sixty children (Glass, Cahen, Smith, & Filby, 1979).

Classes that meet once or twice a week accomplish far less than classes that meet daily. You cannot present as much material in one day or two as you can in five. And children, particularly the younger ones, tend to forget what they learned a week earlier. The teacher who meets a class once a week must plan on spending part of each lesson reviewing last week's lesson. The time spent on review reduces the time that can be spent presenting new information.

If children are to learn and understand a concept or skill, each child will need a number of experiences with a particular task or challenge. When the amount of equipment is limited, all the children must wait and each child has fewer opportunities to use the equipment. One result is that children learn more slowly than they would with adequate equipment that would make it possible to increase learning opportunities.

Equipment also dictates which experiences can be presented. In gymnastics, for example, children who have progressed beyond the initial stages of skill development need apparatus—tables, beams, and vaulting apparatus—that allows them to work off the floor. Only with such equipment will they continue to be challenged. Similarly, nylon hose rackets are appropriate for children who are just beginning to learn to strike with implements. But wooden paddles or rackets are essential if the children are to remain interested in and challenged by the skill theme of striking with implements.

Facilities also influence planning. Kicking can be studied briefly in a limited indoor space. But children can learn much more about kicking when it can be practiced outdoors in a larger area that has a smooth surface. Thus, lack of adequate facilities may prevent you from devoting as much time as you would like to a particular skill theme.

Similarly, the kind of indoor space that is available will influence planning. Most teachers, for example, prefer to teach dance indoors. Hallways, classrooms with furniture that has been pushed aside, school foyers—all these indoor areas can be used for teaching. But these are not ideal settings for teaching many movement themes. It is extremely difficult, for example, to teach locomotor activities in a crowded classroom. However, you can effectively teach the concepts of symmetrical and nonsymmetrical shapes in a crowded, indoor area.

How responsible are the students? The ability of children to function in a variety of environments also influences planning (see Chapters Four and Five). During the first few meetings of a class you can gather observations about the characteristics of the children. This information will be useful when you plan lessons for a particular class. Some classes and some individual children can cooperate with others and work well in less than optimum circumstances. The teacher of such a class can provide experiences that would not succeed with less responsible children. To illustrate, some children in a class are able to work effectively without constant supervision—perhaps in a hall outside the classroom. The teacher of this class can send some children into the hall to work on a particular topic. This decreases the number of children who work in the classroom and so increases the space available to all of the children. A skill theme can be studied more effectively, and for longer, if the class can be split up. The enthusiasm and cooperativeness of a class also influence the way different themes and concepts can be studied.

The factors mentioned thus far are easier to assess than are the skill levels and interests of a class. The teacher must have information about the skill levels and interests of the children, to decide what material is appropriate and how that material is to be presented. You want to challenge the students but not to overwhelm them, so that they will continue to be interested and will want to learn.

If you decide that the class needs to be introduced to the concept of levels (Chapter Fourteen), your plan for this lesson will be determined by many factors, including the ages and skill levels of the children. Young, unskilled children often enjoy the challenge of taking different body parts into different levels—for example, "Can you move your elbow into low level?" "Can you move an ankle into high level?" Intermediate grade children, who might be bored by that task, would probably learn more effectively if challenged to catch or strike a ball at different levels.

When teaching upper-grade children, it is important to consider the types of movement experiences to which they have already been exposed. You will want to take advantage of skills learned in earlier experiences, and you will also want to avoid repetition of material with which students are already familiar. If the children are proficient in the skills used in softball, you may decide to minimize the amount of time spent on the skill theme of striking with bats.

EFFECTIVE PLANNING

The experienced teacher is often able to plan more effectively than the neophyte. A beginning teacher may work hard to plan appropriately, but because of many of the factors listed above the lessons may be unsatisfactory. In contrast, a more experienced teacher can often predict accurately whether a lesson will succeed or fail with a particular class. Many experienced teachers have also developed the ability to modify a plan, during the lesson, to make it more successful. The inexperienced teacher must observe carefully and consider the many factors that influence a class. Gradually, with accumulating experience and hard work, you will find that you are increasingly effective at creating reflective lesson plans.

Reflective planning can best be explained by dividing the process into three steps. The first step involves determining the skill themes and movement concepts that will be taught during a year, as well as the emphasis each theme or concept will receive. This emphasis is expressed in percentage figures. In the second step these percentages are translated into days, organized into a progression, and placed on a daily calendar. The third step consists of planning for each day's lessons.

Step One: Planning the Year   A plan for a year, or one for several years, is really nothing more than an outline of the types of activities (themes) you intend to have the children study during that period of time. Elementary school physical education specialists typically work with the same children for several years, and so long-term planning is as necessary at the elementary level as it is at the secondary level. The content of the plans for the two levels is also different, however.

At the secondary level, physical education teachers typically specialize in certain activities, and the activity in a particular class is changed every few weeks. Thus, many secondary teachers organize the academic year into six-week units. Most elementary schools, however, have only one physical education specialist. This means that elementary teachers have few opportunities to specialize. But the elementary school teacher, who is not bound by arbitrary units

of time, can plan for an entire year. At the elementary level, the instructor has the freedom to focus on a topic for a few days, several weeks, or at intervals throughout the year. A long-term plan can be changed to match the needs and interests of the children. We have learned through experience, for example, that some themes are most effectively taught when presented for brief intervals of two, three, or four days, throughout a year. This is particularly true when teaching younger children. The total time devoted to a theme is the same, whether that theme is presented in one extended period or in a number of brief periods. Variations in the length and continuity of the time devoted to a particular theme can enhance the effectiveness of both planning and teaching.

The School Year Overview Form includes the percentage of time that you decide should be devoted to each skill theme and movement concept in a particular class. When teaching an inexperienced class (Table 3.1) we focus more on concepts than we do when teaching an experienced class (Table 3.2).

PLANNING THE SCHOOL YEAR

The chapters in Section Four are arranged in a developmentally logical sequence. The first three chapters (Chapters Fourteen, Fifteen, and Sixteen) focus on the movement concepts of space awareness, effort, and relationships, respectively. These concepts are initially taught as movement vocabulary words. Once the concepts are understood they are utilized to enhance and embellish the study of individual skill themes (refer to Chapter Two for a more thorough explanation). The remaining chapters in Section Four (Seventeen through Twenty-Seven) offer ideas for developing eleven skill themes.

When planning the school year, it is necessary to focus on the movement concepts before the skill themes. Children need to be taught (or to review) the movement vocabulary before it can be employed successfully in the study of different skill themes. For example, pathways is a movement concept that is a subtheme for skill themes such as throwing and catching, traveling, dribbling and chasing, fleeing and dodg-

ing (Chapter Fourteen contains an explanation of pathways). Rather than breaking the continuity of several lessons on the skill theme of traveling to explain a concept such as pathways, we find it more satisfactory to teach pathways and other movement concepts first. Then when we want children to travel in different pathways, there is no need to stop and explain pathways. The children already know this movement concept and the emphasis can remain on traveling.

We would like to provide an exact, step-by-step progression for the school year, including a day-to-day outline that a teacher could follow with every class they teach. This is unrealistic, however. Teaching situations are too different and varied. The examples of planning guides included in this chapter are intended only as aids to understanding the process of reflective planning. Once an individual obtains a teaching position, it is his or her responsibility to develop yearly and daily plans that reflect the uniqueness of that particular teaching environment.

Table 3.1   Overview of activities for an inexperienced class

MOVEMENT CONCEPT	PERCENTAGE OF CLASS MEETINGS	APPROXIMATE NUMBER OF DAYS
Location	10%	18
Direction, levels, pathways, and extensions	10	18
Relationships with objects and people	10	18
Effort	10	18
SKILL THEMES*		
Travelling	20	36
Throwing, catching, kicking, and punting	10	18
Dribbling, volleying, and striking	5	9
Shapes, turning, twisting, stretching, and curling	10	18
Balancing, transferring weight, and rolling	10	18
Jumping and landing	5	9
	100%	180

Table 3.2   Overview of activities for an experienced class

MOVEMENT CONCEPT	PERCENTAGE OF CLASS MEETINGS	APPROXIMATE NUMBER OF DAYS
Space awareness	5%	9
Effort	10	18
Relationships	10	18
SKILL THEMES*		
Travelling	10	18
Throwing, catching, kicking, and punting	15	27
Dribbling, volleying, and striking	15	27
Shapes, turning, twisting, stretching, and curling	10	18
Balancing, transferring weight, and rolling	15	27
Jumping and landing	10	18
	100%	180

NOTE: These overviews are for a class that meets every day.

*The appropriate emphasis on games, gymnastics, and dance is typically specified in the daily outline.

First, decide which movement concepts and which skill themes you are going to teach, and write these on an overview form. Second, determine what percentage of the class meetings you plan to spend on each concept and theme.

Step Two: Day-by-Day Outline   The next step is to outline the sequence of lessons for each skill theme or movement concept (Table 3.3). For example, let's assume that you have decided to devote approximately 10 percent of the lessons for a particular class to the skill theme of jumping and landing. The day-by-day outline for this skill theme

In most classrooms, . . . there is no time to reflect or hold at a particular point and drift for a while. There is little time to celebrate communal achievement or discuss and respect boredom and weariness. Yet it seems to me that it is crucial that the rhythm of the school year be adjusted to the organic rhythms of individual classes. Learning cannot be parceled out evenly over all the days of the year, and every day cannot be expected to contain the same amount of material to be covered. There must be peaks and valleys, variations in the quality and quantity of work done at different times.

HERBERT KOHL,
On Teaching

Table 3.3   Sample sequence of jumping and landing skill theme: Eighteen-day sequence for an inexperienced class (10 percent of a year's lessons)

DAY	LESSON FOCUS
1	Jump over rope placed on floor, two feet to two feet; hop from one foot to other foot
2	Jump from milk crate, using both feet for two-foot take-off and landing; quiet, balanced landing
3	Jump for distance, using both feet for take-off and landing
4	Jump for height
5	Jump in and out of hoop, using various take-off and landing positions
6	Land in different ways
7	Jump over low obstacles while on the run
8	Shapes while in the air (for example, wide, nonsymmetrical)
9	Rhythmical jumping
10	Use gestures while in the air
11	Invent a series of jumps with slight pauses between jumps
12	Strike an object (balloon, plastic ball) while body is off the floor
13	Jump onto low objects
14	Sequences that include jumping and landing
15	Sequences that include jumping, landing, and various locomotor patterns
16	Rhythmical jumping to different cadences
17	Jumping dance phrases
18	Jumping to throw and to catch

NOTE: These sequence ideas are taken from Chapter Nineteen. They are intended to serve as a starting point but would be varied to suit the needs of classes, groups, and individuals. Some classes, for example, might need to spend several days on jumping for height. Other individuals, who are adept at jumping and landing, could be individually challenged to make shapes in the air while others in the class are still attempting to take off and land on two feet without falling down (intratask variation). Once a teacher understands a sequence, it is easier to logically rearrange the sequence to suit the needs of various individuals and groups.

would be an appropriate progression for that particular theme. In devising that progression, you would take into consideration the factors, discussed earlier, that influence the teaching environment, and you would utilize the information in Chapter Twenty-three. This outline would contain a guideline for each of the days to be devoted to this skill theme. The beginning teacher will often be experimenting in outlining this sequence. This process of sequencing lessons to enhance learning movement concepts or skill themes is a valuable one. With practice, each teacher learns to predict, with increasing accuracy, the appropriate emphasis that a theme or concept should receive in a given class. And experience helps the teacher to adjust the sequence of the lessons to account for individual differences within a class and among classes. Once a sequence has been outlined, the teacher can rearrange that sequence without losing sight of the intended direction or perception of the skill theme or movement concept.

Once the theme or concept has been outlined and arranged into a progression, the next step is to insert the progression into the daily calendar (Table 3.4). Decisions on the number of days in a row to focus on a theme or concept are based on the teacher's knowledge of all the factors that make up the learning environment.

Once an outline is written, it is used only as a guide and is changed as often and as much as a particular situation requires. Outlines should be written in pencil, with lots of space left for changes.

Learning is not totally predictable. If the study of a particular topic is going especially well, we do not change simply because the daily outline tells us to change. If several lessons on a particular topic have proven ineffective, it is possible to change to a different focus even though the daily outline calls for teaching three more lessons on that topic.

The needs and interests of the children are the guide for the lessons to be presented. No outline, however theoretically sound it may be, can unfailingly reflect the progress and the interests of the children being taught.

Step Three: Planning Daily Lessons Short-term planning is typically done after school and in the evenings. This is where the specific variations

Table 3.4 Sample daily sequence of jumping and landing skill theme

MONTH	DAY	PRIMARY LESSON FOCUS
September	17	Jumping over rope on floor; vary landing
	18	Jumping from boxes (milkcrates); quiet, balanced landings
	19	Jumping for distance
	20	Jumping for height
October	10	Jumping in and out of hoop varying takeoff and landing positions
	11	Landing in different shapes
	12	Jumping over low obstacles while on the run
	13	Making shapes while in the air
November	7	Rhythmical jumping
	8	Using gestures while in the air
	9	Inventing a series of jumps while in the air
January	17	Striking objects while airborne
	18	Jumping onto low objects
March	22	Sequences which include jumping and landing
	23	Sequences which include jumping and landing in combination with various locomotor patterns
April	19	Rhythmical jumping to different cadences
	20	Jumping dance phrases

among individuals and classes are taken into account (Chapter Four). Long-term planning is typically done before the school year begins, before a teacher knows the individual children she or he will be teaching. Thus, it is in daily lesson planning that individual variations can be accommodated.

Lesson ideas are generated from a number of sources, including notes from classes, your own observations and those of others, books, workshops, conferences, articles, and discussions. Planning for

lessons involves sifting through sources and then designing lessons to match the needs and characteristics of a particular class. We have found few, if any, predesigned lessons that worked for us the way they supposedly worked for their authors. And so, instead of including specific lesson plans, this book contains Ideas for Development to encourage you to develop your own plans.

The sample guide for Reflective Planning (Figure 3.1) contains vital information that needs to be con-

GUIDE FOR REFLECTIVE PLANNING

CLASS NAME _Mrs. Kobel's 3rd Grade_ CLASS SKILL LEVEL _Control-Utilization_

LENGTH (TIME) OF LESSON _10-10:30_ # OF MEETINGS PER WEEK _2_

EQUIPMENT TO BE USED: 1) _Hoops_ 2) _Stretch ropes_

3) _Blocks and canes_ 4) _Table and mats_ 5) _Milk crates_

ORGANIZATIONAL PATTERN _Scattered; learning centers_ FACILITY _Outdoor blacktop_

MAJOR SKILL THEME OR MOVEMENT CONCEPT _Jumping and landing_

SUBCONCEPT(S) OF THEME(S) 1) _Symmetrical and nonsymmetrical shapes_

2) _____

IN THIS LESSON I WANT THE CHILDREN TO LEARN: _To be able to make at least three different (repeatable) symmetrical and nonsymmetrical shapes during flight._

LESSON COMPONENTS	OBSERVATIONAL FOCUS
INTRODUCTION: Travelling throughout general space — stopping on signal in symmetrical and nonsymmetrical shapes.	Do the children remember the difference between symmetrical and nonsymmetrical? Are they varying their shapes or relying on only one or two shapes?
DEVELOPMENT: Jumping from a running take-off; emphasizing height and a sustained flight phase.	Are the children using their arms to gain height? Knees bent upon landing? On-balance landings?
5 learning centers — children CORE: choose two to work at: (1) jump into hoops; (2) over slanted rope; (3) over blocks and canes; (4) from table onto mat; (5) from milk crates.	Do children make as many nonsymmetrical shapes as they do symmetrical shapes? Are they able to change from a nonsymmetrical shape into a balanced, symmetrical landing? Utilization, proficiency level: Are they sustaining their shapes or simply making them quickly in preparation for a balanced landing?
CONCLUSION: Which shape is easier to make during flight? Which is better for on-balance landings?	

LESSON EVALUATION (USE REVERSE SIDE):

1) HOW CAN THIS PLAN BE IMPROVED?
2) HOW COULD MY TEACHING PERFORMANCE BE IMPROVED?

Figure 3.1   Guide for reflective planning

sidered if one is to plan reflectively. We have found this form useful in planning lessons and in improving our teaching. It is presented here only as a guide. You may want to change it to adapt it to your particular style of lesson planning.

Planning and teaching are facilitated when each lesson is divided into four related parts—introduction, development, core, and conclusion. These four parts constitute what we call the lesson format.

Introduction   Most children are eager to get started when they arrive for class. We try to provide an initial activity that can be organized quickly, is active, and involves all the children. Here are some sample introductory tasks:

"Find a rope. There's one for everyone. See how many times you can jump without a miss."

"Use only your feet to dribble your ball all over the field. See how fast you can go, but be ready to stop, with your ball under control, as soon as you hear the signal."

"Find a partner. Throw the ball so that your partner has to run to catch it."

"The same music is on that was on yesterday. Form the same group you were in yesterday and continue to work on your sequence to the music."

Often, and especially with young children, you will find that it is counterproductive to ask children to listen to a lengthy explanation at the beginning of a lesson when they are bursting with energy. Once children have had a few minutes to dissipate some of that energy, they are more likely to listen to explanations and to focus on practicing new skills.

During the introductory period we try to create interest in the theme of the day's lesson. Technically this is called *set induction* (Graham, 1975). The purpose is to help the children understand the reason behind a lesson. It can be accomplished by describing the movement or activity planned for the day. And it can be enhanced by asking the children questions that encourage them to think about what they are about to do—"How can you make a ball

curve in the air?" or "During the flight phase of a jump, is it harder to make symmetrical or nonsymmetrical shapes?" Set induction can generate enthusiasm, so that children participate, not because they have to, but because they can't wait to begin.

Development   During this part of the lesson, new ideas or concepts for practice are introduced. Try to keep the explanation brief, so that the children have plenty of time to practice. This can be called skill practice time, because the focus during this phase is on improving skill (rather than on winning a game, for example). This part of the lesson varies considerably in length. Sometimes it is brief. But sometimes the children become engrossed in the activity and then this phase takes up most of the class period.

Core   The core period of a lesson is used for two purposes. One is to provide the variety of activities (stimulus variation) that children need, particularly when they are unaccustomed to working at skill improvement (Graham, 1975). The second purpose is to provide a situation that encourages the children to apply the skill they have been practicing in a different but clearly related context. For example, if the children have been practicing rolling in different directions in the development section of the lesson, during the core period they might focus on rolling in two different directions without hesitating between rolls.

Conclusion   Rather than simply saying, "OK, time to head back to your classroom—bring in the equipment," we try to provide a productive ending to each lesson. This phase can serve two purposes (Graham, 1975). First, it is an excellent time to review, to briefly discuss a skill, a concept, or the children's behavior that day. And second, it can be used to help children to slow down gradually so that the transition from physical education class to the classroom is easier for them. Lengthy conclusions are usually counterproductive. But when conclusions

GYMNASTICS? DANCE? GAMES?

This dialogue is a reconstruction of conversations the four authors had about the organization of this book. This section relates specifically to planning.

GEORGE: What about the question of emphasis in activities? One-third games? One-third dance? One-third gymnastics? Or two-thirds games? A little bit of gymnastics? And a dab of dance?

TIM: A lot of teachers, especially starting out, are most familiar with games. I imagine someone with a gymnastics background would focus more on gymnastics and the same would be true for a dancer. One needs to ask whether it is important to provide children with experiences in all areas, regardless of one's background. We agree that it is, but it is not easy. We are trying to help other teachers by describing the kinds of experiences that are successful with children and that children enjoy.

SHIRLEY: We are trying to present dance and gymnastics so that teachers who have been exposed primarily to games will feel confident in providing children with dance and gymnastics experiences.

TIM: It is easy to say that gymnastics equipment is too expensive, and that children do not like to dance. Obviously we have been able to teach in these areas and succeed. It would be nice to have had all kinds of gymnastics equipment or to have children come in and say, "Let's dance today!" But that is not realistic.

GEORGE: Are we not going to include gymnastics, dance, and games *activities*?

MELISSA: No. Our gymnastics, dance, and games ideas transcend these areas. In essence, we are trying to help children become more skillful—rather than teaching games or dance or gymnastics. There are dance experiences that require skills, games experiences use skills. But it is not as if a skill is totally different in games and dance—the purpose is different, but the movement is related.

GEORGE: Some books are divided into games, gymnastics, and dance activities. If you want to find a related theme (a skill in games, gymnastics, and dance), it is difficult to do. We have designed this book differently. We have taken skills and developed them thoroughly. It should be easier for teachers who want to teach two-week dance units to read the chapters and find dance ideas that will logically combine into a dance unit.

are kept brief and are used to deal with important matters, children pay attention and find this brief time together worthwhile.

Changing Activities   How do you decide when to continue focusing on a concept or theme, and when to change? This can be a difficult decision. Probably the least efficient guide is time. That is, it is not usually productive to plan to spend five minutes on one idea and ten minutes on another, or a week on a theme. We have found that observation, using the techniques suggested in Chapter Seven, can provide cues about the skill levels of the children in a class. Some cues are more valuable with some activities than with others.

We use five criteria in reflecting on a particular activity and making appropriate decisions:

1. What is the success rate being achieved, by individual children and by the class as a whole?
2. Are children able to perform this movement effectively, using correct motor patterns?
3. How many children are on-task and how many are off-task?
4. Are the children interested in the activity?

5. How much time has been allocated, in the long-term plan for the year, to this activity?

Because we want the children to succeed more than fail, we prefer the children to experience success 70 to 80 percent of the time. This can be assessed for an entire class by employing a scanning technique (Chapter Seven) to determine how well the children are able to accomplish a task. If, for example, the children have been challenged to "dribble a ball with one hand as you travel through general space" and we observe that most of the children are chasing after the ball rather than dribbling under control, we would refocus the lesson. In contrast, if the task appeared too easy for the class, we would also refocus the lesson.

Information recorded on the Observation Guide described in Chapter Seven is valuable in making decisions related to change. If the children are performing a movement efficiently, using correct motor patterns, that is clear evidence of the appropriateness of a lesson or a sequence of lessons.

A scanning technique can be used to assess the number of children who are on-task and off-task. If a number of the children in a class are off-task, the task may be too difficult or too easy or uninteresting. As a teacher gets to know a particular class, this judgment becomes more accurate.

Verbal and nonverbal indicators can also be cues about the appropriateness of a task. Relatively quiet involvement in an activity, for example, often indicates the appropriateness of a challenge. Unusual loudness, in contrast, may indicate a general lack of interest. Obviously this, too, depends on the class and on the individuals in the class. Some children seem to complain about everything and consequently are inaccurate barometers.

The final criteria that we use is the long-term plan for the year. While this is probably the least important of the five criteria, it does influence decisions about whether to continue with an activity. Even though the children may be infatuated with a particular theme, if a disproportionate amount of time is devoted to one theme or concept, other topics will receive less attention. We do adjust our long-term plans regularly, but we also try to provide children with the variety of experiences that is so important to overall development.

The successful teacher is able to use cues to make informed decisions about the appropriateness of a particular activity. A decision to refocus within a lesson or between lessons is, for an effective teacher, a conscious decision based on data.

Intratask Variation The daily sequence (Table 3.4) provides overall direction for topics that will be presented to a class throughout a school year. Such a sequence should not, however, be considered immutable. We frequently vary the tasks to make them appropriate for individual children, even though the entire class has been given the same challenge (Chapter Four). Technically we call this intratask variation. An example will help to clarify when and how intratask variation is used.

With an inexperienced class, one of the initial throwing and catching challenges we provide is: "Find a small or large ball, a yarn ball, or beanbag that you want to practice with. Throw and catch to yourself. Try to stay in your self-space." For some of the children, this will be an appropriate, interesting challenge. For others, however, the task may be inappropriate. This is when intratask variation would be used.

As we travel around the area, we observe the success rate of individual children, their throwing and catching patterns, and their levels of skill proficiency. Using this information, we can provide individual children with variations of the initial task—variations within the theme of throwing and catching. We might ask one child to "See if you can make your catches at different levels." A more skilled youngster could be challenged to "See if you can jump to catch the ball." A child who is having little success might be asked if a larger ball or a beanbag would be more interesting.

The teacher who uses intratask variation effectively needs a thorough understanding of the appropriate sequencing for the skill theme that is being taught. Careful planning and experience enhance the use of this technique. Keeping track of intratask sequencing for different children is difficult. A checklist, with the names of the children and the appropriate sequence on the same sheet, is useful here. On this sheet you can record the progress of each child. This checklist can serve as a useful tool for measuring the children's improvement and also your effectiveness as a teacher. A sample checklist, included in Chapter Eight, is based on the Sample Daily Sequence (Table 3.4) in this chapter.

Writing Objectives   We are not convinced of the importance of writing objectives in a specified format or style. In fact, we are not convinced that it is necessary to write objectives for every lesson taught. We realize that this contradicts what many preservice teachers learn as undergraduates. Our discussions with experienced and successful teachers reveal that many of them do not write objectives for every lesson. It is obvious, however, that successful teachers always know the purpose and goals of their lesson—they know what they are trying to accomplish, even though their objectives may not be written.

Because we are not convinced that the ability to write objectives correlates highly with teaching effectiveness, we do not tell you how to write objectives. Our experience suggests that, if you are an education major, you have already had (or will have) several courses that emphasize writing objectives. If you believe that it is important to know how to write objectives, there are a number of very good references available (Mager, 1962; Mager, 1973; McAshan, 1970; Kibler, 1970). We do believe that objectives are necessary. We are not convinced, however, that a teacher needs to write them for every plan every day.

Recording Progress   A reflective teacher needs to record the progress that a particular class, group, or individual makes during a lesson. An elementary school physical education specialist may teach eight or ten or twelve classes a day. Each group and each student will progress to a different degree and in a different way. A reflective teacher, whose approach takes these differences into consideration, will need notes on which to base the next day's (or week's) lessons.

Brief comments can be written in a standard planning book or on index cards. Notes summarizing what was accomplished during a lesson are helpful when planning the next day's lessons. Whenever possible, the day's schedule should include five or ten minutes between classes. This time can be used for recording observations and, if necessary, arranging equipment for the next class. When a schedule does not include time to write notes, particularly when teaching a class as individuals (see Chapter Four), a cassette tape recorder is helpful. Just a few words on tape can help you remember the details of an important observation made during the first lesson of the day. What seemed so clear at 9:00 A.M. is often opaque by 4:00 P.M.

LESSON DESIGN

If children are to develop into skillful movers, they must do more than simply play games that foster skill development. Children need opportunities to practice skills in contexts that are meaningful to them. A successful teacher is able to create practice situations that are enjoyable, appropriately designed, and allow for maximum participation. The teacher who can design interesting and exciting practice situations will rarely hear the question—asked so often by highly skilled unchallenged children—"When do we get to play a game?"

Interesting Lessons   Many children, particularly the younger ones, do not understand the need to practice in order to become more skillful. Nor do they care. Many children are interested only in the present and have little concern about the future, which seems remote. Lessons with immediate meaning are more easily accepted and enjoyed by young children. For example, we would not teach second graders how to turn on one foot by having them do a mass drill. Such an exercise would make little sense to them. We might have them jog around the gym and instruct them to "Spin around on one foot when you hear the drum, and then continue jogging." On the next drum beat we might ask them to "Pivot on the other foot" or to "Spin in the opposite direction." Later, when the children are able to travel dribbling a ball, we might ask them to "Spin on the drum beat while continuing to dribble a ball." We do not teach skills as if all children really want to learn the skill because they intend to play on a varsity team in high school—they do not.

Variety in a lesson also makes it more enjoyable. We try to provide children with a number of related practice opportunities in a single lesson, rather than practicing the same skill the same way for the entire lesson.

Appropriate Lessons   Children want to be challenged and successful at the same time. The ideal task is difficult enough so that the child cannot do it as intended every time, and yet easy enough so that the child is successful much of the time. If a small child tries to make a basketball go through a ten-foot high basket, his success rate may be so low that he will quickly lose interest. If the same child is given options—for example, shooting at a basket that is seven feet high or shooting through a hoop suspended from a pole—his interest will remain higher for longer. And so his skills will improve.

Maximum Participation   One of the clearest differences between more effective teachers and less effective teachers is that the students of more effective teachers actually spend more time practicing than do the children of less effective teachers (Gage,

1978; McDonald, 1976). The value of practice may seem obvious, and yet frequently practice is neglected, particularly in teaching games. When a class of thirty children is practicing a skill such as throwing or catching and uses only three or four balls, their skills will probably improve less than will the skills of children whose teacher designs the same lesson so that there is a ball for every two children in the class.

Remember, though, that not all children have learned to practice on their own. Making more equipment available does not guarantee increased practice time. In fact, we have observed instances where the children in a class actually practiced more when there were only three or four balls available because a majority of the students in the class had not yet learned to work on their own.

MAKING PLANNING ENJOYABLE

Planning is hard work. It takes time and energy to plan effective lessons that are exciting and interesting to children. Teachers who fail to plan well tend to return to old standbys—kickball, dodgeball, and four square—that contribute minimally to the physical education of children.

You will always be able to find something to do that is more interesting than planning lessons. So it is a good idea to devise ways to make planning easier and more fun. We have found the following ideas helpful:

1. Set aside some time each day specifically for planning. Then you will not be constantly trying to find time to plan. Some people find that planning at school before they leave for home is effective. Others prefer to arrive at school early to plan the day.

2. Try to become excited about your plans. When you are excited about trying to present an idea in a new and interesting way, planning is fun and your enthusiasm is communicated to your students.

If this project doesn't interest you, leave it alone, don't imagine that you can make exciting for children what to you is only a bore. Find instead something to do that you can throw yourself into. Let the students see you genuinely interested. Let them see your intelligence, imagination, and energy at work.

JOHN HOLT,
Freedom and Beyond

3. Do not hesitate to experiment. The worst that can happen is that a lesson will not work as planned. When this happens, we tell the children we were trying a new idea and it did not work. Children understand and sometimes make worthwhile suggestions about how the idea might be improved.

When you set aside appropriate amounts of time, try new ideas, and attempt to make lessons exciting, planning becomes more enjoyable. And your attitude toward teaching will be affected. Most of us experience uncertainty when beginning a lesson (or anything else) for which we are unprepared. When you have planned a lesson thoroughly, the assurance and enthusiasm you feel can be contagious.

A bride served baked ham, and her husband asked why she always cut the ends off. "Well, that's the way my mother always did it," she replied. The next time his mother-in-law stopped by, he asked her why she cut the ends off the ham. "That's the way my mother did it," she replied. And when grandma visited, she too was asked why she sliced the ends off. She said, "That's the only way I could get it into the pan."

MURIEL JAMES AND DOROTHY JONGEWARD,
Born to Win

SUMMARY

Planning is a crucial, although not necessarily enjoyable, facet of teaching. Successful teachers plan effectively, not only from day to day but for the entire year. Plans should be used as helpful, but not immutable, guides. As the teacher learns about the individual children and the ecology of the particular teaching situation, plans can and should be adapted to these.

Long-term plans provide an outline of the general topics to be covered throughout a year. When this outline is done as a School Year Overview (Tables 3.1 and 3.2), the percentages can be reflected in a Daily Outline (Table 3.4). This outline provides the teacher with a guide for determining what will be taught on a particular day. When daily lesson planning is based on the long-term plans, the teacher can make certain that appropriate topics are adequately studied.

Intratask variation is a technical term used to describe the process of adapting a lesson to individual children when teaching the class as a whole. A teacher may decide to ask some children to continue working on a challenge, to repeat and refine a movement. At the same time, other children may be ready to go on to another skill in the sequence—or to a skill that has not yet been introduced to the entire class.

Each lesson has four phases: introduction, development, core, and conclusion. Approaches to keeping track of individual student progress and writing helpful objectives were also discussed, as were criteria for determining when to change to a different theme or concept.

Guidelines for designing successful physical education lessons for children include ideas for making lessons enjoyable and appropriate and for maximizing the children's desire to participate in physical education lessons.

REFERENCES

Gage, N. L. *The scientific basis of the art of teaching.* New York: Teachers College Press, 1978.

Glass, G. V., Cahen, L., Smith, M., & Filby, N. "Class size and learning." *Today's Education* (April–May 1979): 42–44.

Graham, G. A bridge between what is and what could be. *The Physical Educator* (March 1975): 14–16.

Hanson, M. Professional preparation of the elementary school physical education teacher. *Quest* (June 1972): 98–106.

Holt, John. *Freedom and beyond.* New York: E. P. Dutton, 1972.

James, M. & Jongeward, D. *Born to win.* Reading, Mass.: Addison-Wesley, 1973.

Kibler, R. J., Barher, L. L., and Miles, D. T. *Behavioral objectives and instruction.* Boston: Allyn and Bacon, 1970.

Kohl, H. *On teaching.* New York: Schocken, 1976.

Mager, R. F. *Preparing instructional objectives.* Belmont, Ca.: Fearon, 1962.

Mager, R. F. *Measuring instructional intent, or got a match?* Belmont, Ca.: Fearon, 1973.

McAshan, H. H. *Writing behavioral objectives: A new approach.* New York: Harper and Row, 1970.

McDonald, F. Report on Phase II of the beginning teacher evaluation study: Overview of the ethnographic study. *Journal of Teacher Education* (Spring 1976): 39–42.

CHAPTER 4
CLASS, GROUP, AND INDIVIDUAL INSTRUCTION

The key to success in such trial runs (individualizing),
I've found, is to go at it quietly, carefully and watchfully.
Don't try to change the whole world, even the small
world of your own gymnasium, on the first try.
DOLLY LAMBDIN

What is the best way to organize a class for instruction? Some teachers rarely vary the organization of their classes. Others, however, often do. When deciding how to organize a particular class, the reflective teacher considers such factors as how much responsibility the class is ready for, how many decisions the children are capable of sharing in, and whether the lesson will fail if the students are allowed to choose among several activities. The factors discussed in Chapter One will influence this decision, as will the teacher's experience with different organizational patterns.

Organizational patterns can be described along a continuum from direct to indirect (Table 4.1). At the direct end of the continuum, the teacher makes virtually all of the decisions. The student is told what activity to practice, how to practice, when to start, and when to stop. At the middle of the continuum, the teacher and the child share some of the decisions. The teacher might tell the class what to practice, but each student would decide how to practice and when to start and stop.

At the indirect end of the continuum, each child makes many of the decisions—not only about what to practice, but also about when and how to practice. Some educators have suggested that at this end of the continuum children are permitted to make virtually all of the decisions. Our experience, and that of others, suggests that, at least in American schools, children are never allowed to make all of the decisions related to their learning (Holt, 1976).

Table 4.1 Continuum of teaching methods

Direct	Limited	Indirect
Teacher makes virtually all decisions	Teacher shares some decisions with students	Teacher shares many decisions with students

VIEWPOINT

The continuum, from direct to indirect, could be represented as if each of the approaches were equally good for children. While that may be true in theory, our experience suggests otherwise. Teaching a class of thirty children as a group—as if they had identical interests, abilities, and goals—conflicts directly with our most basic belief. We believe that children are individuals with different abilities and interests, and that all children are capable of learning to make responsible decisions about their learning. We realize that in some situations a class must be taught as a single entity. This does not mean, however, that teaching the class as a whole is the pattern of organization ultimately desired by that teacher.

Starting one's career by teaching at the direct end of the continuum is probably typical because few instructors, as students or as teachers, have been exposed to individualized instruction. "There has been a lot of pious (and generally naive) exhortation to individualize by teacher educators who do not even apply the concept to their own college classes, much less model techniques of individualization in the public schools" (Locke and Lambdin, 1976, p. 26).

We believe that it is unfair to children and professionally irresponsible to continue to use approaches from the direct end of the continuum once you have begun to teach a class and observe differences among the pupils. Children deserve to be taught as individuals. Individualized instruction is not an ivory tower fantasy. Teachers can learn to

We attempt to work with children as individuals

vary the organizational patterns of instruction and to adapt those patterns to specific classes and children. It takes time and work, but it can be done.

In respect to my own growth, whether in tennis or any other aspect of development, I have found it helpful to look at myself as the seed of a tree, with my entire potential already within me, as opposed to a building, which must have stories added to it to achieve a greater height. This makes it easier for me to see that it doesn't help me to try to be what I'm not at any given moment, or to form concepts of what I should be, or to compare myself to other trees around me. I can understand that I need only use all the rain and sunshine that come my way, and cooperate fully with the seed's impulse to develop and manifest what it already uniquely is.

TIMOTHY GALLWEY,
The Inner Game of Tennis

ORGANIZATIONAL PATTERNS FOR INSTRUCTION

Now that you are aware of our views on organizational patterns for instruction, you understand that

we think of the direct end of the continuum as a place to begin or to return to in uncertain or confusing situations. In order to describe some of the approaches we use to individualize instruction, we want to share a practical model based on the direct–indirect continuum described above. This model is divided into three general categories: teaching a class as a whole; teaching a class in groups; and teaching a class as individuals (Locke and Lambdin, 1976). Some methods from each of these categories are presented as examples (see Table 4.2).

Teaching a Class as a Whole   This method of organizing for instruction has been predominant in physical education instruction. The teacher designs the lesson with a theoretical midpoint in mind, aiming between the abilities of those children in the class who are highly skilled and those with minimal physical abilities. Children who are above or below this midpoint in ability are expected by the teacher to participate enthusiastically and with interest, even though the tasks in the lesson are so difficult that they lead to frustration for the minimally skilled or so easy that they bore the highly skilled

Table 4.2   Organizational patterns for instruction

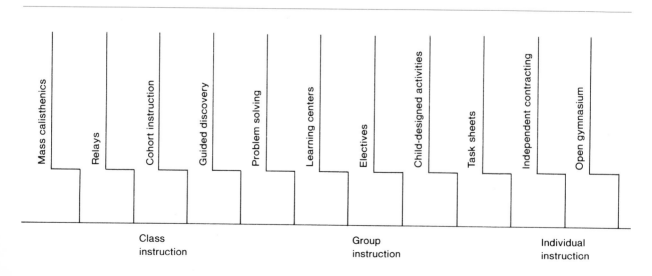

Teaching a class as a whole is a popular method of organizing instruction

children. Mass calisthenics, relays, predetermined activities, guided discovery, and problem-solving are used in teaching the class as a whole.

Mass Calisthenics   For many years mass calisthenics have been considered a typical "gym" activity. Films of physical education classes always seemed to show all the children in a class performing exercises together. Unfortunately some people still believe that calisthenics are the only activity taught in physical education classes.

Calisthenics, performed appropriately, have obvious benefits. But the practice of having an entire class perform identical exercises the same number of times is archaic and educationally unsound. Some exercises are of little benefit to some children in the class, and the number of repetitions probably meets the needs of less than one-third of the children. You may be unfortunate enough to work for a principal who enjoys the organized, uniform appearance of a class performing calisthenics in cadence. But not all pupils benefit from mass calisthenics.

Relays When participating in relay races, children must wait in line for their turns. Because relays are competitive, skill performance frequently declines as children try to win the race. For example, if children are asked to write their names on a chalk board and then the class is organized into teams for a name-writing relay race, the decline in the quality of the children's writing provides a visual illustration of the decline of performance that is observed in gross motor skill relays. Some children enjoy relays. Other children, often the poorly skilled, despise relays. When an entire team heaps blame on a single child for "making us lose the relay," that child may have difficulty remembering that it is only a game—especially when that youngster knows he tried his best.

Cohort Instruction The term *cohort instruction* was defined by Locke and Lambdin (1976) as "teaching the same thing to all students at the same time, by the same method, requiring all the students to practice in the same way, at the same pace, for the same length of time." Technically, mass calisthenics and relays fit under this definition. However, we use the term *cohort instruction* to describe organizational patterns of instruction, other than relays and mass calisthenics, in which the teacher works with a class as a single entity. An example of cohort instruction would be to divide the entire class into two teams that would play Snatch the Bacon, Red Rover, or Brownies and Fairies. Or the children could separate into groups and learn the Virginia Reel or Seven Jumps in the dance area.

Cohort instruction has two advantages: (1) it is an effective way to provide instruction to an entire class, if you want all of the children to be exposed to the same activity or skill; and (2) it is easier to use than other methods because the entire class does the same thing at the same time, and this simplifies observation.

Typically, activities for which a cohort instruction format is used are described in textbooks or learned in methods classes. Such activities can be adapted to match the characteristics of a class as a whole. A predetermined activity can be modified, or the teacher can incorporate the desired skills into

Directions written on posterboards can help shorten waiting lines

an activity appropriate for his or her teaching situation (Riley, 1975).

Guided Discovery and Problem-Solving   When guided discovery or problem-solving are used, all the children work on the same task, but not all at the same pace or in the same way. Some allowance is made for individual differences. The children usually are all active simultaneously, rather than some being active while others wait for a turn.

In a problem-solving format, the teacher sets the problem and each student is expected to find the answer or answers without help from the teacher or from other pupils (Mosston, 1966). For example, the teacher might ask: "Can you find at least two ways to avoid an opponent and still maintain possession (foot or hand dribbling) of the ball?" or "Can you take off on two feet while facing any direction? Which direction do you prefer?"

In guided discovery, the teacher provides the learner with clues as guidance but does not provide the answer (Mosston, 1966). The teacher might ask: "Is this your most balanced position? Could you now be in a position that is in a little bit less balance? Could you now be in the least balanced position?" Typically the problem is posed to the entire class. Each child's ability and interest in discovering her or his physical potential will determine which answer is selected from the range of possibilities.

Teaching a Class in Groups   One alternative to teaching the class as a whole is to organize the children so that they can work in groups. The children will not all be involved in the same activity simultaneously, and so they (and the teacher) should be ready to have more than one activity happening at the same time. Planning, observation, and sometimes management may be more difficult for the instructor. But the teacher will be able to better match the lesson to the varying abilities of the students. Learning centers, electives, and child-designed activities can be used when teaching a class in groups.

Learning Centers   When learning centers (stations) are used, the teacher sets up several activity areas in the teaching space. The class is then divided into groups, one for each learning center. It is wise to start with just a few learning centers—perhaps three. The number of centers can be increased gradually as the children learn to work responsibly at their centers. Stopping when asked, rotating systematically, and not interfering with others are responsibilities that the children accept when they work effectively in learning centers.

One advantage of learning centers is that practice situations can be set up that, if the entire class were involved, would involve waiting in lines for turns (see Figure 4.1). When the children are able to function in the environment of learning centers, they

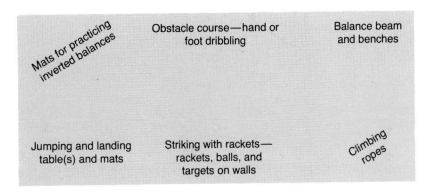

Figure 4.1   Learning centers

can be allowed to choose the learning centers at which they would like to work. Eventually they can rotate from one learning center to another at their own discretion. You may want to write task descriptions on poster boards and place one at each learning center. This technique decreases substantially the time spent instructing the class as a whole.

Electives   When each child is permitted to select the learning center at which he or she would like to work, or to choose between two or more activities during a lesson, the teacher is providing the children with electives.

> "Today you may choose between playing a game of mini-soccer or playing One Step with a partner."

> "Today you may choose to continue working on your partner sequence to *Star Wars* music, or you may practice shooting baskets, or you may continue practicing your sequence focusing on rolling into balanced positions."

> "We have two types of over-the-net for you to choose from today. At this net we will keep score, one team against another. At the other net, the teams will be working together to see how many times they can get the ball to cross the net before it touches the floor."

When a teacher begins to offer electives, it is a good idea to limit the amount of time the children have to practice or play at a given activity. As a class learns to make responsible choices, the time can be extended. You can decide how long to allow them to work on their own by observing how well they practice as intended. Electives are not synonymous with recess. We expect children to practice or play in a responsible, productive manner.

Child-Designed Activities   In the methods described up to this point, the teacher makes most of the decisions about how and what the children are to practice. Eventually, however, you want the children to contribute to decisions about what is to be done, and for how long, in practice sessions. Devising situations in which children can design their own

dances, gymnastics sequences, or games is a step in this direction.

Moderation is the key to success. If you simply say to children, "Make up your own game. It has to include throwing and catching," the result may be a disaster. We know from experience. Try to provide children with more specific suggestions for designing activities.

> "Design beginning and ending movements for the balance, roll, balance sequence you have been practicing."

> "You have been practicing five movements: leaping, spinning, sinking, exploding and freezing. Use them in a repeatable sequence that flows together smoothly."

In time, the situation can be structured so that the children contribute more and more. By initially restricting the children's input, you limit the amount of time the children spend making decisions. These decisions are important to children, and so some children take a substantial amount of time to design an activity. You want the children to contribute to their own learning, but you also want them to be active in physical education class. At times this can be a dilemma!

An environment in which children are designing their own activities is a complex one in which to teach. Should you assist or stay away, encourage or simply observe, offer an idea for restructuring an activity or let the children work it out? And these decisions are even more complicated when a variety of projects are going on simultaneously. Child-designed activities are challenging for the children, and they are challenging for the teacher.

Individualizing is not so much a method of instruction as it is a distinct way of thinking about learning and the respective roles of teacher and student.

LARRY LOCKE AND DOLLY LAMBDIN,
Personalized Learning in Physical Education

Teaching the Class as Individuals Even more challenging and demanding for the teacher is working with children as individuals—attempting to design and successfully teach in an environment in which you account for individual differences. Task sheets, independent contracting, and the open gymnasium are used to individualize instruction.

Task Sheets One approach to individualizing instruction is to provide each child with a series of challenges that she can practice at her own pace. Task sheets (see Figure 4.2) are given to each child. Each task sheet contains a progression of activities and includes spaces for child-designed activities. When a task is successfully accomplished, the student records it on the task sheet, with that day's date, and asks the teacher, a parent, or an older child or partner to observe the accomplishment and sign the task sheet.

Initially an entire class works on the same task

Date Accomplished	Verification	Challenge
		Name _____ Teacher _____
		BALANCE TASK SHEET
		I can walk forward the entire length without falling off.
		I can walk leading with my right side the entire length without falling off.
		I can walk leading with my left side the entire length without falling off.
		I can walk backward the entire length without falling off.
		I can walk forward (with my hands folded on my head) the entire length without falling off.
		I can walk forward the entire length with an eraser balanced on my head.
		I can walk backward the entire length with an eraser balanced on my head.
		I can walk along the beam, pick up a beanbag, and walk to the other end without falling off.
		I can walk along the beam, balance on one knee, and walk to the other end without falling off.
		I can walk the entire length of the balance beam without falling off, keeping my eyes closed all the way.
		I can bounce a ball across the beam without a miss.
		I can roll a ball along a beam without either the ball or myself touching the ground.
		I can walk along the beam, do a complete turn on one foot only, and walk to the end without falling off.
		I can walk along the beam twirling a hoop on one arm, without falling off.
		I can walk along the beam balancing a wand in one hand without falling off.
		I can hop along the beam on one foot without falling off.
		I can throw a ball back and forth to a partner ____ times without a miss, while standing on the end of a beam.
		I can jump rope on a balance beam ____ times without a miss.
		I can do a forward roll on the beam.
		I can jump onto the beam from a spring board without losing my balance.
		I can . . .
		I can . . .
		I can . . .

Figure 4.2   Task sheet

sheet. As the children learn to use the task sheets, we allow them to pick from sheets on several different skill themes. Writing and refining group task sheets is time consuming, but these can be valuable when you begin to individualize instruction.

Independent Contracting   As children become accustomed to working on their own, the teacher can use independent contracting to make instruction more personal (Gotts, 1976; Locke and Lambdin, 1976). A teacher who uses independent contracting is saying to the students, "I trust you to make intelligent and responsible decisions about what you need to practice."

We have used the written contract illustrated in Figure 4.3. Each child writes down the skill or activity she or he will be practicing or playing, the goal to be achieved, the time to be spent practicing each activity, and (when appropriate) the name of a practice partner. Recognizing the dynamic nature of

Name _____

Contract for _____ , 198__
                    (date)

Time	Activity	Goal	Partner

COMMENTS:

1) Did you accomplish your goal?

2) What do you need to work on during the next class?

3) Do you want to tell me about the class?

Figure 4.3   Individual contract

a physical education class, we allow the children to change their contracts during class, as long as they write all changes down. We encourage the children to save time by coming to physical education class with their contracts already completed for that day. In the final few minutes of a class we ask the children to evaluate their accomplishments for that day.

When you first use independent contracting, it is wise to restrict each child to a single skill theme. As the children become accustomed to the system, the number of choices can be increased gradually.

Open Gymnasium   Allowing the children to select among a variety of available activities without requiring them to write down what they will be practicing is a step beyond independent contracting. An open gymnasium is not a setting for free play (Caldwell & Skaff, 1976). We expect children to act responsibly in an open gymnasium setting. An open environment is established to encourage children to practice the activities they are interested in, in ways they like, for as long as they like. An open gymnasium can prepare children for the kinds of settings in which they will experience physical activity once they are on their own, with no one telling them what or when to practice. In this open gymnasium, as in other settings, we encourage the children to seek assistance from the teacher and from other children who are skilled in a particular activity.

As with the other approaches to individualizing instruction, the open gymnasium seems to be more effective if initially it is limited. Generally we provide only a few minutes at the beginning or end of a class for the children to begin to experience the feeling of being on their own. And, initially, we also try to create an exciting environment by providing a limited number of activities that we know are favorites of the children. As the children learn to work successfully in the relatively unstructured environment of the open gymnasium, we gradually increase both the time and the number of learning opportunities in the open gymnasium.

It takes experience, including defeat, failure, and frustration to develop skills as a teacher. It takes years to become established in a new community and then more time to develop an organization strong enough to fight oppressive schools effectively. With the best will in the world, it also takes years to learn to build the right tone in a class and equip the room sensibly, to develop an eye for children in trouble, to know how to support students and how to make demands on them without oppressing them, to know when to add something new or step back and leave the children alone. Teaching is no simple matter. It is hard work, part craft, part art, part technique, part politics, and it takes time to develop ease within such a complex role. However, for many of us the effort makes sense, for one gets the opportunity to see young people grow while one has a positive and caring role in their lives.

HERB KOHL,
On Teaching

MAINSTREAMING

Mainstreaming can be defined as the inclusion of handicapped students in regular educational programs. Public Law 94–142 was passed by Congress to encourage normalization of the education of children with special needs. The law states that the amount of time that special students spend in classes designed for children with handicaps (retardation, visual or orthopedic impairment, emotional disturbance) is to be decreased. This law is based on the premise that handicapped children will be better prepared for life in the real world if they have been involved in ordinary educational experiences. The goal is to provide full educational opportunities for all handicapped children.

Mainstreaming presents a challenge to the physical education teacher in direct proportion to the way a particular class is organized. Can a retarded child or an orthopedically impaired child in a wheelchair be expected to participate in the same ways as other children when the teacher is working with the class as a whole? In this situation the teacher must select activities that are within the skill range of these children. In contrast, the instructor who is teaching by task or employing an independent contract system will have less difficulty in adapting lessons to accommodate special children and facilitate mainstreaming. One of the provisions of P. L. 94–142 requires that each disabled child be issued an Individualized Education Program (IEP). This means that an individual contract must be written for every handicapped child. Obviously the teacher who is already using an individualized approach will need to make fewer changes in accommodating the disabled child. The teacher who ordinarily organizes the class as a whole may have to make substantial adjustments if he or she is to comply with the intent of mainstreaming.

Working under P. L. 94–142, teachers will encounter many different disabilities. Each child is unique, but a few suggestions may prove helpful. The medical report of a child who is being mainstreamed for the first time should be checked to determine whether any activities or situations are contraindicated for that child. Some schools have resource teachers who know the individual children and understand the special needs and abilities of a particular population of children (children with a particular handicap). Care must be taken to avoid placing the mainstreamed child in situations that will lead to embarrassment or ridicule. This is con-

sistent with the need to help all children to be sensitive to the emotional and physical needs of others. The presence of disabled children can enhance the learning experience of all the children.

We believe that using handicapped children to distribute equipment or to keep score is exactly that—using children. All children, including those who are disabled, deserve the fullest physical education experiences their abilities allow. The ideas discussed in the section on Teaching the Class as Individuals will help to provide appropriate learning opportunities. The instructor who has disabled children in a class will have to be innovative, alert, sensitive to the interaction among all the children, and willing to devote time to careful planning. The challenge is great, and so are the rewards.

SELECTING A FORM OF ORGANIZATION

How do you determine which organizational pattern is best for a given class? An assessment of the eagerness and achievement level of a class can provide guidance. The model we use theorizes that classes can be neatly subdivided into high and low eagerness and achievement levels (Figure 4.4)

We assume that children who are eager to participate in physical education require less teacher direction, as do children who have high ability levels. Children who do not enjoy physical education and

		Eagerness	
		High	Low
Achievers	High	Teacher is efficient at organizing, managing an individualized learning environment; teacher is facilitator, helper	Teacher is efficient at motivating, conveys enthusiasm, and accepts differences in interests
	Low	Teacher is efficient at prompting, cueing, reinforcing, and is supportive, considerate, and patient	Teacher is efficient at being direct but is warm, self-confident, and able to work with class as a whole

Figure 4.4   Model for determining class organizational pattern

Teachers have to learn how to provide transitions for their pupils. It is not possible for most young people to make choices after five or six years of being told what to do every minute they are in school. It is equally hard for them to share resources, help other students, or decide what they want to learn after years of being expected to hoard, compete, and conform. Transitional situations often have to be provided. Some students need workbooks for a while; others want to memorize times tables or have weekly spelling tests. Young people are no different from adults. When faced with new possibilities they want something old and predictable to hold onto while risking new freedom. Inexperienced teachers often make the mistake of tearing down the traditional attitudes their students have been conditioned to depend upon before the students have time to develop alternative ways of learning and dealing with school. In their impatience they become cruel to students who do not change fast enough or who resist change altogether. One just cannot legislate compassion or freedom. Teaching as a craft involves understanding how people learn; as an art it involves a sensitive balance between presenting and advocating things you believe and stepping away and encouraging your students to make their own sense of your passion and commitment.

HERBERT KOHL,
On Teaching

do not have well-developed skills seem to require more direct teacher attention. When this is true, the model presented in Figure 4.4 provides a useful, generalized guide for determining the best organizational pattern for a class.

Children who are high achievers and are highly eager are assumed to function well in a personalized instructional setting. Highly eager, low-achieving students seem to do well in an individualized instructional setting, if the teacher is efficient at skills such as prompting, cueing, and reinforcing to keep the children focused on the task at hand. Students who are low in eagerness and high in achievement often seem to function well in groups, particularly if the teacher is enthusiastic and an efficient motivator. Low achievers who are also low in eagerness often require teachers who are direct with them initially, until the children discover success and the personal satisfaction that can be derived from involvement in physical activity.

Obviously this model is an oversimplification and should not be used as a concrete, universally applicable guideline. It does, however, provide a perspective that can help you to decide which organizational pattern to use with a particular class at various times during their physical education experience.

THE TEACHER'S ROLE

Kenny Moore, a famous distance runner and an insightful writer, once wrote: "Each of us is an experiment of one. What is realistic for any of us is what allows us to achieve our reasonable goal. For each of us, our goal and also our body is different from that of another." Because we totally agree with this statement we are continually attempting to move toward the individualization of instruction.

Do not think, however, that all of our classes eventually work in an open gymnasium setting. Time—often years—may pass before some children are ready to work responsibly as individuals. And some children never are (Barth, 1972).

One of the most important variables related to the individualization of instruction is the approach utilized by the children's classroom teacher. If the children are accustomed to working as individuals in the classroom, then physical education instruction usually can be individualized much sooner than is possible with a class that is accustomed to cohort instruction, for example.

The instructor needs time to learn to teach children in groups or as individuals. You will find that the transition from being a director to being a facilitator or helper can be time consuming and difficult. But that process can also be exciting.

SUMMARY

Some methods of organizing for instruction are more effective than others. We believe in trying to involve children in decisions about their learning. Generally, student–teacher involvement in decision-making is depicted along a continuum from direct (teacher makes almost all of the decisions) to indirect (teachers and students share decisions). We have expanded this concept and grouped organization for instruction into three categories: teaching the class as a whole, teaching groups, and teaching individuals.

Teaching the class as a whole involves organizing a class so that all of the children are involved in the same activity simultaneously. Mass calisthenics, relays, cohort instruction, guided discovery, and problem-solving can all be used when you are teaching a class as a whole. Teaching the class as a group is the next step toward individualized instruction. Learning centers, electives, and child-designed activities can all be used with groups. Ideally, all teachers would be able to allow for individual differences in every class they teach. Unfortunately not all teachers are able to reach this goal with every class. Task sheets, independent contracting, and the open gymnasium can be used to facilitate individualized instruction that accommodates different interests and abilities.

An assessment of the achievement and eagerness levels of the students in a class can be useful when you are deciding the organization and the kind of environment that is likely to work best for a particular class.

REFERENCES

Barth, R. S. *Open education and the American school.* New York: Schocken Books, 1972.

Caldwell, S. F., & Skaff, J. The open gymnasium. In D. Hellison (Ed.), *Personalized learning in physical education.* Washington, D.C.: American Alliance for Health, Physical Education, and Recreation, 1976.

Gallwey, T. *The inner game of tennis.* New York: Random House, 1974.

Gotts, S. L. Student–teacher contracts. In D. Hellison (Ed.), *Personalized learning in physical education.* Washington, D.C.: American Alliance for Health, Physical Education, and Recreation, 1976.

Hellison, D. (Ed.) *Personalized learning in physical education.* Washington, D.C.: American Alliance for Health, Physical Education, and Recreation, 1976.

Holt, J. *Instead of education.* New York: E. P. Dutton, 1976.

Kohl, H. *On teaching.* New York: Schocken, 1976.

Lambdin, D. Quiet individualizing: What one teacher did. In D. Hellison (Ed.), *Personalized learning in physical education.* Washington, D.C.: American Alliance for Health, Physical Education, and Recreation, 1976.

Locke, L. F., & Lambdin, D. Teacher behavior. In D. Hellison (Ed.), *Personalized learning in physical education.* Washington, D.C.: American Alliance for Health, Physical Education, and Recreation, 1976.

Mosston, M. *Teaching physical education from command to discovery.* Columbus, Ohio: Charles E. Merrill, 1966.

Mueller, R. Task cards. In D. Hellison (Ed.), *Personalized learning in physical education.* Washington, D.C.: American Alliance for Health, Physical Education, and Recreation, 1976.

Riley, M. Games and humanism. *Journal of Health, Physical Education, and Recreation.* February 1975, pp. 46–49.

CHAPTER 5
ESTABLISHING
A LEARNING
ENVIRONMENT

Many teachers get bogged down in problems of discussion about maladjustment of children when in actuality the children are reacting normally to a poorly organized, undefined, purposeless learning environment.
JAMES DiVIGLIO

One of the most important factors in establishing a learning environment is also one of the least tangible—teacher attitude. The way a teacher feels about himself or herself, about teaching, about physical education, and about children—all these influence attitude. The teacher who is enthusiastic conveys this attitude to the children, and as a result their enthusiasm for physical education is heightened. The teacher who views physical education as a time for learning and work communicates this to the children by the way he or she demands that certain criteria for behavior be adhered to by all the children.

The clearest evidence of the influence of teacher attitude on the atmosphere of a learning environment can be obtained by observing one class of children with several different teachers. The same children may be businesslike and involved with one teacher and apathetic or frivolous with another teacher only thirty minutes later. Clearly teacher attitude has a significant influence on the learning environment.

History, science, even music and art classes are all thought of as work. But it is not uncommon for children, parents, and even some teachers to think of physical education as free time, a break from the work of the academic subjects taught in classrooms. In fact, many teachers refer to physical education class as recess.

Children definitely need a break from routine. Recess is free time and provides that needed break. Physical education, however, is an educational experience designed to enhance motor skill learning and to foster the development of positive attitudes toward physical activity. The difference between physical education and recess must be clear to

children, parents, and teachers if students are to benefit appropriately from the time devoted to physical education.

A physical education teacher's first goal is to establish an environment in which learning will occur. From the first day the pupils must understand that physical education is not a break, but a time for learning skills and activities. Once children understand this, the teacher's task is much easier. Remember, though, that a learning environment is not established in a single lesson. With some classes this process may take several weeks.

Some educators use "developing a learning environment" and "discipline" as if they were synonymous, but we do not. Discipline is required when a child's behavior is disruptive and the teacher needs to prevent the disruption from occurring again (see Chapter Six). When establishing a learning environment, the focus is on fostering behavior and creating an atmosphere appropriate for a physical education class. Some discipline may be required in a physical education class, as in any class. But a positive approach, with an emphasis on cooperation, will reduce the need for discipline and stimulate enthusiasm and learning.

FOSTERING APPROPRIATE ATTITUDES

Most children, when they begin school, have few preconceptions about how a physical education learning environment will be structured. In a short time they learn to behave according to the expectations of their teachers. And once the youngsters acquire a concept of acceptable and unacceptable behavior in physical education class, it becomes increasingly difficult for a teacher to alter the behaviors of children. For this reason it is crucial that an appropriate learning environment be established immediately with the new children in a school. And the same is true when a teacher is new to a school.

Management and waiting activities hinder the development of an appropriate learning environment. Time spent taking out and putting away equipment, lining up, calling roll, and choosing teams (management time) detracts from time spent learning and contributes to off-task behaviors, such as pushing, shoving, and talking at inappropriate times. Off-task behavior also occurs when children are spending time waiting for class to begin, waiting for turns, or waiting for the teacher to rearrange equipment (waiting time). The teacher who has planned effectively and is well organized will involve the children in appropriate activities and so will have less difficulty establishing an environment that fosters learning.

Time spent in learning activities (activity time) is increased when the children are taught to set up and put away equipment. Although initially this detracts from activity time, over a school year substantial amounts of time can be saved. Pre-school children, for example, can learn to work together to move chairs, tables, benches, and mats. When you observe a class of children who efficiently set up and put away a variety of equipment, you can be certain that the teacher devoted some time, probably at the beginning of the year, to teaching the children to quickly and safely carry and arrange equipment.

Teaching the children to work together also fosters attitudes of cooperation and feelings of responsibility toward the class. When the children are expected to assume some of the responsibility for organizing the environment, they begin to view the class as "ours," rather than as the teacher's class. This is an important distinction.

LISTENING SKILLS

When a teacher must spend time quieting the children so that an explanation or comment can be heard by the entire class, the amount of time left for activities is decreased. Physical activity, by its nature, is noisier than classroom activity, and children tend to be even louder on a playground than in a gymnasium. Because this is true, it is imperative that children learn to respond quickly and appropriately to the teacher's signal for quiet. Listening

SIXTY-FIVE WAYS TO SAY "GOOD FOR YOU"

EDWARD S. KUBANY

Every one knows that a little praise goes a long way in any classroom. But "a little praise" really needs to be something more than the same few phrases repeated over and over ad nauseum. Your students need more than the traditional "Good," "Very Good," and "Fine" if encouragement is in the cards. Here are some additional possibilities.

You're on the right track.
That's really nice.
Thank you very much.
Wow!
That's great.
I like the way you're working.
Keep up the good work.
Everyone's working so hard.
That's quite an improvement.
Much better.
Keep it up.
It's a pleasure to teach when you work like this.
Good job.
What neat work.
You really outdid yourself today.
This kind of work pleases me.
That's right! Good for you.

I like the way Tom is working.
That's 'A' work.
John is in line.
Mary is waiting quietly.
Dickie got right down to work.
Ann is paying attention.
It looks like you put a lot of work into this.
That's clever.
Very creative.
Very interesting.
Good thinking.
Thank you for raising your hand, Charles. What is it?
That's an interesting way of looking at it.
Now you've figured it out.
Clifford has it.
Congratulations. You only missed _____.

Terrific.
I bet your Mom and Dad would be proud to see the job you did on this.
Beautiful.
I'm very proud of the way you worked [are working] today.
Excellent work.
I appreciate your help.
Very good. Why don't you show the class?
Marvelous.
Groovy.
Right on.
For sure.
Sharp.
That looks like it's going to be a great report.
That's the right answer.
Now you've got the hang of it.

Exactly right.
Super.
I like the way Bill [the class] has settled down.
Superior work.
Thank you for [sitting down, being quiet, getting to work, etc.]
That's a good point.
That certainly is one way of looking at it.
Sherrie is really going to town.
That's an interesting point of view.
You've got it now.
Out of sight.
Nice going.
You make it look easy.
My goodness, how impressive!

games can be used to teach children to listen as they move and to respond quickly to the signals of the teacher.

SAFETY

A physical education environment must be safe. Children need to be taught that certain actions—such as pushing and shoving, running out of control, and touching another child who is on a piece of apparatus—are inappropriate and unsafe. It helps to explain to the children why these are inappropriate behaviors, while also explaining the possible consequences of actions that are unsafe. Safety is taught at the beginning of the school year. And it is often reviewed because of violations or when an upcoming activity, such as gymnastics, includes unusual hazards. The children need to understand that safety is their responsibility as well as the teacher's.

INFLUENCE OF THE PRESENCE OF DISABLED CHILDREN

Another responsibility that the children can be taught to share is a responsibility for helping their classmates. This is particularly true when a class in-

LISTENING GAMES

In a successful learning environment, noise rarely exceeds a reasonable level that can be thought of as "busy noise." Hollering, shrieking, and yelling are appropriate at recess. In physical education class, the children should not be expected to be silent, but they should be able to hear a teacher speaking in a reasonable tone, considerably below a shout. The games described below can be used to establish an appropriate noise level. The objective of these games is to teach the children to listen for the teacher as they move.

STOP AND GO

Children travel in general space in a scattered formation. Once the children are able to (1) walk without touching others and (2) stay far away from others as they walk, you can begin to play Stop and Go. When you say "stop," the children are expected to stop and freeze instantly. When you say "go," they should begin to travel again. The signals should not be shouted—they should be spoken, so that the children become accustomed to listening for your voice at a reasonable level.

BODY PARTS

This game focuses on the different body parts. Once the children have adjusted to Stop and Go, they enjoy the challenge of touching the floor with different body parts—elbow, seat, knee, wrist, waist, left hand, and right foot—as quickly as they can when you say "stop."

TRAVELING

When children have learned to travel using different locomotor patterns, variations in locomotor patterns are appropriate. Call out different ways of traveling—skipping, hopping, crab-walking, galloping—and challenge the children to change from one to another as rapidly as possible. The challenge of this game is increased when you combine traveling and the concept of direction—for example, gallop backward or hop to the right.

CIRCLES

This game can be played on a painted playground surface or in a gymnasium. Before class, you will draw circles, triangles, squares, and so on, on the ground. The object is for the children to move as quickly as possible to the shape named by the teacher. If you call out "circle," the children stand on a circle as quickly as possible. You can use colors instead of, or in combination with, shapes if the surface you are using is

painted various colors. The terms you use will also be determined by your young pupils' knowledge of colors and shapes.

NUMBERS

In one version of this game, the children stop with the appropriate number of body parts touching the ground. If you call out "three," the correct response would be for the children to stop with three body parts touching the ground.

In a second version, the children stop in groups. The size of the group is determined by the number called by the teacher. This game is helpful when you want the children to form into groups of three, four, or five in a hurry.

COMBINATIONS

As children learn each variation, they find it challenging and fun to play several games at once. For example, you might call out a body part or a color or a locomotor pattern or a number. Children thrive on increasingly difficult games.

SWITCH AND ROTATE

This game is primarily to teach listening, but it is more appropriate for older children. The object of the game is to stay so close to a partner that, when the teacher says "stop" and the players freeze, the follower can still touch the leader. When the teacher says "switch," the partners change roles and the follower becomes the leader.

You can make this game more difficult by increasing the size of the group, from two to three, then four, then five. The object of the game remains the same—each child should be able to touch the person in front as soon as you say "stop." When you add the challenge "rotate," the leader goes to the end of the line and becomes a follower. The challenge of listening and responding instantly while trying to remain close to the children in front of them is fascinating for children. This game can be made more challenging by varying the locomotor patterns—e.g., from walking to skipping to hopping to galloping to running.

PURPOSE OF LISTENING GAMES

These listening games are designed to help the children learn to stop as quickly as possible when responding appropriately to the teacher's verbal challenge. Try not to single children out who are slow, and do not use penalties as a form of discipline. Embarrassment and punishment are both counterproductive. You want children to enjoy exercise, not to think of it as unpleasant.

cludes children with disabilities. As mainstreaming (P. L. 94–142) is implemented, it is becoming more common to have children who are in wheelchairs or on crutches, for example, in classes with ambulatory children. It is virtually impossible for the teacher to give a disabled child all the attention he or she would prefer to give. Classmates, however, can be taught to work with disabled children. For instance, the teacher can show the sighted children the appropriate techniques for assisting a blind person to travel in a limited space—the blind child holds onto the arm of the sighted child and travels slightly behind. Then, each day a different child might be given the responsibility of working with a blind child who is in class. In some situations children consider it a privilege to be trusted with the responsibility of assisting a disabled individual. This frees the teacher to devote more time to all the children and assures that the disabled child has an opportunity to actively participate in the lesson.

LEARNING ENVIRONMENT VERSUS RECESS

The difference between physical education and recess must be made clear to the children from the beginning. If you can arrange to have your first meeting with the children in their classroom, you can explain the difference to them in that more formal environment. Then, when the children enter the gymnasium or playground, they will know what to expect and what is expected of them.

Rules of Behavior   If children understand the behavioral boundaries within which they are expected to function, they are less likely to test your flexibility and more likely to cooperate. A few rules, stated clearly and adhered to consistently by the teacher, can be helpful to everyone.

1. When the teacher gives a signal (whether with words, a drumbeat, or a whistle), the children are expected to stop and listen.

2. Children are expected to work without interfering with other children or preventing others from working.
3. Children are expected to treat equipment carefully, as if it were their own.
4. Children are expected to stay within assigned boundaries.

These rules are basic to group survival. After children understand these rules, explain why rules are necessary. Children are far more cooperative with rules that make sense to them than with seemingly arbitrary regulations.

Standards for Performance   Children are expected to abide by the rules. We attempt to teach with a critical demandingness (Brophy and Evertson, 1976). This means that we set standards and consistently adhere to them, so that the children know exactly what is expected. For example, we have established performance standards for many of the management tasks that occur daily, such as putting away equipment or lining up to go back to the classroom.

You might initially assign a criteria of five seconds as a reasonable amount of time for the children to be stopped and listening after they hear the stop signal. If the entire class is stopped and listening in five seconds or less, we praise them. If they are not stopped and listening, explain that taking more than five seconds is too slow, and they had better practice again because it is a waste of time to take that long. Gradually, raise the standards as the children become more proficient. The children often view these races against the clock as fun games and delight in praise from the teacher when they perform well. They also enjoy trying to beat their own records. This approach provides far more time for activity and instruction. As the children learn the value of spending less time on management tasks, these races against the clock can be eliminated.

SUMMARY

It is important for a teacher to distinguish between physical education and recess. Once children truly understand the difference between "purposeful practice" (physical education class) and "doing your own thing" (recess), they are far more willing to participate in the development of a learning environment.

A new teacher needs to begin to develop a learning environment immediately. So does the teacher who is working with a new class. Designing lessons that involve the children in activity the majority of the time is one positive approach to establishing a learning environment. Excessive management time and waiting time, often the results of poor organization, tend to hinder the creation of an appropriate atmosphere.

When children have acquired suitable listening skills and safety practices, when they accept the responsibility for their own actions and cooperate with others, the alternatives for class organization are increased significantly. The teacher who clearly states and consistently adheres to rules of behavior and standards for performance will have productive lessons and enthusiastic students.

REFERENCES

Brophy, J. E., & Evertson, C. M. *Learning from teaching: A developmental perspective.* Boston: Allyn & Bacon, 1976.

DiViglio, J. Guidelines for effective interdisciplinary teams. *The Clearing House* 47 (1972): 209–211.

CHAPTER 6
DISCIPLINE

Many teacher-trainees are quite simply afraid that they
will not be able to control their students, let alone teach
them anything. They should be afraid. They have had pre-
cious little in their undergraduate curriculum which
would provide the kinds of experiences necessary to understand the problems and gain the skills necessary to feel
confident about their abilities as educators.

DARYL SIEDENTOP

Even the teacher who establishes and explains rules of behavior,
teaches with a critical demandingness, and sets and adheres to performance standards cannot be sure that a class will perform as expected. In many classes there will be some children who find it difficult
to function in a school environment, not only in physical education,
but in other classes as well. Occasionally an entire class has difficulty
adhering to the behavioral boundaries established by the teacher.

Whether an individual, several children, or a majority of a class refuse to abide by the rules, your first response might well be to examine
your performance as a teacher. When children react in unexpected
ways, you may, upon reflection, find that their reactions are justified.
Children are incredibly honest. A teacher may not want to know or
believe that a lesson is a dud, but the children will let him or her
know. Occasionally it is the behavior of the teacher, rather than that of
the children, that needs to be changed.

If you determine that the lesson is appropriate and that your performance as a teacher is satisfactory, you can then look for other causes
of disruptive behavior.

Try not to view disruptive behavior as a personal affront. Instead, try
to understand the reason for the child's behavior and then react
appropriately.

We have found two guidelines to be effective in disciplining children. First, emphasize the positive rather than the negative. Many children who are known throughout a school as discipline problems have
become accustomed to hearing nothing but negative comments about
their behavior. Catching them in the act of doing something right and

The class proceeded through its parody of education, following a formula validated in a thousand classrooms I have visited and countless thousands I have not. First step in the formula is an assumption, an untested hypothesis which becomes valid merely because (and as soon as) it is assumed: Children who do not easily take the imprint of their teacher's own education and values, who are not ductile enough to be drawn wire-thin so that they may slip through traditional holes in the fabric of society—these are not "promising children" and the best that can be hoped for from them is good behavior (silence) and early withdrawal (dropout). Since silence is their most positive attribute, they should be left unmolested during the class hour so long as they practice that virtue.

Perhaps worst of all the many dreadful aspects of this assumption is that the children know it. They know—and will tell you, as they told me, if they are asked—that a few of them are regarded as "good material" and the rest are nothing: "ever' time I go to her class, she make me feel like I was nothin.' " Snapper, Rubbergut's half brother, said it. He said it for all the children who drown in the well of silence.

DANIEL FADER,
The Naked Children

praising them for being on-task can result in dramatic changes in their behavior (Siedentop, 1976).

Second, try to be firm but warm in working with children (Brophy & Evertson, 1976). Threatening or scaring children may bring temporary cessation of disruptive behavior but is not likely to bring about permanent, positive changes in behavior. If children are to learn to function effectively in groups, they need support, not threats. Teachers who are simultaneously warm and demanding are respected by children. The teacher who is friendly and informal with children can also be firm. It takes time, however, for children to learn that firmness and warmth need not be contradictory.

HELPING INDIVIDUAL CHILDREN

Often a stranger can walk into a classroom and, after a few minutes, pick out the "discipline problems" in a group of children he or she has never seen before. Frequently these are the children whose names are constantly being called out by the teacher—"Cecil, are you listening? Daphne, sit down, please." It is not uncommon to see the same children singled out frequently. And typically these children are masters of brinkmanship. They know just how far they can go without actually being disciplined. Because they covet adult attention, they

---

Every person needs recognition. It is expressed cogently by the lad who says, "Mother, let's play darts. I'll throw the darts and you say 'Wonderful.' "

DALE BAUGHMAN

In the inner city, teachers and students do not respect the same rules. Many of the youngsters want their teachers to play the game of teaching and learning by the rules and regulations they know and understand, and that are important to them—not by the rules that are important to their teachers. They want their teachers to be humanly and emotionally tough enough to make them control their behavior, since they in fact gain strength to behave from the emotional strength of their teachers. They want teachers who will "make me work and not let me get away with anything" (told to me and my university students by innumerable so-called inner city school "discipline problems").

HERBERT FOSTER,
Ribbin', Jivin' and Playin' the Dozens

persist in their deviant behavior. For that reason, avoid singling these children out, if possible.

You can learn a great deal by listening to tape recordings of a few lessons. Place a tape recorder in the gymnasium or on a belt around your waist. (This observation and assessment technique is discussed further in Chapter Nine.) After you have taped several lessons with the same class, listen to the tapes. If you hear yourself repeatedly singling out the same few children, you know you have to take steps to change your teaching behavior (see Chapter Nine).

Tape recordings of learning sessions can be used to evaluate verbal behaviors with children

Person-to-Person Dialogue   Another technique that has been successful is the person-to-person dialogue. Arrange a time to meet with a child away from the class (not immediately before or after). You might say to the child, "Willie, you don't seem to be enjoying our physical education class. I'd like you to come to my office after school today so that we can talk about it." The purpose of this meeting is to try to determine the reasons for the child's behavior in your class. This is not a time for a lecture. Instead, teacher and pupil should have a dialogue. We have found that a statement such as the following enables many children to begin a discussion of their concerns: "Willie, I'd like to talk to you about physi-

Person-to-person dialogue can be an effective strategy for reaching alienated students

cal education class. Is there something I do that bothers you?"

This statement takes the focus from the child and places it on the teacher. Many children are quite candid about what is bothering them. Remember, this is a dialogue, not a lecture. Explaining to the child something of how and why you teach is constructive and often productive. Lecturing to the child about his behavior, or threatening him with future punishments is counterproductive. This dialogue is not teacher-to-child, but person-to-person. Often the temptation to lecture, accuse, or blame a child is strong. But succumbing to this temptation is the quickest way to destroy any rapport that may exist between student and teacher. If a child trusts you enough to talk candidly about his concerns and you threaten or lecture him, communication ceases. Many children—especially those who need individual attention the most—have been betrayed before. And so they are likely to be sensitive and wary. Use of teacher power in this situation reinforces a child's belief that he cannot trust teachers and that being honest only gets him into more trouble.

Time-Out Person-to-person dialogue cannot be used during class. But there are times, during class, when you must deal in some way with a disruptive

child. When a child is not abiding by the class rules (stated above), one strategy you can use is time-out. The child is told to withdraw from the class and to stay out of the lesson until he or she is ready to function according to the rules. When the student is ready to return to the class, he or she reports to the teacher and describes what it is that he will be doing differently. For example, such a child might say, "When I hear the stop and listen signal, I'll stop right away and listen." A child who needs to sit out a second time in the same lesson stays on the sidelines for the remainder of that day's lesson.

Some children never want to participate in physical education class. A person-to-person dialogue is often helpful here, as is a conference with the child's other teachers. Some children are simply being obstinate or are genuinely lazy. Others may be afraid of participating in physical activity because they have already had unsatisfactory experiences at home or on the playground. If a child has a legitimate reason, we respect the child and attempt to create a satisfactory alternative. Transferring the child to another physical education class or arranging a one-to-one teaching situation often leads, in time, to participation with the regular class. Forcing a child to participate in physical education classes without first understanding the reason for the reluctance may not be in the child's best interests. Once a teacher understands why a child is reluctant to participate, an informed decision can be made about the most appropriate course of action.

I have tried to respond to what children say rather than to what I expect or want them to say. Responding to children in this way is not a natural act; I have often been chagrined or embarrassed to discover myself listening to myself (rather than to the child) and answering a question both unasked and unintended. Or, worst of all, I have an answer that was not only unwanted but unmanageable by the child. In this, as in so much else, adult responses are inferior to children's, for children are usually too wise to burden adults with information they cannot handle.

DANIEL FADER,
The Naked Children

Tokens Time-out penalizes disruptive behavior. A token system rewards desirable behavior. A token system is implemented when one or several rules are consistently being broken by some of the children in a class. The intent is to reward appropriate behavior and so encourage all the children to behave appropriately.

The teacher initially explains to the class that a particular rule is being violated. For example, some children are not stopping and listening as soon as they hear the stop signal. The teacher explains that, beginning today, as soon as the stop signal is given, checks will be made on a class list next to the names of the children who stop and listen within five seconds after the signal is given. Students who earn five checks during the class will be given a reward.

Some teachers have successfully used a "Mork award," based on the character from the television show "Mork and Mindy." Children who earn a reward are given a badge with Mork's picture on it to wear until the next physical education class meeting. Another version allowed children to write their names on a life-size Mork figure that was prominently displayed in the school cafeteria.

Free-choice times are an alternative that some teachers use to reward children. Children who have earned three tokens, for example, may choose an activity for the last five minutes of class, while the remainder of the class continues with the ongoing activity. Jumping rope, shooting baskets, or climbing on the playground apparatus are examples of free-choice token system rewards.

Gradually the length of time in which a reward is earned can be lengthened from a day to a week to a month. Once children have learned to abide by

ELEMENTARY SCHOOL

PHYSICAL EDUCATION BEHAVIOR REPORT

NAME _____   DATE _____

Educational research has consistently shown that when a teacher spends class time managing discipline problems, less "teaching" and student "learning" occurs. Disruptive behavior, therefore, is a primary reason for poor student achievement.

We regret to inform you that your child exhibited the following misbehavior during physical education class today:

Fought with others	____	Refused to participate	____
Argued with others	____	Lazy; no hustle or energy	____
Mistreated equipment	____	Late to class	____
Disrupted the work of others	____	Disruptive in hallway	____
Discourteous to others	____	Continually off-task; not following teacher's directions	____
Frequently clowned acting foolish and silly	____	Spoke using foul language	____
Talked while teacher was talking	____	Did not listen to teacher	____

Teacher's Comments: _____

_____

_____

_____

Please discuss today's incident with your youngster. We are concerned about the harm your child's behavior is causing himself and his classmates. We will keep you informed of his behavioral progress during the coming weeks.

Thank you for your cooperation.

TEACHER _____

PARENT'S SIGNATURE _____

Figure 6.1   Reports for parents

the rules that are vital for the successful functioning of a large group, token systems become unnecessary.

Letters to Parents   Time-out and token systems work with some children, not with others. When a child continues to misbehave and to present problems, a letter to a parent can be effective in obtaining that child's cooperation. But this technique should be used only after other approaches have proven unsuccessful.

The letter to the parents lists specific violations.

The child is to have the letter signed by a parent and then return it to the teacher. Such a letter is usually followed by improvements in behavior. When that occurs, you can send home a letter, as soon as possible, that reports the improvements as clearly as the earlier letter reported violations. This second letter congratulates the child on his improved behavior and, like the first one, requires a parent's signature. Some parents may have never before received a positive comment about their child from a school. Figures 6.1 and 6.2 present two suggested report forms.

```
                    ELEMENTARY SCHOOL

            PHYSICAL EDUCATION BEHAVIOR REPORT


    Name: _____    Date: _____


        Educational research has shown that when a teacher spends
    class time managing discipline problems, less teaching and less
    learning occurs.  Therefore, when disruptive behavior is non-
    existent in a class situation, greater student achievement is
    likely to result.


        We are glad to inform you that your youngster's behavior
    in physical education class has been super!!!  _____
    consistently exhibits the following exemplary behaviors:


    _____  Listens to the teacher      _____  Is courteous to others

    _____  Is on-task, following       _____  Treats equipment with
              directions                          care

    _____  Is eager to participate     _____  Plays safely


        Your child is doing a wonderful-terrific-dynamite job in
    physical education and we are proud of him/her.  You are to be
    commended for preparing your youngster to function so well in
    school.  We are more effective teachers because of your efforts.


        Thank you for your cooperation.


                    Teacher: _____
```

Figure 6.2   Elementary school physical education behavior report

The Principal   Sending a disruptive child to the principal may or may not be successful. When you send a child to the principal, you are acknowledging—to yourself and to the child—your inability to cope with the situation. You are also placing the child in a situation you cannot control.

Some principals are positive and helpful in working with disruptive children. Others use threats or corporal punishment, techniques that are likely to produce temporary improvements in the child's behavior but permanent damage to the child's enthusiasm and trust.

Only when you have tried every other possible technique to deal with behavior that is detrimental to the child and his classmates should you send a child to a principal. If you must, we hope yours is a principal who can help you and the child to better understand each other's needs and situations, so that you can work together more successfully.

CLASS DISCIPLINE

Some classes have a more difficult time than others in learning to abide by the class rules. When the race-against-the-clock games and performance standards do not result in the desired outcome, it is necessary to utilize more sophisticated techniques. Two approaches that have proven to be successful are class rewards and behavior games.

Class Rewards   Class rewards are earned by a class as a whole for abiding by the class rules. The first step is to establish a reward that will have meaning to a particular age of students. Posters, banners, and free time have been used successfully. When an entire class does well for a day (week, month) it receives the reward. For example, if a class consistently does better than the performance standards established for management tasks over a

FORMAT FOR A BEHAVIOR GAME

1. *The class is divided into four squads and each squad chooses a name.*
2. *Four to six rules are explained to the class and posted for all to see.*
3. *It is made clear to the class that each of the squads can win the game.*
4. *The rewards to be won are determined and the precise relationship between student performance and earning the rewards is stated (this relationship is called a "contingency"). In this case, the reward is 15 minutes of extra recess on Friday if a squad wins 24 of the possible 32 points in the game.*
5. *To win one point, all members of the squad must behave in accordance with the rules.*
6. *A cassette tape is preprogramed (with a bell or buzzer as the sound signal) to go off eight times during a class period. The interval between the sounds is varied so that the class never knows when the signal will go off. When the class begins the teacher turns on the tape recorder.*
7. *When the signal sounds, the teacher quickly glances at each squad and makes a judgment as to their behavior. The points are quickly recorded on a clipboard and any team that loses a point is told why. Teams that win points are praised. (With practice this scoring and record keeping should not take more than 15 seconds at each signal.)*
8. *At the end of the period, the teacher totals the points and posts the total scores for the day on a conspicuous chart.*
9. *At the end of the week, each team that wins gets the extra recess (or gym time or some other reward) while the teams that lose stay in the classroom at their regular assignment.*
10. *If one player on a team loses more than two points for his/her team two days in a row, the team meets and votes as to whether the player should sit out from the gym class for a day.*

DARYL SIEDENTOP,
Developing Teacher Skills in Physical Education

given period of time, it receives a poster or banner to display in its room. Some teachers provide a reward for a class-of-the-week. We prefer, however, to reward every class for doing well, not just one.

Behavior Games   A more sophisticated and persuasive approach to class discipline is described in Daryl Siedentop's *Developing Teaching Skills in Physical Education* (1976). Siedentop suggests the use of a behavior game where the learning of appropriate behavior occurs as a game played by a class. Certain standards for performance are established, and all the students in a class have the opportunity to earn the reward. This format can be modified. The standards can be raised gradually, the number of signals can be decreased, and the time period over which the game is played can be extended, from one week to two weeks to a month. Siedentop emphasizes that the purpose of this game is to elicit the desired behavior, so that the behavior game eventually can be eliminated. Behavior games are not intended to be a permanent feature of a program. Rather, they can be effectively employed when the behavior of a class as a group is exceptionally deviant. As with the class rewards, the key to success is a reward that is desirable to the class as a whole. Remember, what appeals to one class may not appeal to another.

CORPORAL PUNISHMENT

We are unalterably opposed to corporal punishment. For some teachers the administration of a spanking or a paddling seems to serve—inappropriately—as a cathartic that may help the teacher but is even more likely to harm the child. There are times when the temptation to paddle or strike a continually misbehaving child is almost overwhelming. And yet, in our experience, it is the same few children who receive the vast majority of the paddlings. Obviously, this shows that for many children paddling does not achieve the desired result. And simultaneously it proves to these children that physically striking another person is a legiti-

mate alternative when no other course of action appears effective. Interestingly, many of the children who are continually the recipients of corporal punishment are being punished for fighting or hitting others. Occasionally a first paddling achieves the desired result. One cannot help but wonder, however, about the long-term impact of such an experience on a child. Use of corporal punishment is inhumane, it is ineffective, and it is an admission of failure.

DISCIPLINE AND TEACHING

Disciplining children is probably one of the least enjoyable tasks of teaching. But it is something that all teachers must do. The notion that only poor teachers have to discipline children is simply not accurate.

We cannot give love to children. If we do feel love, it will be for some particular child, or some few; and we will not give it, but give ourselves, because we are much more in the love than it is in us. What we can give to all children is attention, forbearance, patience, care, and above all justice.

GEORGE DENNISON,
The Lives of Children

Concern about discipline is normal. Fuller (1969) and Fuller, Parsons, and Watkins (1974) found that the primary concerns that preservice teachers have about teaching can be stated as follows: "Will I be able to control the children?" and "Will the children like me?"

Our experiences with beginning teachers, as well as our own teaching experiences, suggest that these questions are asked by most preservice teachers. The difference between so called good teachers and poor teachers is not in their concern about discipline. All teachers encounter deviant behavior and must find ways of dealing with it. Rather, the more successful teachers are able to minimize the amount of time they devote to discipline.

Kounin (1970) spent a number of years studying discipline and group management in classrooms. He concluded, in his own uniquely descriptive language, that teachers who spend the least time on discipline possess the characteristic of "withitness"—they seem to have eyes in the backs of their heads. They are able to attend to two issues simultaneously ("overlapping"). They can avoid "dangles" (leaving something hanging in midair) and "flip-flops" (terminating one activity, starting another, and then returning to the first activity). Siedentop (1976) followed Kounin's terminology with the terms *targeting* (selecting the student who is misbehaving) and *timing* (the lag between a student behavior and teacher reaction). Use of these skills enables a teacher to avoid what Kounin (1970) called the "ripple effect," which occurs when one class member involves several others in a rapidly spreading circle of off-task behavior. Probably the classic example of the ripple effect resulting from ineffective targeting and timing is attempting to identify who started a fight.

TEACHER: "All right, who started the fight?"

TED: "Ray pushed me first."

RAY: "Well, Ted threw a rock at me."

TED: "But I was aiming for Bobby because he called me a dumbbell."

Until a learning environment has been established and the time spent on discipline has been minimized, it is unrealistic to expect to be able to work successfully with individuals or groups within a class. The teacher who has developed ways to successfully manage a class does not have to spend time, energy, and thought on maintaining an orderly environment.

SUMMARY

During the time needed to establish a learning environment, discipline problems may arise. When this happens, the teacher should make certain that

his or her lesson plans and performance are pedagogically sound. Then the teacher can focus on the behavior of the children. Successful discipline includes emphasizing the positive rather than the negative, and being firm but warm as opposed to threatening.

Techniques for dealing with deviant behavior by individuals include person-to-person dialogue, time-out, tokens, letters to parents, sending the child to a principal, and corporal punishment. Techniques for refocusing an entire class that is off-task include class rewards and the behavior games suggested by Siedentop.

It is important to understand that so-called discipline problems are normal. All teachers experience off-task behavior by children; successful teachers simply adapt effectively to off-task behaviors.

Jacob Kounin has studied the problem of classroom management for a number of years and has created his own language to describe how one might minimize discipline problems in teaching. The teacher who is able to do this teaches in an environment that facilitates the use of a variety of desirable instructional strategies. And so that teacher

---

HUMANIZING PHYSICAL EDUCATION

For the past few years Don Hellison has been teaching physical education to alienated (and other) youth in Portland, Oregon. Don has written an extremely practical, helpful, and empathetic account of his successes (and failures) entitled *Beyond Balls and Bats* (AAHPER, 1978). The book presents the model he has developed in his attempt to humanize physical education for inner-city students. It is more than a few tricks or gimmicks; it is a total system (under construction). In Don's words:

> *The gym has got to become a comfortable place to be, a sanctuary perhaps, where students feel free to explore their connections to their bodies and to physical activities and where teachers can freely interact with the students, caring and sharing who they are and encouraging students to do the same.*

can utilize a variety of instructional strategies, with the class as a whole, with groups, and with individuals.

REFERENCES

Brophy, J. E., & Evertson, C. M. *Learning from teaching: A developmental perspective.* Boston: Allyn & Bacon, 1976.

Dennison, G. *The lives of children.* New York: Vintage, 1969.

Fader, D. *The naked children.* New York: Macmillan, 1971.

Foster, H. L. *Ribbin', jivin' and playin' the dozens.* Cambridge, Mass.: Ballinger, 1974.

Fuller, F. Concerns of teachers: A developmental conceptualization. *American Educational Research Journal* (March 1969): 207–26.

Fuller, F., Parsons, J., & Watkins, J. *Concerns of teachers: research and reconceptualization.* Austin: University of Texas, April 1974.

Hellison, D. *Beyond balls and bats.* Washington, D.C.: American Alliance for Health, Physical Education, and Recreation, 1978.

Kounin, J. *Discipline and group management in classrooms.* New York: Holt, Rinehart & Winston, 1970.

Siedentop, D. "Tilting at windmills while Rome burns. *Quest* (June 1972): 94–97.

————*Developing teaching skills in physical education.* Boston: Houghton Mifflin, 1976.

CHAPTER 7
OBSERVING, ANALYZING, AND PRESCRIBING

It is vital for a teacher to observe children, whatever the subject or situation. It is through observation that the successful teacher assesses the moods, attributes, needs, and potential of individuals and groups.

E. MAULDON and J. LAYSON

The ability to observe—to see with understanding—is crucial for a reflective teacher. The instructor who designs and implements a successful physical education program for an individual school or class must be able to observe accurately and continuously. The ability to observe perceptively and then translate the data gained from the observation into usable information can, and must, be learned by all reflective teachers.

Hoffman (1977), for example, reports on a study that compared the observational-analysis ability of physical education teachers with that of a group of softball players and coaches who had no professional training in physical education. The study revealed that the softball players scored significantly higher than the teachers who had degrees in physical education. Hoffman also provided evidence that the skill of observational analysis can be learned. "Data from the only training study conducted to date have indicated that thirty-five minutes of well-organized discrimination training can bring about significant gain in the ability to detect error in a fundamental skill" (Hoffman, 1977, p. 45). Neither of these studies was conducted in a field-based setting.

Accurate observational analysis is difficult in a nonteaching environment. The complexity is increased considerably, however, when the teacher attempts to observe the movement and behaviorial characteristics of individual children while simultaneously monitoring the work of an entire class during a physical education lesson (Barrett, 1979).

THE PROCESS OF OBSERVATION

The process of observation can be thought of as occurring in four interwoven steps: (1) formulating an
observation guide; (2) observation; (3) analysis; and
(4) prescription. An understanding of these steps
will make it possible for you to develop your own
observation techniques and adapt them to different
children and situations.

Formulating an Observation Guide   Successful
observation begins at home or in the office. Before a
teacher can observe movement with accuracy and
understanding, some homework is required. In this
initial phase of observation, the teacher determines
exactly what to look for during a lesson. Arend and
Higgins (1976, p. 37) provide this description:
"Based upon knowledge of the classification, description, and analysis of the skill, the constraints of
the performance environment, the prerequisites essential for the successful performance of the skill,
and the characteristics of the performer, the ob-

server develops expectancies as to 'what he expects
to see.' "

The process of reflecting on the pertinent bio-
mechanical, neurological, and developmental factors of a movement is best done in an atmosphere of
relative calm. The teacher who tries to observe and
analyze movement during a lesson, without any
preparation, complicates an already difficult task.

Establishing an Observation Guide involves deciding upon one or more critical factors in the
movement to be observed. Once a critical factor has
been identified, it serves as a focal point for the
teacher's observation. In jumping and landing, for
example, the teacher may decide to focus exclusively on the take-off phase of the jump—observing the relationship of the leg and arm actions. As
teachers gain in observation skill and learn more
about the execution of specific movements, they become increasingly adept at identifying one or more
of the critical factors that have a significant impact
on the way a child executes a particular movement.
Initially, however, it is difficult even to identify the

*This vignette describes a two-minute observation made of a
class of 34 fourth-grade children during a gymnastics unit:*

*Teacher is working one-on-one with a student who
has an obvious neurological deficit. She wants him to sit
on a beam and lift his feet from the floor. Her verbal
behaviors fall into categories of reinforcement,
instruction, feedback, and encouragement. She gives
hands-on manual assistance. Nearby two boys perched
on the uneven bars are keeping a group of girls off.
Teacher visually monitors the situation but continues
work on the beam. At the far end of the gym a large mat
propped up so that students can roll down it from a
table top, is slowly slipping nearer to the edge. Teacher
visually monitors this but continues work on the
beam. Teacher answers three individual inquiries
addressed by passing students but continues as before.
She glances at a group now playing follow-the-leader
over the horse (this is off-task behavior) but as she does
a student enters and indicates he left his milk money*

*the previous period. Teacher nods him to the nearby
office to retrieve the money and leaves the beam to
stand near the uneven bars. The boys climb down at
once. Teacher calls to a student to secure the slipping
mat. Notes that the intruder, milk money now in hand,
has paused to interact with two girls in the class and,
monitoring him, moves quickly to the horse to begin a
series of provocative questions designed to reestablish
task focus.*

*As Locke so aptly reminded us after painting this accurate
picture of the complexity of teaching:*

*That was only 120 seconds out of the 17,000 the
teacher spent that day in active instruction. A great deal
of detail was unobserved or unrecorded over those
two minutes, and nothing in the record reflected the
invisible train of thought in the teacher's mind.*

LARRY LOCKE
The Ecology of the Gymnasium

critical factors—let alone analyze them during a movement. For this reason we suggest that teachers initially identify only one or two factors to look for as they focus on a particular movement.

When preparing for effective observation, you must do more than select a skill theme for a lesson and determine the movements to be practiced. Key components of the movements must be identified in relation to the developmental characteristics of the children for whom the lesson is being planned. It is helpful to list these critical factors, as questions, on the same sheet on which the ideas for development of the lesson are listed. In each chapter in Section Four, under the heading Ideas for Observational Focus, questions are listed that will provide guides to observation while teaching. These questions focus on the critical factors of the particular movement being used in the activities under the parallel column of Ideas for Development.

Ideas for Development	Ideas for Observational Focus
Have children attempt to walk along a line that has been painted or taped on the floor.	Do the children utilize their arms to help maintain balance? Do their eyes look straight ahead to the end of the line?
Have the children jump over one hurdle and use a yielding landing, sinking and rolling under a second hurdle.	Do the children bend their knees upon landing in order to smoothly transfer weight in rolling under the second bar?

Often several focus ideas are included with one idea for development. The teacher does not need to utilize all of the focus ideas while observing a lesson. The focus ideas are simply guidelines. When the resulting observations are combined with observations about a child's success rate and interest in

the task, the teacher has clues about the type of prescription that will best meet that child's needs.

Observation   The next three phases—observation, analysis, and prescription—occur during the lesson. In the initial phase of observation, the teacher usually focuses on the class as a whole, watching for these things:

1. Are the children working safely without interfering with others?
2. If any equipment or apparatus is being employed, is this being done within the context of the lesson?
3. Is the assigned task appropriate for the developmental level of the class and of interest to the class?

When you begin to teach specific skills, your observation of a lesson will be guided by the questions you have listed under ideas for Observational Focus for that day's class. Those questions will help you to assess the development of particular skills by individual children and by the class as a whole.

To determine whether the class is functioning appropriately, a teacher must be in a position to observe the entire class. This is referred to as the back-to-the-wall technique. The teacher is on the outside of the area in which the children are working, so that she or he is able to see the entire class. When a

OBSERVING FOR SAFETY

Safety is the primary observational focus of any lesson. Whenever a teacher, during a lesson, observes an unsafe or potentially unsafe situation, that situation must receive the teacher's immediate attention. Constant monitoring is required in order to maintain a safe environment. If a child is injured during physical education because an unsafe situation is ignored or not observed, then the teacher has failed to create and maintain a safe learning environment for children.

*The back-to-the-wall technique allows a teacher to view
all children simultaneously*

teacher enters the middle of an instructional area, he or she is unable to see part of the class. The ability to observe all that is going on, particularly with classes that are difficult to manage, is important for effective classroom management as well as for comprehensive observation. When a teacher is sure that a class is capable of working without constant monitoring, the back-to-the-wall technique can be ignored, except when used for observation of the whole class.

Remember, though, that the teacher who is in a position to observe an entire class, is not necessarily observing effectively. It is not unusual for a teacher to become so focused on the movement or behavior of a particular individual or group that he or she

becomes oblivious to other children within the class.

The teacher who wants to observe the class as a whole can maintain an appropriate focus by scanning (Siedentop, 1976). Using a left to right sweep, the teacher can glance at an entire class in just a few seconds and make an accurate assessment about how all the children are working. For example, if you want to determine the number of children who are actively practicing a given movement, you could quickly observe the class from left to right, counting as you scan. By comparing the number practicing a particular movement with the total number of children in the class, you can rapidly (in no more than fifteen seconds) assess the way the class is working.

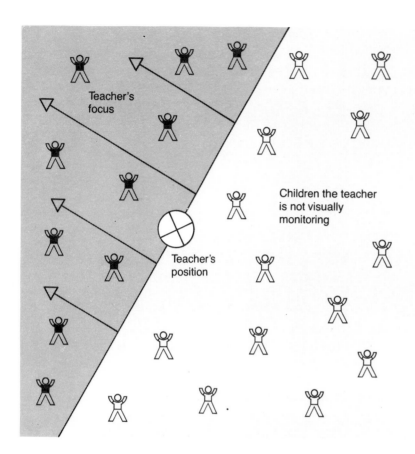

Figure 7.1   An ineffective position for observation

This observation technique can be used for obtaining information about the appropriateness of the movement, the behavior of an entire class, or the behavior of individuals within the class.

Initially the novice teacher may be overwhelmed—there are so many children to observe and so many things to look for and remember. With practice and experience, you will learn to effectively observe and record. The latter part of this chapter includes several practice techniques that will help you learn to observe accurately and quickly.

Analysis   When accurate information about the performance of a class or individual has been obtained, the next step is to compare these data with the intended focus of the lesson. This comparison,

or analysis, is expressed in one of three possible assessments:

1. The class (individual) is functioning appropriately and needs no recommendation for change.
2. A slight refinement or redirection is necessary, but not a total refocusing of the task or challenge.
3. The lesson needs to be refocused for the class (or individual).

A reflective teacher makes these decisions quickly and frequently during the lesson. The process is much more complex if an instructor has no reference point—or observational focus—against which to compare the work of the class.

Prescription   Once the appropriate data have been obtained and analyzed, the final step is to talk with the individuals or class about their work. Hoffman (1977, p. 46) indicates that the prescription phase of the observation process is also complex:

> Physical education teachers experience a great deal of difficulty in communicating messages about movement. Traditional movement nomenclature (flexion, extension, abduction, etc.) designed specifically for scientists may have little meaning for learners. A vocabulary of summary labels and vivid picture words, . . . while occasionally lacking precision of scientific terminology, can be efficient symbols for transmitting meaningful information about movement to learners.

For maximum clarity a teacher's message about a student's movement includes:

1. A brief description of what the teacher observed, stated in terms the student can understand.
2. A contrast between the observed performance and the desired performance.
3. A single suggestion (prescription) as to what the student can practice in order to improve proficiency.

Imagine, for example, that a class is working on the task of throwing a ball to a partner so that the partner can make the catch without having to stop running. As you observe one child throwing the ball, you see that he consistently throws the ball behind the partner, so that the partner has to stop and run back to make a catch. The prescription might be phrased this way: "I notice that Beth is having to stop and turn around to catch your throw. The ideal throw is one that is slightly ahead of her, so that she can keep running to make the catch. Pick out a target that is ahead of Beth and try to throw to the target rather than to the runner."

A particular prescription can be stated in any one of many ways as long as the necessary information is conveyed clearly.

Recently I observed a teacher attempting to teach a child how to run and kick a stationary ball. The child was unable to adjust her run to enable her to arrive at the ball in a proper kicking position. After each unsuccessful attempt (the ball was barely moving as the child appeared almost to step on the ball rather than kick it) the teacher would say to the child, "No, that's not it!" The child knew she had failed as she watched the ball erratically dribble away from her foot, and yet the teacher offered no prescription for improvement. Rather than providing a student with a statement of results they can readily observe, the successful instructor offers a prescription for practice.

LEARNING TO OBSERVE EFFECTIVELY

The skills used while observing movement in a laboratory or classroom differ from the skills required for effective observation of a physical education class. It seems reasonable to assume, however, that individuals who are unable to correctly observe, analyze, and prescribe in a classroom setting will be unable to observe effectively while teaching a physical education class. Even the person who is able to observe in a laboratory setting will not necessarily be able to effectively employ observational skills when given the responsibility of working with thirty children. The practice of observation and analysis of movement must be primarily done in actual teaching situations if it is to be of maximum benefit.

The learning principles that apply to other situations are also applicable in learning to observe movement. Probably the most obvious of these principles, but one that is often ignored, is to proceed from the simple to the complex. The paragraphs that follow provide detailed guidance for the individual who wants to learn how to observe effectively.*

---

*These ideas for practice are based on the pinciples outlined in K. R. Barrett's (1977) insightful paper on the topic of learning to observe.

Movement Focus   Observe a child at play. Describe his or her movements. Be as specific as possible. When possible, compare your observations with those of another observer. Gradually expand your observations to small groups of three, four, and five pupils. Be sure to focus on movement rather than on behavior.

Describing Movement   Observe a physical education class. Focus on one child at a time, and write a brief description of the movements of that child. Try not to spend too long watching any one child. Compare your observations with those of others. The Sample Observation Guide (Figure 7.2) may be helpful.

Observing, Analyzing, and Practicing   When you are able to write brief descriptions quickly and accurately, you are ready to add a step. You can now use a form that includes a third column for the prescriptive phase of observation (Figure 7.3). In that column you will write what you would say to the child after observing and analyzing his movement.

Class Scanning   With a partner or small group, identify a particular question that you want to ask about the performance of the children in a physical education class. For example, you may want to determine how many children are *actively* practicing the task assigned by the teacher. Using the left to right scanning procedure, make a ten-second scan

Theme: Jumping and landing Subtheme: Flow	
Child's Name or Description	Description of Movement
Blond boy in football jersey, #49	Obvious hesitation between landing and roll; difficulty transferring momentum from horizontal to vertical — jumps are long, rather than high.
Susie	Slight flexion at knees seems to cause her to be off-balance upon landing; doesn't use full arm swing to gain height when jumping.

Figure 7.2   Observation guide

Theme: Symmetrical and nonsymmetrical shapes

Subtheme: Matching a partner's movement

Child's Name or Description	Description of Movement	Prescription
Mark and Todd	Using only arms to vary shapes; mostly nonsymmetrical	It seems that you are mainly using your arms to vary your shapes. Have you tried using your legs to make different shapes?
Two girls in red sweatshirts, blue jeans	Movements between shapes are fast and jerky; not staying together	The shapes you have invented are super! Would it be easier to stay together if you slowed down a bit and tried to make your movements smoother?

Figure 7.3   Observation guide with prescription

of the class. Compare your answers and discuss the differences. Ask other questions that can be answered by class scanning, such as, How many children are waiting for a turn? or How many children are maintaining control of the ball with their feet? Record your observations on a two-column Observation Guide form.

Observing as a Part of Teaching   When you are satisfied with your ability to observe, analyze, and prescribe movement as a spectator, the next step is to practice observing in a teaching situation. You may find that a neighborhood playground is a comfortable setting in which to practice.

If at all possible, begin with a single child. Grad-

ually work with more children. Although sometimes it is difficult to arrange to do so, you will find that your teaching and observing skills will develop more rapidly if you work first with one child, then two or a few, and with an entire class only when you have achieved some proficiency.

Ask a friend (or use a tape recorder strapped to your waist) to record your movement descriptions and prescriptions. As soon as possible after teaching, analyze what you have done. Try to determine the appropriateness of your prescription as related to your description. Did the prescription you provided accurately refer to your description? Think about the clarity, in children's terms, of your prescription. Was it understandable to the child?

As you become proficient at observing and pre-

Be gentle with yourself. Don't be disappointed initially if, in the relative tranquility after you have finished teaching, you find that you made some apparently obvious errors. Observation appears easy to the spectator, but the complexity of teaching and observing movement can only be fully appreciated when one assumes the role of the teacher. In time and with practice you will become increasingly satisfied with your ability to observe and analyze movement.

scribing, you can increase the number of children you observe and the length of time you spend practicing.

SUMMARY

The reflective teacher must be able to observe movement accurately and efficiently while teaching. Accurate assessment of the individual variations present in a particular teaching situation is a prerequisite to reflective program design and implementation. In this chapter the process of observation is described as four interrelated phases.

The initial phase occurs prior to actual teaching when the teacher develops an observational focus. This is a list of several critical factors related to the movements to be observed during the lesson.

The next three phases—observing, analyzing, and prescribing—occur during the lesson. In the observation phase, the instructor obtains informa-

tion about how the children are moving. The teacher watches individuals and the class as a whole and records his or her observations.

Analysis, the process of comparing the information obtained through observation to the observational focus written prior to the lesson, is the third phase. The final phase, prescription, involves providing the children with accurate, understandable information about their performances. These three phases are interwoven and virtually inseparable as they occur during the process of teaching a lesson.

REFERENCES

Arend, S. & Higgins, J. R. A strategy for the classification, subjective analysis, and observation of human movement. *Journal of Human Movement Studies* 2 (1976): 36–52.

Barrett, K. R. We see so much but perceive so little: Why? *Proceedings: 1977 National Conference of the National College for Physical Education for Men and the National Association for Physical Education of College Women.* Chicago: Office of Publications Services, University of Illinois at Chicago Circle, 1977.

———Observation for teaching and coaching. *Journal of Physical Education and Recreation* (January 1979): 23–25.

Hoffman, S. J. Toward a pedagogical kinesiology. *Quest*, Monograph 28 (1977): 38–48.

Locke, L. F. The ecology of the gymnasium: What the tourist never sees. *Southern Association of Physical Education for College Women Proceedings*, Spring 1975.

Mauldon E. & Layson, J. *Teaching gymnastics.* London: MacDonald & Evans, 1965.

Siedentop, D. *Developing teaching skills in physical education.* Boston: Houghton Mifflin, 1976.

CHAPTER 8
EVALUATING STUDENT PROGRESS

In light of the influence of self-concept on academic
achievement, it would seem like a good idea for teachers to
follow the precept I saw printed on an automobile drag-
strip racing program: Every effort is made to insure that
each entry has a reasonable chance of victory.
WILLIAM PURKEY

It is naive to assume that children who attend physical education class
regularly are learning to move efficiently and effectively. They may be.
But the only way to be certain is to use an evaluation instrument designed to assess improvement in children's movement abilities.

Evaluation is also a direct way of assessing one's effectiveness as a
teacher. If the children are learning what the teacher intends them to
learn, then the instructor has some assurance that he or she has been
successful. If, on the other hand, the children show little or no improvement, then there is cause to question one's effectiveness as a
teacher.

As physical educators we are concerned with not only the children's
physical development but also their attitudes about physical education
and themselves as movers. Evaluation can provide information about
our success in the affective as well as the motor domains.

SUMMATIVE AND FORMATIVE EVALUATION

Evaluation can be divided into two types—summative and formative.
Summative evaluation (Safrit, 1973; McGee, 1977) is generally performed as a culminating activity at the end of a unit or series of lessons.
It is intended to indicate a student's ability when the study of a particular skill has been completed.

In comparison, formative evaluation involves frequent, even daily,
assessment of a child's abilities, knowledge, or attitudes. This information is incorporated by the teacher into lessons that provide the child
with appropriate experiences. McGee (1977) illustrates the differences

between formative and summative evaluation with the following questions:

Summative	Formative
How far can Terry jump?	How many times can Terry jump?
	Does Terry have enough body control to jump long and short distances?
	What can Terry do to improve his body control?
What is Terry's fitness percentile?	Does Terry have enough strength and endurance to keep moving in the lesson?
	What can Terry do to improve his stamina?
Did Terry learn to jump?	How can Terry use his body in a lot of jumping patterns?
	What can Terry do to get more arm movement into the jump?

Summative evaluation is analogous to taking a trip and finding out, after arriving at what you think is your intended destination, that you took a wrong turn and really were not where you intended to be. Formative evaluation serves as a road map, providing information during the trip through physical education so that changes and corrections can be made along the way. And this is an important aspect of evaluation. Evaluation is used to determine not only how much or how well students have learned, but also what areas should be emphasized in the curriculum.

EVALUATION TECHNIQUES

For many years the major instrument for evaluation in education has been the standardized test. Some would argue that reading and math curricula, in particular, have for too long been determined primarily by how well students have performed on the standardized tests administered every few years. In physical education, however, curricula are not dominated by the specter of students' performance on a single test. This not only allows but actually encourages teachers to develop their own evaluation techniques for determining student progress. Some evaluative instruments that teachers have developed include checklists, individual records of progress, student logs, and tests. Using a variety of evaluative instruments can facilitate and enhance the thoroughness and appropriateness of teacher evaluation of individual children.

Checklists   One of the most practical evaluation aids is the Individual Progress Checklist (Figure

---

The current philosophy of elementary physical education programs stresses the concepts of alternatives, choices, flexibility, variety, versatility, and other such words that refute the concept of only-one-acceptable-way to do a task. While earlier a teacher may have been primarily interested in how far a child could jump, now that teacher is interested in the variety of ways the child can jump with good body control. This change in philosophic position, which has changed the methodology and content emphases of physical education in the elementary schools, has likewise changed the role of evaluation. Both product and process evaluation continue to be needed, but the emphasis has changed from a product to a process orientation. The teacher-centered program was generally product oriented using summative evaluation. The current student-centered program is process oriented stressing formative evaluation. Consequently, the growth process in developing movement patterns is more essential than the final product measure.

ROSEMARY McGEE
Evaluation of Processes and Products

8.1). Each checklist can be designed to correspond to the sequence in which a particular skill theme will be presented to a class of children. The checklist is a natural outgrowth of the planning that is done for each skill theme (Chapter Two). Checklists can also serve as guides for observation (Section Four) and are a source for progress reports to parents. The teacher lists key phrases related to the observational focus for a particular movement. This list is used to check each student's progress periodically during lessons (without setting up special testing sessions).

Individual Records   Keeping individual written records of children's progress is another helpful evaluative technique. Whenever possible, try to write brief comments about several children in a class each time you meet that class, and the next time you teach that class write comments about sev-

Individual Progress Checklist
Skill Theme: Jumping and Landing

Children's Names	Jump down and maintain balance	Two feet to two feet	Run and jump from one foot to other (leaping)	One foot to two feet	Two feet to two feet over object	Hopping	Bent knee landings	Appropriate use of arms in jump	Balanced, quiet landings	Run and jump over low obstacles	Shapes while airborne	Jump to various rhythms	Use gestures while airborne	Series of jumps	Jump to catch an object	Jump to throw an object	Jump over high obstacles	Travel using a series of leaps	Jump and land appropriately from high level	Jump from apparatus to apparatus	Jumps on beam or bench	Jumping to mirror or match	Jumping and turning in a mount or dismount	Jumping using a spring board

Figure 8.1   Individual progress checklist (Skill theme: jumping and landing)

Progress Record Form

George - 5/6 stretched to catch + would come down under ball and give with it - throwing with a mature pattern - rotation and opposition - full extension of arm- Often would throw ball so he had to move slightly to catch it backward as well as side to side.

John - 4/22 when stretching + catching at low level tucked ball + rolled - when fell, often to back 4/28 - rolled w/ ball using opp. arm for support. - stretched so that he was forced to roll.

Derek -

Mimi - 4/25 Beautiful - rolled w/ ball in hand - using opp. arm to push - quickly back up to feet.

Frank - 4/22 hands still on side of ball when catching - often missing - would bring his hands together after the ball had passed them.

Rosemary - 4/10 Very skilled stopping ball with feet + knees. - timing good - used different parts well.

Alfred - 4/22 Throw + catch with small ball - gave with whole body; knees, ankles, hips - hands under ball - caught w/ fingers. 4/28 rolled with ball. Stretched so that he had to roll 5/6 - catching with large ball - better caught from behind ball - would grab with fingers often would miss because of loss of eye contact during flight and would try to catch after ball passed him.

Figure 8.2   Progress record form

Try to stay aware of how you feel about what you are doing. If you feel uncomfortable or confused, don't fight it, just face it and try to identify the cause. A clear picture in your own head is the most important tool you possibly can have. It is a good practice to set aside a short period at the end of the day, or even at the end of each class, to review how things are working out and what your experience is. Just lock the office door or hide in the boiler room. It will take some self-discipline because there always are more pressing things to do. Consulting your head need not take long (a minute or two), but it can pay off. Review of this kind can consolidate a lot of specific detail in your memory for future use that otherwise would be lost in the daily tidal wave of experiences.

DOLLY LAMBDIN
"Quiet Individualizing: What One Teacher Did"

eral other children. If you use sheets (Figure 8.2), prepared in advance with the names of all students and space below each name for notes, you will have less trouble remembering which children you have not yet observed. These sheets will also help you during the first class meeting. Initially you may find that you remember only a few of the children, and that you remember how they behaved but not how they moved. Keeping individual records will help you to become a more efficient observer.

Sometimes you will not have time to write comments between classes. A tape recorder is a handy

A tape recorder is a quick, convenient way to record observations

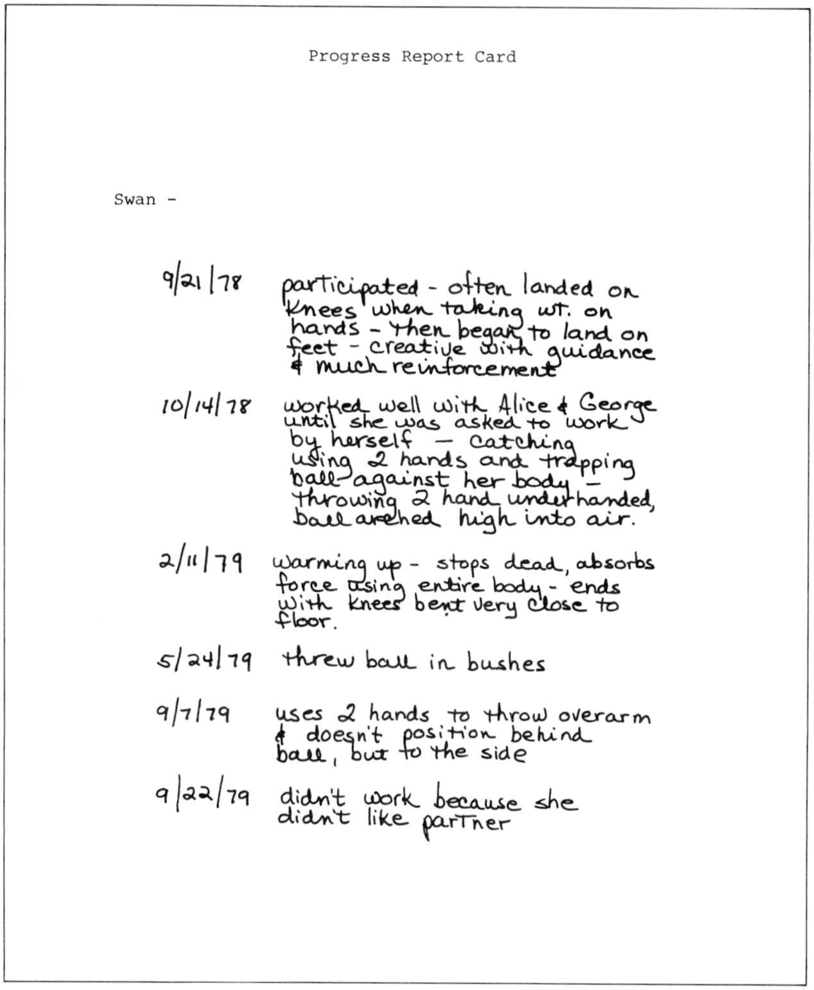

Progress Report Card

Swan -

9/21/78   participated - often landed on
knees when taking wt. on
hands - then began to land on
feet - creative with guidance
& much reinforcement

10/14/78   worked well with Alice & George
until she was asked to work
by herself — catching
using 2 hands and trapping
ball against her body —
throwing 2 hand underhanded,
ball arched high into air.

2/11/79   warming up - stops dead, absorbs
force using entire body - ends
with knees bent very close to
floor.

5/24/79   threw ball in bushes

9/7/79   uses 2 hands to throw overarm
& doesn't position behind
ball, but to the side

9/22/79   didn't work because she
didn't like partner

Figure 8.3   Progress report card

way to record observations quickly. Later, you can transfer taped comments to index cards that can be filed for easy reference (Figure 8.3). The process of transcribing the taped comments to cards will help strengthen your memory of the movements of individual children.

These cards can be used for individual conferences with children or with parents. When you teach several hundred children, you need notes, written over a period of time, to refer to. If you keep such notes for several years, you will have an en-

lightening and encouraging record of how children progress from year to year.

Student Logs   When each child keeps a log related to physical education, these often yield fascinating insights into how individual children perceive physical education class (Figures 8.4 and 8.5). One technique that works well is to provide each child with an individual physical education log (Norris, 1976). College blue books serve this purpose very well.

Child's Class Journal

Sept. 13

Today in class we were working outside with balls and we were throwing over handed and under handed. Erin was my partner today. I had fun. but it was hot. Sometimes I would catch the ball Sometimes and sometimes I would not. I throw the ball ok I guess, That is what I did today.

Sept. 14

Today in class I was working on not too much. But handspings Everybody was with me I had fun. I also worked on round off.

Sept. 15

Today in class we were working with Mats it was fun. we had to roll font and back. rolls we had to land on our feet and not fall down. I tried and I did it. Then we ran and landed in a almost falling over way, I think it was fun.

Nov. 2

Today in class we were doing all diffrent kinds of shapes. it was fun. My partner was Erin D. We worked all diffrent shapes together.

Nov. 3

Today in class we worked with beanbags. My partner was Machiel. She was not a very good worker. My other partner was going to be Corntnay, but miss parker put me with Machiele. It was fun (I guess).

Nov. 21

Today in class we worked on balls of anything that we wanted to do. It was fun. My partner was Corntnay.

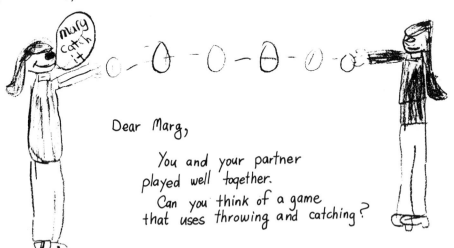

Dear Marg,

You and your partner played well together.

Can you think of a game that uses throwing and catching?

Figure 8.4 Child's class journal

Manie

You need five people four people Get in a square. One of the four people takes a ball. Then when somebody says to go the four people start throwing the ball around the square. The 5th person runs around the square. If the ball get to the fourth person the ball wins but if the person gets the first he or she wins.

Manie—
  I like the way you girls were playing together.
  You also explained your game very well.
  Keep up the good work.
          Mr. Tim

Figure 8.5   Child's class journal

physical education class. We collect the logs periodically and write comments in them when appropriate, and so we have only a few classes keep logs at a time.

Standardized Tests   Although we do not base grades on performances on standardized tests, we believe such tests do have a place in the physical education program. For example, children enjoy and are challenged by comparing their current performances with their past performances on the American Alliance for Health, Physical Education, and Recreation (AAHPER) Youth Fitness Test.

When you administer a standardized test, it is wise to keep the results private, rather than reading them out to each class or posting the scores on a bulletin board. If children choose to share their scores—and many do—that is up to them. Our purpose, however, is not to have children compare themselves with others, but rather to determine whether or not their efforts have resulted in improvement.

Many other instruments can be utilized to assess student progress. Rosemary McGee (1977) has written an excellent reference, "Evaluation of Processes and Products," for those who are interested in obtaining additional information and practical examples of tools for evaluation.

To begin with, I've found that there is no else like me, anywhere, like snow flakes. No one else feels completely the way I do. No one else sees things in the same scope as I do. So my first discovery about myself is that I'm me.

FROM A HIGH SCHOOL COMPOSITION

Whenever possible, encourage children to keep their logs in the classroom and to bring the logs to physical education classes periodically. Usually the students have time to write in their logs sometime during the school day. Many classroom teachers encourage the children to keep up with their logs because they believe this is good writing practice for the children. One of the quickest ways to discourage children from writing in their logs is to correct for grammar, punctuation, and spelling. This is not the purpose of the logs. They are intended to help teachers learn about children's perceptions of

USES OF EVALUATION

Evaluation is used to assess student progress and to determine teacher effectiveness. It is also a basis for grading, a source for progress reports to parents, and a way of determining the individual needs and interests of a child.

As a Basis for Grades Grades are apparently a necessary evil of schooling (Kirschenbaum, 1971). For many years alternative approaches have been advocated, and yet the grading system has remained virtually unchanged. We are philosophically opposed to grading, but most school systems in which we have taught require that students be assigned a grade in physical education.

We are opposed to grading because of the inherent unfairness of basing a child's grade on a comparison of that child's attributes with the attributes of others (norm-referenced grading). An oak tree is different from a maple tree, though both are trees. One provides shade, the other syrup, one has green leaves, the other has red leaves. Too often it is assumed that, because all students are children, they all have the same potentials and abilities. This is nonsense. Children have at least as many differences as trees. If you must grade your students, it is important to be aware of these differences as you go about the process of evaluating individual children.

The practice of grading on dress or on attitudes and participation implies that the student who

---

Whenever a value is set forth which can only be attained by a few, the conditions are ripe for widespread feelings of personal inadequacy. An outstanding example in American society is the fierce competitiveness of the school system. No educational system in the world has so many examinations, or so emphasizes grades, as the American school system. Children are constantly being ranked and evaluated. The superior achievement of one child tends to debase the achievement of another.

MORRIS ROSENBERG
Society and the Adolescent Self-Image

---

wears the required uniform to class, launders it once a week, and conforms to the teacher's guidelines for behavior will earn a high grade in physical education, regardless of physical ability. This approach to grading is indefensible and absurd.

If one must grade students, surely there is a better way. Nevertheless, one study of secondary school physical educators revealed that 93 percent of the high school teachers surveyed based part of a student's grade on whether the student was appropriately dressed for physical activity. Seventy-nine percent considered student participation, and 55 percent based part of each grade on attitude. In contrast, less than 30 percent took the student's skills into account when grading (Morrow, 1978).

Obviously, the information gained from various evaluation instruments often is a factor when a grade must be assigned. Whenever possible, however, a progress report or checklist that is shared with both the parents and the child are our preferred alternative to a single grade on a report card.

As a Basis for Progress Reports to Parents Grading and evaluation are supposedly different processes. In the real world, however, a grade is often used as the single indicator of a child's ability. The teacher who provides students and parents with a descriptive, analytic progress report, rather than a single grade that summarizes weeks of work, is performing a valuable service.

Whenever possible, we design our own progress reports for parents, rather than using the standardized report card forms provided by the school district. This makes it possible to inform parents of their child's progress in a way that is consistent with our beliefs about children and physical education (Figure 8.6). We compare each child's current performance with his or her past performance, not with the performances of others. Instead of providing parents with a single grade, we prefer to tell parents: (1) what their child has been working on in physical education since the last progress report; (2) how their child has improved; (3) the areas in which their child needs additional assistance; and (4) how they might work with their child.

The ideal way to report a child's progress is to have a conference with his or her parents. However, this is not possible in many situations. When such conferences cannot be arranged, informative progress reports are especially important.

Discovering the Needs and Interests of Children
Evaluation can be employed to discover the varying needs and interests of individual children. Formative evaluation techniques are designed for this purpose. Student logs, for example, provide unique and fascinating data about how different children are perceiving physical education classes and how well they feel they are doing in the class. Checklists allow a teacher to evaluate students individually. A teacher can use information obtained through the checklists to make appropriate individual movement prescriptions for a child. Checklists are also excellent catalysts for conferences and discussions,

---

Progress Report to Parents

Name: Sharon

Theme of Study: Throwing and Catching   Area: Games
                   with Emphasis on
                   Traveling in Different
                   Pathways

Brief Description: A study of one aspect of throwing and
catching emphasizing traveling in predictable pathways so as
to facilitate smooth, rather than jerky, catches.   Children
also had the opportunity to throw and catch against opposition
if they chose.   The culminating activity involved designing a
series of plays for receiving a throw. Decisions included
group size, type of balls, and pathways to be traveled.

Demonstration of Theme Understanding:
   Sharon clearly understands the concept of traveling
in different pathways to receive a ball — she is able
to execute straight, curved and zig-zag pathways.

Skill in Execution:
   Sharon catches well when traveling; she is working on
traveling in more predictable pathways so that she will
be a better target; her throwing is improving, although she
still tends to throw behind the receiver.
Group/Partner Interaction:
   Works well with others. Her group did a very nice job
of co-operatively designing a series of "plays." They
preferred not to try them out against opposition.

Additional Comments:
   Sharon continues to improve in throwing and catching.
She enjoys the challenge and would benefit from
practicing at home if the opportunity arises.

   I continue to enjoy working with her.

Figure 8.6   Progress report to parents

with individual children, about their needs and interests in physical education.

EVALUATION IN THE REAL WORLD

No instructor who teaches several hundred children each week—as many physical education instructors do—has the time needed to use all the evaluation techniques described in this chapter. But a reflective teacher is aware of these techniques and uses them with different classes for different purposes. Perhaps you will have one class at a time keeping logs. And you may be able to send only one written report a year to parents.

You can select from the various evaluative techniques those that are most appropriate. Each technique provides a different type of information. The reflective teacher selects the instrument that will provide the type of information that is desired. Logs provide fascinating insights into how children are progressing in designing their own games or dances. A checklist would be far less appropriate for that. In contrast, a checklist is useful for assessing individual abilities of children in a new situation—for example, a class of kindergarten children or during a teacher's first year in a new school.

SUMMARY

Evaluation is a necessary process for determining whether children are actually learning in physical education. Evaluation of student progress is also a direct way of assessing one's effectiveness as a teacher. Summative evaluation is generally performed at the end of a unit or topic of study. In contrast, formative evaluation is an ongoing process of evaluation that provides guidance for future lessons while tending to minimize comparisons between children.

Instruments for evaluating a student's progress include checklists, individual records, student logs, and standardized tests. Evaluation can be used as a basis for grades, as a basis for progress reports to parents, and for discovering the individual needs and interests of children. Progress reports to parents, as an alternative to a single grade, are the preferred mode of reporting student progress whenever feasible.

REFERENCES

Kirschenbaum, H., Simon, S., and Napier, R. *Wad-ja-get? The grading game in American education.* New York: Hart, 1971.

Lambdin, D. Quiet individualizing: What one teacher did. In D. Hellison (Ed.), *Personalized learning in physical education.* Washington, D.C.: American Alliance for Health, Physical Education, and Recreation, 1976.

McGee, R. Evaluation of processes and products. In Logsdon, B. J. et al., *Physical education for children: A focus on the teaching process.* Philadelphia: Lea & Febiger, 1977.

Morrow, R. Measurement techniques: Who uses them? *Journal of Physical Education and Recreation* (November–December 1978): 66–67.

Norris, G. Perceptions of an elementary school physical education learning environment reflective of humanistic tenets as seen by participants and selected observers. Unpublished research paper, University of North Carolina at Greensboro, 1976.

Purkey, W. *Self-concept and school achievement.* Englewood Cliffs, N.J.: Prentice-Hall, 1970.

Rosenberg, M. *Society and the adolescent self-image.* Princeton, N.J.: Princeton University Press, 1965.

Safrit, M. J. *Evaluation in physical education.* Englewood Cliffs, N.J.: Prentice-Hall, 1973.

CHAPTER 9
ASSESSING YOUR TEACHING PERFORMANCE

While it is true that a few individuals have used systematic observation for many years to analyze skill
performance, most have ignored the objective route. Far too
much guess work has been used. Student teachers have
been angered by the high degree of subjectivity shown by
supervisors; practicing teachers have complained about
the prejudicial nature of their promotion evaluations; students have been frustrated in their endeavors to seek
helpful means by which they can work for self-change. In
general, the act of teaching has lacked scientific inquiry.
JOHN CHEFFERS

Accurate and relevant feedback about your teaching performance is necessary if you aspire to become a truly effective teacher. Historically a number of informal and, in many instances, inaccurate approaches to obtaining feedback about teaching have been used. For example, an assessment based on how much the students like a teacher does not provide much useful information about that teacher's performance. Nor does a principal's evaluation if it is made after a five-minute, once-a-year visit to the gymnasium. Some student teachers receive feedback from their supervisors that is both helpful and accurate. Few teachers, however, continue throughout their entire teaching careers to receive the amount and type of feedback that is vital to improving teaching performance. And this is unfortunate.

The notion that anyone who receives a teaching certificate is a qualified teacher is gradually becoming discredited. And it is about time. No airline would hire a novice pilot to fly an airplane containing two hundred people. No doctor would be permitted to perform a major operation, by himself, the day after he graduated from medical school. Pilots and doctors must complete extensive internships before they are assigned major responsibilities. But this has not been true for teachers.

In most states, when a teacher is certificated (usually with only brief student teaching experience) he or she is given complete responsibility for a class of children. The assumption is that anyone who is cer-tificated knows how and what to teach and requires little, if any, as-sistance. But in teaching, as in all human activities, experience enhances proficiency. And beginning teachers can benefit from profes-

Try to stay aware of how you feel
about what you are doing

sional guidance. With appropriate assistance they will become better teachers sooner.

Some school districts, recognizing the need of inexperienced teachers for professional guidance, employ educators who use clinical supervisory techniques (Krajewski, 1976) to work with beginning instructors. In other school districts, however, inex-

perienced teachers must discover for themselves how to teach and what to teach. Individuals who are trying to improve their teaching effectiveness without assistance from school district or university personnel can use self-evaluation techniques. We have divided these techniques into three categories: (1) techniques that can be utilized without assistance; (2) those that require student assistance; and (3) those that use peer assistance.

UNASSISTED ASSESSMENT TECHNIQUES
You can learn a lot about your teaching without relying on others for observation, interpretation, or analysis. You can learn, for example, the amount of time that you spend actually talking to the entire class or to individuals within a class. You can discover which children receive the majority of your attention and whether you spend more time discussing their movement or their behavior. How do children react to your teaching performance? How, and how often, do you use positive or negative comments? How much time do the children spend getting out or putting away equipment? These and other key questions can be answered with self-assessment techniques.

Tape Recorder Self-Analysis   One of the simplest techniques for analyzing teaching performance is to tape record verbal interactions and instruction. If you strap a portable cassette tape recorder around your waist, you will be able to record interactions with individual children as well as instructions to the entire class. The children quickly become accustomed to seeing the tape recorder, and before long they forget about it. By taping different classes, you can obtain answers to such important questions as:

What percentage of a lesson did I spend talking to the entire class? To groups? To individuals?

Are my verbal comments clear? Do I repeat myself frequently?

What percentage of my comments to the children are positive? Negative? Neutral? Do I nag children?

Do I interact with many children in a class? Or do I focus on just a few, constantly calling their names?

These are only a few of the many questions that

can be answered by making tape recordings. Once you have obtained baseline data about your teaching performance, you can measure improvement over a period of weeks or months.

You may find it challenging to set teaching goals for yourself: "During this class I want to interact at least once with every child in the class," or "During this class I want to make at least 80 percent of my comments positive." When you listen to a tape after a class, you will learn whether you have achieved your goal.

Written Instruments   A written instrument, completed by the children, can provide information about your teaching. The children can circle appropriate faces (Figure 9.1) to indicate their responses (Cheffers, Mancini, & Zaichowsky, 1976; McGee, 1977). You can hand out answer sheets (see Figure 9.1) and then read the questions to the whole class. This technique minimizes reliance on children's ability to read or to write.

Be careful in interpreting the results of such an instrument, and remember that it is only one of many techniques that can be used to obtain information about your teaching performance. Judiciously employed, however, such an instrument can provide valuable insights about the children's reaction to your teaching.

STUDENT-ASSISTED ASSESSMENT
Mature, responsible students can help you assess your teaching performance, using techniques that can be learned in just a few minutes. The instruments in this group will provide information that cannot be obtained by the techniques described above.

Teacher Pathway   Provide the student with a sketch of the teaching area—the gym or playground. The student is to trace the pathway that you make during the lesson. This is especially help-

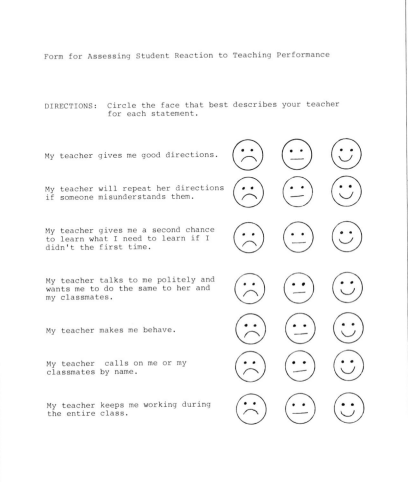

Form for Assessing Student Reaction to Teaching Performance

DIRECTIONS: Circle the face that best describes your teacher
              for each statement.

My teacher gives me good directions.

My teacher will repeat her directions
if someone misunderstands them.

My teacher gives me a second chance
to learn what I need to learn if I
didn't the first time.

My teacher talks to me politely and
wants me to do the same to her and
my classmates.

My teacher makes me behave.

My teacher calls on me or my
classmates by name.

My teacher keeps me working during
the entire class.

Figure 9.1   Form for assessing student reaction to teaching performance

ful when you are learning to increase your effectiveness as an observer (Chapter Seven). You can also teach the student to make a mark on the pathway each time you interact individually with a child.

Interaction Patterns   It is important to interact, verbally or nonverbally, with each child during each lesson. The Interaction Checklist (Figure 9.2) can be used to obtain information about your patterns of interaction with an entire class.

Select a student who knows the names of all the children in the class. Provide that student with a checklist form on which you have listed the names of the entire class. And ask that student to make a tally, in the appropriate column, across from the name of each child you talk to, touch, or smile at during one class period. At the conclusion of the lesson, you can use the completed checklist to analyze your teaching pattern.

You may also find interesting information in an

```
                Interaction Checklist Form


CHILDREN'S NAMES                TYPES OF INTERACTION
                      ┌───────────┬───────────┬──────────┐
                      │ TALKED TO │ SMILED AT │ TOUCHED  │
    Nick              │    ||     │           │    |     │
    Tom               │    |||    │     |     │          │
    Anna              │    |||    │     |     │          │
    Ken               │     |     │     |     │    |     │
    Melinda           │           │           │          │
    Laura             │           │     |     │          │
    Hal               │    ||     │           │    |     │
    Megan             │           │     |     │          │
    Kelly             │     |     │           │          │
    Patrick           │     |     │           │    |     │
    Jeanette          │     |     │    ||     │          │
    Josh              │           │           │          │
    Benjie            │           │     |     │          │
                      │           │           │          │
                      │           │           │          │
                      └───────────┴───────────┴──────────┘
```

Figure 9.2   Interaction Checklist Form

analysis of the sex and race of the children you interact with. If you are, however unintentionally, favoring one group over another, you should be aware of that.

Another type of analysis that can be conducted allows the teacher to determine whether there is a disparity in his or her interactions with different children. Is the teacher interacting more with the children who are most skilled than with those who are least skilled? Or do the interaction patterns indicate some other distribution of attention? Again, the teacher uses the information on an Interaction Checklist that has been filled in by a student. The teacher selects the students who have been observed to be the most skilled and the least skilled—each of these groups should include about 25 percent of the class. From an analysis of the interactions with each of these groups and a comparison of these two interaction patterns, the teacher can de-

termine the group to which he or she is devoting more time.

Practice Opportunities   Effective teachers provide plenty of practice opportunities for children. One way to indirectly assess the number of practice opportunities that students are getting in a class is to teach a student helper to observe and record the number of practices for selected students (Figure 9.3). You may want to select the children to be observed. Or the student helper, if qualified, can select two or more children to observe. This technique works best when the lesson focuses on easily observed movements, such as rolls, catches, or kicks, that can be written on the form before the lesson.

Students can be trained to collect data
on teaching performance

PEER-ASSISTED ASSESSMENT

Some children could learn to utilize the data-gathering systems described below, but it is more realistic to seek the help of a colleague who is willing to help you assess your teaching performance. Such an arrangement can be mutually beneficial, since the systems described in this section can be easily adapted for use in a classroom setting. Thus, if there is only one physical education specialist in the school, a classroom teacher could work as peer assistant, with the specialist.

Feedback and Practice Opportunity Checklist

This system goes a bit further than the Practice Opportunity Checklist described in the previous section. Using the form shown in Figure 9.4, a colleague selects several children, without your knowledge, and records their practice opportunities. She also codes feedback statements made by you to the students being observed. Each statement is coded as related to the child's movement or behavior. And each statement is coded as positive or negative when possible—that is, if the statement is clearly positive or negative. Neutral statements are not recorded under the behavior heading.

The statement "Nice catch, Virginia" would be coded on the checklist as Movement, Positive. The statement "Jeff, you never listen!" would be coded as Behavior, Negative. This observation system is relatively simple to learn and can be used reliably after just a few minutes of practice.

DATE ______________________

Teacher ______________ Observer ______________

Theme of Lesson ______________________________

OBSERVATIONAL DATA

Practice Opportunities

Names of Children	Roll	Catch	Kick	Throw

Figure 9.3 Practice opportunity checklist

Figure 9.4   Practice opportunities and
teacher feedback checklist

DATE **February 12**

Teacher **Linda Kobel**   Observer **Judy Mitchell**

Theme of Lesson **Kicking and catching**

OBSERVATIONAL DATA

Names of Children	Practice Opportunities		Teacher Feedback			
			Movement		Behavior	
	Kicks	Catches	Positive	Negative	Positive	Negative
MARK	HHT HHT IIII	HHT IIII	II	I	II	
VIRGINIA	HHT II	III	IIII		II	
TODD	HHT HHT HHT HHT	HHT HHT HHT III	III		I	I
JEFF	I HHT HHT	HHT HHT		HHT	I	III
SUSIE	HHT HHT HHT III	HHT HHT II	III	I	II	I

*Instructional time is recorded when
the opportunity to learn is present but
the students are not active*

Management time is recorded when the opportunity to learn is not present and students are involved in activities that are only indirectly related to the class learning activity

Waiting time can be the time when students are waiting for class to begin

Activity time is recorded when the children are involved in movement that is consistent with the goals of the teacher

Duration Recording System Duration recording, which is a bit more difficult to use than the Teacher Feedback Checklist, provides an indirect assessment of teacher performance by measuring what the students are doing (Siedentop, 1976). This system includes four categories of student behavior: (1) instruction time; (2) management time; (3) activity time; and (4) waiting time. The total amount of time, in minutes and seconds, is determined for each of the four categories. These minutes and seconds can then be converted into percentages that permit comparisons with previously coded lessons.

The Duration Recording System form (see Figure 9.5) contains three time bars. Each bar represents ten minutes and is organized by ten-second segments. The form lists the code to be used by the peer assistant to report what is happening: I, for instruction; M, for management; A, for activity; and W, for waiting time.

The peer assistant records the exact time the lesson begins—the time at which the teacher gives a starting signal or the children begin to practice one or more activities. From that moment until the end of the lesson, the peer assistant, using a watch with a second hand, marks the time bars to reflect what is happening in the class. The assistant draws a line through the bar when there is a change in student behavior and indicates the change by writing the appropriate letter over the next space in the bar. At the end of the lesson, the time is recorded. The peer

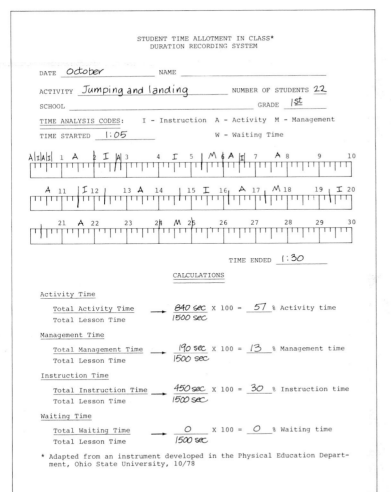

Figure 9.5   Student time allotment in class duration recording system

assistant uses the definitions and examples in Table 9.1 as guides to accurate coding.

After the lesson the teacher uses the information of the Duration Recording System form to figure out what percentage of class time was spent on each category. The following procedure should be used: Add up the time for each of the four categories. Divide each category total by the total lesson time, and then multiply each by 100. The calculations at the bottom of Figure 9.5 illustrate how the percentages for that sample lesson were determined.

In the beginning the peer assistant may be uncertain about how to code a particular event. This is not uncommon when one is learning to use any type of analysis system. The assistant should make a decision and then code other such events the same way. That will enable you to compare a succession of lessons to determine what progress you are making.

COMBINING ASSESSMENT TECHNIQUES

Many observation systems have been developed to analyze the teaching performance of physical education teachers (Siedentop, 1976; Cheffers, 1977; Barrett, 1977). As one becomes accustomed to using different systems it is possible to begin to code additional teacher or student behavior simultaneously— for example, how many students are off-task at a particular moment, or how many positive and negative feedback statements are made by the teacher. Remember that what is measured or how it is measured is less important than the continuing effort to systematically assess and improve one's teaching performance. Relying on one's subjective judgment ("I think I'm getting better"), or that of a colleague ("That lesson looked good"), is not nearly as effective as collecting and analyzing relatively objective data that can be referred back to in a few days, months, or even years.

Table 9.1   Duration recording system coding guide

CATEGORY	DEFINITION	EXAMPLES
Instruction	Time when students have an opportunity to learn. They may be receiving verbal or nonverbal information. Most students (51 percent or more) are *not* engaged in physical activity.	Listening to a lecture, watching the teacher or another student demonstrate a skill, participating in a class discussion, or answering questions from the teacher.
Management	Time when the opportunity to learn is *not* present. Most students (51 percent or more) are involved in activities that are only indirectly related to the class learning activity. There is no instruction, demonstration, or practice.	Changing activities, numbering off for an activity, listening for roll call, getting out or putting away equipment, or getting into line.
Activity	Time when most students (51 percent or more) are involved in physical movement that is consistent with the specific goals of the particular lesson.	Performing exercises, designing a game, dance, or gymnastic sequence, participating in a group or individual game, providing assistant for a partner, or waiting in line for a turn.
Waiting	Time not defined by the other three categories.	Waiting for class to begin, or waiting for instruction to resume when it has been interrupted by another teacher, student messenger, parent, principal, or public address system.

SOURCE: Adapted from an instrument developed by the Physical Education Department, Ohio State University, Columbus, Ohio.

A SUPPORT GROUP

The techniques described above for analyzing one's teaching performance are effective approaches to improving teaching performance. But successful teaching is more than utilizing specific teaching behaviors in predetermined ways. Teaching can never be totally reduced to specific formulas of behavior that guarantee success for all teachers with all classes. However, systematic observation can help to answer some questions and provide information that can influence a teacher's success. There are other questions that require careful thought and analysis, questions that cannot be answered solely by systematic observation. Sometimes we need to sit down with colleagues who will listen carefully and help us to understand (analyze) a particular situation. This is what a support group does. Teachers form support groups to build helping relationships between two or more individuals who have learned to trust one another. These individuals share their concerns, questions, dreams, and hopes about themselves as teachers.

If one is not careful, teaching can be a lonely and difficult profession. As the poster depicting an exhausted teacher at the end of an obviously difficult day reminds us: "No one ever said teaching was

Elementary school physical education teachers have been observed who clocked as little as three and a half minutes of significant face-to-face contact with other adults between the hours of 7:30 A.M. and 4:30 P.M. The teacher can be psychologically alone in a densely populated world. The physical (architectural) isolation of the gym located away from the political heartland of the school and the social isolation of the physical educator role which may make the teacher peripheral to the real business of the school, both seem to sustain and intensify the feeling of isolation. Teaching physical education in some schools is a lonely job, awash in an endless sea of children.

LARRY LOCKE,
"The Ecology of the Gymnasium: What the Tourist Never Sees."

going to be easy." When your teaching is not going well, or when you have had a spectacular day, a support group can provide comfort and encouragement. It is reassuring to have a stable group of colleagues who will listen carefully, verbally applaud your successes, and help you analyze your concerns.

Most teachers occasionally gripe about teaching conditions, parents, administrators, or fellow teachers. We all have our down days. Within a support group, however, complaining is inappropriate because it is often toxic and tends to contaminate the thinking of others. A support group is designed to make people feel better about their teaching, not worse.

Teaching will never be an exact, predictable science. There will always be some art to teaching effectively. Systematic observation techniques and support groups are two approaches to improving both teaching performance and one's personal satisfaction and enthusiasm for teaching.

SUMMARY

Teaching is a developmental process. Because effective teaching involves learning, it takes time and experience to become a successful teacher. Unfortunately, many school districts do not seem to recognize this. As a result, many inexperienced teachers find themselves on their own before they are actually ready to face teaching alone. Various observation techniques can be used to obtain data that *are* helpful to the teacher who wants to become more effective. These techniques have been classified into three categories: (1) techniques that can be used without assistance; (2) those that require student assistance; and (3) those that use peer assistance.

When there is no one available to help, a teacher can use written instruments and tape recorder self-analysis to obtain information about his teaching performance. A teacher's pathways, interaction patterns, and the number of practice opportunities provided to children can be assessed with student assistance. A peer can provide even more technical information, by utilizing a feedback practice opportunity checklist and a duration recording system.

A very different but equally valuable aid is the support group. Such a group, made up of fellow teachers, can provide comfort and encouragement for all participants. When a group of peers actively listens to each other's questions and helps clarify each other's thoughts, the teaching attitude of all the members is improved.

REFERENCES

Barrett, K. R. Studying teaching: A means for becoming a more effective teacher. In B. J. Logsdon et al., *Physical education for children: A focus on the teaching process.* Philadelphia: Lea & Febiger, 1977.

Cheffers, J. Observing teaching systematically. *Quest* 28 (1977): 17–28.

Cheffers, J., Mancini, V., & Zaichowsky, L. The development of an elementary physical education attitude scale. *The Physical Educator* 32 (1976): 30–33.

Krajewski, R. J. (Ed.) Clinical supervision. *Journal of Research and Development in Education* (Winter 1976): 58–66.

Locke, L. F. The ecology of the gymnasium: What the tourist never sees. *Southern Association of Physical Education for College Women Proceedings,* Spring 1975.

McGee, R. Evaluation of processes and products. In B. J. Logsdon et al., *Physical education for children: A focus on the teaching process.* Philadelphia: Lea & Febiger, 1977.

Siedentop, D. *Developing teaching skills in physical education.* Boston: Houghton Mifflin, 1976.

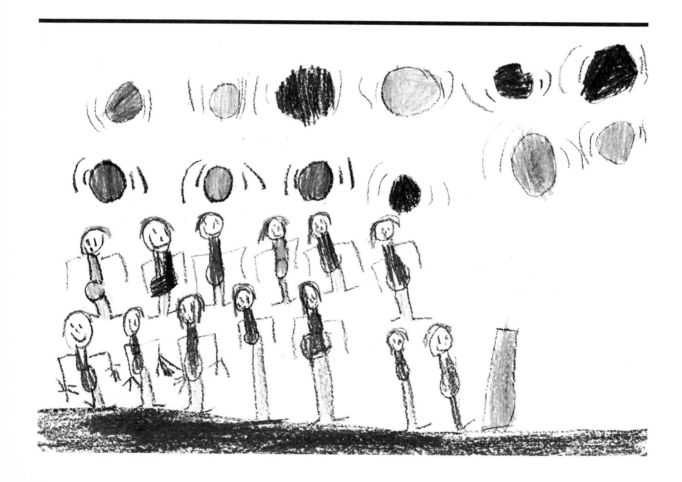

SECTION 3
PROGRAM
CONTENT

The four chapters in this section discuss what is included in a program of physical education and how it is presented. Because our programs are not organized by grade level or age, the first chapter in this section—Chapter Ten, Determining Generic Levels of Skill Performance—discusses our approach to organizing program content according to general levels of skill proficiency. Chapters Eleven, Twelve, and Thirteen describe the teaching of games, dance, and gymnastics.

Because this book is organized by movement concepts and skill themes and does not contain the traditional sections on games, dance, and gymnastics ideas, we have included sections in the index that provide guides to games, dance, and gymnastics ideas. This should be of value to those who prefer to organize program content around games, dance, and gymnastics activities.

CHAPTER 10
DETERMINING GENERIC LEVELS OF SKILL PROFICIENCY

Public school curricula are full of programs that work under "special circumstances," that is, conditions unobtainable in the average school system.

DANIEL FADER

Historically elementary school physical education textbooks have used grade levels as guidelines for determining what to teach and when to teach it. Activities thought to be appropriate for first grade children are described in one section, second grade activities in another section, and so forth. We found, when teaching, that organizing content by grade levels does not work well. One third grade class is different from another third grade class, in both ability and interest. And within each third grade class, the range of differences is substantial. The convenience of organizing curriculum by grade level cannot be denied. But we wanted an approach that would better match the range of differences that are characteristic of children. Both age and sex are inadequate guidelines for curriculum construction. Six-year-old boys have a wide range of abilities and interests, as do ten-year-old girls. And so we began to examine the possibility of organizing a curriculum based on children's levels of motor skill proficiency.

The concept of levels of motor ability is not new. It is supported by research in motor development (Wickstrom, 1977; Roberton and Halverson, 1977; McLenaghan and Gallahue, 1978; and Seefeldt and Haubenstricker, 1978); motor learning (Gentile, 1972); and curriculum theory (Jewett and Mullan, 1977). The problem was to assimilate the available research and formulate a practical model, grounded in research, that could be utilized effectively in actual teaching situations. Stanley (1969) proposed four levels of skill proficiency—precontrol, control, utilization, and proficiency. We have adapted these levels as a guide to organizing lesson content to match the skill abilities of children.

LEVELS OF SKILL PROFICIENCY

Precontrol   This initial level is characterized by lack of ability to either consciously control or intentionally replicate a movement. A child at the precontrol level who is bouncing a ball spends more time chasing after the ball than bouncing it—the ball seems to control the child. A child at this level who tries to do a forward roll may complete a revolution on a mat. Or the child may get stuck, not rolling at all, or rolling half forward and half to the side and finishing flat on his or her back. Efforts by a child at this level to strike a ball with a racket are characterized by frequent misses, mis-hits, and a striking pattern that is inefficient and inconsistent. Successful skill performances are accidents.

Control   The control level is characterized by less haphazard movements—the body appears to respond more accurately to the intentions of the child. A movement that is repeated becomes increasingly uniform and efficient. A cartwheel performed by a child at this level is identifiable as a cartwheel; a child is able to travel in a previously identified direction while briefly taking full weight on his or her hands. When a child at this level tries to throw a ball at a target, the ball travels in the direction of the target, usually.

The child's movements at this level are often characterized by intense concentration, because the movements are far from automatic.

Movements at the precontrol level are characterized by inconsistency, and successful skill performances are often accidental rather than intentional

At the control level, movements are often characterized by intense concentration

Utilization   As a child's movements become increasingly automatic, the child is said to be at the utilization level. Children at this level are able to use a movement in different contexts, because they do not need to think as much about how to execute the movement. The task of dribbling a ball in a situation similar to a game is appropriate for a child at the utilization level. When children at the previous (control) level try to dribble a ball, they spend more time chasing the ball than dribbling. At the control level, children are unable to focus on dribbling a ball while trying to travel away from an opponent. A cartwheel, as one in a sequence of three movements, would also be an appropriate task for a child at a utilization level.

Proficiency   The fourth level, proficiency, is characterized by somewhat automatic movements that begin to seem effortless. This is the level when children gain control of a specific movement and are challenged by the opportunities to employ that skill in changing environments that may require sudden and unpredictable movements. The challenge of repeating movements exactly and with ever increasing degrees of quality is also appropriate for children at this level.

At the utilization level, movements are more reflexive and require less concentration

Children at the proficiency level are challenged by dynamic, unpredictable situations

OBSERVABLE CHARACTERISTICS OF THE GENERIC LEVELS OF SKILL PROFICIENCY

Precontrol Level

1. Child is unable to repeat movements in succession; one attempt does not look like another attempt to perform the same movement.
2. Child utilizes extraneous movements that are unnecessary for an efficient performance of the skill.
3. Child seems awkward and frequently does not even come close to a correct performance of the skill.
4. Correct performances are characterized more by surprise than by expectancy.
5. When the child practices with a ball, the ball seems to control the child.

Control Level

1. The child's movements are less haphazard in appearance and seem to conform more to the intentions of the child.
2. Movements are more consistent in appearance and repetitions are somewhat alike.
3. Correct performances of the skill begin to occur more frequently.
4. When the child tries to combine one movement with another or perform the skill in relation to an unpredictable object or person, the attempt is usually unsuccessful.
5. Because the movement is not automatic, the child needs to concentrate intensely on what he or she is doing.

Utilization Level

1. The movement becomes more automatic and can be performed successfully, with concentration.
2. Even when the context of the task is varied (slightly at first), the child can still perform the movement successfully.
3. The child has developed control of the skill in predictable situations and is beginning to be able to move skillfully in unpredictable situations. The skill can be executed the same way consistently.
4. The skill can be utilized in combination with other skills and still be performed appropriately.

Proficiency Level

1. The skill has become almost automatic, and performances in a similar context appear almost identical.
2. The child is able to focus on extraneous variables—such as an opponent, an unpredictable object, the flow of travel—and still perform the skill as intended.
3. The movement often seems effortless as the child performs the skill with ease and seeming lack of attention.
4. The movement can be performed successfully in a variety of planned and unplanned situations as the child appears to modify his performance to meet the demands of the situation.

TASK-SPECIFIC LEVELS

The levels of motor skill proficiency are task specific and not age related. This means that a child who is at a proficiency level in one skill (for example, at striking a ball with a racket) is not necessarily at the proficiency level in related skills (such as striking a ball with a bat or a club). Thus, a child's level of motor skill proficiency is evaluated for specific skills.

Age is not an indicator of motor skill proficiency.

If it were, all adults would be skillful at ball games, for example, and we know this is not true. It is not unusual to observe children in the fourth and fifth grades who are at a precontrol level when a new skill is introduced, one that they have never practiced. Generally, however, because of their physical maturation and previous experiences, they move from the precontrol level more rapidly than younger children.

DEVELOPMENTAL STAGES OF MOTOR SKILLS

Some research in motor development has focused on developmental stages of specific skills, such as throwing, jumping, and kicking. This work relates directly to the generic levels of skill proficiency (Roberton and Halverson, 1977; Wickstrom, 1977; McClenaghan and Gallahue, 1978; and Seefeldt and Haubenstricker, 1978). Researchers typically have used photography to analyze the movements of children as they perform specific motor skills. From photographs, researchers have been able to formulate developmental stages that characterize the skills studied. This information is important to teachers of physical education because it gives them descriptive information about children's motor patterns, from immature to mature (skillful) stages.

When a teacher understands a child's present stage of development and knows the characteristics of the next stage, as indicated by research, the teacher can provide that child with appropriate feedback. An instructor who is unaware of developmental stages may err by providing a child with information that is not only confusing, but possibly irrelevant because it is too advanced.

Descriptions of developmental stages have been included with those chapters in Section Four for which there is available research. At the first two levels, many of the tasks are designed to enhance the development of mature motor patterns, and the observation guides are designed accordingly.

USING SKILL LEVELS IN TEACHING

The levels of motor skill proficiency provide a basis for the design of experiences that are appropriate to each level of skill ability. In most classes you will find that the children range across three levels for a particular skill. When this is true, a single game or task will be inappropriate for at least some of the children. Typically in physical education, tasks or

games that seem to be appropriate for the middle skill level have been selected. When that is done, children at the extremes are either bored or left behind because the activity is too hard or too easy. (Some would argue that in physical education we have typically focused predominantly on the highly skilled children, the athletes, and virtually ignored the remainder of the children.) The instructor who assesses the skill levels of pupils can develop a curriculum that matches the children's abilities and interests—a curriculum that reflects the characteristics of the individual children and other facets of the ecology of his particular teaching situation.

SUMMARY

Organizing curriculum by grade level or by age is convenient. And yet, because of the range of skills found at any grade level or age, age and grade level are inadequate indicators of children's skill levels. We adapted the concept of generic levels of motor skill proficiency. Assessment of children's skills in terms of these levels provides a basis for planning appropriate activities. The four levels of motor skill proficiency are: (1) precontrol, (2) control, (3) utilization, and (4) proficiency.

Children at a precontrol level are unable to consciously control or replicate a particular movement. At the control level, the child's body appears to respond more accurately to the child's intentions, and movements become increasingly similar. Movements are even more automatic and reflexive at the utilization level. Children at this level can use a movement in a variety of contexts. At the proficiency level a child has gained control of a movement and is challenged by the goal of repeating movements exactly or using movements effectively in dynamic, unpredictable situations.

The generic levels of skill proficiency are task related—that is, a person who is at the utilization level in one skill may be at the control level in another skill. Age and skill level are not necessarily related.

REFERENCES

Fader, D. *The naked children.* New York: Bantam, 1971.

Gentile, A. M. A working model of skill acquisition with application to teaching. *Quest* 17 (January 1972): 3–23.

Jewett, A. E., & Mullan, M. R. *Curriculum design: Purposes and processes in physical education teaching–learning.* Washington, D.C.: American Alliance for Health, Physical Education, and Recreation, 1977.

McClenaghan, B., and Gallahue, D. *Fundamental movement.* Philadelphia: W. B. Saunders, 1978.

Roberton, M. A., & Halverson, L. E. The developing child: His changing movement. In B. J. Logsdon, et al. *Physical education for children: A focus on the teaching process.* Philadelphia: Lea & Febiger, 1977.

Seefeldt, V., & Haubenstricker, J. Developmental sequences. From materials presented at the University of Georgia, Athens, Georgia, June 1978.

Stanley, S. *Physical education: A movement orientation.* Toronto: McGraw-Hill, 1969.

Wickstrom, R. L. *Fundamental motor patterns.* (2nd ed.) Philadelphia: Lea & Febiger, 1977.

CHAPTER 11
TEACHING GAMES

All too often when it comes to the physical education of children we steal away this world of the child by dictating games to them. We do this under the assumption that it is good for all children to learn about our major sports through lead-up games involving kickball, dodgeball, Newcomb, line soccer, steal the bacon, and the like. Most of these games, however, are characterized by large groups, lack of participation, elimination, and stress on winning. Those who are not ready because of interest, motivation, strength, size or skill often turn to a search for stimulation in activities other than the game. These symptoms can be seen when children begin daydreaming, playing with dandelions in the grass, shoving, pushing, pulling, or looking for mischievous action with a friend.

PETER WERNER

Games* are probably the easiest subject to teach. Unlike dance and gymnastics, games are self-propelling. Once students grasp the basic concepts of a game, they require little teacher intervention; except for resolution of misunderstandings and arguments.

The ease with which a subject can be taught should not be the primary determinant of the content of a physical education program. The current and future needs and interests of the children in the program are the key factors to consider when planning an overall program. The instructor who teaches children to play games successfully and effectively does more than simply provide opportunities for children to play games. He or she must create a variety of learning opportunities. These will include situations in which the children play games and situations in which they practice skills. The children in such programs acquire a foundation of movement skills that enables them to participate successfully in a broad variety of games and sports. Once children have acquired the prerequisite game skills, sport becomes an attractive leisure time alternative for them throughout their lives.

GAME EXPERIENCES
Children need practice experiences that will lead to acquisition of game skills and an enjoyment of games. We organize game lessons into

---

*Throughout the book we refer to the activities typically played by children in elementary schools as games. Sports, with standardized rules and procedures (for example, football, basketball, and baseball), are designed primarily for adults.

three types of experiences based on the children's skill levels: invariant game skill experiences, dynamic game skill experiences, and games playing experiences (Figley, Mitchell, Wright, 1977; Barrett, 1977).

Invariant Game Skill Experiences The first experiences we provide for most children are ones that involve basic skills. Such experiences allow the pupils to focus on a specific skill. The experience is structured so that the task is as identical as possible each time—the experience is invariant in that the

Kicking a ball at a target from behind a designated line is an example of invariant gamelike practice

child is not required to predict the flight of a ball or the movement of an opponent, for example. Such experiences are appropriate for a child who is at the precontrol or control level of skill proficiency (see Section Four) and would have difficulty executing a skill in a dynamic or open situation. As a child's proficiency in a skill increases, you can increase the difficulty of the tasks while retaining the relative predictability of the skill. For example, when a child is learning to throw a ball to hit a stationary target, the distance to the target can be increased. If the child is learning to run and leap over a low obstacle, the height of the obstacle can be increased.

When a child who is not able to perform a basic skill consistently (precontrol) is placed in a game that requires that skill and the ability to perform it in a dynamic situation, the results are often counterproductive. A child in that situation often experiences failure and frustration because of his or her continuing inability to execute the prerequisite movements of the game. And the other children are frustrated when the flow and enjoyment of the game is interrupted by an unskillful player.

When I first started teaching, I was looking for games that were recommended for first grade children and did not require a great deal of game skill. Brownies and Fairies, a simple running and chasing game, was prescribed in one text as appropriate for six-year olds. The first time the game was played, two children fell down and bloodied their knees when they tried to run in a crowd of children. They could run without falling by themselves. But when they were placed in a dynamic situation that involved both running and dodging, they were unsuccessful. They probably forgot that experience many years ago—once their knees healed. I haven't.

Recent research suggests that the child who practices skills in an unchanging situation probably does not benefit as much as the child who practices in a dynamic setting (Arnold, 1978; Schmidt, 1977;

McKinney, 1977). The skill acquired by a child who throws and catches a yarn ball with a partner may have minimal transfer to the skill of throwing and catching as used in baseball or basketball. For this reason we try to create situations in which skills can be used as they are in games, as soon as the child is able to perform skills successfully in an unchanging situation.

The appropriate time to switch from invariant skill experiences to dynamic situations is determined as the teacher classifies the abilities of the children according to the generic levels of skill proficiency (see Chapter Ten). Some children enter school ready for experiences that require skills used in games (utilization level). Other children are not ready to use a skill in a dynamic setting until they are much older.

Dynamic Game Skill Experiences When children have learned to successfully perform skills under relatively static conditions, they need and are challenged by opportunities to practice skills in cir-

cumstances similar to actual sport situations (utilization level). Shooting a basket with no opposition is in some ways a different skill from the skill needed to make a basket immediately after stopping a dribble or when guarded by an opponent. Children should be exposed to many experiences that relate to a variety of sports. Not only do we expose children to experiences from sports that are played in America, but we also attempt to expose children to game-type experiences that require different combinations of skills that have no apparent relationship to any sports that we are familiar with (Section Four). Such experiences encourage children to develop techniques and applications of skills in unique situations, because no doubt they will experience games that have yet to be invented and which require skills and abilities yet unheard of.

Providing experiences that require children to use game skills is different from teaching games. You can create practice opportunities that simulate the way skills are used in games but do not include scoring and competition. For example, you could ask children to try to keep a ball away from a part-

Striking a ball past a defender into a goal is a skill experience similar to a striking game situation

COMPETITION/COOPERATION

Some children love to compete; others prefer (and seem to learn better) in games that encourage cooperation. We attempt to respect the preference of each child by providing choices, trying never to place an entire class in a competitive situation. Instead, we allow children to choose between two or more games or ask children to make up their own games. The degree of competition is heightened or lessened by the teachers. Teachers who constantly shout out the score, post team won and lost records, and reward the winners (thereby punishing the losers) place an emphasis on competition for which some children are not ready. If you don't believe us, talk to the thousands of adults who were unskilled as children and yet were placed in highly competitive situations. They can describe, in vivid detail, the feelings of being picked last, shouted at for dropping a ball, and ridiculed for "letting the team down." Such distasteful experiences usually have lasting and negative influences on the individual's willingness to participate in sports.

Skill acquisition lesson: teacher challenges children to dribble a ball through an obstacle course

ner using only a dribble (hand or foot), or to work in a group of three to keep a ball moving in the air without actually catching the ball. These tasks are close to the dynamic situations of games and sports.

Games Playing Experiences   When providing children with games playing experiences, we try to acquaint the children with many different types of games. These activities can help children experience the enjoyment, satisfaction, excitement, and sense of accomplishment that can be the outcome of a developmentally appropriate game.

Some skill development results from playing games. But game playing is not the most efficient way for all children to improve their game skills. For this reason, it is useful to distinguish between lessons in which the primary purpose is to improve skills (invariant and dynamic game skill experiences) and lessons in which the primary purpose is to develop enthusiasm for and a playing knowledge of a variety of games (games playing experiences).

Nettie Wilson (1976) conducted a study to determine the number of throwing, catching, and kicking opportunities in the game of kickball, as played by third and fourth grade children under the direction of a classroom teacher. She found that:

1 less than one-half of the game was actually spent using the criterion skills.
2 the average number of catches attempted in the kickball games was slightly more than two—35 percent of the children never caught the ball. Eighty-three percent of the children who didn't catch the ball were girls.
3 the average number of throws made in the kickball games, excluding those made by the pitcher and catcher, was slightly more than one—52 percent of the children never threw the ball at all during the entire game, and 67 percent of those who never threw the ball were girls.

Lessons devoted to skills acquisition are punctuated by a number of starts and stops. The teacher continually refocuses or redefines the tasks, providing feedback to individuals and groups in an attempt to enhance the quality of their movements.

The games playing environment is somewhat different, however. The enjoyment and satisfaction derived from playing games frequently is a product of playing a game without interruption. In the limited time most of us have to teach our classes, there is hardly enough time for skill practice and game playing in a single lesson. Try to observe the types of skill work that children need as they are playing games, and focus on those needs during later classes. Try not to stop or interfere in the children's games to teach skills, unless the game has become unsatisfying and boring because of lack of ability. Adults prefer not to be interrupted during a game, even by someone who wants to provide feedback. Children share this feeling, and it must be respected if the teacher wants to create positive attitudes toward games.

GAME LESSON DESIGNS

A teacher can use five types of lesson designs in structuring games experiences. These are predesigned games, modified predesigned games, games designed by the teacher, games designed by the teacher and the children, and games designed by children (Riley, 1975).

Predesigned Games   Predesigned games are the games described in textbooks or learned in a methods class and taught to the children without modification. Such games, the textbooks imply, will be appropriate for your pupils as well as interesting and exciting for them. Brownies and Fairies, Red Rover, Four Square, and Snatch the Bacon are well-known predesigned games.

Predesigned games are easy to teach because they require little preparation or teaching skill. The teacher selects a game and explains it to the children. When the children understand the game, they start to play. And the game continues until the lesson ends or the teacher changes to another activity.

Unfortunately, few predesigned games are appropriate for all of the children in a class. A few skilled or popular children often dominate such games, while others are minimally involved, both physically and emotionally. You may occasionally have a situation in which a particular predesigned game is appropriate for a class or group of children. Usually, though, you will find that, while many of

---

I would like to contrast the richness of children's natural play with the stultifying rigidity of play that is organized by adults. No better example can be found than that of the Little League, for what boys, left to their own devices, would ever invent such a thing? How could they make such a boneheaded error as to equate competition with play? Think of the ordinary games of boys—in sandlots, fields, parks, even stickball in the street. They are expansive and diverse, alternately intense and gay, and are filled with events of all kinds.

Between innings the boys throw themselves on the grass. They wrestle, do handstands, turn somersaults. They hurl twigs and stones at nearby trees, and yell at the birds that sail by. A confident player will make up dance steps as he stops a slow grounder. If an outfielder is bored, he does not stand there pulling up his pants and thumping his glove, but plays with the bugs in the grass, looks at the clouds. . . . There is almost always a dog on the field, and no part of the competition is gayer or more intense than that between the boys and the dog, who when he succeeds in snapping up their ball, leads them off in a serpentine line that is all laughter and shouts, the dog looking back over his shoulder and trotting with stiff legs, until finally he is captured and flattens his ears as they take back their ball. No one has forgotten the score or who was at bat. The game goes on. The game goes on until darkness ends it, and the winners can hardly be distinguished from the losers, for by then everyone is fumbling the ball and giggling and flopping on the grass.

GEORGE DENNISON
The Lives of Children

the ideas in a predesigned game are worthwhile, the structure of the game needs to be modified to match the game to the abilities and interests of different children.

Modified Predesigned Games   Modifying a predesigned game requires greater planning and organizing ability than is needed to pick a game from a book. The chances that a game will be more appropriate for a particular class are increased when a teacher modifies a predesigned game. You might decide to narrow or widen the playing area; require that different skills be utilized in the game (e.g., throwing instead of kicking or volleying) or change a rule to make the game less complex, (e.g., allow two tries instead of one)

During the lesson the instructor may use the same teaching skills required to teach a predesigned game—explaining the game and intervening only when that is necessary to keep the game going. Evaluation of the game is more complex. You will have to decide, after observing the children, whether the game should be modified further or is satisfactory as currently structured.

Teacher-Designed Games   Sometimes a teacher cannot find a game that is appropriate for a particular class, and modifications of predesigned games do not seem effective. In such a situation, the teacher may design a game that satisfies a specific goal. Designing a game places a greater demand on the creative abilities of a teacher than do either of the game lesson structures already discussed.

The teacher needs to understand the children's skill abilities and interests and needs to be able to use this knowledge to design a game form that the children will find interesting and enjoyable. For example, a teacher could design a game to focus on striking a ball with a bat. The object would be to strike a pitched ball and then run around a cone and back before the other players could catch or collect the ball and touch the home base with the ball. If the children used rather narrow boundaries and played in small groups, they would be assured of

Children enjoy playing a modified game of soccer

more striking, throwing, and catching opportunities than if they played the standardized nine-per-side version of softball. The teacher could design the game to be played by two teams. Or it could be designed so that each child goes back "to the field" once she or he hits the ball and runs around the cone. Section Four includes a number of additional ideas that can be used when designing games for children. Once you have created the game, the teaching skills used are virtually identical to the skills needed to successfully teach a modification of a predesigned game.

Each of the three game lesson structures discussed so far places on the teacher the responsibility for selecting or designing a game. One advantage of these games structures is that the children spend most of the time—once the game has been explained and organized—playing the game. But the children do not contribute to the design of the game, nor do they have anything to say about whether they would like to continue playing the game as it is or change the game to make it better. The two game lesson structures discussed below involve the children in the design of the game. They also require more advanced teaching skills if they are to be effective.

Teacher-Child-Designed Games   When the children and the teacher design a game together, the teacher presents the purpose of the game and the restrictions. The children and the teacher then work cooperatively to decide on the rules, scoring, and equipment to be used.

You will find that it is wise to stipulate that, once the game has begun, only the team with the ball (or the advantage) can stop play to suggest a change. (Unless the children are restrained by this rule, they are likely to stop the game and suggest a change every time the other team gains an advantage.) After a brief discussion of the proposed change, the class votes and the majority decision prevails. If a rule needs to be made to assure safety, you can offer solutions to be voted on or ask the children to propose a solution.

One example of a teacher–child designed game is Magladry Ball, named by the children after their school. The teacher was concerned about the inability of the children to travel and pass a ball or other object to a teammate who was also traveling, particularly when an opponent attempted to intercept or prevent the pass from being made. After describing the purpose of the game, the teacher imposed two restrictions—children could not touch each other, and once the ball (object) touched the ground it was automatically in the possession of the team that did not touch it immediately prior to hitting the ground. The object of the game was to throw the ball (bean bag, frisbee) through a hoop suspended from a goal post by a rope at either end of a field. Once the game began children made decisions about how long one child could remain in possession of the ball (object); what type of ball (object) to play the game with; boundaries, violations, and penalties; and scoring.

Teacher–child designed games evolve slowly. You may spend several lessons creating games that children are excited about and enjoy playing. Once the time and effort have been spent to create a game, the children will want to have opportunities to play it.

The instructor in a teacher–child designed game serves as a facilitator, enhancing and expanding ideas rather than imposing his or her ideas on the children. The teacher helps the children modify the games, offers suggestions, and manages a group of eager, charged-up children who are anxious to get the game going again. This is not an easy task, and it often takes some time to master this approach.

A true game is one that frees the spirit—the true game is the one that arises from the players themselves.

PETER AND IONA OPIE
Children's Games in Street and Playground

Child-Designed Games   In the discussions of the first four games lesson structures, the assumption has been made that the entire class is playing the same game together (even though, in actuality, you may have children playing several games at the same time). In discussing child-designed games, however, we assume that a number of games are being played simultaneously, and that few, if any, are identical. Such an environment is a far more complex one in which to teach. The teacher is assisting groups of children to develop different games

Youngsters in this class have designed their own games focusing on the skill theme of striking with rackets

"We made it up ourselves. You don't need nine guys on a team, or grownups, or uniforms. . . . It's like baseball, only better!"

The Family Circus by Bil Keane, Reprinted Courtesy The Register and Tribune Syndicate, Inc.

and is also responsible for observing a number of different games and assisting or staying away when appropriate.

Child-designed games have some definite advantages. Children in groups of similar skill ability (given a choice, children typically choose to be with others of similar ability) are allowed to design games that are interesting and exciting to them. These may be cooperative or competitive, active or passive, depending on the intent of the children.

You may consider it a disadvantage that some children take a great deal of time to design games. Children who have had little experience in designing their own games may spend as much as half of a lesson seriously working out the way they want a game to be played, perhaps without ever actually playing the game. But you will find that, as students gradually become more adept at designing games, playing time increases substantially. One way to increase the time the children are active is to suggest structure—purpose, boundaries, rules—when children are beginning to design their own games. As the children learn to make decisions about their games, the amount of imposed structure can be decreased (Chapter Four).

WHICH GAME DESIGN IS BEST?

The ecology of the particular teaching situation determines which game design is best. When selecting a game design for a class, you will want to take into consideration the skills and interests of the children, and the playing area and equipment available.

We always try to involve as many children as the situation will allow. Sometimes two games going on simultaneously are better than one, because that allows twice as many children to actively participate. And three games are usually better than two for the same reason. Some games are better with more participants; others can be played with fewer children.

Gradually each class begins to need less teacher monitoring of games, and the teacher becomes more effective at delegating responsibility. When this happens, the teacher can begin to design lessons that offer children a choice between two different games played simultaneously. Remember, the children will need to have played both games if they are to make informed, responsible choices. You can expand the selection to three or four games as the children become more adept at decision-making (Chapter Four).

Most children enjoy participating in the design of their own games. But the children must be ready—they must be able to function successfully in a small group (two or three is an appropriate number) when playing a game they know. Then they can begin to design games. Some teachers, even of younger children, can use child-designed games from the time they began teaching and have exciting, successful lessons. But when a teacher—even one who believes in the philosophy represented by child-designed games—tries to have children design their own games before the children

(and the teacher) are ready, the outcome can be a disaster. Start with the design that you think is most appropriate to a class and situation, and proceed from there.

A FINAL THOUGHT

During the past few years much has been written about the inappropriateness of adult versions of sports for children (Tutko & Bruns, 1976; Orlick, 1978; Thomas, 1977). The child who seeks sport experiences can find them outside of the school. Most communities in the United States offer adequate sports in junior and senior high school, in after-school programs, and in programs sponsored by youth agencies.

Physical educators have a responsibility to provide instruction for all children, to help them become skillful games players who enjoy participating in games and are eager to play games on their own time. We must do more than produce a few good athletes. In a successful physical education program, all of the children improve their games playing skills and are eager and excited about playing games.

SUMMARY

Because games are self-propelling, they are easier to teach than dance or gymnastics. Ease of teaching, however, is an educationally unacceptable rationale for curricular decision-making. Teachers need to provide children with appropriate experiences that lead to the development of games playing skills. We provide children with experiences that involve invariant game skills, dynamic game skills, and games playing.

Invariant game experiences focus on skill acquisition in a predictable, closed environment where the movement is essentially the same each time. Dynamic game experiences require the children to use game skills in unpredictable, open situations where they must focus on more than the execution of a particular skill. Games playing experiences are designed to expose the children to the joy and satisfaction that can be found in games. These experiences can be divided into five categories: (1) predesigned games; (2) modified predesigned games; (3) teacher designed games; (4) teacher-child designed games; and (5) child designed games.

The teacher's work is more complex when children are encouraged to help create their games. But the enthusiasm that is generated when children do invent their own games makes this process worthwhile.

REFERENCES

Arnold, R. K. Optimizing skill learning: Moving to match the environment. *Journal of Physical Education and Recreation* (November–December 1978): 84–86.

Barrett, K. R. Games teaching: Adaptable skills, versatile players. *Journal of Physical Education and Recreation* (September 1977): 21–24.

Figley, G. E., Mitchell, H. C., & Wright, B. L. *Elementary physical education: An educational experience.* Dubuque, Ia: Kendall/Hunt, 1977.

Fluegelman, Andrew, ed. *The new games book.* Garden City, N.Y.: Doubleday-Dolphin Books, 1976.

Friends Peace Committee. *For the fun of it! Selected cooperative games for children and adults.* Philadelphia: Nonviolence and Children Program, 1976. Available from 1515 Cherry St., Philadelphia, Pa. 19102.

Mauldon, E., & Redfern, H. B. *Games teaching.* London: MacDonald & Evans, 1969.

McKinney, D. E. . . . But can game skills be taught? *Journal of Physical Education and Recreation* (September 1977): 18–21.

Morris, G. S. *How to change the games children play.* Minneapolis: Burgess, 1976.

Opie, P. & I. *Children's games in street and playground.* New York: Oxford University Press, 1969.

Orlick, T. *The cooperative sports and games book: Challenge without competition.* New York: Pantheon Books, 1978.

———*Winning through cooperation: Competitive insanity, cooperative attitudes.* Washington, D.C.: Acropolis, 1978.

Riley, M. Games and humanism. *Journal of Physical Education and Recreation* (February 1975): 46–49.

———, ed. Games teaching. *Journal of Physical Education and Recreation* (September 1977): 17–35.

Thomas, J. R., ed. *Youth sports guide for coaches and parents.* Washington, D.C.: Manufacturers Life Insurance Company and the National Association for Physical Education and Sport, 1977.

Tutko, T., & Bruns, W. *Winning is everything and other American myths.* New York: Macmillan, 1976.

Werner, P. *A movement approach to games for children.* St. Louis: C. V. Mosby, 1979.

———. Inexpensive equipment for innovative games. *Journal of Physical Education and Recreation* (September 1977): 28.

Wilson, N. The frequency and patterns of selected motor skills by third and fourth grade girls and boys in the game of kickball. Unpublished master's project, University of Georgia, 1976.

CHAPTER 12
TEACHING DANCE

One of the great values in the education of children
comes from the experience of making their own forms to
express, to communicate, to enjoy. Each child is unique in
his individualism and in his environment. He needs a
chance to say what he is, how he feels, what his world
means to him.
RUTH MURRAY

Dance is probably the hardest teaching area for the same reason that
games are the easiest. Most teachers have an extensive background in
games playing, but few teachers have experience as dancers. And most
of us do teach best what we know best. Many teachers, because they
have only limited backgrounds in dance, omit dance altogether or
provide only a few dance experiences in their programs.

None of the authors of this book is a dancer, and yet each of us has
learned to provide children with exciting, interesting, and educational
dance experiences. In fact, for most of us dance has become one of the
most enjoyable areas for us to teach because of the children's enthusiasm and excitement about dance. We are convinced that individuals
who have had a minimum of formal training in dance can learn to
teach dance successfully.

PURPOSE OF DANCE IN ELEMENTARY SCHOOL

One of the keys to providing children with successful dance experiences is to develop an understanding of dance and its purpose in an
educational program. When we teach games, our purpose is not to produce varsity athletes. Similarly, when we teach dance, our purpose is
not to train children to become professional dancers. Few, if any, physical education teachers have the expertise to train children to become
professional dancers. And few children want to dance professionally.
Dance experiences in physical education classes should provide children with:

Many children are enthusiastic and excited about dance

THE MOVEMENT MOVEMENT

When we are children most of us can run and tumble and roll in the grass. We can yell and laugh and cry. We can sing our inner songs and dance our personal dances. Our feelings are visible in our actions. When we're unhappy, we stomp and mope. When we're happy we turn cartwheels and splash in puddles. Our imaginations have a direct line to our arms and legs. We can take giant steps and be giants. We can flap our arms and they will fly us away over houses and mountains. We can do all of this and more, for a while.

And then, somewhere between five and twenty, we stop.

We stop running just for the fun of it. We stop letting out the shouts and belly laughs. We stop looking at the treetops and start walking the city sidewalks staring at the pavement. We begin, somewhere along the line, to "keep a stiff upper lip," to put "starch" in our spines, to speak softly and when spoken to. Our behavior becomes "acceptable" and, in the process, we are cut off bit by bit from ourselves and therefore from each other. If my impulses can't get through to me, how can I possibly share them with you? As we lose touch with our bodies our heads take over and begin to monitor our actions, to restrict our responses until the simple interaction of children becomes an elaborate and inaccurate communication system between Brain A and Brain B.

Jules Feiffer pictures one of these disconnected, clever heads floating around complaining about its headless, funny-looking, malfunctioning body. "It's lucky," Feiffer's head says, "that I need my body to carry my head around . . . otherwise . . . out it would go."

Too drastic.

We can fit our heads back onto our bodies. We can rediscover the links between the headbone and the toebones. We can regain the freedom to spread our arms out wide; to run and shout without feeling awkward or embarrassed. We can learn to fall down, jump up, and bend over without breaking. We can unlock the sounds of our sadness and our joy. We can tune in to the beat of our pulse and stamp our feet to our inborn sense of rhythm. We can explore the sounds and the gestures of our feelings and our dreams. We can reclaim our bodies and our voices; free them to rediscover our inherent sense of balance and design; and use them to show each other who we are and what we hope to be.

KEN JENKINS, *"The Movement Movement,"* in *California Living: The Magazine of the San Francisco Sunday Examiner and Chronicle.* January 25, 1976, p. 19.

1. The ability to use their bodies to express feelings and attitudes about themselves and others;

2. A sense of self-satisfaction that can be derived from an effective utilization of one's body as an instrument of expression;

3. Enjoyment and appreciation of dance as a worthwhile experience for all, not for just a few;

4. An appreciation of dance as an art medium that can have value for both the participant and the spectator; and

5. The ability to interpret and move to different rhythms.

When children begin school, many are still in touch with their bodies as an instrument of expression. The task of the teacher of young children is not so much to teach them how to use their bodies as instruments of expression as it is to enhance the expressive abilities of the body that young children already possess. By helping children at an early age to become aware of how they use their bodies for expressive purposes, you can help each child avoid a mind–body dichotomy. You are able to help children develop an increasing awareness of their bodies as instruments of expression. Too many of us, once we are able to communicate verbally, no longer use our bodies as tools for communication.

DANCE FORMS

Expressive or creative dance is easier for most teachers to teach to younger children. Certainly it is not impossible to involve older children in creative dance experiences that are enjoyable and educational for them. But it generally takes a skilled, self-confident teacher to introduce creative dance to older children who have had little or no previous creative dance experience. Our major emphasis in teaching dance to children is on creative or expressive dance. We have nothing against folk, ethnic, or square dances—we enjoy them ourselves. We have found, however, that creative dance is easier and more enjoyable, for the children and for the teacher, when it is taught to the younger pupils. As children enter secondary school and become more

Dance experiences can be designed to build children's expressive abilities

interested in partner dances, they can begin to learn more of the cultural dances that are an important part of a society's heritage.

Children in the upper grades may find it interesting to learn a dance that is representative of a particular topic they are studying in the classroom—for example, the culture of Greece or the pioneer period in American history. But, from an educational standpoint, the brief time allowed in most schedules for physical education can best be spent on expressive dance. Other dance forms can be introduced at the secondary level.

THE CONTENT OF EXPRESSIVE DANCE

The movement framework, depicting the interaction of skill themes and movement concepts (Chapter Two), is used as the foundation for expressive dance experiences for children. The majority of skill themes categorized under locomotor skills (walking, running, hopping, skipping, and galloping) and nonmanipulative skills (turning, twisting, rolling, balancing, transferring weight, jumping and landing, and stretching and curling) are utilized in expressive dance. Virtually all of the movement concepts (Chapter Two) are used to heighten and expand the child's ability to express feeling and emotion through movement (see Table 12.1).

The focus in expressive dance is not on simply executing a particular movement—a turn or a balance—but on performing the movement so that it communicates the message intended by the child. Once children are able to perform turns efficiently,

Table 12.1   Overview of the content and rationale of teaching expressive dance to children

We want children to acquire:	By learning a movement vocabulary:	That can be used to express such emotions and thoughts as:	Stimulated by such catalysts as:
An ability to use their bodies as a means of expression	of movement concepts	Friendship	Sounds
	Space awareness	Warmth	Music
	Effort	Anger	Poetry
The sense of self-satisfaction that can be derived through expressive movement	Relationships	Unhappiness	Art
		Peace	History
	and of skill themes:	Hostility	Motion pictures
		Joy	Personal experiences
An enjoyment and appreciation of dance	Locomotor	Satisfaction	
	Nonmanipulative	Harmony	
An ability to interpret and move to different rhythms			

SOURCE: Adapted from K. R. Barrett, "Educational Dance," in B. Logsdon et al., *Physical Education for Children: A Focus on the Teaching Process* (Philadelphia: Lea & Febiger, 1977), p. 128.

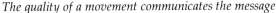
The quality of a movement communicates the message

they can begin to experiment with different qualities of turning. Slow, hesitant turns, or fast, sudden turns are two possibilities. Eventually these qualities of turning can be used to express inner feelings or attitudes. Slow, hesitant turns might be used to depict sadness or uncertainty. Sudden, quick turns could be used to express anger, frustration, or perhaps joy. Turning, by itself, communicates little. It is the quality of the turn that communicates a message, as it is the quality of any movement that is expressive. This is the reason that it is so important to provide children with a movement vocabulary if they are to become expressive movers.

Imagery is the use of a creative stimulus as a catalyst for movement. Many people believe, inaccurately, that imagery provides the content of dance. The content of expressive dance is movement. Imagery is a helper. Asking children to use imagery as the content of expressive dance is like asking children to write a story when they have a vocabulary of only fifty words. One or two extraordinarily intelligent pupils might do well. Most, however, would fail miserably, because they had not yet ac-

quired the tools needed for successful story writing.

The same principle can be applied to expressive dance. Children must be provided with the tools of dance, the ability to use a variety of movements effectively. Only when children have developed these skills can they successfully combine the movements into dances that express what the children want to communicate. Movement vocabularies, however, are not acquired through imagery. An example will help to illustrate this point.

A teacher focusing on the concept of slow, heavy movement may ask children to travel as if the floor were coated with six inches of peanut butter. But using the peanut butter image without first teaching the concept of slow and heavy travel is of little value. Children who are adept at such movements at the beginning of the class will remain adept. Those individuals who were unable to travel slowly and heavily might move in the desired manner when stimulated by the image of a peanut butter floor. But they will not have acquired a functional understanding of slow, heavy movement as a concept that can be transferred to other movement situations. In short, imagery can be useful as a reinforcer for certain movements. But imagery by it-self does not enhance the quality of children's ex-pressive movement.

DANCE EXPERIENCES

Dance experiences provided for children can be classified into two types—rhythmic and creative. In rhythmic experiences children are taught about different rhythms, to develop awareness of rhythm and the ability to move in relation to various beats. In creative experiences, you can devise situations that invite children to insert their own ideas into the lesson. Many rhythmic experiences involve a correct response. Creative experiences have no right or wrong answers. Rather, the children are asked to provide interpretations or responses to a particular problem or situation.

The teacher challenges a class to move an elbow to the beat of a drum

Rhythmic Experiences   Initially, rhythmic experiences for children at the pre-control level are very basic and are used to reinforce the movement concepts and themes the children are already studying. For example, you might ask the children to move body parts (head, feet, knees) to a simple beat you produce by playing on a rhythm drum, tambourine, or wood block. Or you might ask the children to skip three beats in one direction and then change to skipping in a different direction on the fourth beat. This experience focuses on the skill theme of skipping and the movement concept of direction.

Once children have grasped the basic concepts of rhythm and are able to respond correctly to different rhythms, rhythm can be used as a guide to the creation of simple sequences. For example, body part awareness can be enhanced by asking children, who are sitting on the floor "yoga style," to bounce their heads up and down four times to the right, four times to the left, and four times straight ahead in accompaniment to a beat. A record with an obvious beat heightens the children's enjoyment of this type of experience. You can also use shakers and drums, like those illustrated in Figure 12.1.

In another body awareness sequence that children enjoy, they are asked to imagine that someone is sneaking up on them from behind. The children are sitting on the floor. On the count of one, they move only their eyes; on two, they turn their heads; on three, they fall back; and on four, they return to a sitting position. Control level experiences are often designed to involve the children in remembering a sequence of movements that are to be performed to a rhythm.

Utilization level experiences require children to be able to perform a variety of movements while focusing on an extraneous, outside factor—rhythm. For example, you might say to your pupils: "Skip to the beat, moving away as far away as you can from where you are in the room. On the twelfth beat be back where you started." Children at the utilization level can also begin to discover inherent rhythms in some movements—for example, the lay-up in basketball, running and jumping over a hurdle, a gallop.

DRUMS

Tin can drum

Remove the top and bottom of any size tin can. Cut two circles, about an inch larger in diameter than the tin can, from an inner tube. Punch about six small holes around the edge of each rubber circle. Place one circle over each end of the can. Tighten by lacing strong string or nylon cord through the holes. Bells or bottle caps may be added for additional sound.

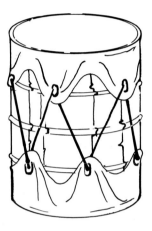

Bleach (or milk) jug drum

Screw top of jug and secure with tape or glue. Hit with dowel rod. The children can decorate the jug with paint or colored tape.

CLACKER

Cut two pieces of board to the same size. Drill holes in one end of each and join the boards with nylon cord or wire. The children can decorate the boards.

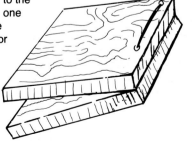

SHAKERS

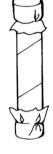

Tube shaker

Cover one end of an empty paper towel tube with heavy paper or aluminum foil. Fill with small round stones or dried beans. Then cover the other end. Shakers can then be decorated by the children.

Pie pan shaker

Place small round stones or dried beans in an aluminum pie pan. Staple another pie pan of the same diameter on top.

Balloon shaker

Pour sand, rice, beans, or a combination of these into a balloon. Then partially inflate the balloon and tie the end.

Cup shaker

Partially fill a paper or plastic cup with small stones, beans, or bottle caps. Tape another cup on top.

Figure 12.1   Easy-to-make rhythm instruments

Proficiency level experiences are characterized by movements that are repeated, often to a varied rhythm. Triplets, when the children run and dip on the first beat and stand tall on the second and third beats, exemplify one type of proficiency level experience. Another occurs when you ask children to create a rhythm for a partner's sequence, using available rhythm instruments. Children at this level enjoy discovering the different rhythms in records, both classical and popular. (Appendix 1 contains a list of records that are suitable for various kinds of movement.)

Creative Experiences   Creative and rhythmic experiences in dance are not separated in our pro-

*A child travels to the rhythmic
pattern played on a rhythm drum by
a classmate*

gram; many of the creative experiences are performed to rhythm. In fact, it is not uncommon for us to switch the focus several times during a lesson, sometimes focusing on the rhythm of the movement, other times focusing on the expressive qualities of the movement. When concentrating on rhythmic experiences, the primary focus is on the ability of the children to move to the rhythm. In contrast, creative experiences are intended to provoke creativity and expression. Creative experiences for children are designed to evoke the expressiveness and lack of body inhibition that is so characteristic of the young child.

At the precontrol level, experiences are designed to help children develop sensitivity and awareness to movement by focusing on fundamental body actions and travel skills. Stretching, curling, bending and skipping, galloping, and leaping are movements frequently used with precontrol children. Initially it is a good idea to focus on providing children with opportunities to explore a wide range of movement possibilities. Once this has been accomplished, shift the emphasis to the spatial quality of the movements. For example, have the children do a complete, full stretch or a very tight curl, and use the movement concepts to enhance the children's sensitivity to the potential of movement. The primary emphasis, however, is still on the movement rather than the expressive or communicative possibilities of the body.

At the control level, begin to clarify for children the expressive and communicative aspects of movement. The focus now centers more on the effort and relationship concepts (Chapter Two). Through these concepts movement is explored as a tool for expressing an idea, attitude, or feeling. Movement is no longer studied primarily as an entity in and of itself. Rather, movement is viewed as a medium of expression.

Challenge the children to structure their movements to an imposed beat or rhythmic pattern. Or have them verbalize how their movements feel and describe their emotional reactions to the expressive movements of classmates.

EXPRESSIVE AND COMMUNICATIVE ACTIVITIES

Time Travel or gesture in slow motion.

Travel to an externally imposed beat or rhythmic pattern, such as a handclap or drumbeat.

Rise and sink suddenly or slowly.

Force Travel or perform nonlocomotor actions to a strong beat.

Travel or perform nonlocomotor actions to light, gentle, delicate music.

Freeze in a strong, dramatic pose.

Flow Combine two travel skills, such as running and leaping, always moving smoothly.

Display hesitant, jerky, mechanical flow to create the illusion of being a robot.

Feel and observe the differences in combining a step with a turn, first with smooth, continuous flow, then with pauses (stillnesses) interspersed between each step and turn.

Relationships

Experience the sensation of matching, mirroring, or shadowing the movements of a partner.

Explore the expressive possibilities of group formations—for example, sculpture for the city park, or a mountain range.

Experience the feeling of contrasting the movements of a partner—for example, as one partner rises the other sinks, or one partner travels in a geometric path (square) while the other travels in a random path.

SEQUENCE ACTIVITIES

Design a sequence that combines light, gentle, delicate leaps with smooth, fluent, step-turns interspersed with dramatic stillnesses.

Combine appropriate travel skills and gestures with the rhythmic patterns of several Tom Foolery rhymes.

Have groups of children organize into group formations and then continually transform themselves into different formations.

Design a sixty-second phrase depicting the plight of a caravan of lost travelers crossing the Sahara Desert.

A child freezes in a strong pose

Children at the utilization level have learned to efficiently perform the movements studied at the precontrol level and to modify the movements intentionally by focusing on different movement concepts. At this level children can begin to structure their communicative movements into organized forms. This is often termed *sequencing* or *phrasing*.

It is usually a good idea to narrow the focus of a sequence or phrase to one, two, or at most three skills and concepts. When youngsters at this level

Youngsters explore the expressive possibilities of partner formation

are given too many possibilities, they are often unable to decide where to begin. The ability to move, however, combined with a working knowledge of movement concepts, enables pupils to elicit varying and qualitative responses to a single challenge.

DANCE-MAKING

Dance-making—structuring several sequences or phrases into a whole—becomes the focus at the proficiency level. The idea behind a dance can be stimulated by an infinite variety of sources, such as machines, natural phenomena (flowers, snowflakes), sculpture, music, poetry, or painting. Appendix 1 lists some recordings suitable for this activity.

Design of Dance   We have found it valuable to have upper-grade children view the dance-making process as composed of the following procedures:

1. Selection of the purpose, idea, or theme of a dance.
2. Identification of appropriate movements and movement concepts to express the intended idea, attitude, feeling, or theme.
3. Design of a powerful opening statement for the dance.
4. Design of a series of actions rising to a climax.
5. Design of the portion of the dance that is to be the climax or peak of the action.
6. Design of the resolution or concluding statement of the dance.

The possibilities for dance-making are infinite. Two examples illustrate how dances can be designed to portray different emotions or thoughts. The first is an abstract dance contrasting tradition with the forces of change. One group arranges itself as a solid square facing in one direction. Symmetrical movements prevail. Actions are firm, sustained. The other group is scattered widely, facing in random directions. Nonsymmetrical movements, free use of space, and variety are employed.

The second is a dance based on the theme of freedom. Joyous, vibrant movements prevail. Free use of space, meeting and parting are appropriate. Displays of strength, courage or pride are also suitable.

Evaluation of Dance-Making The evaluation of dance-making is a continual process that results in constant refinement and revision of a dance. Children need to be satisfied with the final product. Evaluation examines all movement skills and concepts incorporated into the dance by the teacher and children. Considerations might include:

The beginning location and pathway of each youngster—how the children choose to locate themselves at the beginning of the dance and the pathway they choose to express various feelings.

The selection of travel skills (leap, skip) and the quality with which they are performed— whether the children are using a variety of travel skills and executing them clearly and precisely as intended with the desired impact.

The relationship of the children to one another—whether the children are reacting to each other with sensitivity and whether the timing, strength, and speed of their responses are appropriate.

The flow of the dance—how the parts of the dance are connected in order to give a unity of expression.

THE PROCESS OF TEACHING DANCE

Teaching creative dance is different from teaching functional movements. A functional movement is performed correctly or incorrectly, and the task of the teacher is to guide the child toward an appropriate execution. Dance movements, performed to express an idea or emotion, are more difficult to define clearly, and so the task of the teacher is different.

Because the child is trying to express feeling or attitude, observation and feedback are also more complex. In games and gymnastics, the purpose of a movement is obvious; this is not true in creative dance. When teaching dance the teacher, initially, encourages, expands, and embellishes, rather than correcting or refining. As the teacher comes to know the children and understand them as individuals, and as the children begin to trust the teacher, sensitive and supportive feedback from the teacher will be sought. Remember, though, that human expression is very fragile and easily misinterpreted. Nothing stifles expression more quickly than insensitivity or lack of understanding. The teacher of creative dance needs to be constantly aware of how easily creativity is threatened.

You do not have to be a dancer to be a successful teacher of children's dance. The following thoughts may help those who are searching for ideas that will help them to develop effective programs of creative dance, even though they are inexperienced, both as dancers and as teachers of dance.

Don't Call it Dance! Children who have had little exposure to creative dance experiences often react negatively to the prospect of studying dance. Children in the upper grades have been known to express their hostility to the idea with groans, frowns, sighs, and even emphatic refusals to participate. This resistance can be understood when you realize that too often, children in the upper elementary grades have had few opportunities to move creatively. Too often even those few opportunities have been poorly presented. Children have been forced, for example, to participate in uninteresting, unstructured forms of dance that had no purpose or reason for involvement that was apparent to the children. When that has happened, children turn away from the joy of dance, instead of becoming excited about creative movement. The teacher who, initially, avoids the word dance can involve the children in enjoyable, challenging movement experiences before they realize they are dancing. As the youngsters' awareness that dance can be exciting and stimulating grows, the stigma attached to the word dance will disappear.

Begin Gradually The first experiences that a class has with creative dance need not last for an entire class session. A few minutes at the beginning or

CHILDREN DESIGNING THEIR OWN DANCE: A DESCRIPTION OF A PROCESS

One of the goals in teaching dance is to work with children so that they learn to design dances to express feelings or thoughts that are important to them. This description of the process of creating a dance tells how one teacher worked with a group of upper grade children, assisting them to create their own dance. The description is intended to reveal the process of creating dances; it is not presented as a pre-designed dance to be taught to other children.

Background

The population of the community in which the children in this class lived was predominantly Black. The eight children in this group wished to create a dance that expressed pride and respect for their Afro-American heritage.

We began by using several methods to develop an outline for the dance:

1. One student wrote a short paper describing what he considered the most important events in the movie *Roots.*

2. The school librarian provided several sources of information. Individual students read these and outlined them for the remainder of the group.

3. Several students interviewed teachers and classmates about their family backgrounds. They also asked people to describe what emotions they had about their heritage.

Without question, the movie *Roots* had the biggest influence in determining the students' conception of Black history. The pride and courage of Kunta Kinte and his descendants were the qualities the children wanted most to exhibit in their dance.

An Outline of the Dance

After gathering and reviewing this information, we discussed a sequential outline for the dance. It was agreed that:

1. We would begin by depicting, in some way, the period of slavery.

2. The arrival of freedom would be expressed. Interestingly, the children did not want this portion of the dance to be happy or exhilarating for several reasons. They felt that Blacks were always free, despite slavery; that many freedoms were long in coming; and that

the struggle for equality continues today.

3. Upon arrival of freedom, it was important to display the pride and courage of Afro-Americans in overcoming many injustices, both as individuals and as a people.

4. The conclusion of the dance would be spiritual, exhibiting respect and thankfulness to God for blessing a cherished people.

Creation of the Dance

Children focused on each section of the dance before putting it all together. For each portion the youngsters needed to decide upon and write on paper:

1. The beginning location of each dancer.

2. The sequential travel pathway of each dancer or of the entire group.

3. The expressive qualities they intended to exhibit in their movements.

4. The sequence of specific gestures and travel skills incorporated to express desired qualities.

Once the group could perform one section to the teacher's and their own satisfaction, work was begun on the next phase of the dance.

Slavery

After discussing the accumulated information, the children agreed to begin the dance by exhibiting the qualities and actions of field slaves laboring under a hot sun.

Freedom

This phase of the dance was the most difficult for the children. After experimenting with several ideas, the youngsters asked if they could select music to serve as background for the dance. They thought that if they had appropriate music as a stimulus, they would be able to solve their dilemmas. After listening to several cuts from the *Roots* soundtrack album, the children unanimously agreed that the words and slow pulse of the song "Many Rains Ago (Oluwa)" was perfect for their purposes. They decided to express freedom by simply putting down their tools and slowly and smoothly beginning to interweave with one another, making eye contact with others for the first time. This was intended to express

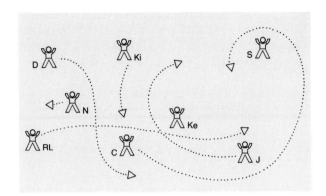

Travel pattern for freedom

Travel pathways:
Random, dancers weave in, out, and
   around one another.
Qualities:
Smooth, wavy, uncertain, looking to others for help
Actions:
Wavy gesturing of arms, held upward for
   protection or reaching out
Hips smoothly waver
Eyes contact others
Stepping is slow with changes in direction and levels

changed circumstances, in which they were free and proud but still struggling. During this phase, the youngsters' facial features exhibited fear and uncertainty about the future. The travel pattern was random.

Gathering Together: Strength as a People
To express their solidarity and pride as a people, the children's random travel began to be directed toward the center of the room where they gathered one by one, grasped one another's hands tightly, and formed a strong, unified statue.

From this point the youngsters were able to complete their dance with little teacher suggestion or intervention.

Dispersing: Strength As Individuals
Youngsters dispersed from center stage with new vigor and traveled along definite travel patterns.

Gathering Again: Strength, Pride, Confidence
Children leaped to center of room, where suddenly and simultaneously they clasped hands with one another overhead and formed a statue.

Respect and Thankfulness to God
From the statue position, youngsters slowly bowed and traveled to semi-circle formation. Slowly they dropped to their knees, and then slowly they raised their hands and heads upward.

Conclusion: We Are Strong and Proud
Youngsters slowly bent to curled position . . . Suddenly and simultaneously they rose on knees to grasp one another's hands to form a statue as a final statement of strength and pride.

Travel pattern for gathering again: Strength, pride, confidence

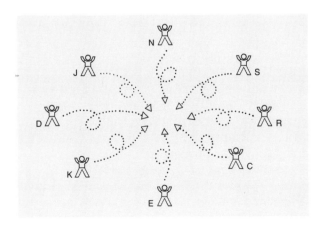

Travel pathways:
All dancers suddenly and simultaneously
   gather in middle with a run, leap, and turn.
Qualities:
Strong, confident, proud, smooth, and fluent.
Actions:
Smooth, fluent leap and landing, when
   the dancers grasp each other's hands
   overhead and freeze into a stillness.

end of a class is often sufficient to introduce creative movement concepts—and simultaneously build your confidence as a creative dance teacher. One idea that we have found particularly effective can be used as a conclusion to an active lesson. Ask the children to lie on the floor, close their eyes, and using only their fingers (toes, arms, legs, elbows) to move to music. Short segments of lively music are most effective. With their eyes closed, children are less inhibited. The teacher, with eyes open, sees the creative dance potential that seems to be an inborn characteristic of the young child.

Start with a Cooperative Class   Some classes are more agreeable to work with than others. Select a class that is generally cooperative as the first one to which you will teach creative dance. You do not need to start dance programs with all of your classes at the same time. Instead, pick one class that you feel comfortable with. As your confidence builds, start dance programs in other classes. Use the first class as a testing ground for your ideas.

Use Props   Creative dancers derive great pleasure and satisfaction from focusing on how they can move their bodies. In contrast, immature dancers often feel insecure when asked to focus on how they are moving. Props can serve as catalysts, redirecting the child's attention and so reducing self-consciousness. The use of such props as scarves, ropes, hoops, newspapers, balloons, dowel rods, stretch nylon, and even shadows can effectively divert the attention of uncertain children from their bodies. For example, when attempting to duplicate the light, airy movements made by a floating sheet of newspaper, the child's attention is focused on moving as the newspaper does, rather than trying to travel lightly. As confidence builds, the children's attention can be gradually focused to their own movements.

Start with Exciting Movement Experiences   Fast, vigorous, large movements are attractive and appealing to young children. A lesson that focuses on running, leaping into the air, landing, and rolling evokes the exuberance associated with speed and flight. Gradually the teacher can begin to focus on the quality of the leaps, the effectiveness of the landings, and the use of gestures while in flight.

Dance to the Music   One of the most devastating experiences for poorly skilled children occurs when a teacher plays some music and simply says "Go ahead and dance to the music." This can be a terrifying experience for youngsters with little background or confidence in creative movement, children who have not yet acquired a vocabulary of functional movements. The challenge "Move to the Music" can be appropriate later, when the children are putting together movements they have acquired.

A FINAL THOUGHT

One instructor's initial attempts at teaching creative dance are still vivid. She recalled teaching an entire lesson that focused on running, jumping, and turning to different rhythms to a second grade class. Afterwards she remarked to a friend that it was the best workout that the children had experienced the entire year and added that she was going to teach another lesson because of the physical fitness benefits. After another lesson was received as enthusiastically as the first, she was struck with the realization that the reason the children had been so actively involved was that they were totally immersed in the exciting atmosphere that was generated by exploring fast and slow turns, acceleration and deceleration leading into jumps. The children loved creative dance.

The physical education instructor who does not offer creative movement experiences is being professionally irresponsible. You may be more qualified

THE AWFUL BEGINNING
A TRUE STORY, UNFORTUNATELY

JAMES A. SMITH

I looked across the desk at my big girl. She'd come for help in planning her semester schedule.

"Look," I said, "you have some electives. Why don't you take a course or two for fun? You've worked hard and really should take something outside your major that will be pleasurable."

"Like what?" she asked.

My eyes scanned the college schedule of courses. "Like Dr. Mann's Creative Writing or Dr. Camp's Painting for Beginners or something like that."

She threw back her head and laughed. "Who me? Paint or write? Good grief, Dad, you ought to know better than that!"

"And this," I thought, "is the awful ending."

It was not always like this. I remembered an early golden September day when I went to my garage studio and gathered together my easel, paintbrushes, and watercolors. I sensed someone was watching me and looked up from my activity to see her framed in silhouette in the doorway. The breeze and the sun tiptoed in the gold of her curls. Her wide blue eyes asked the question, "Whatcha doin'?"

"I'm going to the meadow to paint," I said. "Want to come along?"

"Oh, yes." She bounced on her toes in anticipation.

"Well, go tell Mommy and get your paints."

She was off but returned in no time carrying the caddy I had made to hold her jars of paint and her assortment of brushes.

"Paper?" she asked.

"Yes, I have plenty of paper. Let's go."

She ran down the hill before me, pushing aside the long soft grasses of the meadow. I watched closely for fear of losing her golden top in the tops of the goldenrod. She found a deserted meadowlark's nest and we stopped to wonder at it. A rabbit scurried from under our feet. Around us yellow daisies and goldenrod nodded in friendly greeting. Above, the sky was in infinite blue. Beyond the meadow, the lake slapped itself to match the blue of the sky.

On the lake, a single white sailboat tipped joyously in the breeze. My daughter looked up and saw it. "Here!" she said.

Trusting her wisdom as I always did, I set up our easels. While I deliberated over choice of subject and color, she had no such problem. She painted with abandonment and concentration and I left her alone, asking no questions, making no suggestions, simply recognizing uncontaminated creative drive at work.

Before I had really begun, she pulled a painting off her easel.

"There!" she said. "Want to see?" I nodded.

I cannot describe the sense of wonder that flooded over me as I viewed her work. It was all there—that golden September day. She had captured the sunlight in her spilled yellows, the lake in her choppy, uneven strokes of blue, the trees in her long, fresh strokes of green. And through it all, there was a sense of scudding ships and the joyousness of wind that I experience when I sail, the tilting and swaying of the deck, the pitching of the mast. It was a beautiful and wondrous thing and I envied her ability to interpret so honestly, so uninhibitedly, so freshly.

"Are you going to give it a name?" I suggested.

"Yep! Sailboats!" she responded, as she taped another sheet of paper to the easel.

There wasn't a single sailboat in the picture.

She began school the following week. One dreary November day she came into my study with a sheet of paper in her hand.

"Daddy," she asked, "will you help me draw a sailboat?"

"Me? Help you draw a sailboat?"

My eyes turned to the wall where her golden September painting hung in a frame I had made for it.

"Me? Help you draw a picture of a sailboat? Why, sweetheart, I could never paint a picture like the one over there. Why don't you paint one of your own?"

Her blue eyes looked troubled.

"But, Daddy, Miss Ellis doesn't like my kind of painting."

She held up her sheet of paper in the middle of which was a dittoed triangle.

"Miss Ellis wants us to make a sailboat out of this."

And that was the awful beginning!

to teach gymnastics or games. But you will always be teaching some children who might eventually choose creative dance as their primary form of participation in the motor domain. Depriving children of opportunities to experience creative movement is no more acceptable than eliminating all opportunities to practice throwing and catching. You may have to devote a lot of time and work to developing a successful program. But any teacher, even one who has little background in creative dance, can provide children with effective creative movement experiences.

SUMMARY

Teachers who lack experience and educational background in dance find that it is difficult to teach. But any teacher who is willing to try new and possibly unfamiliar ideas can learn to successfully teach dance to children. Children look forward to and enjoy dance experiences presented appropriately.

Because of the ages and abilities of children in elementary schools, we have found creative or expressive dance to be the most successful. Creative dance is also consistent with the nature and characteristics of young children, who are already adept at fantasizing and expressing their thoughts and feelings through movement.

The content of expressive dance is derived from the movement concepts and the majority of locomotor and nonmanipulative skill themes. The initial emphasis is on executing particular movements. As children learn to perform these skills efficiently, the emphasis shifts to varying the quality with which the movement is executed.

Children should have both rhythmic and expressive dance experiences. In rhythmic experi-

ences, the focus is on moving in relation to different rhythmic beats. Creative dance experiences, in contrast, focus on expressive interpretation by children as they expand their movement vocabulary for communicating feelings and moods.

Through a process of trial and error we have discovered numerous techniques that are helpful in making dance lessons for children both interesting and educational. For example, we suggest that teachers initially avoid the word *dance* because it has negative connotations for some children. Inexperienced dance teachers may find it helpful to begin by teaching dance to one cooperative class. Using props and designing lessons that are vigorous and action packed are also strategies that help to excite children about dance.

REFERENCES

Barlin, A. L. *Teaching your wings to fly.* Santa Monica, Calif.: Goodyear, 1979.

Boorman, J. *Creative dance in the first three grades.* New York: David McKay, 1969.

Carroll, J., & Lofthouse, P. *Creative dance for boys.* London: MacDonald and Evans, 1969.

Docherty, D. *Education through the dance experience.* Bellingham, Wash.: Educational Designs and Consultants, 1977.

Fleming, G. A. *Creative rhythmic movement.* Englewood Cliffs, N.J.: Prentice-Hall, 1976.

Joyce, M. *First steps in teaching creative dance.* Palo Alto, Calif.: Mayfield, 1973.

Murray, R. L. *Dance in elementary education.* (3rd ed.) New York: Harper and Row, 1975.

Russell, J. *Creative movement and dance for children.* Boston: Plays, Inc., 1975.

Slater, W. *Teaching modern educational dance.* London: MacDonald and Evans, 1974.

CHAPTER 13
TEACHING GYMNASTICS

If gymnastics is to be for everyone, including the handicapped child, then all children cannot be asked to do the same gymnastic movement at the same time, in exactly the same way, for clearly some children are going to be underchallenged and some are going to be overchallenged.
ANDREA BOUCHER

Gymnastic movements are fascinating to children. Climbing trees, balancing on logs, swinging from limbs, and maneuvering through playground apparatus are all responses to the same question—"How well can I avoid falling down as I explore different challenges?" The skills of balance, transfer, and support of weight on different body parts and combinations of body parts are intriguing to children for at least three reasons.

First, these accomplishments are easy to measure. The child knows that he did something today that he could not do yesterday or last week. Second, the feedback a child receives about the success of the attempt to defy gravity is instant and self-revealing. The child does not have to rely on others to determine whether she has been successful. And third, children naturally find many of the possibilities in gymnastics on their own; in dance and games they are typically introduced to possibilities by outside sources, such as a coach or teacher or television.

Many gymnastic movements are referred to as *self-testing*. For children, especially younger children who still find it difficult to work with other children, the challenge of testing themselves in appropriate environments designed by a teacher is exciting and enduring.

In recent years—primarily because of television coverage of gymnastics featuring Olga Korbut, Kurt Thomas, and Nadia Comeneci—interest in gymnastics has increased. Young children watch these exceptional performances by skilled gymnasts, and are fascinated by the speed and difficulty of these gymnastic movements. In years past, most children were introduced to this sport in physical educational classes. Today, most children learn about Olympic gymnastics through television.

How well can I defy the force of gravity?

PURPOSE OF GYMNASTICS

Educational gymnastics (as taught in physical education classes) and Olympic gymnastics are not the same. They are related but have different purposes. In educational gymnastics, we are not training children to become competitive gymnasts. We do not have the time. Nor do many physical education teachers have the expertise. And not every child has a desire to be a competitive gymnast. We provide children with gymnastic experiences to teach them

to maneuver their bodies effectively against the force of gravity, both on the floor and on apparatus.

Rather than providing children with a relatively narrow gymnastic program focused specifically on learning to execute a series of predetermined stunts, we attempt to provide children with a foundation of gymnastic experiences that increases their skills and introduces them to the types of activities that are characteristic of gymnastics. Specialization in specific skills can be gained elsewhere.

Some children who are interested in gymnastics enroll in programs sponsored by youth agencies, and others join school programs available at the sec-

The joy of gymnastics can be instantaneous

THE LITTLE GYMNAST
DAN ZADRA

Come with us, now, to a very nice place where little
  children swing on rings.
Where laughter is king—and happiness queen—and
  everyone likes who they are.

On a little green island called Mercer, in a big blue Washington lake surrounded by trees, is a wonderful building assembled by people who think it's important for children to play. And learn. And find out what they can do.

The building is called the Jewish Community Center, and children come from miles around to follow a Pied Piper of a man named Robin West.

Robin grew up in South Africa and then went to college at the University of Saskatchewan in Canada. Now he teaches movement, tumbling and gymnastics to hundreds of boys and girls in the United States. One of his favorite classes is "kiddie gymnastics," for little gymnasts, four to six.

Most four-year-olds already know how to run, jump and play when they come to their very first day of kiddie gymnastics. But in no time at all, Robin can open their eyes to hundreds of new ways to move, swing, roll, bend and balance their bodies with success.

"Success for everyone" is the motto in kiddie gymnastics. It's such a simple motto—so easy to follow—that sometimes even Robin and the children's parents must stop to remind themselves of its magic.

A child is a butterfly in the wind. Some can fly higher than others; but each one flies the best way it can. Why compare one against the other? Each one is different. Each one is special. Each one is beautiful.

In kiddie gymnastics, everyone flies and nobody fails. There's plenty of praise for the attempt well-tried. To balance on a beam for the very first time is discovery. To be praised and applauded for the very same motion is joy.

In just a few short weeks the children in Robin's class have learned to move with a confidence, poise and imagination that surprises and pleases both themselves and their parents.

But they've also learned something else along the way. You can see it in their eyes when they tug so gently on Robin's bushy black beard. You can see it in the way they lie on their backsides and stare at the ceiling and giggle. It's as if they've learned something deep and exciting about themselves.

"I'm me . . . I'm special . . . I can try."

"If I make a mistake, it's all right. I'll start over . . . I'll learn . . . I'll get better."

"Look at my friend. I'm helping him stand on his head. He's special, too."

"We're good. We're children. We're okay."

ondary level. Some elementary schools offer programs before and after school for children who want additional practice in gymnastics. These programs are for children who want to specialize in gymnastics.

Specialization in physical education class can lead to education of a few, while the majority are left behind. Educational gymnastic programs should be designed to assist all children, regardless of ability, to improve their gymnastic skills—to become better able to control their bodies in the variety of planned and unplanned encounters they will have, as children and as adults, with the force of gravity.

CONTENT OF EDUCATIONAL GYMNASTICS
Educational gymnastics can be divided into floor experiences and apparatus experiences. Floor experiences are movements, executed on grass, mats, or carpeting, that do not require equipment to enhance the challenge. Apparatus experiences involve moving in relation to one or several pieces of equipment (tables, benches, beams, bars, and vaulting boxes). Children are introduced to these only after they have achieved sufficient skill on the floor. Many movements performed on the floor are replicated on apparatus, but executing a balance or a roll is more difficult on apparatus. Initially the majority

of gymnastics lessons are devoted to floor practice. Then, as children become more skillful, a larger percentage of the lessons are devoted to apparatus experiences.

Floor Experiences   With children at the precontrol level, the initial focus is on placing body parts close together and maintaining round body and body part shapes. Once children have learned to curve their bodies and body parts and keep them rounded, they can focus on rolling in different di-

rections. Children at the precontrol level can also learn to transfer weight to different body parts, to balance on different body parts, and to travel on lines or ropes on the floor.

Control level experiences include rolling from standing positions, and traveling and rolling. Nonsymmetrical balances and inverted balances are also introduced. The concept of stillness is studied as an interesting contrast to rolling or as a goal for a particular type of balance. Children are challenged to begin simple combinations of two related skills— for example, moving from a two-part balance into a

*One of the first objectives is to have children
learn to keep their bodies rounded*

*Children work on the floor before
progressing to apparatus*

three-part balance without using the body parts from the two-part balance.

More advanced and increasingly complex sequences of movements are enjoyable and challenging to children at the utilization level who have developed control over movements executed singly. Transferring weight from feet to hands, exploring "almost off" balance, and taking part or all of a partner's weight are other tasks appropriate for children at this level.

The concepts of acceleration and deceleration, strong and light, bound and free are stressed with

Inverted balances are introduced at the control level

children who are at the proficiency level. These children have learned to perform some gymnastic movements with relative ease and enjoy the challenge of focusing on the quality of the execution. Matching or mirroring the movements of a partner, repeating sequences of several gymnastic movements, and experiences that involve several children supporting each others' weight are all proficiency level gymnastic experiences on the floor.

Apparatus Experiences   As children become skillful at floor work, we introduce them to experiences on apparatus. Balance beams, parallel bars, side horses, vaulting boxes, and still rings are Olympic gymnastics equipment. Some elementary schools have this official gymnastics apparatus. But many elementary school programs use benches, tables, chairs, hoops, the edge of a stage, blocks and canes, climbing ropes, and climbing frames to provide gymnastic experiences on apparatus. Unofficial equipment is often more compatible with the abilities of children. And children have fewer preconceived notions about what is expected when they work with an unfamiliar piece of equipment.

You can introduce the children to a piece of apparatus by encouraging them to explore the equipment, never forcing a child onto a piece of apparatus. A child at the precontrol level can start by walking along a low beam or bench, jumping from a chair or low table, hanging from a climbing rope, or traveling along a climbing frame. Obstacle courses designed from available equipment—tables, benches, chairs, hoops, ropes, blocks, and canes—are also challenging to children at this level as they learn the concepts of under, over, along, and through.

Children at the control level, while continuing to explore apparatus, can begin to focus on different ways to move in relation to the equipment. They can try different ways of traveling along a beam, hanging from a bar or rope, jumping from a table or chair, or traveling from side to side on a climbing

GYMNASTICS NOTATION

Steve Sanders, an elementary school physical education specialist at Joseph T. Walker School in Atlanta, Georgia, with his students devised a gymnastics notation system. His purpose for developing the system was twofold. First, he viewed such a system as a way of enhancing the movement vocabulary of children, so that they would better understand the meanings of the terms in the movement analysis framework. His second purpose was to enhance the amount of thought and creativity that went into the student's work in building gymnastics sequences.

The notation system, inspired by Rudolf Laban's notation in dance, uses a symbol for each of the framework elements most frequently used in gymnastics. For example, middle level is represented by ——□—— , movement in a backward direction is represented by ◄———— , a roll is represented by ~~~~ , and a movement done at a slow speed is represented by ● ● ● ● . In a written description of a gymnastic movement, the skill is listed first and the movement concept(s) are written underneath the skill.

EXAMPLE OF GYMNASTIC NOTATION

Routine

Student starts routine by running very fast, doing a forward roll, balancing on one foot, and skipping to the balance beam. Routine is continued by student mounting the beam, doing a forward roll, two jumps, and a cartwheel; dismount off the beam. Routine is ended by doing a backward roll and a balance on one foot.

Notation of Routine

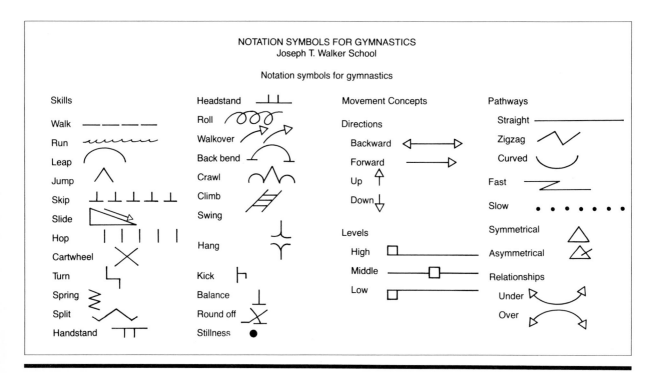

NOTATION SYMBOLS FOR GYMNASTICS
Joseph T. Walker School

Notation symbols for gymnastics

Skills		Headstand	Movement Concepts		Pathways	
Walk		Roll	Directions		Straight	
Run		Walkover	Backward		Zigzag	
Leap		Back bend	Forward		Curved	
Jump		Crawl	Up		Fast	
Skip		Climb	Down		Slow	
Slide		Swing			Symmetrical	
Hop			Levels		Asymmetrical	
Cartwheel		Hang	High		Relationships	
Turn		Kick	Middle		Under	
Spring		Balance	Low		Over	
Split		Round off				
Handstand		Stillness				

Left *Children are encouraged to explore apparatus*

Below *Children enjoy creating symmetrical body shapes while in flight*

frame. As children develop the ability to function with relative ease and security on apparatus in a variety of ways, you can begin to challenge them to transfer skills that they learned on the floor to the apparatus.

Children at the utilization level can try different ways to get onto equipment, vaulting over equipment, and forming shapes in flight while moving from apparatus to the floor. Experiences that involve supporting weight on different body parts, asymmetrical balances, and inverted balances are also appropriate for children at this level.

When children reach the proficiency level, they should continue to focus on increasingly demanding balances, shapes, ways of traveling, and ways of supporting the body weight. As with gymnastic experiences on the floor, the children should be encouraged to focus on the quality of their movements as they practice repeating movements exactly and combining movements into sequences that flow together smoothly and fluently.

THE PROCESS OF TEACHING
EDUCATIONAL GYMNASTICS

Teaching gymnastics is different from teaching either dance or games, because apparatus is used and because of the self-testing nature of gymnastics. Successful educational gymnastics teachers are able to match interesting and challenging tasks to the ability levels of children. This is a teaching skill learned only with time and practice.

Some teachers avoid gymnastics because they are concerned about the safety of the children and are afraid that children might be injured. Remember, though, that injury is always a possibility in physical education classes. When gymnastic experiences are presented sequentially, and in an appropriate environment, gymnastics is no more dangerous than any other physical education activity. You will find the following ideas helpful in creating successful and safe gymnastic experiences for children.

Vary the Task   When all the children in a class are expected to perform the same skill in the same way, two things are likely to happen. Many of the children in the class will be bored, because they can already perform the task successfully. Some of the children will be frightened, because the task is too difficult for them and they know it. When you offer children some choices about how they will perform a task, each child can select an appropriate level of activity. For example, it is unlikely that all the children in a particular class will be able to do a handstand. Some children may not be strong enough to support all of their body weight on their hands. Some will not be able to land safely if they lose their balance. Instead of telling the entire class to do a handstand, you could tell the children to find a way to place some or all of their weight on their hands. An instruction that allows for individual differences in ability affords all children an opportunity for success.

Gymnastics Environment   An appropriate environment in gymnastics is one in which safety is

emphasized. Encourage children to be responsible for their own safety. Explain that you cannot be everywhere in the gym. Stress that if they do not think they can do something, they should not do it or they should ask you for help. Games of "I dare you" and "follow the leader" are inappropriate in gymnastics classes. When you encourage children to be responsible for themselves, you will find that they rely less on you and more on themselves to determine what is appropriate. The development of self-reliance should be one of the goals in teaching gymnastics.

Children are encouraged to be responsible for themselves

Spotting   Spotting—the practice of physically assisting a child as he performs a movement—is not commonly employed in educational gymnastics classes. Children who depend on such help are likely to be unsure and even afraid unless a teacher is nearby. And, conversely, spotting encourages children to attempt movements for which they may not be ready. We have observed a number of programs, including our own, in which children have progressed to a relatively high level of skill proficiency without any spotting.

Demonstrating   Some teachers feel that, because they are not skilled gymnasts themselves, they will not be able to teach gymnastics effectively. Certainly a thorough background in a teaching area is an asset in teaching. But even teachers who are not skilled gymnasts can provide children with appropriate gymnastic experiences. In educational gymnastics, the instructor does not need to be able to correctly demonstrate a skill, because the children are never expected to perform the same skill in the same way. If you want to provide children with additional ideas or to emphasize a particular movement quality or concept, you can invite some of the more proficient children to demonstrate for the rest of the class. This technique has the added advantage

Some of the children who are working on gymnastics at an outside club or program may come to class with gymnastic skills that exceed your teaching knowledge and ability. Since you are responsible for the safety of all of the children, the activities of these club gymnasts may cause you some uneasiness.

If you explain your concern to these children, you will find that they appreciate your candidness. Tell these young gymnasts that you are working to learn about the movements they are practicing. Assure them that, once you are skilled enough to help them practice appropriately and safely, you will be delighted to have them resume practice in class.

This approach makes it clear that you are not criticizing but instead are respecting their proficiency. Students will, in turn, respect you for acknowledging your limitations and seeking their cooperation. And teacher–student rapport will be enhanced.

of reinforcing those children who are working especially well.

Moving Equipment   In some situations, if the teacher had to move the gymnastics equipment alone, gymnastics would never be taught. Gymnas-

Children learn early to transport apparatus safely and efficiently

tics apparatus is heavy, cumbersome, and difficult for one person to move. You can devote some time during each of the first few gymnastics apparatus lessons to teach the children how to move the equipment. Once they learn to maneuver apparatus safely and efficiently, a gymnastics environment can be set up or taken down in a short time. It is wise to have the children follow a few simple rules when they move equipment:

1. An adequate number of children (as determined by the teacher) must be present before equipment can be moved.
2. Children are to lift the equipment together and lower it together, being careful of toes and fingers.
3. Each piece of apparatus has its own storage space to which it is to be returned after the lesson has been concluded.

Children need several lessons (and some classes will need even more) to learn to handle the apparatus efficiently. Once the children learn to maneuver the equipment, their help saves a lot of time.

Stations   One of the most effective ways to organize a gymnastics lesson is to divide the children into groups (once they are able to work this way) and set up stations (learning centers) in different parts of the teaching area (Chapter Four). Each group works on a different skill and uses different equipment. Sample tasks could include: jumping from a table or chair onto a mat, landing and rolling; traveling different ways along a bench or beam; climbing a rope; practicing putting weight on hands; and vaulting over a table.

This method of organization allows the use of various pieces of equipment and eliminates long lines. When the children have learned to function successfully in this environment, you can write tasks on poster boards and tape them to the wall near each station. Since children usually read far faster than teachers talk, practice time will be increased.

Club Gymnasts   Because of the increased interest in gymnastics, you may find some children in your classes who are studying gymnastics independently, perhaps in a club or recreation program. Most of these club gymnasts are more skilled than the other children—many are at the proficiency level in many skills. And so they provide an interesting dimension to gymnastics lessons. The other children will look to the club gymnasts as models and as sources for new ideas. Although you will not be teaching Olympic gymnastic skills, you certainly can encourage the club gymnasts to practice the skills they have learned elsewhere. The presence of club gymnasts in a gymnastics class results in an interesting blend of child-created gymnastic skills and Olympic gymnastic skills.

A FINAL THOUGHT

Teaching educational gymnastics is, in some ways, more difficult than teaching Olympic gymnastics. In Olympic gymnastics the desired outcomes are clear—the teacher wants the children to learn to execute predetermined skills in specific ways. The desired outcomes of educational gymnastics are less easily defined. The skills to be learned are not predetermined, nor are they to be executed in one correct way. Instead, the teacher helps the children to improve their abilities to move in relation to the force of gravity, to learn self-confidence and self-reliance in interpreting tasks and determining the best ways to execute skills. Often it is more difficult for a teacher to share decisions with children than it is for the teacher to make the decisions. You will find, however, that the process of sharing decisions in educational gymnastics can be exciting for the teacher and rewarding for the children, regardless of their gymnastic abilities.

SUMMARY

Because of the self-testing nature of gymnastics, most children are fascinated by the challenge of attempting to defy the force of gravity. It is important to distinguish between educational gymnastics and Olympic gymnastics. Educational gymnastics focuses on enhancing the ability of each child to more effectively maneuver his body against the force of gravity. Olympic gymnastics emphasizes the learning of specific gymnastics stunts, usually for the purpose of entering individual or team competition.

Many gymnastics movements are learned on the floor (mats) first and then practiced on apparatus. Gymnastics apparatus can be purchased, or equipment available in schools—such as tables, chairs, and benches—can be adapted to serve the same purposes.

Because of the increased likelihood of injury in gymnastics, it is important that an appropriate learning environment be established so that children avoid games like "follow the leader" or "I dare you." Gymnastics tasks can be presented in ways that allow for individual differences. This should be done so that children are not tempted to try movements for which they are not ready.

REFERENCES

Boucher, A. Educational gymnastics is for everyone. *Journal of Physical Education and Recreation* (September 1978): 48–50.

Kirchner, G., Cunningham, J., & Warrel, E. *Introduction to movement education* (First edition). Dubuque, Ia: William C. Brown, 1970.

Mauldon, E. & Layson, J. *Teaching gymnastics.* London: MacDonald & Evans, 1965.

Morison, R. *A movement approach to educational gymnastics.* London: J. M. Dent, 1969.

O'Quinn, G. *Developmental gymnastics.* Austin: University of Texas Press, 1978.

Parent, S. (Ed.) Educational gymnastics. *Journal of Physical Education and Recreation* (September 1978): 31–50.

Williams, J. *Themes for educational gymnastics.* London: Lepus Books, 1974.

SECTION 4
MOVEMENT CONCEPT AND SKILL THEME DEVELOPMENT

T he first three chapters in this section explain the concepts of space awareness, effort, and relationships. Because these are concepts rather than actual skills, levels of skill proficiency are not discussed. As children study these concepts, they learn to demonstrate, through movement, their understanding of the meaning of each concept. Once this functional understanding has been acquired, the concepts are used primarily as subthemes to enhance the range and quality of skill development that result from the study of the various skill themes.

The next eleven chapters provide information about teaching skill themes. These skill themes can be presented to the children in the same order they are presented here. Or you may, on reflection, find that with a particular class or in a specific environment a different order of presentation is desirable.

The eleven skill themes presented here are the ones that we focus on in our physical education programs. Other skill themes could have been included. It is our hope that you will be able to use the format described in Section Four to independently develop additional skill themes needed for particular classes or groups of children.

Each of the skill theme chapters is organized according to the generic levels of skill proficiency. After an introductory section, Ideas for Development are included for each level of skill proficiency. We attempt, as much as possible, to avoid suggesting methodology in these ideas. It is possible, for example, to use the same idea as a predesigned game or as a focus around which children can design their own game, or to teach a specific movement in developing a dance idea or to have children develop their own dance with the same idea.

The way a class is organized for instruction depends on the pupils' abilities to accept responsibility, rather than on a specific movement. Each movement can be studied successfully in different ways with classes of various levels of eagerness and ability to work on their own.

Each skill theme chapter also includes Ideas for Observational Focus. These contain suggestions about what to look for while teaching. They provide information that is useful when making decisions about whether to change to a different skill theme or to stay with the same theme for a while longer.

CHAPTER 14
TEACHING SPACE AWARENESS

All movement takes place in space. Children who develop a keen space sense will be better able to move safely as they travel through physical education environments. For this reason, it is beneficial to focus on the concept of space awareness at the beginning of the physical education program.

Children can be made aware of the different aspects of space and then challenged to think about spatial considerations as they engage in game, gymnastic, and dance experiences. As children move their bodies in differing ways through varying spatial conditions, they begin to feel and understand space in new ways. As relationships between the body and space become clear, adeptness at controlling movements in functional or expressive physical education activities is enhanced. For example, a child learns to maneuver across a large span of climbing equipment, traveling around, over, and under other youngsters without bumping any of them or losing control of his or her own movements.

Activities are planned to introduce children to the six categories of space: (1) self-space; (2) general space; (3) directions; (4) levels; (5) pathways; and (6) extensions. We usually begin by acquainting youngsters with the two basic orientations, *self-space* and *general space*. Self-space refers to all the space that the body or its parts can reach without traveling away from a starting location. General space is all the space, within a room or a boundary, that the body can penetrate by means of locomotion.

The remaining four categories describe the relationships of the body to the space aspects of directions, levels, pathways, and extensions. *Di-*

When appropriately challenged, young children become enthralled with the process of exploring space

rections in space are the dimensional possibilities into which the body or its parts move or aim to move—up and down, right and left, forward and backward. *Levels* in space are divided into high, low, and medium areas. High level is the space above the shoulders. Low level is the space below the knees. And medium level is the space in between, when the child is in a standing position. *Pathways* in space are the floor patterns (straight, curved, and zigzag) the body can create by traveling through space. The term *pathways* also denotes the possible floor or air patterns of a thrown or struck object—for example, the arched flight of a volleyball set shot, or the curved path of a pitcher's curveball. The last category, *extensions,* includes the size of movements of the body or its parts in space (for example, small arm circles or large arm circles) and the distances from the center of the body that the parts reach to carry out a movement. The tennis serve performed by a skilled player is a far extension, while a tennis serve executed by a beginner is often close to the body. The ideas for developing each of the space concepts are stated in direct terms. Remember though, that the method used for the study of each concept can be varied according to the purposes of the teacher and the characteristics of the children in the class (see Chapter Four).

DEVELOPING THE CONCEPT OF SELF-SPACE
Understanding of the concept of self-space increases children's awareness of movement possibilities in the space immediately surrounding

their bodies. Without a keen sense of the relationship of self to surrounding space, the range of potential movements is restricted. When young children are introduced to a wide repertoire of movement skills in self-space, they begin to build a foundation of nonlocomotor skills (such as twisting and turning) that can be used to enhance the development of concepts and of other skills.

Each individual is surrounded by a self-space as he or she travels—the possible movements into space immediately surrounding the body will be the same regardless of location. But children will understand this concept most easily if they learn it while remaining stationary. Staying in one location will clarify for the children the difference between the movements possible in the space immediately surrounding the body and the movements possible when the body travels through a general space.

Youngsters discover that a variety of nonlocomotor movements are possible within a self-space

Teaching the Concept of Self-Space

Overview   We provide the children with movement tasks they can accomplish in one location, without traveling. In addition to building their movement vocabularies, the absence of locomotion enhances kinesthetic awareness of stretching, curling, twisting, and swinging (nonlocomotor) movements.

IDEAS FOR DEVELOPMENT

IDEAS FOR OBSERVATIONAL FOCUS

Have the children sit or stand and ask them to move specific body parts—leg, arm, elbow, head—around their bodies into as many places as possible while remaining in the same location (without traveling).

Do the children remain in the same location (self-space)?

Do the children move different body parts into many areas of self-space (down low, up high, in front of the body, behind)?

Have the children put various body parts in as many places as possible using specific actions—bending, stretching, twisting, shaking; remain in self-space.

Does each child remain positioned in self-space while moving a single body part?

Challenge children to move their entire body mass while remaining in self-space—curling their bodies tightly, stretching their bodies as high as possible, twisting their entire bodies.

Do the children remain in self-space—not touching anyone else—while moving the entire body mass?

Challenge children to put weight on different body parts without moving out of self-space—on knees, bottom, hands, head and hands.

Do the children remain in self-space while putting weight on different body parts? Do they refrain from touching or bumping into other children?

DEVELOPING THE CONCEPT OF GENERAL SPACE

General space is all the space, within a room or boundary, into which an individual can move by traveling away from the original starting location (self-space).

We help the children learn different ways of traveling safely through general space by providing appropriate movement tasks. Once the children are able to travel safely (without bumping and under control) in general space, they are ready to experience more complex tasks

Teaching children to travel safely through a general space is one of our first objectives

that include several concepts in combination, such as speed, pathways, and directions. Manipulating balls as one travels through general space presents an even more difficult challenge.

Teaching the Concept of General Space

Overview   Tasks in this section are designed to help children learn to travel safely and efficiently through general space. The complexity of the tasks is increased by focusing on the concepts of speed, pathways, and directions and on the manipulation of objects through general space.

IDEAS FOR DEVELOPMENT

IDEAS FOR OBSERVATIONAL FOCUS

Ask children to find a self-space—spread about the room, not close to others—and to be still. On signal (for example, a drum), the children leave their self-space and walk around the room, trying not to touch anyone else and not to leave any empty spaces (areas with no children). On the second signal, the children stop immediately, at whatever location or body position they find themselves.

Do the children remain relatively evenly spaced throughout the room or boundaried space?

Do the children keep space between themselves and others, or do they cluster together?

Do some children bump into others? Are the children watching for others (traveling defensively)?

When the children are able to walk safely through general space without bumping or losing control, the following tasks are appropriate: Jogging through general space; running through general space.

When the stop signal is given, do the children stop quickly or does it take a while for everyone to come to a position of stillness?

Are the children finding open spaces to move into, rather than staying close together or bunched up?

Are the children watching for others and avoiding bumping one another?

When the stop signal is given, the teacher can further concept development by providing feedback to the children. For example:

1. Praise youngsters who stop in isolated areas.
2. Praise youngsters who stop quickly and safely.
3. Point out congested or vacant spaces.
4. Praise youngsters who have avoided collisions by traveling defensively.

Challenge children to travel safely through general space by skipping, galloping, and leaping.

Do the children use different locomotor patterns in traveling through general space?

Do the children remain relatively evenly spaced and avoid collisions with others?

The speed of the children's travel can be varied depending on their abilities to move safely— to watch for others and control their travel.

Half of the class begin on one side of the room and half on the opposite side. The children are challenged to walk to the other side without touching anyone.

Do the children walk without bumping into others?

Encourage the children to travel in different ways across the room without touching. Have them crawl, then skip, then walk backward.

Do the children travel without bumping into others?

Ask children to spread out throughout the room and find a self-space. On signal, the children travel safely through general space. When the second signal is sounded, the children return quickly and safely to their original starting location (self-space).

Do the children spread themselves evenly throughout general space?

Do the children remain relatively evenly spaced and avoid bumping into others?

Are the children able to return safely and quickly to their exact starting locations?

Encourage the children to travel safely through the area. Have them go over, under, or around the obstacles (hoops and ropes on the floor, milk crates, low benches). Have them try not to touch any obstacles or other children.

Do the children travel without touching the obstacles or other children?

Do the children spread about the room or cluster together?

Challenge children to move continuously in the space, but to stay between you and the wall you are facing. As they move, walk slowly forward so that the space they have to move around in becomes smaller and smaller.

Do the children move continuously and without bumping?

Do the children adjust their speeds to the smaller space?

DEVELOPING THE CONCEPT OF DIRECTIONS

Directions in space are the dimensional possibilities into which the body or its parts move or aim to move—up and down, right and left, forward and backward. There is no universally correct direction. Rather, direction is a function of the body's orientation in space. Forward and backward, for example, depend on the way a person is facing rather than a location in a room. Left and right refer to the respective sides of the body, not a certain wall or location in a gymnasium. Because the concepts of right and left (sideways) require cognitive as well as physical maturation for correct execution, it is not uncommon to find that children learn the directions forward and backward and up and down before they learn the directions of right and left.

Teaching the Concept of Directions

Overview   These tasks provide ideas for helping children understand the concepts of forward and backward, up and down, sideways, and right and left. As they become more capable, the complexity of the tasks is increased—the children are challenged to combine two or more direction concepts and to move in different directions in relationship to objects or people.

IDEAS FOR DEVELOPMENT

Have the children sit or stand spread about the room. Challenge them to point in various directions with different body parts.

1. In a forward direction with the feet.
2. Backward with the elbows.
3. To the left side with their hips.
4. Forward with the left foot.

Challenge children to travel through general space in different directions.

1. Forward.
2. Backward.
3. Sideward.
4. To left and then right; right and backward; left and forward.

Challenge children to move around the room and change the direction of travel according to this signal code:

1. On one beat of drum, go forward.
2. On two beats of drum, go backward.
3. On quick beat of tambourine, go sideward.
   or
4. On one beat of drum, go right.
5. On two beats of drum, go left.

Challenge children to change the direction of their travel quickly when a signal is sounded—children may change to whatever direction they choose.

Challenge children to change the direction of their travel quickly when a signal is sounded. But this time they cannot change to a direction that

IDEAS FOR OBSERVATIONAL FOCUS

Do children point in the appropriate direction?

Can the children tell you which direction is which?

Do children point in the appropriate direction with the correct body part?

Do children travel in the appropriate direction?

Can the children travel backward and sideward without bumping into others? Do they watch where they are going?

Do children travel in the designated direction, facing the appropriate direction?

Does the child respond to the signal by changing the direction of travel quickly?

Does the child change direction quickly? Or does he hesitate before changing?

Does the child change the direction of travel quickly?

Does he change direction once (for example, from forward to backward) or more than once (for example, from forward to backward to left)?

Is the child able to quickly change the direction of travel to one that is not opposite to the direction in which he or she was traveling?

is opposite the one in which they were traveling. That is, if a child was traveling forward, he cannot switch to traveling backward.

Do the children hesitate?

While they are waiting for the signal, have children think about how they are going to change direction.

Stand in the middle of the room with a drum with children spread about the room. When you say "Go," have the children use a slide pattern to travel around you while they face the outside of the room. When you hit the drum, have the children quickly turn to face the middle of the room without stopping their travel. When drum sounds again, have the children turn to face the outside of the room.

Can the child quickly change the direction she is facing without interrupting her travel?

Ask the children to work with a partner. Have one partner toss the ball so that the other partner must take a step forward, backward, to the right, or to the left in order to touch or catch the ball.

Does the child stand in a balanced position, ready to step in any direction to touch or catch the tossed ball?

Can the child tell you in which direction she stepped?

DEVELOPING THE CONCEPT OF LEVELS

Levels are the horizontal layers in space where the body or its parts are positioned or can move.

Low level is the space below the knees, close to the floor. A stamp or twist of the foot is an action at a lower level. Crawling, creeping, or rolling are locomotor actions performed at a low level.

High level is space above the shoulders, toward the ceiling. Although one cannot move the whole body into high level, actions such as stretching the arms up high or standing on the balls of the feet will bring body parts into a high level. A jump can take much of the upper body into a high level while part of the body remains at a medium or low level because of the pull of gravity.

Medium level is the space between low level and high level—the area between the knees and shoulders. Catching a thrown ball, for example, typically occurs in middle level.

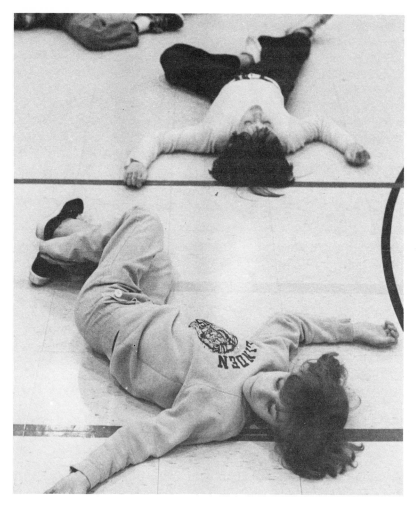

Children explore low level, as close to the floor as possible

Teaching the Concept of Levels

Overview   This section provides movement challenges that help children learn to move the body, body parts, and objects into different levels in space.

IDEAS FOR DEVELOPMENT

IDEAS FOR OBSERVATIONAL FOCUS

Challenge children to travel around the room. On the signal, have them stop with their entire body at a low level.

Does the child exhibit a position of stillness close to the floor?

Have children travel through space. Upon hearing the signal, have them stop in a position where as many body parts as possible are:

1. At a low level.
2. At a medium level.
3. At a high level.

Low	Does the child position his body close to the floor?
Medium	Does the child place his upper body parts about halfway between the floor and his head (waist level)?
High	Does the child stand on the balls of his feet and stretch arms up high over his head? Or does he stand on his hands with feet in the air?

Challenge children to travel while keeping as many body parts as possible at a low level. At the first signal, have them change to travel with as many body parts as possible at a high level. At the third signal, have them travel with as many body parts as possible at a medium level.

When traveling with body parts at a low level is the child close to the floor (crawling, creeping, rolling)?

When traveling with body parts at a high level, is the child on the balls of his feet? Does he jump?

When traveling with body parts at a medium level, is the child placing his head, shoulders, and hips in a space about halfway between his head and knees?

With the children spread about the room, hit eight beats at a slow tempo on a drum. Have the children begin at a low level in a position of stillness. Ask them to rise slowly until they hold a position of stillness with as many body parts as possible at a high level. Then, have them slowly change back to a low level.

Does the child accurately hold shapes at a high level and a low level?

Is it a slow transition, with the child in a medium level at the third, fourth, and fifth beats?

Challenge the children to travel around the room at a low level. Hit four beats on a drum with the accent on the first beat (slow tempo):

1,	2,	3,	4
loud	soft	soft	soft

On the accented beat, have the children quickly jump and stretch into a high level and immediately return to a low level of travel until the next accented beat.

On the accented beat, does the child quickly jump and extend her arms into a high level?

Does the child quickly return to a low level?

Is the child moving to the beat?

Ask the children to work with a partner. Have one partner toss a yarn ball so that the other partner catches it at different levels.

Does the child accurately maneuver her body or arms and hands to the level where the ball is presented?

Is the catch made at the desired level? Or is the ball caught and then moved into the intended level?

Challenge children to place body parts into different levels. Have them:

1. Place feet at low, medium, and high levels.
2. Place knees at low and medium levels.

Can the child place body parts into the designated levels?

What body parts can the child take into all three levels?

DEVELOPING THE CONCEPT OF PATHWAYS

A pathway is an imaginary design created along the floor or through the air by the body or its parts when moving through space. A pathway is also the trail of an object (a ball or hockey puck) as it travels from one player to another or toward a goal.

At first, young children may have difficulty understanding the concept of pathways in space. However, a class of young children can become enthralled with the process of discovering and experimenting with the many pathways the body can travel. A teacher can plan experiences that enable youngsters to recognize pathways and to effectively use knowledge of pathways to improve control of travel. For instance, even very young children can come to understand that a curved or angular pathway is effective in avoiding collisions when traveling through a crowd.

Teaching the Concept of Pathways

Overview   Children learn to travel in straight, angular, and curved pathways, and in combinations of these pathways, by experiencing the tasks in this section. More difficult tasks involve manipulating various objects in pathways and traveling in relation to others along various pathways.

IDEAS FOR DEVELOPMENT

IDEAS FOR OBSERVATIONAL FOCUS

Place tape on the floor in various patterns as shown in Figure 14.1. Have the children try to properly identify a pathway and travel along it. Vary the directions of travel. First, have the children move forward along the pathway; then have

Can the child name the various pathways?

Can the child travel along the pathways without varying from them?

them move backward along it, and then sideways. Then have them hop along the pathway,
then skip, then gallop.

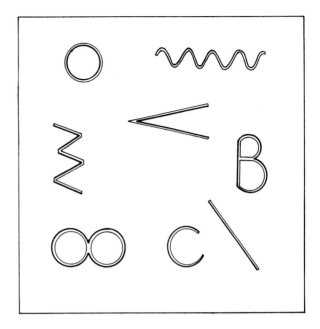

Figure 14.1   Pathways taped on floor

Give each child a card, similar to those in Figure
14.2, depicting a pathway. Encourage the children
to try to walk a pathway on the floor that is like
the pathway on the card.

Can the child accurately replicate the diagramed
pathway along the floor?

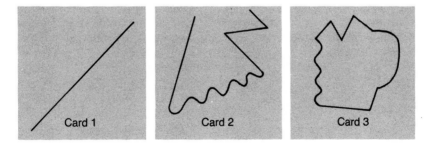

Figure 14.2
Pathway cards

Card 1   Card 2   Card 3

Have the children travel the same pathway in a
small area. Then ask them to travel it in a large
area (an entire room).

With the children sitting on the floor spread
about the room, ask them to look at a spot somewhere else in the room and plan a pathway from
their sitting location to their chosen spot. On

In traveling to their chosen spots, do the children display a wide range of pathway selections
(are some pathways straight, some zigzag, some
curved)?

signal, have them travel along their planned pathway to their intended destination and stop. Challenge them to travel along the same pathway back to their original starting locations.

Ask the children to work with a partner. Let one partner be the leader, the other the follower. On signal, have the leader travel a pathway somewhere in the room. On the second signal, have the leader freeze and the follower try to move along the same pathway as the leader until he catches up with him. Then have the partners switch roles.

Do the children exhibit the same pathways?

Do they find it difficult or easy to retrace their pathways?

Do the leaders design different pathways?

Do the followers accurately travel along the pathways taken by the leaders?

MR. JENNING'S KINDERGARTEN CLASS DISCOVERS PATHWAYS

Teacher: "Hey gang! How did we get to the physical education space today?"

Children: "We walked!"

Teacher: "Yes! And what parts of our bodies did we use?"

Children: "Our feet . . . our legs."

Teacher: "You got it! Tell me, did we leave a trail behind us? Any footprints on the floor?"

Children: "NO!" (loud and laughing)

Teacher: "I don't see any either. But what if our shoes were muddy. Would we have left a trail?"

Children: "Yeah! But Mrs. Farmer (the principal) sure would be mad!"

Teacher: "I think she would be, too! But if we did leave muddy footprints from your classroom all the way to the physical education space, what would our path look like?"

Children: "Long. . . . Messy. . . . We go by the library."

Teacher: "I think you're all right. I have an idea . . . Let's look at the chalkboard. Here is your room way over here and this is where the physical education space is. Look at our pathway. Although we didn't leave any real footprints we did follow a path. We follow this same pathway each time we come to the physical education space. Tell me, is our path just one straight line or did we make any turns?"

Children: "We turned when we came out of the room. At the library."

Teacher: "You people are sharp today. Hey! Can you think of any other pathways you follow each day?"

Children: "We go to lunch. . . . Walk to school. Down to the playground."

Teacher: "We follow a lot of pathways each day. Let's see if we can have some fun with pathways today. Pick a spot somewhere on the outside of the room (for example, a brick, a picture) and when I say 'Go' you stand up and walk in a straight line to your spot and freeze. Here we go!"

Ask half the children in the class to spread about the room and assume positions of stillness (for example, as bridges or statues). Have the other children sit around the perimeter of the room and plan pathways over, under, or around the people obstacles. On signal, have the travelers carry out their pathways. Then have them switch roles.

Place round pieces of carpet around the room in a random arrangement, and give each child a piece of paper on which there is a similar random arrangement of dots. Encourage the children to connect the dots on the paper to design a pathway. Then have them travel the path from one carpet "dot" to another. Have the children trade papers with one another and follow each other's pathways.

Does the child's pathway seem planned (deliberate, with clear beginnings and ends, and not too long), or is it haphazard?

Does the child travel without bumping into any other children?

Can the child repeat his pathway *exactly*?

Do the children diagram a variety of pathways?

Is each child able to accurately travel along his pathway?

Can the youngsters accurately follow each other's pathways?

An angular pattern can be extended to create a zigzag pathway:

A completed curved pathway is a circle:

A circle doubled in the opposite direction creates a figure-eight floor pattern:

DEVELOPING THE CONCEPT OF EXTENSIONS IN SPACE

Extensions in space are best understood as two separate possibilities. First, extensions can be thought of as spatial relationships of body parts to the entire body. Body extremities can be held in close to the body as a curl. Or body extremities can be opened up, as in a stretch. Extension also refers to the size of the movement in space. Movements with extremities held close to the body are small movements, and those with the extremities extended or opened up are large movements. Putting a golf ball is a small movement. Driving a golf ball is a large movement.

Teaching the Concept of Extensions in Space

Overview The concept of extensions is taught through learning experiences that provide children with an operational understanding of the differences between large and small and near and far extensions (movements).

IDEAS FOR DEVELOPMENT

IDEAS FOR OBSERVATIONAL FOCUS

Challenge children to attempt to touch all the space close to their bodies with their fingers.

Are fingers kept close to the body? Are extremities close to the body?

How close to the body can the child place her fingers without touching the body?

Challenge children to attempt to reach out to touch all the space far away from their bodies with their fingers.

Does the child stretch out in all directions to explore space?

Does she reach into high, low, and medium levels of space?

With children spread about the room, hit eight beats at a slow tempo on a drum. Challenge the children to slowly rise and open up their bodies (extending extremities), ending in an open stillness at a high level on the eighth beat. Then, have them slowly sink and bring their extremities close to the body, ending in a closed stillness at a low level on the eighth beat.

When at a high position of stillness, does the child have her extremities extended far from the body center?

When at a low position of stillness, does the child have her extremities held close to her body?

Instruct the children to travel around the room and stop on signal. Upon stopping have them hold a position where the bodily extremities are ei-

Does the child exhibit body stillness with extremities extended far from the body? With extremities held close to the body?

ther reaching out into space as far as possible or held in close to the body.

Ask children to travel around the room. When a signal is given, have them jump. While in the air have them extend their arms and legs away from the body. When they land, have them hold a still position with their arms and legs close to the body.	Does the child extend body extremities away from the body while airborne? Does the child pull the extremities in close to the body upon landing?
Have children pretend to carry an object they are trying to hide or protect (for example, money, a baby bird, or a million-dollar jewel).	Are extremities held close in, covering the object?
Have children pretend to carry an object which they are proud of and want to show off (for example, their picture in the paper, or a trophy they have just won).	Are extremities extended and open, perhaps raised to a high level?
Challenge the children to toss a yarn ball up in the air. Ask them to catch it close to the body or far away. Challenge them to toss using only one arm or their whole body.	Does the child sometimes catch close to the body? At other times fully extended? Does the child throw with small extensions (little range of motion by a few parts)? Is the child able to move a number of body parts through a wide range of motion in throwing?

APPLYING THE CONCEPT OF SPACE AWARENESS

Self-space and general space are often appropriate beginning concepts for children who have had little experience in formal physical education classes. One of the important skills that children need to develop early is the ability to occupy an area or to travel in an area while maintaining awareness of others. Self-space and general space are helpful concepts to use when teaching these skills.

The concepts of directions, levels, and pathways are usually introduced after children have developed the ability to differentiate between self-space and general space. Until the children actually acquire a functional understanding of directions, levels, and pathways (high and low levels, forward and backward directions, straight and curved pathways), the observational focus is primarily on the concept rather than on correct performance of a skill. For example, if you asked the

The child responding to the challenge of catching at a low level must have a functional understanding of the concept of space

children to throw so the ball starts off at a high level, you would be less interested in the actual mechanics of throwing than in the ability of the child to release the ball in a high level. Once you are confident that the children are able to apply the concepts, you can focus more on appropriate skill technique.

Most children take a longer time to grasp the concepts of right and left, air pathways, and extensions. Thus it is wise to introduce the other concepts to children before focusing on these three ideas.

The ability to understand the concept of right and left is related to cognitive maturation. Some children will need more time and more practice opportunities than will others to master left and right. Cognitive understanding of the concepts of extensions and air pathways for objects is easily acquired by many children. But most require a certain degree of skill before they can express these ideas in movements. Children with immature throwing and kicking patterns, for example, have difficulty propelling objects so that they travel in different (but intended) air pathways. Children with immature striking or catching patterns are unable to consistently catch or strike an object far from or near to the body.

If you wait until children have developed the skills that are related to these concepts, you will find that the pupils grasp the concepts more easily than if you try to teach the concepts and then the skills. There is no universally successful sequence for the introduction of these concepts. The reflective teacher utilizes all available information and makes judgments about the most appropriate time, sequence, and duration for introducing and studying the concepts of space awareness and their application to specific skill practice situations.

CHAPTER 15
TEACHING EFFORT CONCEPTS

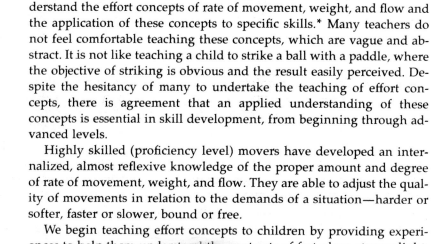

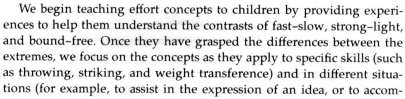

Too often no conscious, planned attempt is made to help children understand the effort concepts of rate of movement, weight, and flow and the application of these concepts to specific skills.* Many teachers do not feel comfortable teaching these concepts, which are vague and abstract. It is not like teaching a child to strike a ball with a paddle, where the objective of striking is obvious and the result easily perceived. Despite the hesitancy of many to undertake the teaching of effort concepts, there is agreement that an applied understanding of these concepts is essential in skill development, from beginning through advanced levels.

Highly skilled (proficiency level) movers have developed an internalized, almost reflexive knowledge of the proper amount and degree of rate of movement, weight, and flow. They are able to adjust the quality of movements in relation to the demands of a situation—harder or softer, faster or slower, bound or free.

We begin teaching effort concepts to children by providing experiences to help them understand the contrasts of fast–slow, strong–light, and bound–free. Once they have grasped the differences between the extremes, we focus on the concepts as they apply to specific skills (such as throwing, striking, and weight transference) and in different situations (for example, to assist in the expression of an idea, or to accom-

---

*Some movement analysis frameworks include the concept of space (direct and flexible) as a quality of movement. In our teaching, however, we use this concept so infrequently that we have chosen not to include it in the discussion of the qualities of movement.

plish a particular strategy). As children become more skillful, we focus on the gradations between the extremes. To illustrate, initially we might ask children to travel rapidly and to travel slowly. As children develop the ability to differentiate between the extremes, we focus more on the movement possibilities between the extremes—faster, slower, accelerating, decelerating, sudden changes of speed.

Many of the Ideas for Development in this chapter use imagery to help children distinguish between different effort concepts. It is important to keep in mind that the focus is on the movement qualities of the various images, rather than on the images. For example, when we say "move like a hippo," we are not asking the children to pretend to be hippos. Rather, we are using this task to help the children envision a slow, lumbering movement. Chapter Twelve contains additional information about the appropriate use of imagery in teaching movement.

DEVELOPING THE CONCEPT OF RATE OF MOVEMENT

Time to a young child is the ticktock of a watch, the cuckoo on a clock, or the numbers racing by on a digital timepiece. When spoken of in relation to movement, time is fast—being able to run like the wind, being the fastest in the class, zip, dash, zoom.

Young children enjoy the sensation of a fast run

Slowness is necessary in executing a headstand

In an activity in which speed is often the measure of success, children often have difficulty comprehending slowness and seeing the importance of this rate of movement. Yet the concept of slowness is grasped by the performer executing a walkover on the balance beam, and by the leaping dancer who seems to remain suspended in the air while the hands and arms express a certain feeling or emotion.

Changes in rate of movement usually occur without forethought as children adapt to different situations—speeding up or slowing down, to maintain possession, to avoid being tagged, to get in open space and receive a pass. Many movements and specific skills dictate the rate of movement. A handspring is done quickly, but a back walkover is done slowly. In some activities the child is free to assess a situation and then perform a skill at the best rate. For example, a movement executed quickly in dance or gymnastics elicits feelings of power and speed; the same movement executed slowly expresses the ultimate in control.

We begin teaching the concept of rate of movement to young children by contrasting the extremes. Gradually we advance to work that focuses on degrees of speed along a continuum—the ability to execute movements at varying speeds for the purpose of adapting, changing, or creating a situation.

Teaching the Concept of Rate of Movement

Overview   These tasks are designed to help children develop a functional understanding of rate of movement by providing them with experiences that contrast fast and slow actions of the total body and body parts, experiences that focus on acceleration–deceleration.

IDEAS FOR DEVELOPMENT	IDEAS FOR OBSERVATIONAL FOCUS
Challenge the children to travel quickly through space, stopping on signal in a balanced position; have them execute the same movement slowly.	Are the two speeds noticeably different?

> When children are traveling fast, try to keep the
> activity period short to avoid undue fatigue.

Encourage the children to begin their travel with a burst of speed, continue at maximum speed for a short distance, and then stop quickly.	Does the action begin suddenly or gradually?
Ask the children to contrast the following images: 1. A tortoise and a hare. 2. A race car and a Model T. 3. Excitement and dread. 4. A sprinter and a distance runner.	Can the child express the contrast by fast and slow traveling, as well as by body configuration or facial expression?

5. A mouse running from a cat and a hippopotamus with full tummy.
6. A dart and a crawl.
7. A dash and a waddle.

Encourage the children to think of their favorite sport or television character and to execute his or her movements as if the film is on fast speed. Ask them to repeat the movements in slow motion. Have them demonstrate only one activity, such as:

1. A catch and run.
2. A pursuit.
3. A lay-up.
4. Bionic power.

Does the rate of movement change?

Is the pattern of action the same in both sequences?

Suggest to the children that they travel through space, beginning slowly and gradually increasing to maximum speed. Ask them how they would travel as a car starting on a very cold morning or how their car would come to a stop if it ran out of gas?

Is the acceleration clearly observable?

Does the child's travel gradually increase and decrease, as opposed to a burst of speed and an abrupt stop?

From their self-space, ask children to focus on a spot to which their travel will be directed. Have them slowly begin to travel around their spot while keeping the focus (like a lion stalking prey). Gradually have them increase to maximum speed while circling in toward the spot. Just before they reach the spot, have them begin to slow down, slowly circle, then *pounce*! Have them pick a new spot and begin again.

Is the sequence characterized by one continuous motion of acceleration and deceleration from start to finish, as opposed to a series of extremes in speed with abrupt stops between them?

Children often equate slowness with heavy, jerky, stiff actions rather than with graceful movement. Examples of slow-moving animals can be useful here.

Challenge the children to bring their hands toward each other, *very slowly*, as if closing in to catch an insect. At the last moment before hands touch, have them quickly separate them, as though they are surprised.

As the hands move toward each other, can the child stop the movement at any time?

When the hands separate, do they move suddenly?

On the loud beat of a drum, have the children move their bodies suddenly—burst, explode, like a tightly coiled spring releasing, then pounce.

Are the child's actions quick, short in duration, one motion from start to finish?

Sustained movement is slower, longer. On the soft beat of the drum, have the children pretend to inflate, deflate, float like a balloon or a feather dropped from a high building.

Are the actions slow, controlled throughout—does the child deflate or collapse?

Does the action appear to be ongoing for a long period of time?

DEVELOPING THE CONCEPT OF WEIGHT

Weight is the contrast of muscular tension. The extremes are described as strong and light. There are, however, obvious gradations between the extremes.

Just as speed to a young child is "as fast as you can go," weight often means trying to bat a ball as hard as possible, whether the situation calls for a bunt or an outfield placement. A preschooler is likely to use the same degree of force to throw a ball three feet as to throw it ten yards.

We usually introduce the concept of weight by combining it with a skill that has been developed to the control level and preferably to the utilization level. Think, for example, of the child at a precontrol level who is learning to strike a moving ball. He is so fully concentrating his attention on making contact with the ball that the concept of weight would be an unnecessary and probably confusing thought. Hard and easy hits can come later, once the child is able to hit a ball consistently.

The qualities of strong and light movements are exemplified by the dancer as she or he expresses aggression, strength, and power, and by the gymnast in a free-floor exercise routine (tumbling on a large mat) as firm and fine actions and balances are combined in a demonstration of muscular control and strength.

Teaching the Concept of Weight

Overview   This section provides suggestions for teaching children to understand the concept of weight. Activities presented help youngsters develop an operational understanding of the strong (firm) and light (fine) actions of body parts and of the entire body.

This young boy freezes in a strong shape, with his muscles tensed

IDEAS FOR DEVELOPMENT

In their self-space, ask the children to make a shape with their entire body that demonstrates strength and firmness. Ask them to make a shape that is light, delicate, and airy.

Challenge the children to travel about the room with heavy actions, as if they are indestructible and all powerful forces.

IDEAS FOR OBSERVATIONAL FOCUS

Do the different body parts (arms, hands, and fingers) as well as trunk show firmness and muscular strength?

Does the observer sense lightness (absence of tension) in the body?

Does body appearance, as well as the movement through space, show firmness and muscular tension?

Ask the children to travel about the room as if they are floating, gliding, light as a feather, carefree in the wind.

Does the movement show a lack of tension?

Ask the children to imagine they are pads of butter that someone has left out in a warm kitchen on a hot day. Suggest that when they are finally returned to the refrigerator they will become solid and have a different shape.

Do the child's actions and shapes change from firm to light to firm?

Have the children use these image sequences to show contrast:

Do the child's actions show the contrast of firm–fine weight?

> Portrayal of a bold villain, a delicate damsel in distress, a courageous hero.
>
> Frosty the Snowman—first as a single snowflake, *gentle, light,* airy in movement and design, then as snowflakes taking on another form, such as a *sturdy, solid* snowman, or slowly melting and sinking as the sun comes out.

Have the children express the seasons to demonstrate understanding of contrast. Ask them what comes to mind when they hear the name of a season.

Are the child's movements firm or light?

Is the child able to tell you why he used strong or light movement?

Do his perceptions of strong and light agree with your perceptions?

Spring,	with new buds and growth, flowers, gentle breezes, and soft rains.
Summer,	with hot weather, swimming, thunderstorms, and leafy, sturdy trees.
Fall,	with going back to school, a football player, and falling leaves.
Winter,	with a single snowflake, an accumulation of snow, and stark, sturdy trees.

Suggest to the children that they select an item from each season to contrast strong–light in shapes and actions.

Imagery sequences designed by the teacher provide experiences in extreme contrasts. The degrees along the continuum (the subtle changes) are focused on in conjunction with the actual skill, such as jumping and landing, or balancing.

Have the children think about each pair of words and ask them to move to express contrasting strong–light images:

Punch/flick
Creep/pounce
Sneak/scare
Float/collapse
Glide/stomp
Raindrop/thunderstorm
Friends/foes
Play/work.

Are the differences in the terms clearly expressed in strong and light movements? Are you able to identify whether each movement is strong or light? Does the child agree with your observation?

> Young children often equate the concept of strong weight with the concept of size. Care should be taken not to pair all imagery examples as such—for example, big–firm or small–fine.

A heavy hippo, a lion stalking his prey, an awakening bear, or a swift deer would use different weight qualities in their movements. Have the children use the different qualities suggested by these images as they travel around the room.

Do the actions of body parts and the total body express firm or fine qualities, not just shape?

Have the children try to express these images to show the building and maintaining of tension:

An ant under a rock attempting to lift it.
An Olympic weight lifter.
A laser beam, first contained, then free.

Does the child maintain the muscular tension throughout the sequence?

> Actions of concentrated movement and muscular tensions are very tiring, and so the activity periods should be kept short.

DEVELOPING THE CONCEPT OF FLOW

Watch a very young child running down a hill. His actions are unstoppable, almost out of his control, until he reaches the bottom. The swing of a batter at a baseball, the smash executed by a tennis player, the giant swing of a gymnast on the high bar—all of these are examples of free flow in movement, when it seems that the performer is lost in the movement. The movement, not the performer, seems to control the situation.

Bound actions are stoppable, cautious, and restrained. The performer is in control at all times. Pushing a heavy object, traveling an angular pathway while trying to stay within boundaries, executing a slow cartwheel with a pause for a handstand before traveling on—these are examples of bound flow.

Teaching the Concept of Flow

Overview   This section provides tasks that assist children in understanding and demonstrating the difference between free flow and bound flow. The tasks encompass a variety of movements that are important for both skill performance and safety.

IDEAS FOR DEVELOPMENT

Challenge the children to travel about the room and to pause the instant you give the signal.

IDEAS FOR OBSERVATIONAL FOCUS

Is the child able to stop instantly, rather than several seconds after the stop signal is given?

Children tend to anticipate the teacher's signals; vary the intervals.

Challenging children to travel while balancing beanbags on their heads is one way to elicit bound flow

Ask the children to travel as though they are completely free—like an eagle, a prisoner with a complete pardon, or a really happy person, totally carefree.

Does the child's action appear free, without a direct goal, without caution or reluctance?

Music can greatly enhance the feel of bound or free flow.

Have the children try these actions to express bound flow:

Press the floor with feet, hands.

Push a heavy box.

Carry a too full glass of milk without spilling any.

Pull a full bucket on a pulley up from a well.

Are the child's bound actions stoppable at any point? Do they appear controlled, restrained?

Have the children try these actions to express free flow:

Flick away a fly.

Slash the air in uncontrolled anger.

Tap Morse code.

Jerk head, hands, away from danger.

Shake a dust mop.

Do the child's free actions appear unstoppable once movement begins?

Write a sentence of actions on the board—for example, "Walk, run, jump." The commas are signals to pause or hesitate, and the period means stop. Have the children begin on the signal.

Are the child's actions characterized by bound flow, with pauses between actions and stops when necessary?

Children enjoy using interpretations of different punctuation marks, such as the comma, exclamation point, and question mark, as different ending shapes.

Now have the children travel the same series of actions with *no* pauses between, as one movement from beginning to end.

Do the actions move unstopped from beginning to end, in obvious contrast to the previous challenge?

From the action words below, have the children select a series for their movement sequence. Remind them that the punctuation is the key to their pauses and stops.

Walk   Jump
Run   Turn
Gallop   Roll
Skip   Hop
Leap

Have the children select actions to express free flow, in which each action leads into the next, without any pause.

Are there obvious contrasts between bound and free actions? Does the child clearly pause between actions?

Children beginning sequence work often need guidance in restricting the length of the sequence; generally two or three actions are appropriate for the initial sequence.

APPLYING THE EFFORT CONCEPTS

We focus on concepts until the children have learned the basic terminology related to the effort qualities of movement. When they are able to accurately demonstrate the differences between the extremes of each concept, we no longer focus on the concept. Instead we focus on how the concept relates to the performance of a particular skill—fast dribble, fluid roll, or light gallop. We want the children to learn the effort concepts so that they can apply the concepts to actual skill learning situations.

The ability to use gradations of movement qualities distinguishes the inept performer from the skilled one, the sloppy movement from the polished one. An individual can learn to execute the basic requirements of a cartwheel, for example, so that it can be recognized as a cartwheel. But when that cartwheel is executed in a ragged, uneven, uncontrolled manner, it is clearly and easily distinguishable from a cartwheel performed by an experienced, trained gymnast. We teach children to apply the qualities of movement to their skill performances to help them become skillful movers.

Generally the concept of rate of movement (fast–slow) is easier for children to grasp than either the concept of weight (strong–light) or the concept of flow (bound–free). And so you may need to focus more on weight and flow than on rate of movement. Time can be studied as an applied concept—fast and slow skips, rolling fast and rolling slow, accelerated and decelerated change of levels—before weight or flow can be. The difference is that in teaching a concept our observational focus is primarily on the ability of the children to understand and apply the effort concept (Chapter Two). In contrast, when we use a concept as a subtheme, we know that the children already understand the concept from previous lessons, and therefore our teaching focus is primarily on the skill and how it can be executed utilizing varying movements.

CHAPTER 16
TEACHING RELATIONSHIPS

Our lives are made up of relationships—to people and to objects. These occur not only in physical education classes, but in everyday life. Driving to and from work in an automobile, maneuvering through a crowded aisle in a supermarket or dodging around an icy spot on a sidewalk—all these activities involve complex, dynamic relationships. And each involves several contexual variables (bodies, body parts, and objects) in simultaneous interaction.

DEVELOPING THE CONCEPT OF RELATIONSHIPS
When introducing the concept of relationships to children, we start with the simplest relationships. Because many young children are still at the "I" stage, the initial lessons focus on self-relationships. These include the relationships of body parts to one another, and the movements of body parts to change the relationships of those parts to make different shapes. As children develop a functional understanding of the relationships among body parts, the emphasis is shifted to moving in relationship to different objects. And finally we focus on relationships with others, initially with partners. When the children develop the social and physical maturity needed to work with others, we focus on relationships within groups and between groups.

Relationships as they occur in the areas of dance (for expressive purposes) and in games and gymnastics (with a more functional intent) are typically within the context of a particular situation. Within a given context the appropriate emphasis is then placed on the dynamics of a specific purposeful relationship. In simpler terms, once the children

"Touch ears with hands"
Young children at the "I" stage
benefit from tasks designed to clarify
the relationships among body parts

"Point to the door with your elbow"
A young girl responds to the teacher's
challenge

have grasped the basic concepts, the emphasis on a relationship is modified to suit the demands of a particular movement situation.

DEVELOPING THE CONCEPT OF THE RELATIONSHIPS OF BODY PARTS

Before children can focus on relationships between body parts, they need to be able to identify specific body parts. Thus, it is essential that each child acquire a functional vocabulary of body part names. Tasks that can be used in teaching this vocabulary include:

1. Pointing to the ceiling with elbow (knee, nose).
2. Touching the floor with wrist (waist, stomach).
3. Traveling with only feet, hands, and seat (elbows and knees) touching the floor.
4. Traveling around the room and, on the signal, stopping and touching heels (shoulders, heads) with another person.

Once the children have learned the names of the body parts, lessons focus on making shapes (round, narrow, wide, twisted, symmetrical, and nonsymmetrical) and using body parts in relationship to each other. For example, we might ask children to:

1. Travel and stop in a twisted shape.
2. Change from a symmetrical to a nonsymmetrical shape.
3. Make a wide shape during flight.
4. Move their feet so that they are higher than their head.

"Freeze in a low and wide shape"
This task requires children to consider the relationships among body parts

The following Ideas for Development contain additional suggestions for teaching the concept of relationships of body parts. They are described as direct statements, but you are encouraged to change the method of organization to suit the characteristics of the class with which you are working, as described in Chapter Four.

Teaching the Concept of Relationships of Body Parts

Overview   This section provides suggestions for teaching children to identify and utilize different body parts and to develop an understanding of how different body parts can relate to one another. Suggestions for teaching the concepts of various body shapes and body part shapes also are presented.

IDEAS FOR DEVELOPMENT

IDEAS FOR OBSERVATIONAL FOCUS

Have the children touch different body parts as they are called out:

nose	arm
chin	ankle
ear	foot
elbow	temple
wrist	neck
shoulder	eyebrow
eye	teeth
cheek	leg
forehead	knee
thumb	mouth
side	hip
lip	earlobe

Is the child touching the appropriate parts as they are called out?

Are there any parts that the children confuse with each other?

Does the child hesitate before touching body parts, or does she respond immediately?

Have the children touch different hands to different body parts—for example, left hand to right knee, right hand to left elbow, left hand to left shoulder.

Does the child know the difference between right and left?

Can the child identify parts quickly, or does she hesitate?

Suggest that the children play a game of Simon Says. (Don't have the children who miss sit out, because it is usually these children who need the work the most.)

Can the child quickly identify the parts that are called out?

Is the child listening to the directions?

Have the children touch different body parts to-gether—knee to elbow, hands to waist, head to knees, foot to shoulder.

Is the child able to figure out how to place different parts together?

Challenge the children to balance on different body parts:

1. On one part—foot, stomach, seat, back.
2. On two parts—feet, knees, hand and foot, head and foot.
3. On three parts.
4. On four parts.
5. On more than four parts.

Ask them which is easiest to balance on and why.

Is the child choosing appropriate parts to balance on? The right number of parts and parts that will support his weight?

Is he able to tell you how many parts he is balanced on?

Does he think that feet and knees are one part or two?

Mark Xs on the floor with tape, one for each child. Ask the children to place certain parts of their bodies on the X—finger, nose, elbow, or knee—making different shapes with their bodies.

Is the child able to place the appropriate parts on the marks?

Does the child simply place the parts on the marks or is he able to form different body shapes?

Is the child able to tell which part he has placed on each mark?

Have children support their weight on:

1. Matching parts—for example, on their feet.
2. Similar parts—on their arms and legs.
3. Different parts—on their seat and feet.

Does the child have to use other parts besides those called for to maintain his balance?

Can the child verbally tell you what kind of parts (matching, similar, or different) he is using?

Challenge the children to travel around the space on their:

1. Feet
2. Hands and feet
3. Elbows and knees

Is the child able to identify the proper parts and then able to use them?

Does the child actually travel? Or does she stay in one place?

Have the children travel around the space. On the signal, have them touch the part of the body that is called out with the same part of another person—for example, heels to heels, shoulders to shoulders, knees to knees.

Are the children able to touch parts together? Or do they simply stand beside each other?

Can they touch parts together without having to lean on each other?

Ask children to travel around the space and, on the signal, touch the called-for part to the floor.

Can the child find the appropriate part to touch to the floor?

Does she find each part quickly? Or does she have to watch others?

Is the child able to touch the part to the floor without falling down?

In their own space suggest that the children make:

1. A twisted shape
2. A round shape
3. A narrow shape
4. A symmetrical shape
5. A nonsymmetrical shape.

Is the child making the shape that is called for?

Is the child's entire body involved in the shape, or only the limbs?

Is she able to tell you which shape she is in?

Using a block and cane (see Figure 16.1) have the children:

1. Travel over the block and cane in any way possible—for example, by jumping, by using their hands and feet, or by using only their hands.
2. Take part of their weight on their hands, and bring their feet down in different places around the block and cane—for example, close to it, far away, on the side, close to-gether, far apart.
3. Travel under their block and cane—some-times on their stomach, sometimes on their back, feet first, head first.

Is the child actually traveling over the block and cane, or does he go around it?

Are the lagging parts clearing the block and cane, so that they do not knock it down?

Is the child able to vary where he brings his feet down? If there is variance, is it by accident?

Can the child tell you where he is bringing his feet down?

Can the child control his body, so that he can get under the block and cane without knocking it over?

Is the child able to vary the way that he gets under the equipment?

In their own space, have the children change from:

1. A wide to a narrow shape
2. A twisted to a round shape.

Are the different shapes clear and distinct?

Is the child able to move fluidly between shapes?

Have the children start in their own space in a round shape and stretch open to a wide shape on

Are the differences in the child's shapes clear?

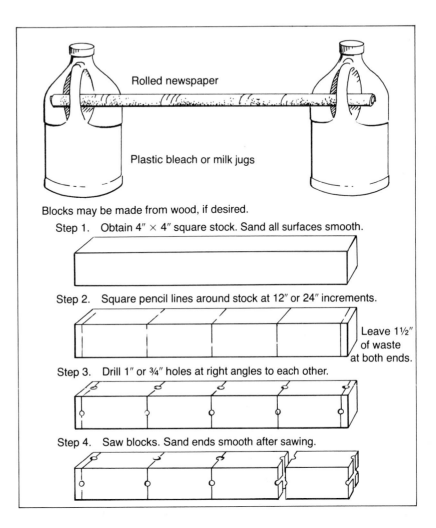

Rolled newspaper

Plastic bleach or milk jugs

Blocks may be made from wood, if desired.

Step 1. Obtain 4″ × 4″ square stock. Sand all surfaces smooth.

Step 2. Square pencil lines around stock at 12″ or 24″ increments.

Leave 1½″ of waste at both ends.

Step 3. Drill 1″ or ¾″ holes at right angles to each other.

Step 4. Saw blocks. Sand ends smooth after sawing.

Figure 16.1   Block and cane construction

six beats. Have them curl back up on the next six beats.

Then have them open quickly on one beat to a wide shape and twist back to a closed shape on six beats.

Have the children work with partners and mold their partners into a shape. The statues stay frozen; the sculptors move around the room and change the other statues. Have the children change roles.

Do they have definite beginnings and ends?

Do the movements match the beat?

Do the movements flow together?

Are the children able to tell you what shapes they are using?

Can they mold others into clear shapes?

Children love to play the roles of statues and sculptors but tend to get silly during this activity. They need to be warned that no horseplay will be allowed. They also need to be cautioned to place others only in shapes that they can hold without too much difficulty, so that no one gets hurt.

Have children practice making symmetrical shapes (in which the two sides look alike). Have them try making nonsymmetrical shapes (in which the two sides do not look alike). (See Figure 16.2.)

Is each child able to create shapes that are identical on both sides (symmetrical)?

Is each child able to create shapes that are nonsymmetrical?

Do the children know the difference between the two kinds of shapes?

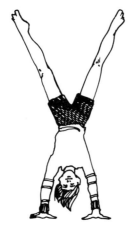

Figure 16.2   Symmetrical and nonsymmetrical shapes

Use museum postcards of paintings, statues, or sculptures as examples. Have the children mold one another into symmetrical and nonsymmetrical shapes.

Is the shape symmetrical or nonsymmetrical according to the picture?

Have the children travel around the room. On the signal, ask them to stop and make a wide shape, then a narrow shape, then a twisted shape.

Is the child able to stop and form each shape immediately, or does she have to watch others?

Can the child form the shapes without falling down?

Are the shapes clear? Are they the ones called for?

Have the children jump off a box, a low beam, or a table. While in the air, have them make a wide shape. Then have them land and roll. Repeat the sequence, asking them to make a narrow shape, a twisted shape, a round shape, a symmetrical shape, and a nonsymmetrical shape.

Does the child form the shapes in the air or after she lands?

Are the shapes clear?

Can the child tell you which shape she is making?

DEVELOPING THE CONCEPT OF RELATIONSHIPS WITH OBJECTS

Some concepts are studied in relationship to objects. Others have more meaning when they are practiced in relationship to people. The concepts of on and off, along, through, over, under, around, and surrounding apply primarily to relationships with objects. The concepts of near and far, in front, behind, and alongside are generally studied as person-to-person relationships. The concepts discussed in this section can be studied as relationships to objects or to people. Because objects are more predictable (less dynamic) than children, however, we focus on the concept of relationships with objects before focusing on relationships with people.

It is interesting to note that children frequently identify a lesson by the object they related to rather than by the concept they studied. For

Children travel cautiously through a narrow space; each constantly monitors his relationship to the obstacle

example, after a lesson in which hoops were used to study the concepts of traveling over, under, and through, children might say, "Hey, that was fun! Are we going to play with hoops again tomorrow?" In time, however, children begin to understand and use the terminology that we use. For instance, a child might say "It is easier to go over and under the hoop than it is to go through the hoop."

Within the context of a game or a dance lesson, specific terms are classified as objects. In dance, for example, wands, streamers, newspapers, or scarves are considered objects. Goals, boundaries, nets, and targets are objects with which the child learns relationship concepts in a game context.

The Concept of Teaching Relationships with Objects

Overview   Ideas for development included in this section are intended to enhance the children's awareness and ability to function effectively in relation to the objects that exist in various physical activity contexts.

IDEAS FOR DEVELOPMENT

Have the children travel over a hoop (Figure 16.3) or a rope (Figure 16.4) in any way they can.

IDEAS FOR OBSERVATIONAL FOCUS

Is the child actually traveling over the equipment? Or does she travel around it?

Does the child travel in various ways?

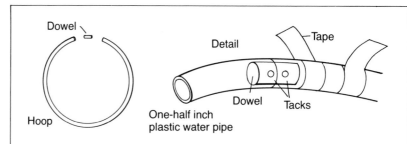

Hoops can be cut from one-half inch plastic air conditioner or water pipe. The connection is made with a dowel rod that is held in place with staples or tacks. Special pipe connectors or fusion with heat can also be used to close the gap. For a hoop with 30-inch diameter, you will need 95 inches of pipe; for a 36-inch hoop you will need 113 inches of pipe; and for a 42-inch hoop, 132 inches of pipe.

Figure 16.3   Construction of a hoop

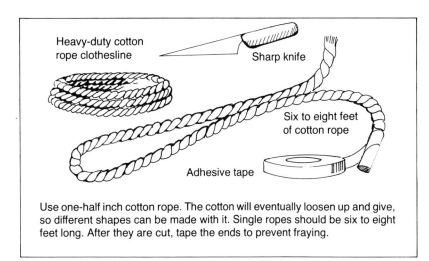

Use one-half inch cotton rope. The cotton will eventually loosen up and give, so different shapes can be made with it. Single ropes should be six to eight feet long. After they are cut, tape the ends to prevent fraying.

Figure 16.4   Construction of a rope

Ask them to:

1. Stay as close to the object as they can when they travel over it.
2. Stay as far away from the object as they can as they cross it.
3. Put their weight down inside the equipment as they travel over it and then continue.

Is each child crossing the object by keeping her body close to it? Or is only one body part close to the object?

Is the child's entire body far away? Or are just the upper extremities away and the lower parts still close?

Is the child able to understand the term *inside,* so that she actually puts her weight inside the hoop or rope at some point?

Moving in relationship to a rolling hoop is a fascinating challenge for the skilled child

Have the children travel onto and off small boxes or milk crates.

1. Ask them to try as many ways as possible (at least three) to get on and off the box.
2. Suggest that they add a hoop on the floor beside their box, and then travel into the hoop and then onto and off the box.

Is the child using a variety of ways to get on and off of the equipment (hands leading, rolling, jumping, stepping)?

Is the child actually traveling inside the hoop before mounting the box? Or does she travel over it?

Have the children use a box and hoop and make up a sequence that includes the ideas of on and off, then in and out and around. Have them practice each sequence until they can repeat it.

Can the child put all ideas together into a sequence?

Does the child understand the concepts of on and off, and in and out and around, so that he can verbalize exactly where each is used in the sequence?

Have the children use streamers or ribbons to create a circular pattern in the air, then a figure-eight pattern, and then a curved pattern.

Is the child able to keep the streamer in the air?

Can he move it around his body to create the appropriate patterns?

Ask the children to take their streamers under, over, in front of, in back of, and around different parts of their bodies—legs, head, trunk. Ask them to try to keep it moving at all times.

Is the child actually moving the streamer over, under, and around different body parts?

Suggest that the children make up a sequence where the streamer always keeps going and they take it over, around, or under at least three different parts.

Is the child able to keep the streamer going?

Can the child move it around three parts?

Challenge the children to travel along a low balance beam or table by:

Walking
Running
Hopping
Waddling
Skipping
Sliding

Is the child able to move along the piece of equipment that he is working on?

Can he adjust his body movements to keep his balance in different situations?

Ask the children to travel under the beam or table.

Can the child travel under the equipment by holding on to it somewhere?

Does each child have most of her body under the equipment?

Have the children travel with part of their weight on the equipment and part off it.

Can the child travel with her weight supported between the equipment and the floor?

Suggest that the children explore various pieces of gymnastic equipment by traveling over, under, around, along, and through each—for example, parallel bars, climbing frame, vaulting boxes, ropes, and chairs.

Is the child able to discover the different possibilities of each piece of equipment?

Can she tell you which concept she is using?

Set up an obstacle course of elastic or regular ropes at various heights around the room. Challenge children to go through the course going over and under the ropes. As they get more proficient, you may want to suggest that they try to go over high ropes instead of under them and under lower ropes instead of over them.

Does the child use a variety of ways to go over and under the ropes?

Have the children work with partners. Suggest that one partner make a shape and freeze while the other partner tries to see how many ways she or he can move around, in and out, and through the shape. Ask them to try going around, over, under, through, away from, and toward.

Does the child find a variety of ways to move in relation to her partners?

Is she able to tell you which ways she has used?

Encourage the children to use their partners as obstacles (see Figure 16.5):

Do the partners consider the ability of the other to cross the shape?

1. Have one partner make a shape while the other tries to cross the shape in any way without touching. For example, one partner makes a small curved shape, and the other jumps over.

Are children creating shapes that are too hard for the crosser?

Are the partners crossing the shape or are they going around it?

2. Have the children match the shape of the obstacle as they cross it.

Are the partners matching the shape of the obstacle as closely as possible in the air?

3. Have them contrast the shape of the obstacle as they cross it. For example, if the obstacle is wide, the crosser is narrow. If the obstacle is curled, the crosser is stretched.

Are the children crossing the obstacles with shapes that are appropriate—wide over narrow, curled over stretched?

Do the children know the differences between different body shapes? Can they name the different shapes?

Can the children form shapes rapidly enough for the other to cross without stopping?

4. Encourage the children to work cooperatively with a partner. As soon as one partner crosses a shape, he forms a shape for the other partner, and both are continually exchanging places.

Can the children recover from one action fast enough to perform the next?

Figure 16.5   Using partners as obstacles

5. In a space that is well defined, have both partners travel around the space. Suddenly one forms a shape for the other to cross. As soon as he sees it being formed, the partner crosses it and the two keep moving. The timing is split second, so that the shape is barely made before it is crossed. See if the children can do this several times without breaking the flow of the movement.

Are the children working cooperatively to accomplish the task?

Can the partners cross the shapes as soon as they are made?

Can the children keep moving without breaks while forming the shapes and crossing them?

Are the children able to vary the way that they cross the obstacles (for example, sometimes feet first, sometimes hands first)?

Can the children move without bumping into each other?

Children need to be reminded that elastic ropes can be dangerous. They should attach the ropes to body parts where they do not tend to slip off. Under no circumstances should a child let go of a rope so that it snaps back.

Have the children work with partners and stretch ropes or elastic ropes.

Are the children actually as close as they can be or just closer than usual?

1. With both partners standing still, ask them to hook the rope to some part of their bodies and see how close they can get to each other.

2. Ask them to see how far apart they can move the parts to which the rope is connected without moving.

Is far away really far?

3. Ask them to see how close they can get.

Can a difference be seen between near and far?

4. Ask them to see how far apart they can get and to be aware of where other children are.

Elastic ropes may be purchased from some equipment companies. If you want to make your own, you can. Cut a six-foot piece of heavy duty elastic and sew the ends together. Elastic ropes can also be made out of heavy rubber bands.

Have children throw an object toward different targets marked on the wall.

Can the child aim toward the target?

Ask them to move closer to the target and throw, and further from the target and throw.

Can the child adjust the throw according to the distances that he is from the target, so that he can still hit it?

Ask the children to change the place from which they are throwing so that they are not always directly in front of the target, but sometimes at one side or the other.

Can the child still hit the target from different places? Or has he put himself completely out of range?

Have children select a partner and move around the room. One partner follows the other's pathway. Ask them to pick three combinations of pathways and write a sentence describing them. Then ask them to draw maps showing their sentences and to make them clear enough so that someone else can follow them. Have the children trade maps with another group and follow their map.

Is the follower able to keep up with the leader?

Is he actually following the leader?

Is it obvious which children are following which children?

1. Ask children to follow their partners as they change pathways, speeds, and form of locomotion.

Are the children able to combine several different concepts and still follow the intended pathway?

2. Ask them to travel, following their partners. When they stop, have them form identical shapes. The shapes can be beside, behind, in front of, or surrounding their partner.

Are the shapes identical?

Do the children vary where they make their shapes?

Are they able to verbalize where the shape is made?

3. As the children follow their partners, suggest that they be beside, behind, or in front of them.

Can the children still match actions from different locations?

Do they understand the concepts of behind, in front of, and beside?

4. Have partners develop a movement sequence together. Then, instead of one following and one leading, have them learn it so well that they can move together.

Are the children doing the same thing at the same time, or is one still following?

Have the children travel with partners throughout the space.

Is it clear which children are partners?

1. As they travel, have them suddenly meet their partners, then go off again. Ask them to always be able to see their partners.

Are the meeting and parting phases clear?

2. Have them meet and part from their partners with the same body shape but in opposite directions (for example, one partner going forward, the other backward).

Can the children keep their body shapes identical while also moving in the opposite direction from their partners?

3. Have them travel in a small confined space, meeting and parting from each other while avoiding contact. Have them travel over, under, and around their partners, and increase the speed of their movement.

Can the children meet and part as well as travel over, under, or around their partners?

Is the meeting and parting still clear?

4. Have partners travel throughout the space, meeting and parting. While they do this have them use opposite speeds—one partner moves quickly, and the other partner moves slowly.

Is the meeting and parting and the change of speed obvious?

5. Have them combine meeting and parting and speeds with an opposition in level to their partners. For example, one partner approaches with a high fast level, while the other approaches with a low slow level.

Are the children able to combine all three concepts and keep them clear?

Have children work with a partner (or in groups). Challenge them to form cooperative designs:

1. Both partners hold identical symmetrical shapes.
2. Partners support one another's weight in forming a symmetrical or nonsymmetrical design.
3. Both partners form nonsymmetrical shapes but create an overall symmetrically designed shape.

Have the children observe their classmates' creations and describe the qualities displayed—jagged, pointed, smooth, ugly, graceful.

Can the children describe the symmetrical/nonsymmetrical nature of their designs?

Do the children display a variety of interesting designs?

Can the children describe the expressive qualities of symmetrical/nonsymmetrical designs (for example, graceful, smooth, calm, rough, jagged, busy)?

DEVELOPING THE CONCEPT OF RELATIONSHIPS WITH PEOPLE

When children understand the concept of relationships with people, they have increased awareness of the interplay that occurs—in games, dance, and gymnastics—among the persons involved in the movement. This interplay is seen when dancers converse and move around, between and beside each other, paired acrobats balance and flip each other, trapeze artists catch and throw each other, and soccer players work as a unit to advance a ball downfield.

Children often think of relationships to others simply as children working with other children. The term *relationships,* as we use it in physical education, is generally unknown to them. When teaching children about relationships with people, we focus on alone in a mass, solo, partners, groups, and between groups. These relationships can occur in a variety of ways: Each child dribbles a ball in general space (alone in a mass); one child demonstrates a sequence before an entire class (solo); a child mirrors or matches the movement of a partner (partners); children meet or part in a dance with a group to express an idea (groups); and individuals work with others as a team to accomplish a task against another team (between groups).

Alone in a mass. This relationship occurs when all children move simultaneously, with no intent of observing one another, and is fre-

A child matches the rocking movement of a partner

quently seen in lessons using a problem-solving or guided discovery approach. In these lessons, the children are indirectly relating to one another as they move throughout general space. In contrast to a solo relationship, the children say they feel they are truly on their own, even though they are surrounded by classmates. A child is alone in a mass when dribbling his or her own ball through general space. So, too, is each child when an entire class is running simultaneously to a predetermined location.

Solo. A solo relationship is that of the individual to the audience before whom he is performing and by whom he is being observed. Examples are the pitcher on a baseball team, a featured performer in a ballet, and a gymnast. Because some children experience unpleasant pressure or tension when they are the center of attention, we make solo performances voluntary, rather than mandatory. This is particularly important for the poorly skilled child who often feels increased tension and pressure when asked to perform in front of an audience. On the other hand, some children enjoy the challenge of solo performances and actually seem to do better when watched by a group. The feeling experienced when moving and being observed by others is an interesting phenomenon and one that we want children to explore, but in a safe, nonthreatening environment. In all classes we discourage the children from laughing at or criticizing the performances of other children.

Partners. Partners are two individuals relating to each other through their movements. As children become increasingly skilled and socially mature, the partner relationship is introduced. Partner relationships include two dancers moving in synchronization to express harmony or peace, two people paddling a canoe, and two acrobats performing a routine together. Relationship concepts that are introduced as children work with partners (or groups) include:

1. Meeting and parting—traveling toward or away from a partner.
2. Unison and contrast—both partners intentionally do the same thing (unison), or they intentionally do the same thing in different ways.
3. Leading and following—one partner leads, the other follows.
4. Matching—partners are side by side and attempt to duplicate one another's movements instantaneously (to make the same movement at the same time).
5. Mirroring—partners face one another and form the reverse reproduction of the partner's movements, as if looking in a mirror.

Groups. Group relationships occur when more than two children work together for a common purpose. These relationships include children working together to express an emotion in dance, to build a shape supporting one another's weight, or as a team trying to keep a ball from touching the floor, but without catching it.

As the size of the group increases so, too, does the complexity of the relationship. A partner relationship involves being aware of one other child, while a successful group relationship necessitates an awareness of two or more children. The difficulty of decision-making also increases proportionately with the size of the group. The concepts of meeting and parting, unison and contrast, and leading and following all become increasingly challenging as the size of a group increases.

We typically assign specific tasks to children in groups. This enables them to develop the skills of moving in relationship to others before they try group tasks that require children to make decisions—such as those required when children make up a game or invent a sequence. Asking children who have had little opportunity to work in groups to make group decisions about their work has proven counterproductive. Once children become proficient at group relationships, however, they are challenged by the adventure and creative opportunities of group decision-making.

A group of children work together for a common purpose

Between groups. This relationship occurs when two or more children relate to two or more children. It is the most complex of relationships because it involves not only being aware of one's own group, but also a responsibility to relate to another group. This relationship is extremely challenging, as demonstrated by the wide appeal of sports that match one team against another. We initially keep intergroup relationships small (three on a side) and try to allow choices about whether or not to participate in an intergroup relationship.

The Ideas for Development that follow can be used to enhance the awareness and ability of children to work with others.

Teaching the Concept of Relationships with People

Overview   These tasks are designed to improve the ability of children to function successfully with other individuals and groups in a variety of situations.

IDEAS FOR DEVELOPMENT

OBSERVATIONAL FOCUS

Have partners travel throughout general space, with one child following the other.

Are the children accurately matching the shape made by their partners, with their extremities too?

1. Ask the children to stop on signal and the follower to match a shape made by the leader.

2. On signal, have the leader use pathways with sharp changes of direction to try to lose the follower. Ask the follower to try to stay right with leader.

Is the follower able to follow the leader?

Are the children able to stay together?

Does the follower copy the leader's movements and changes of directions?

COMPETITION

Many intergroup relationships are competitive, with one group attempting to perform more skillfully than the other group. The emphasis on winning creates an intense emotional involvement that can produce disturbing feelings in some children. We talk with children about these feelings, which usually occur in competitive, predesigned team situations, and we explain how these feelings can be understood and dealt with effectively. Cooperative situations, in which children in a group work to accomplish a common goal, involve relationships that are easier for young children to handle.

Some might suggest the competitive relationships between groups are inappropriate for children. The affective and cognitive ramifications of competition include the feelings associated with winning and losing, false feelings of superiority or inferiority, and determination to beat an opponent. It has been our experience that competitive relationships, with many affective and cognitive ramifications, occur anyway, at recess or after school situations. And so we are convinced that it is the teacher's responsibility to help children develop a healthy attitude about competitive situations.

It is important for children to understand that it is acceptable to choose not to participate in a competitive situation if they feel threatened or insecure. Similarly, they should understand that everyone makes mistakes in games, and that when they make mistakes, the other children are not unhappy with them as individuals, but rather with the situation. These affective concepts are not typically included in a discussion of relationships between groups. But it is in these types of relationships that we so often observe children developing the distaste and disaffection for physical activity that can endure for a lifetime if not dealt with effectively. And so we believe that it is important to discuss them.

> The leader must be aware of the follower's capabilities, so that she or he challenges the partner but doesn't frustrate her or him with movements that are too difficult.

Suggest that partners mirror each others' actions. Have the children decide for themselves who is the leader and when and how they will change roles:

Are the children actually mirroring each other, or are they matching actions?

Is the speed of the actions appropriate for mirroring?

1. Ask the children to follow all that the leader does with just their hands and arms. Remind them that they are mirrors—if the leader moves his left arm, the follower must move his right arm; if the leader moves backward the follower must move forward.

Do partners watch one another closely?

2. Have the children mirror their partners by moving all body parts, but without traveling.

Are the children able to mirror effectively with parts other than the hands and arms?

Are they mirroring the appropriate parts?

3. Have the children change the speed with which they move the body parts—sometimes very slowly, then suddenly fast.

Can the children keep up with the changes of speed?

4. Suggest that, with their partners, the children try to tell a story with mirroring actions—for example, suggest that they act like babies first discovering a mirror and making faces; or that they practice for a play; or imitate a grown-up—their mothers putting on makeup, or their fathers shaving.

Are the children working together to tell the story?

Have the children move toward their partners with body shapes that express how glad they are to see him or her.

Does the partner relationship obviously tell which children are partners?

Have partners meet and part in a way that expresses curiosity and inquiry.

Can the relationship of meeting and parting be observed?

Have partners meet and part without touching, in a way that expresses "Mother said we must apologize."

Are the children able to work together to portray the feelings they want to express?

Have partners meet and part as if they are about to greet someone and realize that they do not know him.

Have partners pass, throw, or kick a ball, always staying the same distance apart.

Are the children able to stay the same distance apart or do they start to move close to one another?

Have partners begin to travel toward a particular mark while passing, throwing, or kicking their balls. As they travel, have them stay the same distance from each other.

Do the children position themselves ahead of their partners so they can receive the pass easily and keep traveling?

This idea works well if a lined field (such as a football field) is available and the children can use the lines as guides.

Have a group (four or five) pass, throw, or kick a ball while moving in one direction. Ask the children to keep the same distance from one another and to work together to keep the action going.

Can the children as a group keep distance between them or do they crowd to the middle or cut into someone else's space?

Are the children able to cooperate to keep the action going?

Do the receivers move ahead of the passers so as to receive the ball on the move and keep moving?

Do the passers send the ball ahead of the receivers so they can receive it without having to stop?

Have partners pass, throw, kick, or strike a ball as they move in the same direction toward a fixed mark. Have them stay the same distance away from their partners while trying to keep the ball away from two others who are moving in the opposite direction and trying to take their ball.

Can the children collaborate with their partners to move the ball in the direction they choose without letting the other group take it?

Are the children able to stay away from each other so they do not crowd or confuse the situation?

Do they use changes of speed to evade their opponents?

Is each child able to pass ahead of the partner so he or she can receive it on the run?

Does the receiver move ahead of the passer?

Does the passer pass when forced to or because she is supposed to?

> When children begin to work with others in collaborative and competitive situations involving a manipulative skill, the skill level tends to deteriorate briefly if they are concentrating on the relationship. This needs to be expected and explained. The children, though, do need to have a certain level of manipulative ability before beginning these situations, or the task will become very frustrating to them.

Have a group of children (four or five) play follow the leader; have the leader change on a predetermined signal.

1. Suggest that the leader change pathways to add sharp changes (zigzags).
2. Have the group determine a signal (such as a clap) and follow the first leader until the signal is heard. After the signal the second person in line takes off in his own direction, changing the way of traveling, and the line follows him. This continues until each child has been a leader. Ask the group to move continually, with no breaks in action.

Can each child keep up with the actions of the group?

Do the children stay far enough apart so that they can follow each other?

Are all the children alert to their movements, keeping their part of the group going?

Have a small group (three or four children) start together to form a shape of their own. Then, on signal, have them suddenly part as if they must leave in a hurry; take only one to two steps, freeze, and form a body shape on their own. On the next signal have them quickly come back to their group shape. Suggest that they practice until they are able to make the same group shape each time.

Are the children able to work together to form a group shape, without giggling or laughing?

Does the shape actually look like a group shape or more like a lot of individual shapes?

Can the children pull apart, yet still have the effect of a group?

Can they come back together as a group and form their shape, or is it fragmented?

Have a small group (six to eight children) play a dodgeball game. After one member is hit, he be-

Are the children able to stay out of each other's way in the middle and dodge the ball?

comes a thrower on the outside of the circle. Have the children concentrate on what it is like to be in the middle and to have to be aware of the others in the middle and of the ball.

Are they able to move away from the ball?

Are they able to dodge the ball even when someone is in front of them?

Have children start together as a small group and form a group shape. Then have them break away, one at a time, travel in their own way, and return to the group as they feel like it. Have the children hold their position in the shape until all have returned and to work on this until their group can do it without stopping or talking. (This idea will take quite awhile for children to perfect, as they will have to learn to wait for the other group members to complete sequences of various lengths. Encourage them to wait rather than to rush what they are doing.)

Is the group shape clear in the beginning?

Is it obvious when the children break away?

Are the children actually taking the time to move on their own?

Can the group get back together again?

APPLYING THE CONCEPT OF RELATIONSHIPS

The concept of relationships with objects and people is considered a beginning theme in the gymnastics and dance areas, as the children are taught the concepts of over, under, in, out, alongside, and on. There the focus is on whether the child understands the concept, rather than on whether he or she can accomplish the skill that is involved. For example, you would observe whether a child was actually jumping symmetrically over a block and cane, rather than whether he or she was crossing without knocking it over. Once you are sure that the child understands the concept, then you begin to focus on the skill. Once a concept has been learned, it can also be used for expressive purposes in dance situations.

Relationships with objects in the games area are not introduced until children have developed an adequate degree of skill in the manipulative area. Children must learn to manipulate objects with some consistency before they can reasonably be expected to manipulate them in relationship to objects or people. If children are given tasks involving manipulative skills and relationships too early, they tend to become frustrated and bored.

The concept of relationships with others is the last concept to be introduced. Socially children enjoy working near other children at a very young age, but often physically and cognitively they are not able to function effectively in relationship to others. For example, children of the precontrol level do not possess enough skill to be able to consistently work with a partner—when such a child is asked to throw an object back and forth, only one out of three throws is likely to reach the partner. Therefore, relationships with others as a *concept* should be dealt with when the children's skills are adequate and when they have matured enough socially so that their abilities are enhanced when they work with other children.

The strategy and challenge of working in groups and between groups is derived only when a skill has developed sufficiently so that the children are able to focus on the relationship while still performing the skill efficiently. There are no magical ages or times for introducing the different relationship concepts. Each teacher must reflect on information about the environment, the children, the skill, and herself or himself as a teacher to determine the best time for introducing the concepts of relationships.

CHAPTER 17
TRAVELING

A child is first capable of changing the location of his body at about three months of age when he turns himself over from his back to his stomach. Unless seriously handicapped, he will soon begin to crawl, then creep. At about one year he will take his first step. And by the time he enters school, he will exhibit relatively mature walking and running patterns. Unlike other skills—such as throwing, catching, and striking—the basic locomotor patterns develop naturally in most children.

Most school-age youngsters, therefore, are beyond the precontrol level in walking and running. Nevertheless, the teacher's first task is to evaluate performance of these patterns to ensure that any youngsters who exhibit severely immature or inefficient patterns will receive remedial assistance.

Similarly, it is important to ascertain how many students can perform the fundamental locomotor skills that emerge from the walk-run pattern—leaping, sliding, galloping, hopping, and skipping.

TRAVEL PATTERNS

Walking   Walking is a process of alternately losing balance and recovering it in a forward direction while in an upright position. While moving forward, the body should display little up and down or side to side movement. The arms and legs move in opposition. A mature walking pattern appears smooth and is accomplished with an ease of manner.

When a class is challenged to travel about a general space, the teacher can observe individual children for possible inefficiencies

In assessing the walking pattern of children, look for these inefficiencies:

1. A bouncy walk—too much vertical push.
2. Excessive swing of the arms away from the sides.
3. Failure to swing the arms at the shoulders.
4. Feet held too close together, so that the entire body has a jerky appearance as the child walks.
5. Feet held too far apart—duck walk.
6. Toes turned out.
7. Toes turned in—pigeon-toed.
8. Head too far forward—body leaning forward before the lead foot touches the ground.

Running   During the earliest stage of running (at about twenty-four months) a child's new speed produces precarious balance. Exaggerated leg movements are made (see Figure 17.1). In particular, the knee of the recovery leg swings outward and then around and forward in preparation for the support phase. This knee action is accompanied by a toeing out of the foot of the recovery leg. These exaggerated movements gradually disappear as the legs become longer and stronger.

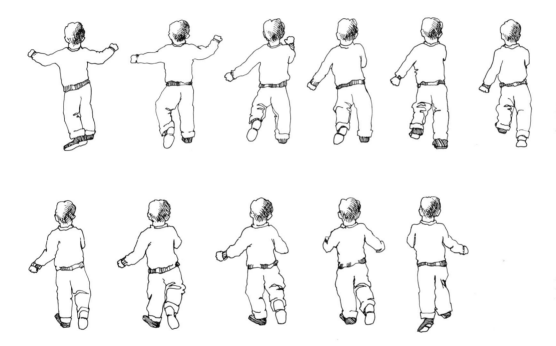

Figure 17.1   Earliest stage of running (child is about twenty-four months old)

Most school-age youngsters are able to run with relatively good speed and can change direction while running with a fair amount of success. In a mature running pattern (observed when children are attempting to run at maximum velocity), each leg goes through a support phase and a recovery phase, and the full sequence produces two periods of nonsupport (see Figure 17.2). Wickstrom* has summarized the essentials of the mature pattern as follows:

1. The trunk maintains a slight forward lean throughout the stride pattern.

---

*R. L. Wickstrom, *Fundamental Motor Patterns*, 4th ed. (Philadelphia: Lea & Febiger, 1977), pp. 37–57.

Figure 17.2   Mature form in running

2. Both arms swing through a large arc and in synchronized opposition to the leg action.

3. The support foot contacts the ground approximately flat and nearly under the center of gravity.

4. The knee of the support leg bends slightly after the foot has made contact with the ground.

5. Extension of the support leg at the hip, knee, and ankle propels the body forward and upward into the nonsupport phase.

6. The recovery knee swings forward quickly to a high knee raise and simultaneously there is flexion of the lower leg, bringing the heel close to the buttock.

Hopping A hop involves a springing action from one foot, in any direction, to a landing on the same foot (see Figure 17.3). The push into the air and the absorption of the landing shock are accomplished primarily by the work of the ankle joint. The knee seldom straightens fully.

Because the weight of the body is supported by one foot, the arm action is restricted. The arms push up and down to help the hopping action and to maintain balance, rather than swinging for height or distance.

Figure 17.3 Hopping pattern

Leaping A leap is an extension of a run—greater force is utilized to produce a higher dimension than a run (see Figure 17.4). A one-foot take-off propels the body upward to a landing on the opposite foot. As the take-off leg bends in preparation for extension and forceful propulsion, the arm on the opposite side of the body comes down and back. Then it swings forward and upward with the forceful extension of the take-off leg.

As take-off is completed from one leg, the other is swung forward to receive the weight. Usually, there is an emphasis on body extension for height or for distance. In preparation for landing, the arm opposite the take-off leg is brought forward and then downward. The landing leg bends to absorb the force of the body on touching the floor. Simultaneously, the opposite arm and leg are extended diagonally, the leg backward and the arm forward.

Figure 17.4   Leaping pattern

Skipping   The skip is a combination of a hop and a step, first on one foot and then on the other (see Figure 17.5). The pattern has the alternation and opposition of the walk, plus the same-sided one-foot hop. The sequence is repeated in any direction. A characteristic quality of the skip is the uneven rhythm:

hop–step   hop–step   hop

L   R   R   L   L

Figure 17.5   Skipping pattern

Sliding   The slide is a combination of a step and a run. The lead step is quickly followed by a closing of the free foot to replace the supporting foot (see Figure 17.6). The lead foot quickly springs from the floor into a direction of intended travel. The sequence is repeated.

Thus, there are two transfers of weights in a slide, with the same foot always leading. The rhythmic pattern is the same as that of a skip.

Figure 17.6   Sliding pattern

Galloping   The gallop is an exaggerated slide composed of a step and a leap. The lead leg is lifted and bent, then thrust forward to support the weight. Quickly, the rear foot closes to replace the supporting leg as the lead leg springs up into its lifted and bent position. The sequence is repeated. The rhythm is uneven, the same as that of a slide:

step–close, step–close, step–close, step–close
or
long–short, long–short, long–short, long–short.

LEVELS OF SKILL PROFICIENCY

In many school situations, the vast majority of five- and six-year-old children will already have mastered these traveling skills, and their classmates will be quick to catch on. Such youngsters are usually found in communities where parents provide their preschoolers with a wealth of movement experiences.

We also have observed some situations where a number of the students were unable to perform many locomotor skills beyond walking and running. Such children are in need of precontrol level travel experiences, so that they will learn to:

1. Crawl along the floor.
2. Creep on hands and knees.
3. Walk along a line on the floor.
4. Crawl underneath a low bar without touching it.
5. Step over a low obstacle without touching it.
6. Hop, leap, slide, gallop, or skip.

Once youngsters can identify and perform the basic modes of travel with relative ease and efficiency, they are ready for control level challenges. These include several types of activities. First the children can attempt variations of basic travel skills: walking at a low level, skipping backward, galloping, changing direction on signal, and running in a crowded room without touching anyone.

Children enjoy traveling at a low level

Then they can try traveling in a rhythmic or expressive manner: skipping to the uneven pulse of teacher's drum, running and leaping on the accented beat, walking as if on hot sand, and walking mechanically, like a robot.

And then they can try to perform another skill while traveling: keeping a long ribbon from touching the ground by traveling swiftly, or striking a balloon and traveling to keep it up.

Once children are able to perform a variety of locomotor skills with ease and can use their travel abilities to carry out a primary objective, they are ready for utilization level activities. At this point, the youngsters' repertoires of travel skills can be refined and expanded through involvement in challenging situations.

The children can combine two or more travel operations into a short sequence, such as run–jump–roll, or run–leap–turn in air–run.

They can improvise or plan in detail expressive travel for short dance phrases, focusing on:

1. The purpose, idea, or theme of the phrase—harmony, a battle, autumn.

The airborne sensation that results from combining a run and a leap provides a thrill for children

ORIENTEERING

Orienteering is rapid travel over rugged terrain, guided only by a map and compass. This activity is becoming increasingly popular. The inclusion of orienteering in a curriculum obviously depends on the availability of the necessary components—compasses and a wooded area close to the school grounds. Teachers who have access to these will find a helpful article, "Orienteering," in the February 1978 issue of *Teacher*, pages 72 and 73. Ellsworth Boyd, the author, describes how orienteering can be taught in a school setting.

2. The pathway of travel that is most appropriate—straight, angular, curved, or symmetrical.
3. The specific travel skills to be incorporated—running, leaping, collapsing.
4. The travel qualities to be exhibited—smooth-flowing, jagged-jerky.

They can utilize effective travel skills and strategic pathways in dynamic game situations:

1. React quickly to a batted ball by charging forward, to the left or right, to collect a ground ball and throw accurately to a teammate.
2. Run a planned pass pattern, utilizing fakes and quick changes of direction to lose an opponent and receive a ball thrown by a teammate.

When students are observed to consistently utilize a variety of travel skills and pathways effectively in game, dance, and gymnastic settings, they are ready to put all of these together through participation in proficiency level experiences:

Games: Youngsters play teacher and/or student designed games that demand alert and accurate performance of travel skills and strategic use of travel pathways.

Dance: Students and teacher work together to design dance studies. Specific travel pathways and locomotor skills are decided upon, practiced, revised, and refined. This process ends in a completed dance that clearly reflects the theme or idea that stimulated the study.

Gymnastics: Students and teacher cooperatively design travel patterns and select specific locomotor skills (as well as positions of stillness—balances) for individual or group gymnastic routines.

The sequence for developing the skill theme of traveling at the precontrol, control, utilization, and proficiency levels is shown in Figure 17.7. The Ideas for Development of traveling skill proficiency at these levels are stated below in a direct style. As discussed in Chapter Four, you are encouraged to vary the method of organization to suit the objectives of the particular lesson.

Figure 17.7   Sequence for developing the skill theme of traveling

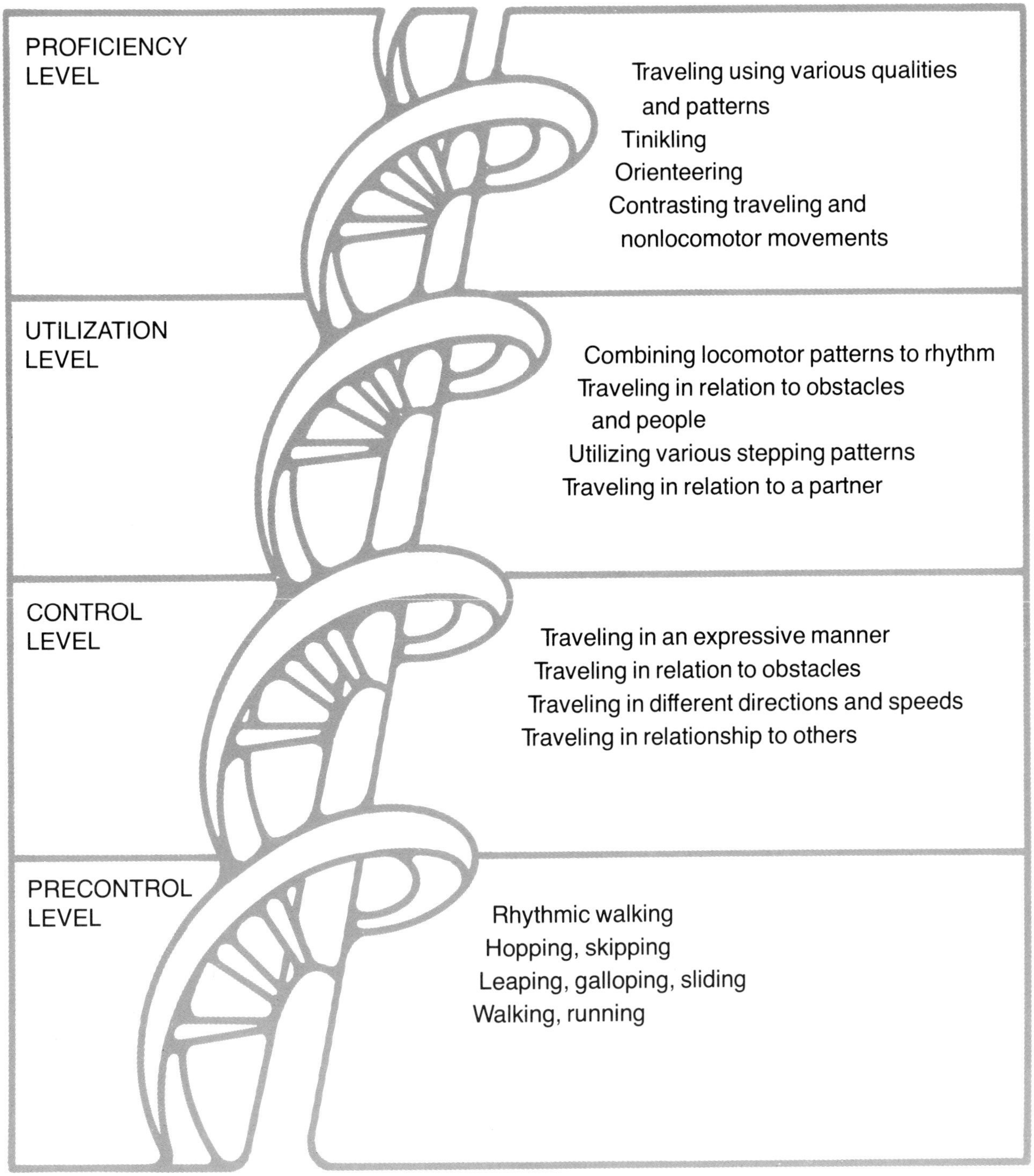

PROFICIENCY
LEVEL

Traveling using various qualities
   and patterns
Tinikling
Orienteering
Contrasting traveling and
   nonlocomotor movements

UTILIZATION
LEVEL

Combining locomotor patterns to rhythm
Traveling in relation to obstacles
   and people
Utilizing various stepping patterns
Traveling in relation to a partner

CONTROL
LEVEL

Traveling in an expressive manner
Traveling in relation to obstacles
Traveling in different directions and speeds
Traveling in relationship to others

PRECONTROL
LEVEL

Rhythmic walking
Hopping, skipping
Leaping, galloping, sliding
Walking, running

Precontrol Level

Overview   The following tasks are designed to acquaint children with the fundamental locomotor patterns. A variety of activities are presented to assist youngsters in the development of mature and efficient travel skills.

IDEAS FOR DEVELOPMENT	IDEAS FOR OBSERVATIONAL FOCUS
A bamboo pole or wooden dowel is placed across two milk crates. Have the children attempt to crawl or creep under the bar without touching it.	Does the child remain low and travel cautiously? Is the child moving the arm and leg on the same side of the body simultaneously?

Children who normally exhibit cross-pattern crawling and creeping often revert back to using arm movement and then leg movement when challenged to travel under an obstacle.

Challenge the youngsters to balance on one foot, first with eyes open, then with eyes shut. Tell the children you are going to count and challenge them to see how many seconds they can hold their balance.	Does the child wobble and lose balance? Can she remain on one foot without much difficulty, or does she wobble?
Ask the children to travel in different ways throughout general space—first leaping, then sliding, then galloping, then hopping, then skipping.	Does the child exhibit the correct motor patterns?

Children who don't know how to hop, leap, slide, gallop, or skip will benefit from opportunities to practice and from watching others. Try not to single them out in class, in front of the other children. If you want to work with them, try to do it individually. They may not be developmentally ready yet, but they will be in a few months.

Have youngsters attempt to walk along a line painted or taped on the floor.

Does the child keep both feet on the line?

Does he use a cross-step pattern or does he slide the front foot and close with the rear foot?

Does he use his arms to help maintain balance?

Do his eyes look straight ahead or down toward the feet?

The teacher beats a cadence of one, two, three, four/one, two, three, four . . . on a drum. The children clap and step on each beat, walking around the room.

Does the child step and clap in time with the drum?

Challenge children to walk on their toes, then to walk on their heels.

Is the child able to travel while taking weight on the toes and heels?

Does he maintain balance?

Is opposition of arm and leg movement apparent?

A rope or tape is placed on the floor in a straight line. The children stand on one foot and try to hop over the rope or tape to the other side. Have them try it again.

Is the child able to hop over the line without losing balance?

Can she hop back and forth in quick succession?

Have youngsters run and leap over a line taped (or painted) on the floor.

Does the child exhibit cross-pattern running?

Does the child take off and land on one foot?

Does she hesitate before leaping, or does the run flow smoothly into the leap?

How high does she leap over the line?

Challenge youngsters to travel carefully between two closely placed objects without touching either. This is done in a narrow space, which can be formed between two desks, or between a chair and a wall.

Does the child move slowly and cautiously?

Does he make a narrow shape with his body?

What locomotor pattern does he use? Slide-step? Walk?

Children seem to skip simply for the sheer pleasure they experience in doing so!

Control Level

Overview   This section provides experiences to help children expand their traveling abilities. Tasks are presented that challenge youngsters to use different traveling patterns with other concepts, such as speed and direction.

IDEAS FOR DEVELOPMENT

IDEAS FOR OBSERVATIONAL FOCUS

Children walk, skip, gallop, or hop around the room without touching anyone else. When the teacher gives a signal, the youngsters quickly stop traveling.

Does the child travel without collisions?

Does the child stop quickly on signal?

Do the children remain equally spread about the room or boundaried space?

Is the child traveling without bumping into another child?

Do the children distribute themselves evenly throughout the room or boundaried space?

Have the children travel (walk, run, hop) and change the direction of travel on signal. Ask them to move sideways, backward, right and left, or use combinations, such as backward and right.

Does the child change the direction of her travel quickly when the signal is sounded?

Does the child travel in all directions, forward, backward, right, and left?

Have the children travel (hop, skip, gallop) through an obstacle course (see Figure 17.8) without touching any people or objects, just the floor.

Does the child run over, through, under, and around the obstacles without bumping them or any of the other children?

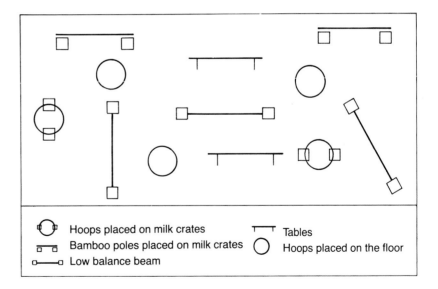

Hoops placed on milk crates   Tables

Bamboo poles placed on milk crates   Hoops placed on the floor

Low balance beam

Figure 17.8   An obstacle course

Does the child visit all areas of the room or boundaried space? Do the children remain fairly evenly distributed?

Ask the children to use a slide-step, and change direction on signal.

Does the child change the direction of travel quickly?

As the child changes direction, does she lead her slide-step with the same foot or the opposite foot?

Ask the youngsters to slide using a big first step, then slide using a short step.

Can the child verbalize about the different feelings or qualities of the two travel variations?

Divide class into two groups. Half will begin curled up, spread around the room on the floor. The other half will begin by running and leaping over the curled up children. On signal, the runners will collapse to the floor and curl up. The other children will pop up and begin running and leaping. (Repeat.)

Does the child leap high over his classmates?

Does he land on one foot, smoothly continuing his run?

Does the child watch for others, traveling away from congested areas?

SAFETY RULES:

1. No children can touch any others.
2. When signal is given, the curled up youngsters count to three before popping up.

Have each youngster hold a sheet of newspaper against his chest. As they begin to travel fast, tell them to let go of the paper and continue running. The newspapers cling to their chests.

Does the child travel fast enough to keep the newspapers against his chest?

Tell the children *not* to touch their papers when they *stop*. The newspapers fall to the floor.

After several attempts, is the child able to figure out why the papers stick to his chest while running and fall to the floor when he stops?

Discuss the concepts of speed and wind resistance with the children.

Discuss the concept of speed in relation to travel.

Does the child travel at speeds that match the speed of the music?

Place a 33⅓ rpm record on the phonograph, preferably an instrumental selection. Instruct the youngsters that when the record or music is fast (speed set at 78 rpm), they are to travel quickly. When the music speed is normal (33⅓ rpm) they are to travel at regular, everyday speed. When the music speed is adjusted to 16 rpm, they are to travel in slow motion. If the music stops, they are to freeze, or stop traveling.

Does the child quickly change speeds when the speed of the music changes?

Instruct the children to be quiet and attentive to the music, so that they may change the speed of travel as soon as the speed of the music is altered.

Lines are taped on the floor as shown in Figure 17.9, one line for each child.

Does the child stay along the line?

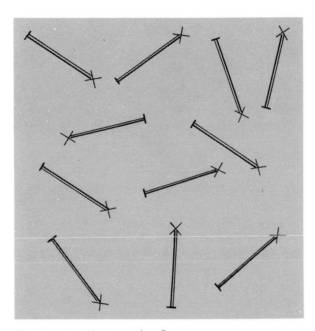

Figure 17.9   Lines taped on floor

Challenge children to start at one end of their line, travel across, and back. They are to use at least three traveling skills (for example, walk, hop, skip) while keeping as much of the body as possible over the line.

Does she exhibit at least three travel skills?

Does the class display a variety of locomotor skills or only a few?

Have each child roll a ball along the ground. Then run and leap over the ball, turn, and pick it up.

Does the child run and leap quickly and smoothly?

Does she judge the correct time to leap (does she clear her ball by a few feet)?

Does she turn while airborne or after landing?

Does the child position herself in front of the ball and successfully grasp it?

This task is accomplished best outside in a grassy area.

Design a short dance phrase focusing on changing the speed of travel.

Discuss the characteristics of water with the youngsters. Explain that at normal temperature, water is a liquid with the molecules moving at a medium speed. When the temperature is increased, the water molecules move faster and faster and water is transformed into steam. When the temperature is decreased the water molecules move slower and slower, and finally freeze together, forming ice, which is solid.

   With or without accompanying music, have the class travel around the room, instructing them to make their travel reflect the change of water from ice to liquid to steam and back again.

Are the child's transitions in speed of travel slow and gradual rather than sudden and dramatic?

To assist the youngsters in changing the speed of their travel gradually, the teacher can tell the story of water molecules aloud as the children travel.

Challenge children to travel in a way that is like:

1. Walking through a thick jungle.
2. Running on slippery ice.
3. Walking through a completely dark haunted house.
4. Walking on the ledge of an eighty-story building.
5. A slow motion replay of an athlete.
6. Traveling across a high wire on a windy day.
7. Traveling during an earthquake.

Does the child's travel reflect the qualities one would expect to observe in the imagined situations? For example, when "walking through a jungle," are her movements slow and cautious? Does she feel out in front with short steps or extended arms? Does she use arms to slash or push jungle brush out of the way? Does she duck or climb over an object?

Utilization Level

Overview   This section provides activities that challenge children to travel in increasingly complex ways. Tasks are designed to develop the travel skills used in many dance, game, and gymnastic activities.

IDEAS FOR DEVELOPMENT

IDEAS FOR OBSERVATIONAL FOCUS

Ask the children to stand back-to-back with a partner. On signal, each partner travels in the direction he or she is facing (away from each other). When the second signal is given, they travel backward along the same pathways to reunite with one another. (See Figure 17.10.)

Do the children exhibit a variety of pathways?

Do they return to their initial locations by traveling exactly along the same pathways?

Do they reunite with their partners in the exact locations from which they started?

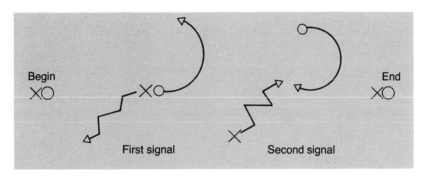

Figure 17.10   Traveling along pathways away from and toward a partner

Separate the children into facing pairs, standing one or two steps apart. One is the leader, the other the follower. The leader slides right or left, changing direction at will. The follower tries to stay with the leader. Then instruct the children to switch roles.

Does the follower closely match the travel of the leader?

Does the follower quickly react to the change in direction by the leader?

Have each child work with a partner. One is leader, the other follower. Leader travels fast, changing direction on signal. Partner (follower) tries to travel, staying right behind the leader. Then have the children switch roles.

Does each child choose a partner of similar ability?

Does the leader change the direction of travel sharply or move in a curvy or wavy manner?

Does the follower keep his eyes focused on the hips of the leader, reacting quickly to his changes in direction?

This is a tiring activity and should not be done for long periods of time.

Challenge youngsters to use varying step-combinations in traveling into and out of the hoop placed on the floor. For example, two steps in, then two steps out, or one step in, then two steps out, or two steps in, then one step out.

Have the children begin slowly, and gradually increase the tempo.

Children participate in a dance study of the contrast between the slow, lethargic walk of an old, old person and the travel of an excited young teenager. Discuss the movement qualities of a very old person—shaky, bent over, trembling, slow, sliding feet rather than stepping.

Ask the youngsters to travel about the room as an old, old person walking down the street. Suddenly, they see a bottle in the gutter that says Fountain of Youth Juice. They drink a few swallows and suddenly are transformed into an ecstatic youth who travels vigorously down the street.

Is the child able to perform the intended step pattern?

Can she do it rhythmically to the voice of the teacher?

Are the children able to travel in a manner that displays the movement qualities of an old person?

As the children drink the youthful tonic, how do they express the shock and excitement of its effects? For example, do their eyes widen? Do their bodies shake vigorously? Do their jaws drop?

How do the children travel once they have swallowed the tonic?

Do they jump and click their heels? Do they throw their canes away? Do they clap and stamp as they slide?

Talk the children through the story and play slow, classical music as they travel as old folks. Once they drink the Fountain of Youth juice, play fast, Earl Scrugg's type music!

Have youngsters design a short dance phrase based upon an imaginary situation:

1. a rag doll that comes to life for just a minute

What travel qualities do the children display?

Are the qualities appropriate?

2. a helium balloon that floats across the sky gradually, then leaks and falls back to earth
3. the wind blowing a paper cup across town

One interpretation: Rag doll slowly comes to life with jerky, uncoordinated movements, falls over, has trouble gaining control and balance, gradually improves until she is running and leaping, turning in the air and enjoying life. Then she suddenly stops, slowly walks back to starting location, sits and sighs, freezes, and is a doll once again.

Discuss with the children the travel qualities that are appropriate for each task. It is a good idea to structure the dance phrase so that it has a clear beginning, rises to a climax, and then winds down to a conclusion.

Ask the children to move as they would if they were escaping from prison.

Apparatus is set up around the room by the teacher or students, as in Figure 17.11. Children plan an escape pathway across the room, attempting not to make any noise and not to touch the floor.

Does the child travel quietly?

What travel skills are utilized?

Does the child control her travel in order not to touch the floor?

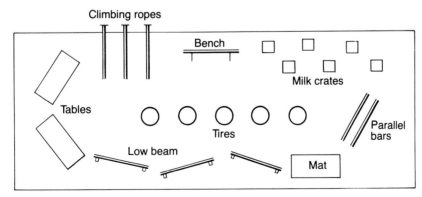

Figure 17.11   Escape-from-prison setup

Children and/or teacher design a humorous dance that combines several locomotor patterns to

Do the children start and stop each segment of the dance together?

the rhythmic pattern of Tom Foolery rhymes. Children can recite the rhymes as they travel. For example:

Soft feet, gentle, quick run:
  Pit-a-pat, pit-a-pat, pit-a-pat, *jump back*!

Swaying, rocking steps:
  See-Saw Mar-ger-y Daw,
  Jack shall have a new mas-ter.
  He shall have but a pen-ny a day,
  Be-cause he won't work an-y fast-er.

Skipping:
  Here's a word to the wise:
  Don't get soap in your *eyes*!
  I hope the dope who thought up soap
  Has to eat it—I repeat it, *Eat it*!

Bouncy Jumps:
  Boinggg, boinggg, boingg, boingg, boingg,
    boingg, boingg, *bammmm*!

Some children may be able to write their own Tom Foolery rhymes.

Are the travel skills displayed accurate reflections of the rhythmic patterns of the Tom Foolery rhymes?

Proficiency Level

Overview   These activities permit youngsters to use their travel skills and knowledge of travel patterns to design and perform dance studies, gymnastic routines, and strategic game maneuvers.

IDEAS FOR DEVELOPMENT

Design dance experiences that focus on the different messages communicated by contrasting styles of travel (for example, jumping and crawling) and stationary, nonlocomotor movements. For example, teacher and/or students can design a dance that contrasts rigid tradition with the forces of change.

IDEAS FOR OBSERVATIONAL FOCUS

Tradition: A group could arrange itself in a solid shape (for example, a square). Movements of group members might be identical and simultaneous. A firm, sustained quality would be appropriate. This group might ignore or turn its back on the alternative movement suggestions of the other group.

Forces of change: Group members would not align themselves in a single formation or limit themselves to a narrow range of movements. They could approach space from different directions and utilize a large area. They could travel in different pathways and exhibit a wide variety of traveling movements (for example, leaps with turns in flight, a vibrant run, a series of bouncy jumps).

Figure 17.12   Basic tinikling setup

Provide Tinikling experiences for children. Bamboo poles, wooden dowels, or plastic piping can serve as poles. Ten-foot lengths are recommended. Two poles are opened and closed while dancers step in and out without touching the poles. (See Figure 17.12.)

Once children learn the basic steps, as described in Figures 17.13, 17.14, and 17.15, they can invent their own steps.

Polers: Are the polers using the following pattern in relation to the rhythm?

1. Crack poles together
2. Crack poles together
3. Tap floor
4. Tap floor
5. Crack
6. Crack
7. Tap
8. Tap

Dancers: Are the dancers using the appropriate steps in rhythm to the music?

Count 1—Hop on left foot outside poles	
Count 2—Hop again on left foot outside poles	
Count 3—Step on right foot between poles	
Count 4—Step on left foot between poles	
Count 1—Hop on right foot outside poles	
Count 2—Hop again on right foot outside poles	
Count 3—Step on left foot between poles	
Count 4—Step on right foot between poles	

Figure 17.13   Tinikling: singles steps

Figure 17.14   Tinikling: doubles steps

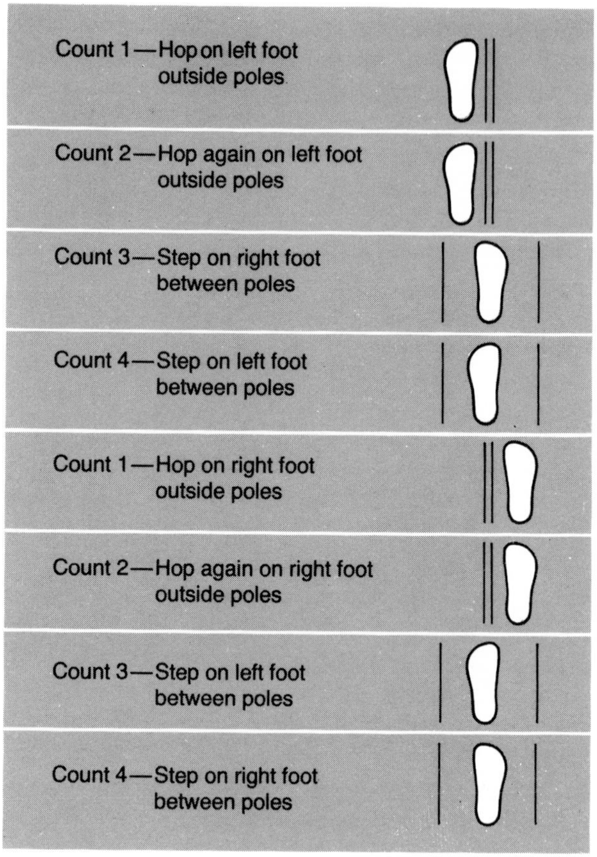

Figure 17.15   Tinikling: hopping

With the children design a dance that focuses upon the qualities of primitive people. Before beginning, discuss the qualities of primitive people with the youngsters. Display cave drawings of tribal dances. The children may say such things as: "primitive people were low to the ground," "primitive people were rooted in the earth," "the joints of primitive people appear angular and jagged," "their movements seem jerky and sharp, rather than smooth."

Now develop a story for a primitive dance. For example, you might divide the class into two tribes. Each tribe begins by creating a dance to prepare for battle. In a circle around the fire, they move close to the ground with elbows and knees bent.

You know your students. If open-ended questions will result in unproductive answers, don't ask them. You are trying to help the children become aware of the movement qualities of primitive people and then to display those qualities while traveling.

Do the children travel vigorously?

Do they display gestures representative of combat, such as punching, jabbing, kicking, and slashing?

Count 1—Jump on both feet outside poles	
Count 2—Jump on both feet outside poles again	
Count 3—Jump on both feet between poles	
Count 4—Jump on both feet between poles again	
Count 1—Jump on both feet straddling poles	
Count 2—Jump on both feet stradding poles again	
Count 3—Jump on both feet between poles	
Count 4—Jump on both feet between poles again	

Count 1—Hop on left foot outside poles	
Count 2—Hop again on left foot outside poles	
Count 3—Hop on right foot between poles	
Count 4—Hop again on right foot between poles	
Count 1—Hop on left foot outside poles (other side)	
Count 2—Hop again on left foot outside poles	
Count 3—Hop on right foot between poies	
Count 4—Hop on right foot between poles	

Now, have the two tribes face one another across the room, ready to do battle. They attack, moving quickly toward one another, remaining low and displaying jagged, sharp movements. (It is best to make a rule that no child may *touch* another.)

On signal the tribes can retreat and regroup to attack again.

Do they travel low to the ground, with elbows and knees bent?

Do they remain low and angular as they attack?

Do the two tribes mingle, with all the youngsters traveling forward, backward, left, and right?

Do the children remain low and angular while exhibiting battle gestures?

As the tribesmen retreat, do they do so in a cautious, protective manner. Are they watching the enemy and also keeping their arms up for protection?

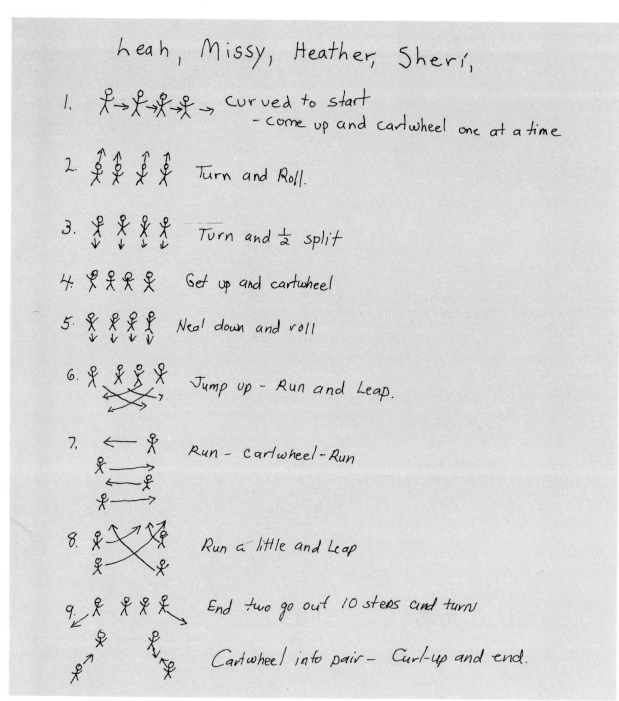

Leah, Missy, Heather, Sheri,

1. Curved to start
   - come up and cartwheel one at a time

2. Turn and Roll.

3. Turn and ½ split

4. Get up and cartwheel

5. Neal down and roll

6. Jump up - Run and Leap.

7. Run - cartwheel - Run

8. Run a little and Leap

9. End two go out 10 steps and turn

   Cartwheel into pair - Curl-up and end.

Figure 17.16   Children's travel patterns

Do they attack with renewed vigor?

How do the "injured" children travel? Do they drag their legs? Crawl? Help fellow tribesmen?

Is their travel heavy, slow, sullen, reflecting defeat?

Have youngsters design and diagram travel patterns for their sequences (see Figures 17.16 and 17.17).

Can the children accurately diagram their travel patterns? How do they feel about their patterns? Do they want to make any changes?

What locomotor patterns did the children incorporate along their pathways?

Are the movements appropriate for the purpose or theme of the sequence?

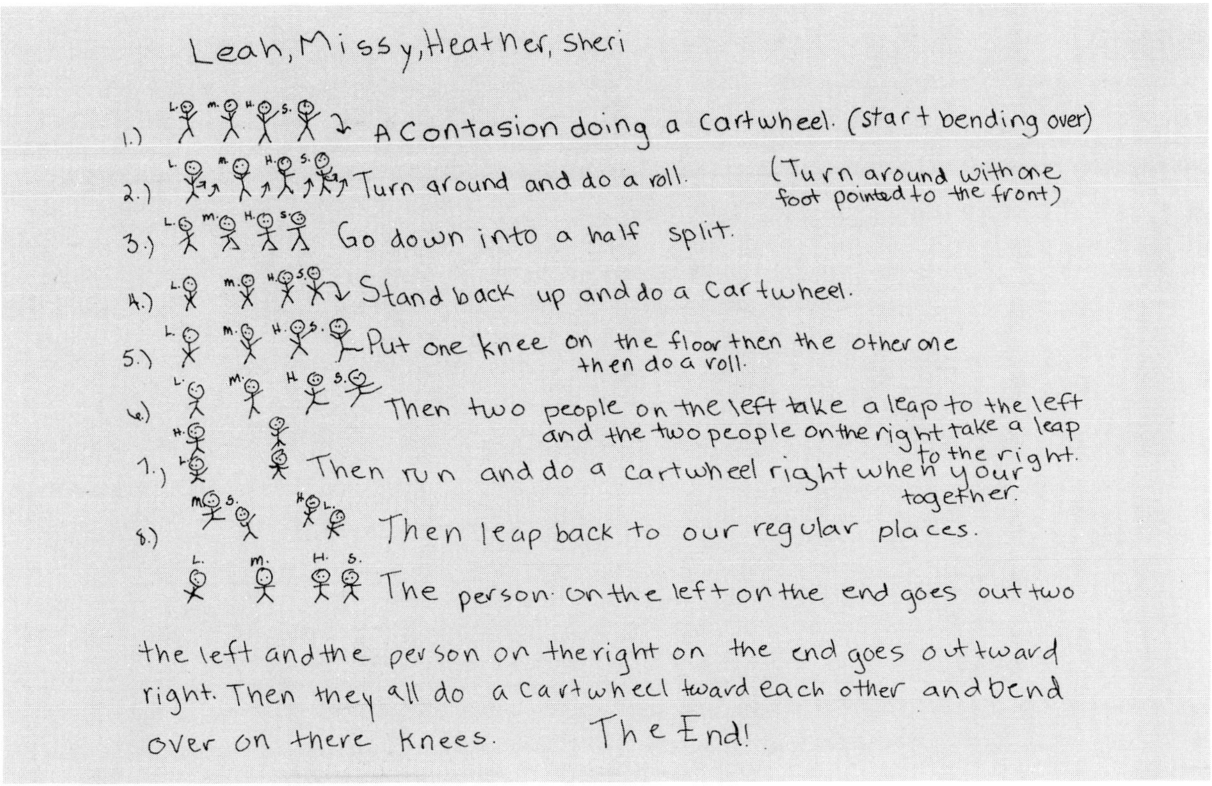

Leah, Missy, Heather, Sheri

1.) A Contasion doing a cartwheel. (start bending over)

2.) Turn around and do a roll. (Turn around with one foot pointed to the front)

3.) Go down into a half split.

4.) Stand back up and do a cartwheel.

5.) Put one knee on the floor then the other one then do a roll.

6.) Then two people on the left take a leap to the left and the two people on the right take a leap to the right.

7.) Then run and do a cartwheel right when your together.

8.) Then leap back to our regular places.

The person on the left on the end goes out two the left and the person on the right on the end goes out tward right. Then they all do a cartwheel tward each other and bend over on there knees. The End!

Figure 17.17 Children's travel patterns

DESIGNING FLOOR PATTERNS FOR DANCE STUDIES

Various ways of travel are used for expressive purposes in dance. There variations are not accidental. Rather, they are planned and carefully designed. In designing the travel pattern of a dance study the teacher and children can focus upon the following concerns:

1. What idea stimulated the dance study? Was it a selection of music? A bull fight? A wiggly snake?

2. What qualities are inherent in the theme of the dance or the selection of music? Is the tempo slow, moderate, or fast? Is the rhythm even or uneven? Is music harmonious? Vibrant? Mellow?

3. What pathway best expresses the feelings or emotions you sense? Advancing, attacking? Retreating? Collapsing? Gathering? Departing? Wavy? Angular? Jagged?

It is a good idea to have the children keep notes and diagram their pathways as they design them. This is done for several reasons: First, the child will clearly visualize what the floor pattern looks like and be better able to evaluate its suitability for the dance. Second, children usually use several classes to put together a completed dance study, and often fail to remember ideas they had in earlier classes. And third, when children finish a dance study, they take with them a written record of their accomplishments.

It is often beneficial to post several examples of pathways around the room on the walls. These give children an idea of what is expected.

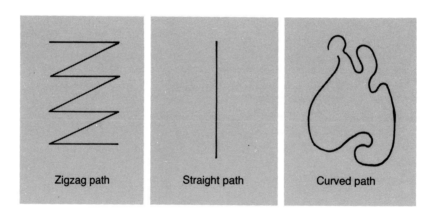

Zigzag path   Straight path   Curved path

An effective teaching aid is to post drawings of locomotor skills and positions of stillness that the children have experienced. Rather than trying to diagram a sequence from memory, youngsters can look at these posters and select movements to incorporate along their floor patterns.

Even those of us with no artistic abilities can trace beautiful diagrams using an opaque projector!

CHAPTER 18
CHASING, FLEEING, AND DODGING

Since ancient times children have delighted in countless chasing, fleeing, and dodging games. Most of these can be grouped into two categories—tag games and dodgeball games. In tag games, all free players flee
or dodge the touch of the chasing tagger. In dodgeball games, one or
more players throw a ball to strike the fleeing or dodging players.

Physical education programs can build on the innate pleasure that
children experience in playing these games. By providing a variety of
challenging tasks and game situations, a teacher can help youngsters to
develop chasing, fleeing, and dodging skills (see Figure 18.1). Experience suggests that it is best to focus on chasing, fleeing, and dodging
skills after children have developed a working understanding of space
awareness concepts.

Chasing, fleeing, and dodging activities are best played outdoors in
large, grassy areas.

CHASING

Chasing can be defined as traveling quickly to overtake or tag a fleeing
person. In many game situations, the fleeing player is given a head
start—he or she is allowed a time period to run away before the chaser
can begin traveling. The fleeing player tries to avoid being caught or
tagged. Thus, the chaser needs to be able to run at full speed and to
react quickly to changes in the direction of the travel of the fleeing
player.

FLEEING

Fleeing can be defined as traveling quickly away from a pursuing person or object. In most game situations, the fleeing person tries to keep as much distance as possible between himself and the chaser. When the pursuer does close in, the fleeing player uses any maneuver possible to avoid being tagged or hit by a thrown object—the fleeing person dodges, changes direction quickly, or runs full speed. This continual demand on the fleeing player—to react quickly to emerging, threatening situations—is what makes tag and dodgeball games thrilling activities for children.

Children enjoy the thrill and excitement of chasing, fleeing, and dodging activities

Figure 18.1   Sequence for developing the skill theme of chasing, fleeing, and dodging

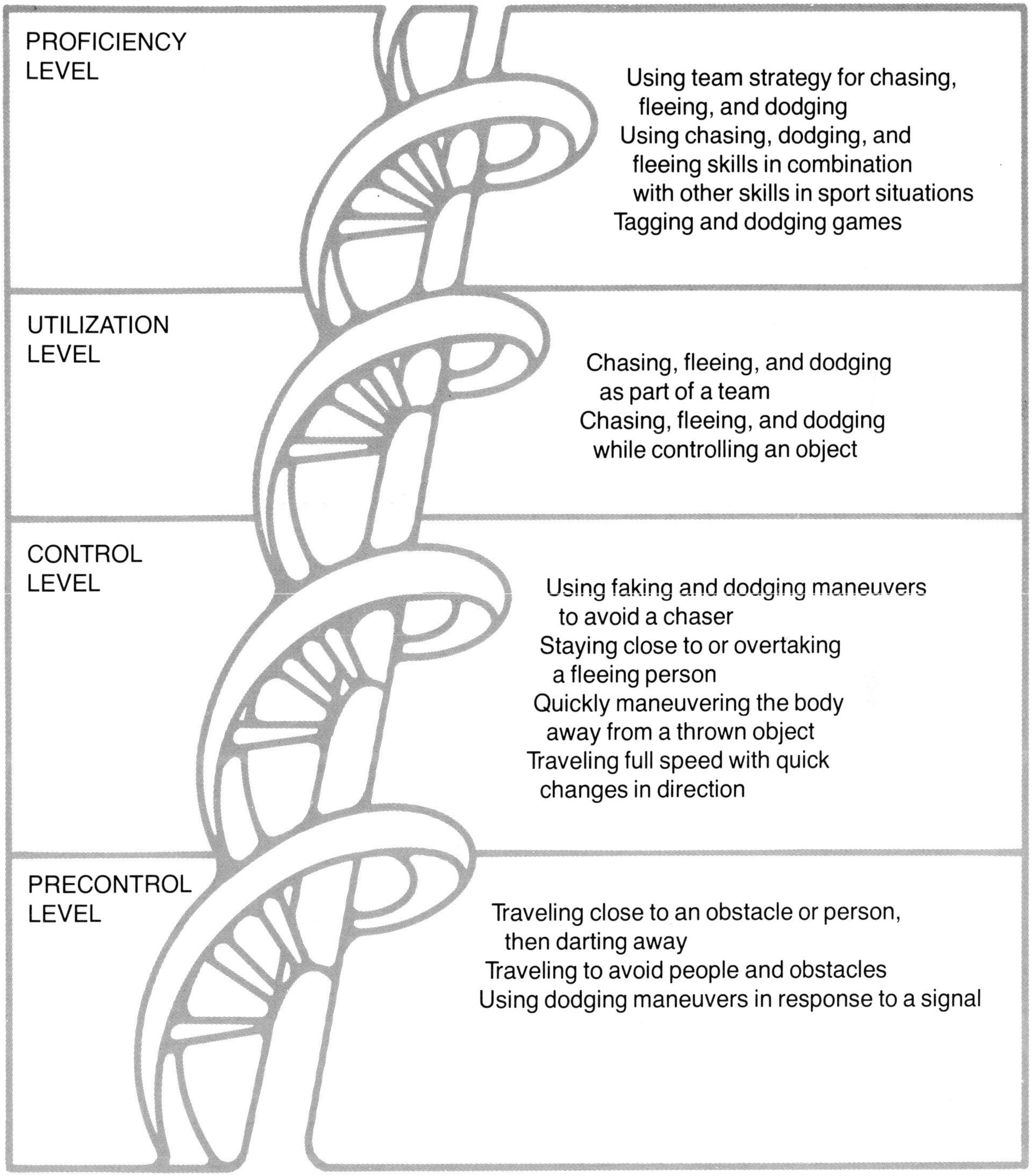

PROFICIENCY
LEVEL

Using team strategy for chasing,
fleeing, and dodging
Using chasing, dodging, and
fleeing skills in combination
with other skills in sport situations
Tagging and dodging games

UTILIZATION
LEVEL

Chasing, fleeing, and dodging
as part of a team
Chasing, fleeing, and dodging
while controlling an object

CONTROL
LEVEL

Using faking and dodging maneuvers
to avoid a chaser
Staying close to or overtaking
a fleeing person
Quickly maneuvering the body
away from a thrown object
Traveling full speed with quick
changes in direction

PRECONTROL
LEVEL

Traveling close to an obstacle or person,
then darting away
Traveling to avoid people and obstacles
Using dodging maneuvers in response to a signal

Dodging a thrown ball requires agility as well as the ability to anticipate the path of a moving ball

DODGING

Dodging is the skill of quickly moving the body in a direction other than the original line of movement. This includes any maneuver a person undertakes to avoid being touched by a chasing person or struck by a thrown object. Dodging may occur while fleeing or when stationary. Effective dodging actions include ducking, jumping, twisting, stretching, collapsing, and rolling.

LEVELS OF SKILL PROFICIENCY

We have found that most school-age children are familiar with a variety of tag and dodgeball games. But some youngsters whose chasing, fleeing, and dodging skills are at the precontrol or control level of proficiency have limited success in playing these games. That is, although many children can chase, flee, and dodge, they cannot perform these skills effectively in dynamic game situations. In a game of tag, for instance, the child doing the chasing is often unable to overtake or tag any of the fleeing players and quickly tires of playing the game. In their classic study of children's games, Iona and Peter Opie noted that chasing games were often plagued with arguments and ended prematurely in heated disputes.*

A teacher's initial task, therefore, is to assist youngsters in developing those skills prerequisite to becoming a capable chaser, fleer, or dodger in various game situations. In some school situations where preschool youngsters have limited opportunities to play with other children, a teacher may need to provide precontrol chasing, fleeing, and dodging activities. Examples might include:

1. Run as fast as possible from one location to another.
2. Travel around a room, change the direction of travel quickly when a signal is sounded.
3. When a signal is given, quickly perform a designated dodging maneuver, such as jumping or collapsing.
4. Run as fast as possible away from your partner; on signal, run quickly toward your partner.

Children who can competently perform a variety of quick, dodging maneuvers while running fast are at the control level. A teacher can provide challenging tasks designed to have these children keep their eyes focused on a target child and react quickly to the movements of that child—by chasing, fleeing from, or dodging him or her. For instance:

1. Stay as close as possible to a fleeing, dodging partner.
2. Chase after a person who has been given a slight head start and is fleeing from you.
3. Use a dodging maneuver to avoid being hit by a ball thrown at you by a partner.
4. Try to run across a field while dodging one or more chasers.

When children are able to effectively dodge a thrown ball or chasing person and can react quickly and accurately to the swift, darting movements of others, they are ready for utilization level activities. Now the youngsters' chasing, fleeing, and dodging skills enable them to enjoy testing their abilities in ever-changing and complex game environments. Challenging activities include the following:

1. The players of one team flee and/or dodge the players of an op-

---

*I. & P. Opie. *Children's Games in Street and Playground* (New York: Oxford University Press, 1969).

posing team while controlling an object (such as a football, frisbee, or basketball).

2. One team chases down the members of an opposing team; that is, instead of fleeing, one team tries to run past the chasers without being touched.

At the proficiency level children are able to use chasing, fleeing, and dodging skills effectively in a wide variety of game contexts. Both the chasers and the fleeing, dodging players are skilled. At times the chaser gets the target, and at others the fleeing, dodging player escapes. Advanced chasing, fleeing, and dodging skills are evident in situations such as these:

1. A runner in a football-type game darts quickly past the defense, dodging around the players who are chasing him.

2. A soccer player dribbles a ball past a defense player by faking one way and then traveling quickly in the opposite direction.

3. A defense player in a football-type game runs twenty to thirty yards to overtake an offensive runner heading for a score.

4. A basketball player races down court to score a layup even though a defense player is chasing right behind him.

In elementary school settings, children at the proficiency level enjoy playing teacher- and student-designed games in which chasing, fleeing, and dodging are the primary movements.

Precontrol Level

Overview   Activities at this level are designed to assist those youngsters of limited movement experience who do not understand the concepts of chasing, fleeing, or dodging.

IDEAS FOR DEVELOPMENT	IDEAS FOR OBSERVATIONAL FOCUS

Teach a simple fleeing game.

Objective: To run as fast as possible against a time standard.

Rules: 1. Children stand behind a starting line.

2. On signal, they must run across a field and line up on a finish line ready to run back. They are given a specific time limit, such as 30 seconds.

Do the children run quickly?

Are they lined up, ready to run again, after the specified interval has elapsed?

Youngsters work with a partner. They stand opposite one another about ten feet apart. On signal, they walk toward one another slowly until they are as close as they can be without touching. Then, they quickly jump backward and walk backward to their starting locations.

Vary the locomotor pattern—instead of walking, have the children jog or skip.

Vary the speed, so that the children move a little faster each time.

Do the children get very close (face-to-face) before jumping back?

Do they perform their jumps simultaneously and suddenly?

Objects are placed about the room on the floor (for example, carpet squares, hoops, milk jugs, or ropes).

Challenge children to travel about the room or boundaried space without touching anyone else or any of the obstacles on the floor.

Do children travel without touching obstacles along the floor?

Do any children bump into others?

Are the children traveling carefully?

Is the noise level low?

Are the children's eyes focused on obstacles along the floor?

Are the children spread about room, rather than clustered together?

Do any of the children lose balance and fall to the floor?

Do some children hesitate, allow others to go by, and then continue travel?

Have the children walk around the area. On the signal, ask them to pretend they are going to travel in one direction and then quickly change to a different direction. Challenge them to try not to let you know which direction they will travel when the signal sounds.

Encourage children to travel backward as well as sideways.

Speed can be varied as children grasp the concept.

Are children actually faking or are they simply changing direction?

Are the children able to fake without falling down or bumping into others?

Control Level

Overview   Tasks are designed for those youngsters who chase, flee, and dodge with limited success. These activities help children utilize their skills effectively in relation to an unpredictable and often equally skillful classmate.

IDEAS FOR DEVELOPMENT

IDEAS FOR OBSERVATIONAL FOCUS

Ask the children to travel around the room or boundaried area. They are to approach another person, getting as close as possible, and then quickly dart away and look for another person with whom to repeat the sequence.

Do the children travel very close to one another before darting away?

Are children bumping or colliding into others as they dart away?

Is there a noticeable increase in the children's speed of travel as they move away from others—a burst of speed?

Partners begin together in a room or boundaried space. On the first signal, one partner darts away from the others. After five seconds, another signal is sounded. The stationary partner chases after the fleeing partner, trying to tag him before a twenty to thirty second period has elapsed. Partners switch roles and repeat the sequence.

Does the fleeing child get as far away as possible during the five-second head start?

Does he use fakes (dodging maneuvers or changes in the speed of travel) to avoid the chaser?

Does the chasing child keep an eye on fleeing partner's whereabouts?

Does he pursue the partner full speed, attempting to trap the partner in a corner of the boundaried space?

If the fleeing partner gets away, does the chaser give up or continue the pursuit?

This task is appropriate when the children have learned to travel in general space without bumping into one another. Initially large areas make this an easier task for children, because they are able to focus more on their partners and less on avoiding other children.

Three children work together. One child stands between the other two. The players on the sides try to throw a yarn ball or plastic ball to hit the child in the middle (below shoulder level).

Does the dodger (player in middle) continually face whichever player has the ball and keep eyes focused on the ball?

Does the dodger remain relatively low, balanced (feet spread about shoulders width), not flat-footed?

Does the dodger avoid being hit by using maneuvers such as diving, ducking, jumping, collapsing, turning away, twisting, or running away?

Six children work together in a boundaried space. Two players begin as taggers. On signal they have one minute to try to tag the other four children. If tagged, a player counts to ten out loud before returning to the game again. The object is for the taggers to have the fleers all caught at the same time. After a minute, players switch roles and repeat.

Do the two taggers work as a team to try to trap and tag one player at a time?

Do the fleeing children use a variety of dodging maneuvers in trying to avoid being caught?

Do they change direction quickly, use sudden stops and quick bursts of speed, duck, or roll?

Four youngsters stand close together in the middle of a boundaried space. One of the youngsters tosses a ball straight up in the air and shouts the name of another player.

The child whose name is called is to catch or collect the ball as quickly as possible while the other children scatter. When the player chasing the ball grasps it and shouts "Stop," all players must freeze.

The player with the ball may take a maximum of three steps and then throws the ball to hit another player. The dodging players can only take one step in any direction to avoid being hit.

Does the player whose name is called quickly position himself to catch or collect the ball?

Do the other players quickly travel away from (flee) the location of the ball?

Does the player with the ball take three steps toward the closest player?

Do the other players keep an eye on the thrower and use a variety of dodging maneuvers to avoid being hit with the ball?

Youngsters must run across a playing field, through a tag zone, and avoid being touched.

Do the children use fakes and try to surprise the taggers as they dart through the tag zone?

Do they turn and twist, bend and roll, or utilize other effective dodging maneuvers in bursting through the tag zone?

Four children stand in a relatively small bound-aried area. Two other youngsters stand on opposite sides of the area.

The two players on the outside try to throw a ball to strike the players below the shoulders. The children within the area try to avoid being hit.

Do the dodgers keep as much distance as possible between themselves and the thrower?

Do the dodgers keep their bodies relatively low, balanced (feet spread about shoulders width), and facing in the direction of the thrower?

Do the throwers quickly collect and release the ball toward the dodgers, or hold the ball, allowing the dodgers to get further away and rest for a few moments?

A child who is hit by a ball need not be penal-ized or eliminated. The challenge of avoiding being hit by the ball is an adequate motivator.

One group of youngsters begins on one side of the room, the other group on the opposite side. On signal, the two groups are to switch locations; no child is to touch another.

The difficulty of this task can be increased by hav-ing the children travel at different levels (with body parts at different distances from the floor), facing in different directions, or supporting their weight on three or more body parts.

In crossing the room, how many children touch with others?

Do the children spread themselves from side to side or cluster together?

BEGIN SLOWLY. Have the children walk. Speed can be increased as children are observed to travel without any collisions.

Dodging players stand in a boundaried area. One foot must remain pivoted in one spot.

Two youngsters outside the designated area are to try to strike the dodging players by throwing a ball.

Have the children play a game of Tag, in which all players must remain on the lines painted on floor or pavement (See Figure 18.2). Children who

Do the dodging players keep one foot pivoted?

Do they effectively avoid being hit with the ball by using maneuvers such as bending, stretching, or ducking?

Do the children keep their feet on the desig-nated lines?

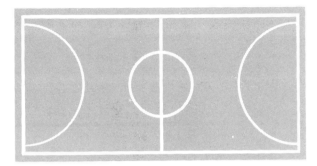

Figure 18.2

are caught, stand on one foot for thirty seconds before returning to the game; they count to themselves.

Have the children play a game of Tag on a playground or climbing apparatus. Fleeing children are given thirty seconds head start. No player may touch the ground.

Are the children able to watch for the chaser while keeping their feet on the lines?

Do they travel backward and sideward at times to keep the tagger in view?

Do the children play safely, without horseplay or showing off? Do they travel without bumping into others?

Does the chaser travel quickly toward a target person to corner him?

Do the fleeing children try to keep as much distance as possible between themselves and the chaser?

In some school yards we have observed classes of children playing a game popularly called Bombardment or Killer. As these names imply, the game can be dangerous. Typically, a class is divided into two teams, with a middle line separating them. Each team tries to throw a hard ball to strike players on the opposing team, often at close range and toward an unsuspecting child. We do not recommend this activity. Many alternative dodge-type experiences that are safer, allow more children to participate, and are more apt to result in skill development can be planned.

Utilization Level

Overview   Children at this level are ready to test their skills in increasingly complex and gamelike situations. These activities necessitate frequent faking and dodging maneuvers in quick reaction to the deceptive movements of others.

IDEAS FOR DEVELOPMENT

Youngsters are divided into two groups. Tape or chalk marks are placed on the floor to designate where the members of one team must place their feet. (These marks are approximately an arm's length apart; see Figure 18.3.)

The team members standing on the marks cannot move their feet. This group is the taggers.

The other group begins at one end of the room or boundaried space. They try to travel through the maze of taggers without being touched.

The taggers can be instructed to touch the runners in various ways—for example, to touch runners' left knees with right hand, or to touch runners' right knees with left hand.

IDEAS FOR OBSERVATIONAL FOCUS

Do the runners twist, turn, jump or duck to avoid being touched by the line of taggers?

Do the runners fake going between two taggers and then quickly dart through the maze at a different location?

Do the runners take their time and anticipate the right moment to dart through the maze (for example, as tagger reaches to one side to try to touch another player, does a runner quickly dart to other side of tagger)?

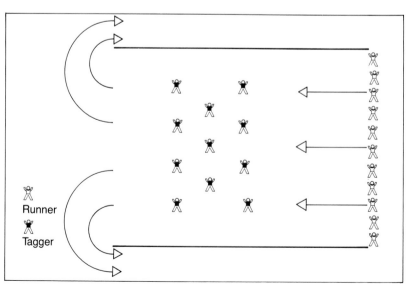

Figure 18.3   Diagram of dodging and fleeing activity

The runners return around the outside of the room and continue until a stop signal is given. Then the two groups switch roles.

Each player of one group is paired with a player on the opposing group.

On signal one group tries to travel to the other side of the boundaried area without its players being tagged by the paired players on the opposing side. Player A of one group can only be tagged by Player A of the other group.

The groups switch roles.

Teach Body Part Tag.

Objective: To tag runners on a given body part (if a chaser) or to evade being tagged (if a runner).

Rules:
1. About ten players in a boundaried area; two are chasers.
2. Chasers attempt to tag runners on a specified body part (for example, a knee).
3. If tagged, fleeing children must freeze.
4. These children may travel again if touched by a free player on a different body part (for example, an elbow).
5. Taggers are given a time limit (for example, three minutes) to attempt to tag all the fleeing players.
6. Switch roles.

Partners run toward one another head on. Use a slow run at first; speed can gradually be increased. As partners are about to collide, they turn away from one another (avoiding contact) and continue running.

Do they use fakes (for example, take one quick step to left, then quickly run right, or jerk head to right, then run left)?

Do they use teammates' bodies as obstacles, or blockers, to avoid their tagger?

Do the taggers overrun their target runners?

Do they use a controlled run that allows them to change directions quickly and tag an opponent?

Do the two taggers work together?

Do the chasing children select a target person and relentlessly go after him, trying to corner or tire the chasing players?

Do the fleeing children travel quickly and display a variety of dodging maneuvers (for example, duck, change of speeds, stop and go)?

Do the children barely miss one another?

With practice, can they perform the sequence of "run-turn-away-run" in quick succession?

Children get excited when they can perform this maneuver quickly, timing their turn with their partners' just before contact is made. They enjoy watching one another perform this task.

Boundaried areas about the size of a basketball key circle are marked on the floor or pavement.

Do the children keep their bodies between their balls and opposing players?

Two or three children begin within each area, bouncing a ball. Each player tries to knock the others' balls out of the area while protecting their own. Dribbling with feet can be used.

Do the children remain low (knees bent) and use a low, quick bouncing action?

Are the children able to continue bouncing their own balls with control, while reaching to strike an opposing player's ball?

Proficiency Level

Overview   Children at this level are ready to use their skillful chasing, fleeing, and dodging abilities in a variety of complex and ever-changing game situations. Activities are provided that require two teams of players to chase, flee, and dodge one another to accomplish game objectives.

IDEAS FOR DEVELOPMENT

IDEAS FOR OBSERVATIONAL FOCUS

Two teams of three players place flag belts around their waists.

Does the team with the ball try to have its players spread out?

On signal, one team tries to pass or run a ball from its goal to the opposite goal without having the ball touch the ground *or* having the opposing team grasp the flags of the player with the ball.

Do these players continually travel full speed while trying to flee their chasers?

Is the general direction of their movement toward the intended goal area?

Does the player with the ball use throwing fakes, sudden starts and stops, or other dodging maneuvers to keep the chasers from grabbing his flags?

Does each player on the chasing team try to stay with one player on the opposing team? Do they stay as close as possible?

Each child has a flag belt with flags around the waist. Children try to snatch other children's flags without losing their own flags. When a flag is pulled, another child must replace it—children cannot replace their own flag.

Do they keep their eyes focused on the target player and react quickly to his or her travel changes?

Are the children able to simultaneously chase and flee?

Start with groups of six children. As the children become more proficient, the size of the groups can be enlarged.

Teach a game of tag that includes safety bases (see Figure 18.4).

Objective: A team of runners tries to cross a designated area without being touched by a team of taggers.

Rules: 1. A large boundaried area is marked. Several hoops—safety bases—are placed on the ground within this area.

   2. The runners begin at one end of the field; the taggers begin at the opposite end. On signal, the runners try to cross the field without being tagged; the taggers try to prevent any runners from crossing the field.

   3. The runners are safe—cannot be tagged—when they are in any of the hoops.

   4. The runners have two or three minutes in which to cross the field.

   5. After a designated time limit, the teams switch roles.

Are they able to keep track of one another for both helping and avoiding purposes?

Do they use effective dodging maneuvers—for example, jumping away from another child, turning or twisting to avoid flags being pulled?

Do the runners make good use of the safety areas? For example, are they observed to quickly duck or jump into a safety base as they are about to be tagged?

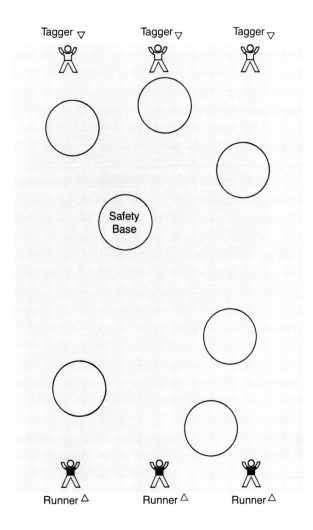

Figure 18.4   Tag game with safety bases

Teach a chasing, fleeing, and dodging game
called Pirate's Treasure (see Figure 18.5).

Objective: The free players try to steal the
                 treasure (beanbag) from the middle of
                 a boundaried area and return it to
                 the perimeter without being tagged
                 by the pirate (a chaser, who is protec-
                 tor of the treasure).

Rules: 1. Five players to a game.
            2. A square playing area is marked. A
               hoop is placed in the center with a
               beanbag inside.
            3. The pirate attempts to protect the
               treasure by preventing any other play-
               ers from taking the beanbag outside
               the square.
            4. On signal, the perimeter players
               have two minutes in which to steal
               the beanbag and take it outside the
               square. They must do so without
               being touched by the pirate.
            5. When the beanbag is successfully
               brought outside the square by a player
               or when two minutes has passed, a
               new pirate is selected and the game
               continues.

Do the perimeter players work together—for example, does a player on one side fake an attempt
to grasp the beanbag and a player on the opposite side quickly grab it and run?

Does the pirate (chasing player) stay close to the
center of the square and keep looking in all
directions?

Does the pirate player remain alert, quickly reacting to the stealing maneuvers of the perimeter
players?

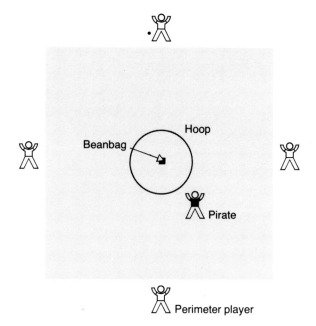

Figure 18.5   Pirate's treasure

In many primitive tribal games, it was believed
that the chaser was evil, magic, or diseased, and
that his touch was contagious. Although today's
games are a far cry from fleeing possible death,
one has a hard time believing otherwise when observing the intensity and all-out effort displayed
by children fleeing a chaser!

Teach Guarding the Dynamite (see Figure 18.6).

Objective: Two players try to prevent the other players from throwing a ball to strike the dynamite (for example, a stack of tin cans).

Rules:
1. Six players to a game.
2. A large square playing area is marked . . . In the middle of this area a circular area is designated. Inside this central circle a pin is placed or several cans are stacked.
3. Four "demolition" players stand outside the perimeter boundaries and attempt to throw a ball to explode the dynamite—strike the pin or cans.
4. Two guards stand within the square area but outside the circular area. They attempt to collect or catch the balls thrown from the demolition players, to prevent the dynamite from exploding.
5. When the dynamite is hit or after thirty seconds, the children rotate so that two new guards protect the dynamite.

Figure 18.6   Guarding the dynamite

Do the perimeter players work together? Do they pass to one another? Do they travel along the perimeter rather than remaining stationary?

Do the demolition players demonstrate a variety of effective throws? Do they bounce the ball along the ground? Do they loop the ball over defender's head?

Do the guarding players work together? Is one guard responsible for watching two players or sides of the field while the other watches the remaining players or sides? Do the guards talk aloud to one another in preparing to block or catch a thrown ball?

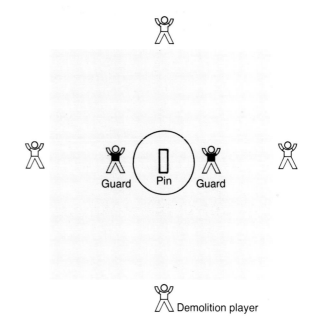

Demolition player

Teach Rip-Flag.

Objective: To remove flags from opposing team members while protecting one's own flags.

Equipment: Each team member wears a belt with two flags around his waist. Opposing teams wear different color flags. Thus, hanging from each belt

Do the players continually travel and *not* remain in one location for too long a time?

Do the players use turning, twisting, and rolling actions to avoid losing their flags?

Do team members work together (for example, do they converge on one opposing player and then another)?

are two flags which can be easily ripped-off and then refastened.

Rules:

1. Two teams of four players each wear flag belts.

2. A boundaried field space is marked. One team begins at one end, the other team at the opposite end.

3. On signal the two teams travel within the playing area attempting to grasp flags belonging to opposing team members while protecting their own. On the second signal the two teams return to their sides and count how many flags they were able to steal.

CHAPTER 19
JUMPING AND LANDING

Jumping is a locomotor pattern in which the body propels itself off the floor or apparatus into a momentary period of flight. As an isolated maneuver or in combination with other basic patterns, jumping—particularly the flight phase when the body is unsupported in the air—is a fascinating body action.

FUNDAMENTAL JUMPING PATTERNS

Wickstrom* suggests that infants are developmentally capable of performing a jumping operation at approximately twenty-four months of age. He describes the types of jumps achieved by preschool children in terms of progressive difficulty:

Jump down from one foot to the other.
Jump up from two feet to two feet.
Jump down from two feet to two feet.
Run and jump from one foot to the other.
Jump forward from two feet to two feet.
Jump down from one foot to two feet.
Run and jump forward from one foot to two feet.
Jump over object from two feet to two feet.
Jump from one foot to same foot rhythmically.

*R. L. Wickstrom, *Fundamental Motor Patterns*, 2nd ed. (Philadelphia: Lea & Febiger, 1977), p. 63.

Young children often jump up and down like bouncing balls, enjoying the sensation of propelling the body off the ground for a momentary period of flight

THE FIVE BASIC VARIATIONS OF THE JUMPING PATTERN

1. Two-foot take-off to a one-foot landing
2. Two-foot take-off to a two-foot landing
3. One-foot take-off to a landing on the same foot (hop)
4. One-foot take-off to a landing on the other foot (leap)
5. One-foot take-off to a two-foot landing

It is safe to assume that, within an average class of young children, some will be incapable of performing one or more of the above jumping tasks. Initial observations will probably reveal a wide range of jumping abilities. Typically, kindergarten students are at the precontrol level. They tend to exhibit jumps of little height or distance, performed on two feet to ensure maintenance of balance. Children at this level seem to be jumping merely to enjoy the sensation of momentarily losing contact with the ground and the challenge of maintaining balance upon landing.

A teacher can build on this natural fascination by providing learning activities that progressively lead children toward the mature performance of jumping and landing in different dance, game, and gymnastic situations (see Figure 19.1).

The fundamental jumping pattern consists of five basic variations, but the specific actions of the body in performing a jump will vary depending on the purpose or intention—for example, jumping to catch, or jumping to dismount from apparatus.

VERTICAL AND HORIZONTAL JUMPING

A jump is performed for one of two reasons: (1) to raise the body vertically (straight up) for height; or (2) to raise the body with a forward momentum to travel over a distance. Children who learn to effectively jump for height and jump for distance are prepared for a multitude of game, dance, and gymnastics activities in which the performer needs to be a skilled jumper.

LEVELS OF SKILL PROFICIENCY

When we begin to focus on jumping, we have children think of the skill as three successive phases:

Take-off: actions of the body as it is propelled off the ground
Flight: actions of the body while off the ground and in the air
Landing: actions of the body as contact is reestablished with the ground

We present tasks designed to have the children discover and experiment with the five possible take-off and landing combinations. Children begin to sense which take-off procedures result in the highest

Figure 19.1   Sequence for Developing the Skill Theme of Jumping and Landing

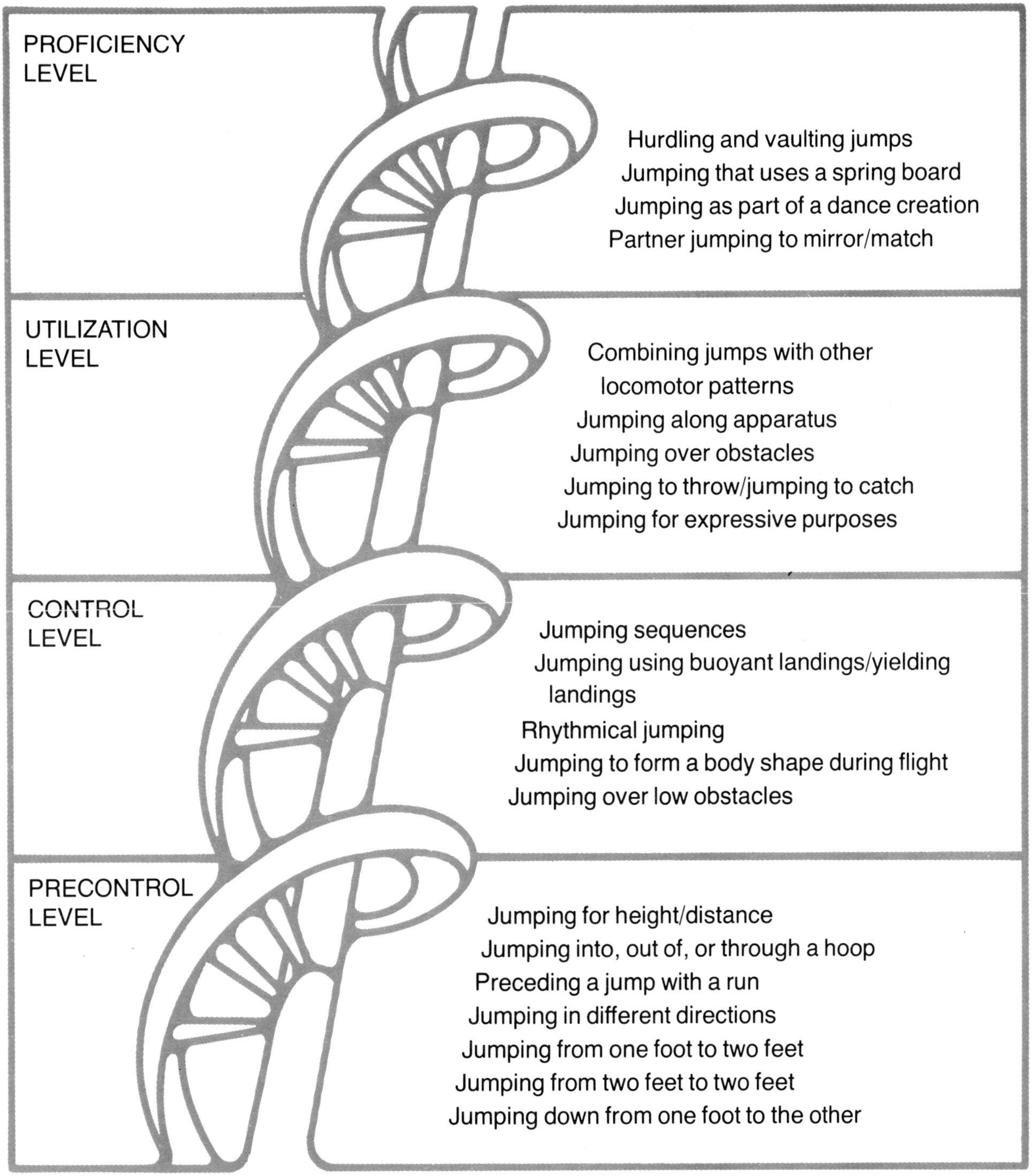

PROFICIENCY
LEVEL

Hurdling and vaulting jumps
Jumping that uses a spring board
Jumping as part of a dance creation
Partner jumping to mirror/match

UTILIZATION
LEVEL

Combining jumps with other
    locomotor patterns
Jumping along apparatus
Jumping over obstacles
Jumping to throw/jumping to catch
Jumping for expressive purposes

CONTROL
LEVEL

Jumping sequences
Jumping using buoyant landings/yielding
    landings
Rhythmical jumping
Jumping to form a body shape during flight
Jumping over low obstacles

PRECONTROL
LEVEL

Jumping for height/distance
Jumping into, out of, or through a hoop
Preceding a jump with a run
Jumping in different directions
Jumping from one foot to two feet
Jumping from two feet to two feet
Jumping down from one foot to the other

jumps as opposed to those that result in the longest jumps. They find that actions of the legs, arms, torso, and head during the flight phase influence the trajectory of the jump. And they come to recognize the unique giving action of the ankles, knees, and hips in absorbing the shock of landing.

Once children can accurately perform the five basic jumping variations using vigorous take-offs and balanced, controlled landings, they

---

DEVELOPMENTAL STAGES OF THE VERTICAL JUMP

Different jumping performances will be elicited from children depending on whether they are asked to jump as high as they can or to jump and try to touch a high object. Typically, children challenged to jump high tend to hunch their shoulders, position their arms outward in balancing actions, and draw their legs up well under the body immediately after take-off. When youngsters are asked to jump and reach or to touch a high object a more mature jumping pattern is exhibited— the arms are lifted high and the whole body is fully extended.

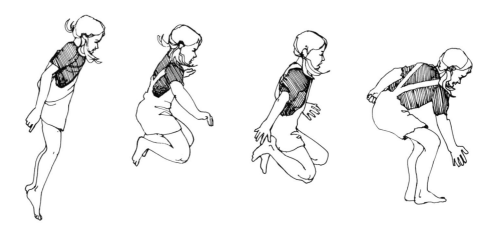

STAGE 1   There is a minimal preparatory crouch of the legs. The arms and shoulders are slightly elevated. A small forward lean of the body is apparent at take-off. The hips and knees flex quickly following take-off.

STAGE 2   There is a gradual and progressive increase in the crouch. Upward movement is initiated by the hips, knees, and ankles. Leg extension at take-off and in flight improves. The arm lift becomes more effective, but the action of the nonreaching arm may not be particularly effective. The extension of the trunk at the crest of the reach is steadily increased. And the head and eyes, in focusing upward, increase the body extension.

MATURE STAGE   The hips, knees, and ankles flex in a preparatory crouch. The jump begins with a vigorous forward and upward lift by the arms. The thrust is continued by forceful extension at the hips, knees, and ankles. The body remains in extension until the feet are ready to retouch, and then the ankles, knees, and hips flex to absorb the shock of landing.

SOURCE: Ralph L. Wickstrom. *Fundamental Motor Patterns,* 2nd ed. (Philadelphia: Lea & Febiger, 1977).

DEVELOPMENTAL STAGES OF THE STANDING LONG JUMP

STAGE 1   The force of take-off is usually exerted more in an upward rather than a
forward direction. The arms move
backward, acting as brakes to stop the
momentum of the trunk as the legs
extend in front of the center of the
body mass.

STAGE 2   The arms move in a forward and then a backward direction during the preparatory phase, but move sideward (winging action) during the "in-flight" phase. The knees and hips flex and then extend more fully than in stage one. The angle of take-off is still markedly above 45° rather than in a more forward direction. The landing is made with the center of gravity above the base of support, with the thighs perpendicular to the surface rather than parallel as in the "reaching" position of stage four.

STAGE 3   The arms swing backward and then forward during the preparatory phase. The knees and hips flex fully prior to take-off. Upon take-off the arms extend and move forward but do not exceed the height of the head. The knee extension may be complete but the take-off angle is still greater than 45°. Upon landing, the thigh is still less than parallel to the surface and the center of gravity is near the base of support when viewed from the front.

MATURE STAGE   The arms extend vigorously forward and then upward upon take-off, reaching full extension above the head at "lift-off." The hips and knees are extended fully with the take-off angle at 45° or less. In preparation for landing the arms are brought downward and the legs thrust forward until the thigh is parallel to the surface. The center of gravity of the body is far behind the base of support (feet) upon foot contact, but at the moment of contact the knees are flexed and the arms are thrust forward in order to maintain the momentum to carry the center of gravity beyond the feet.

SOURCE: Adapted from Ralph L. Wickstrom. *Fundamental Motor Patterns*, 2nd ed. (Philadelphia: Lea & Febiger, 1977).

are ready for control level challenges. At this point more emphasis is placed on the flight phase of children's jumps. For example, they can begin to explore bodily actions in flight such as:

Jumping and making a wide body shape
Jumping and gesturing with an arm (for example, punching)
Jumping and twisting the hips
Jumping and turning clockwise.

Low apparatus is used to create new jumping situations, such as:

Jumping over a block and cane
Jumping onto a milk crate
Jumping through a hoop
Jumping from a table.

When children can repeatedly jump to fulfill a variety of objectives and their jumps continually exhibit a mature pattern, then utilization level tasks are appropriate:

Jumping on an accented beat
Performing a series of light, gentle leaps
Jumping to catch a ball
Jumping to mount or dismount apparatus
Jumping to a hanging support (for example, ropes)

Performers at the proficiency level are able to jump high enough to carry out complex maneuvers in the air and to utilize a variety of jumping operations to express a feeling, idea, or attitude. Some examples of proficiency level performances are:

Jumping and throwing a ball to a target
Hurdling
Leaping reception of a football against an opponent
Standard patterns of jumping (for example, long jump, high jump).

"Make a wide shape in flight"

Precontrol Level

Overview These activities provide a variety of jumping experiences that lead to the ability to use jumping patterns and land without losing balance. Children will be able to distinguish between actions that result in going high and those that result in going far.

IDEAS FOR DEVELOPMENT

IDEAS FOR OBSERVATIONAL FOCUS

A rope is placed in a straight line along the floor. Challenge the children to stand on one side of the rope and jump over it to the other side:

1. two feet to two feet
2. hop over rope
3. one foot to the other foot
4. quickly from one side to the other

Does the child accurately perform the prescribed take-off and landing combination?

Does the child jump high over the rope or does she barely get over it?

Are the landings on-balance, knees bent? Does the child's body wobble?

Can the child jump back and forth in quick succession, so that the landing of one jump serves as the take-off for the next jump?

Children stand on a milk crate. Challenge them to jump off using a two-foot take-off and a two-foot landing.

Does the child use a two-foot take-off?

Does she bend her knees and swing her arms backward in preparation for take-off?

Does the child forcefully extend her legs and bring her arms forward and upward at take-off?

Do both feet leave the crate simultaneously?

Does the child propel herself upward off of the crate, or jump downward toward the ground?

Does the child land on two feet simultaneously? Do her knees bend upon contacting the ground?

Does she land on-balance or in an unstable manner?

Challenge children to jump, landing quietly:

1. Jump off a milk crate.

Does the child *not* jump very high?

2. Jump from two feet on the floor and land with both feet on the floor at the same time.

Upon contacting the floor, do the knees, ankles, and hips flex? Does the child do a deep knee bend?

Are the arms held low to act as brakes?

Children stand behind the starting line. They try to jump as far past the line as they can using a two-foot take-off to a two-foot landing.

Does the child place his feet close to the starting line, about shoulder width apart?

Does he bend his knees and swing his arms backward in preparation for take-off?

Do the arms extend vigorously forward and upward on take-off?

Do the hips and knees extend fully on take-off?

Do both feet leave the ground at the same time?

Does the child prepare for landing by bringing the arms downward and thrusting the legs forward, ahead of the body mass?

Do both feet recontact the ground at the same time?

At the moment of foot to floor contact, do the knees flex and is the body weight thrust forward?

If the child is off-balance upon landing, does his weight continue forward?

Challenge children to use a running start (about fifteen to twenty yards) and then jump as far as they can. Provide a soft landing area (for example, mat, sawdust, sand).

As the child prepares to jump, does he slow down and hesitate before jumping, or does the momentum of the run transfer smoothly into the jumping action?

Does the child use a one-foot take-off? Does the lead leg kick high at take-off?

In preparing for landing, do the legs extend forward of the body mass?

As the feet contact the ground, do the ankles, knees, and hips flex as the body mass is thrust in a forward direction?

Children can learn to land safely by jumping off low benches or milk crates onto grass or a mat

Challenge children to jump as high as they can to touch an object.

Markers are taped at different heights to a wall and youngsters try to jump and stretch an arm to touch a marker.

One partner stands on a chair and stretches an arm outward. The other partner attempts to jump and stretch to touch his partner's hand.

A rope is stretched across the area with objects suspended at varying heights. Challenge children to touch different objects.

Do the knees bend and are the arms held low in preparation for take-off?

Does the jump begin with a forceful upward lift of the arms?

Does the body fully extend in the air? Does the reaching arm extend upward as the other arm swings downward?

Do the eyes focus on the marker or object to be touched?

Does the body remain in extension until the feet are ready to recontact the ground?

As the feet touch the ground, do the ankles, knees, and hips flex? Is landing balanced or unstable?

Place a hula hoop on the floor. Challenge the children to jump into and out of the hoop using varying take-off and landing combinations.

1. Hop into and out of hoop.
2. Jump into hoop, landing on two feet. Jump out of hoop landing on one foot.

Is the child able to accurately exhibit the type of jump asked for?

Does the child need to hesitate between jumps, or can he perform several in quick succession?

Does the child always jump in the same direction (for example, forward)? Or are the jumps in different directions?

Control Level

Overview   We encourage children to practice the execution of both long and high jumps until the landings are balanced and controlled. We also provide opportunities to explore variations in the flight phase of the jump and to jump in relation to different rhythms.

IDEAS FOR DEVELOPMENT

IDEAS FOR OBSERVATIONAL FOCUS

Ask children to jump into a hula hoop placed on the floor. As their feet contact the ground challenge them to freeze their entire bodies in a wide shape. Then, on signal, they are to jump out of the hoop and hold a narrow body shape upon landing. Repeat.

Does the child exhibit body shapes that fulfill the task?

Does the child prepare her body to hold the prescribed shapes while in the air prior to landing?

Does she freeze just as her feet contact the floor?

Have children work with a partner. A signal is sounded by the teacher. As one partner jumps out of a hula hoop and holds a still shape, the other jumps into the hula hoop and holds a still shape. Repeat.

Do the children jump immediately upon hearing the signal?

Do both partners leave the ground at the same time and land at the same time?

As their feet recontact the ground, are their bodies completely still?

Children jump over low obstacles while on the run (for example, a bamboo pole placed atop two milk crates).

Is the child able to travel over obstacles without touching them or bumping into other youngsters?

Does the child utilize a one-foot take-off?

Is the momentum of the child's jumps primarily forward and over the obstacles, rather than high and over?

Does the trail leg remain high enough to clear the obstacle?

Does the jumping action noticeably disturb the child's run or do the two flow together smoothly?

Youngsters at the control level enjoy running and jumping over low obstacles

JUMPING ROPE

Teddy bear, Teddy bear, turn around.
Teddy bear, Teddy bear, touch the ground.
Teddy bear, Teddy bear, say your prayers.
Teddy bear, Teddy bear, say goodnight.
Teddy bear, Teddy bear, turn out the light.

Jumping rope is an American pastime that children enjoy tremendously. Although young girls have traditionally been more interested in and more adept at jumping rope, the popularity of Muhammed Ali and the movie *Rocky* have caused many boys to become jump rope fanatics.

In a typical class of first year students, some children will already be experts—they will be able to demonstrate rope jumping tricks that many adults cannot perform. Other children, however, will not be able to jump rope even once without faltering. And so the teacher needs to assess the rope jumping abilities of all the students to determine how to begin with each class.

In our teaching, children have followed a skill progression of jumping rhythmically without ropes, jumping over long ropes turned by others, and then jumping using individual ropes. At first, youngsters need to practice buoyant jumping in time to an even pulse sounded by the teacher on a drum, for example. As children are observed to jump in cadence to a steady beat, they can begin to jump over long ropes turned by classmates.

Once children are able to jump five to ten times over a long rope without a miss, they can begin to practice jumping with individual ropes. Each child should have a rope of an appropriate length. Have each youngster stand with both feet on the middle of a rope and lift the ends of the ropes. The rope is the right length if the ends reach to chest level.

Once children are able to jump individual ropes five to ten times, their rope jumping skills can be further developed through frequent, repetitive practice. For instance, once or twice a week allow children to jump rope at the beginning or end of a learning session. As the youngsters' abilities improve, they will enjoy attempting jump rope routines set to music or to popular rope jumping rhymes. We have found the following ideas valuable in planning jump rope activities for children.

Tape or paint a one-foot by one-foot square on the floor. Jump up and down rhythmically, keeping both feet in the box.

Does the child keep both feet together?

Does the child utilize a buoyant (springing) landing?

Do the child's feet remain in the box?

Does the child look forward rather than down at his feet?

Practice turning long ropes with another person or with the other end attached to a fence, pole or chair.

Do the children turn the rope by moving their arms and hands in large, circular pathways?

Do they keep their arms and hands in front of their bodies rather than pulling back?

Jumping rope is a favorite pastime of children

Try to jump over a long rope—staying in one box—while two other children turn the rope.

Children are given individual ropes. Ask them to turn the rope so that it comes to rest in front of their feet, then, jump over the rope and turn it again, waiting until the rope comes to rest before jumping again. Gradually, the speed can be increased. The same sequence is used in learning to jump backwards.

Do the children time their jumps to avoid the turning rope?

Do the two turners move the rope in large, slow, rhythmic, circular pathways?

Are the children using appropriate length ropes? Are the children attempting to progress too quickly, turning the ropes swiftly and not timing their jumps accurately?

Ask children to form various body shapes while airborne—a wide shape, a compact shape, a symmetrical shape, a nonsymmetrical shape.

Is the child able to perform the intended body shapes while airborne and still land safely? Are knees bent? Does body maintain balance?

The teacher sets the beat on a drum. Children are challenged to perform big, high jumps on slow tempo and quick, small jumps on fast tempo.

Is the child able to coordinate her jumps with the tempo?

Can the child stay with the beat while using different take-off and landing combinations—for example, one foot to other foot, two foot to two foot?

Have children jump rhythmically to the sounds of tools or machines—hammer, saw, ax, plunger, washing machine, coffee percolator. (Sounds can be played on tape recorder.)

Is the child able to jump in time with the rhythm of the tool or machine? Do her feet leave the ground as the sound of the tool or machine is heard?

Challenge children to rhythmically combine other locomotor patterns with jumps—for example, run, run, leap/run, run, leap, while rhythmically saying aloud "run, run, leap . . . run, run, leap" or clapping the beat.

Can the child accurately perform the locomotor patterns in time with the predetermined rhythm?

Do all the children jump at the same time?

Do some jump too early? Too late?

Ask children to use gestures while jumping to express joy—kicking heels while airborne, clapping hands, arms reaching upward and wide while turning in the air. Use exciting music in the background.

Are jumps quick or sluggish?

Are facial and bodily mannerisms exhibiting excitement and exuberance in jumping?

Challenge children to perform a series of jumps with slight pauses between each jump (yielding landing).

As the child lands, do the knees bend and do they hold a still shape for a moment?

Is the momentum noticeably downward (toward the ground)?

Have children perform a series of jumps in which the landing of one jump flows into the take-off of the next jump and there are no pauses in the series of jumps (buoyant landing)

As the child lands, does he quickly bend his knees and immediately spring upward. Are the knees extended?

Is the momentum of landing quickly transferred upward?

Each child has a balloon. Have them keep the balloon up high by jumping to strike it with one or both hands.

When the child strikes the balloon, are both feet off of the floor?

Does he reach the striking arm up high to hit?

Have children jump over one hurdle and use a yielding landing. Sink and roll under a second hurdle.

Does the child bend his knees in landing and smoothly transfer weight in rolling under the second bar?

Ask children to jump over one hurdle and use a buoyant landing to jump over a second hurdle.

Does the landing from the first jump serve as the take-off for the second jump? Is there any hesitation between jumps?

Have children jump onto a small box, milk crate, or low bench. Use a buoyant landing to quickly spring off into another jump to the floor.

Does the child touch the obstacle for only an instant before springing off?

Does the child appear in control (for example, balanced, smooth jumps) or awkward and clumsy (off balance, jerky movements)?

Have children jump onto a small box, milk crate, or low bench and, using a yielding landing, maintain a position of stillness for a few moments and then jump to the floor.

Does the child give at the ankles, knees, and hips upon landing on the milk crates?

Does she hold a position of stillness for an instant?

The teacher designs a sequence that challenges children to remember a succession of movements flowing from an initial jump. Ask the children to jog around a given area and on signal to:

Does the child continually exhibit quality jumps—does she jump high and land balanced?

Is the child able to remember the sequence?

Are the transitions between movements smooth and fluent?

1. Jump high, land balanced, freeze.
2. Jump high, turn in the air, land balanced, freeze.
3. Jump high, turn in the air, upon landing collapse to the floor, curl and freeze.
4. Jump high, turn in the air, upon landing collapse to the floor, curl and freeze for an instant, quickly resume jogging.

Challenge children to combine one or two other locomotor patterns with their jumps:

Does the child smoothly combine her movements? Are transitions between locomotor patterns fluent?

1. Jog, explode, roll
2. Run, leap far, run again (without stopping)

When combining other actions with the jumps, does the child lapse back into inefficient jumping patterns? Do the knees bend at take-off? Are jumps not very high or far? Are landings wobbly?

Is the child performing the combinations too quickly?

Utilization Level

Overview   At the utilization level, we provide contexts that help children to use jumping and landing in combination with other movements, with complicated rhythms, and as a means for expression.

IDEAS FOR DEVELOPMENT

IDEAS FOR OBSERVATIONAL FOCUS

Challenge children to jump rhythmically into and out of a hoop. Have them vary the foot pattern:

1. One foot in/two feet out
2. Two feet in/one foot out
3. Two feet in/two feet out

Possible variations might include:

1. Having the youngsters step on the balls of their feet.
2. Varying the tempo, from slow jumps to very fast jumps.

Does the child accurately display the desired take-off and landing combination?

Can the child continue the jumping pattern for thirty seconds without becoming confused and losing control?

Does the child jump in and out in the same direction or does he vary direction?

Using a drum, the teacher sounds a cadence— one, two, three, four—with an accent on the first beat. Have the children jump on the accented beat and step on the second, third, and fourth beats.

Does the child react quickly to the sound of the drum?

Do the children all jump on the first beat? Are the jumps too early? Too late?

Ask the children to jump and while airborne exhibit big and strong gestures of body parts—a kick of the leg or a punch of the arm.

Does the child propel himself high enough in the air to perform a strong gesture?

Is the exhibited gesture vigorous?

Does the body part that is used move directly through space in a forceful manner?

Does the child land on-balance?

Have children jump and while airborne exhibit soft, gentle gestures—a graceful stretch of arms sideward, or a light turning of head sideward.

Is there a noticeable contrast between the strong gestures and the light, gentle gestures?

Challenge children to create jumping dance phrases based on action ideas:

1. Walking on hot sand.
2. Winning $100,000.
3. Running in outer space.
4. Jumping on a high wire.
5. Being a bouncing ball.
6. Being a piston engine.

Does the child appear stymied in attempting to use the skill of jumping in an expressive exercise?

Do the jumps exhibited display the qualities inherent in the action idea that stimulated the movement?

> When you are trying to create an atmosphere in which children can let themselves go and use movement expressively, humor is a valuable aid.

One child stands on a low bench, chair or milk crate. A partner tosses a yarn ball or plastic ball, so that the child must jump to catch. Children must land on two feet with a balanced landing.

Do the children land safely?

Are the children able to track the path of the ball while also orienting their bodies through the air for landing?

Do the knees bend on landing? Is balance maintained or are the landings wobbly and unstable?

Ask children to jump and while airborne throw a ball through a goal—a basketball hoop or a hula hoop hanging from a basketball hoop.

Is the momentum or direction of the jump in the direction of the goal?

Is the ball thrown forcefully or without much speed?

Is the throw accurate?

Have an opponent try to prevent the ball from reaching the goal without touching the thrower.

Does the thrower fake a jump before leaving the ground?

Does the thrower jump high enough to throw over the defender?

Does the child throw with one hand or two?

Children work with a partner. One partner tosses the ball up to a net or rope. The other partner approaches the ball, jumps, and forcefully strikes the ball over the net to a targeted area. Switch positions.

Challenge children to jump as high as they can over an obstacle (for example, high jump bar or wooden dowel on chairs). A safe landing area of foam rubber or crash mats is essential.

Design a game focusing upon jumping.

Objective: To be off the ground when *any* player touches the ball.

Rules:
1. Two to six players stand in a circle, a beachball is the only equipment.
2. The youngsters use any body part to strike the ball and attempt to keep it up high.
3. When any player strikes the ball he must have both feet off of the ground.

Design a game in which children must jump to catch and jump to throw.

Objective: To have the ball touch the floor on the opposing side of the net.

Rules:
1. A player must be off the floor when she or he throws or catches the ball.
2. Three players must catch and throw the ball before it goes back over the net.
3. A team scores a point when the ball touches the floor on the opposing side of the net *or* when an opposing player throws or catches the ball while touching the floor.

Does the striker utilize a two-foot take-off?

Do the arms initiate the jump and then quickly adjust for the striking motion?

Do the eyes focus on the object to be hit?

Does the child use a running take-off with the lead foot thrusting upward?

Does the jumper lean backward on the other foot?

Are the arms brought upward in a vigorous motion?

Does the trail leg extend, lifting upward?

Is the child able to get both feet off the ground when striking the ball?

Is the child able to time her jumps so that she meets the ball at the peak of the jumps, rather than going up or coming down?

Is the child jumping to throw and catch?

Is the child able to keep the ball in the air for an extended period of time?

Children at the utilization level can explore a variety of ways to jump onto and off apparatus

Ask children to jump and land safely from a relatively high location, for example a beam or a vaulting box. A mat should be placed in the landing area.

Design a course of apparatus so that children can jump safely from one apparatus to another:

1. From the floor onto a milk crate.
2. From a milk crate onto a bench.

Is the child hesitant and somewhat afraid to jump from a height?

Does the child step down off of the high obstacle, or does he jump up from the obstacle?

As the feet contact the floor, do the knees bend to absorb the shock?

Can the child jump onto an apparatus and still maintain equilibrium? Can he use his arms as brakes and keep his weight back as he lands?

Do the knees bend on landing?

3. From a bench onto a beam.

4. From a beam onto a vaulting box.

Is the body weight behind the feet?

5. From a vaulting box to a hang on the ropes.

Are the arms held low behind the body mass?

6. From the ropes back to the floor.

Challenge children to design a sequence on one apparatus that includes at least two jumps. For example: Hop on one foot across the bench. Jump and while airborne turn the body so that, as the feet recontact the bench, the body is facing the opposite direction. Perform a series of small leaps across the bench to the edge. Jump high and to the floor.

Is the child able to design a sequence that includes at least two jumps?

Can he repeat the sequence exactly?

Do the various locomotor patterns of the child's sequence flow together smoothly or in an awkward, hesitant manner?

When the child lands on the apparatus, do the knees bend and is balance maintained? Or, does the child wobble and appear unstable?

Once children become skillful on the bench, they may want to try their sequence on a low beam, then on a high balance beam.

Challenge children to run, jump, and spring from a buoyant landing into another action, such as a cartwheel or a handspring.

Does the springing action create momentum for the subsequent action?

Proficiency Level

Overview   Experiences at the proficiency level provide dynamic dance, game, and gymnastic activities designed to help youngsters utilize, refine, and enjoy their jumping abilities. Jumping will almost always be in relation to objects or other people (or both), and children will be able to use jumping for both expressive and functional purposes.

IDEAS FOR DEVELOPMENT

IDEAS FOR OBSERVATIONAL FOCUS

Two tables, vaulting boxes (see Figure 19.2), or beams are placed about fifteen to twenty feet apart, with a large mat in between.

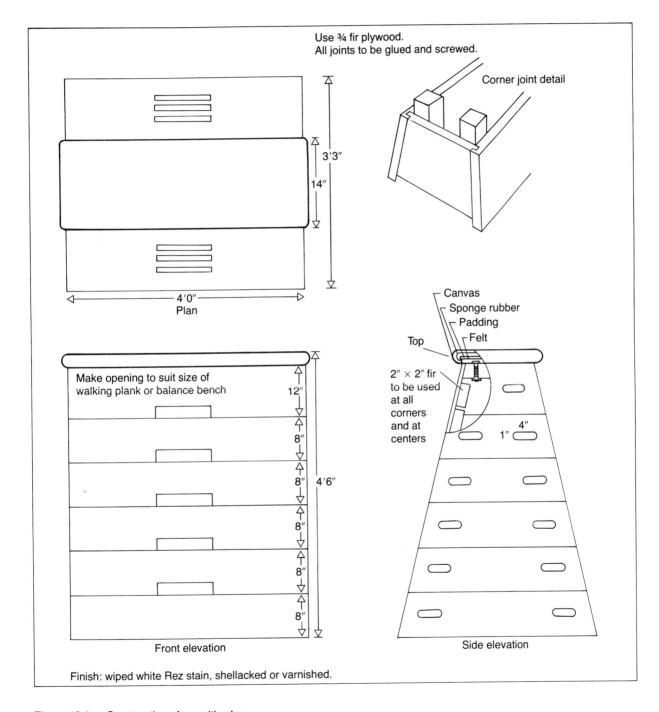

Use ¾ fir plywood.
All joints to be glued and screwed.

Corner joint detail

3'3"

14"

4'0"
Plan

Canvas
Sponge rubber
Padding
Top
Felt

2" × 2" fir
to be used
at all
corners
and at
centers

Make opening to suit size of
walking plank or balance bench

12"

8"

8"

8"

8"

8"

4'6"

4"
1"

Front elevation

Side elevation

Finish: wiped white Rez stain, shellacked or varnished.

Figure 19.2   Construction of a vaulting box

Children work with a partner. They stand opposite one another and try to execute jumps that exactly mirror one another. These may include gestures, turns in the air, or actions such as rolls when landing.

Have children create a dance using a jump as the key action. Have them focus on selecting gestures that will make clear the expressive intentions behind the actions. For example, a Fight Dance would call for such gestures as punching, slashing, jabbing, protecting, retreating, and dying.

Have children use jumps in creating a dance stimulated by natural phenomenon, such as the flight of a bird or leaves rustled in the wind.

Have youngsters focus on:

1. The qualities of the phenomenon stimulating the dance (for example, strength or weakness)
2. The starting location of each person
3. How the dance is to rise to a climax and then how it is to wind down to a conclusion
4. The pathways of the dancers
5. The types of jumps and gestures that will be most effective
6. Whether music or percussive sounds will be used

A jump ball situation, as in basketball, can be created by groups of three—two jumpers and one thrower. Some children may want to design a game based on this task.

Are the children able to mirror one another's movements exactly?

Do the children take off and land at the same moment?

Do the jumps and gestures express the qualities they are intended to represent?

Can the child repeat her dance interpretations?

Is the child able to verbalize the gestures she incorporated into the jumps and why she did so?

Did the child's dance seem to have a beginning, a rise to a climax, and then a resolution or conclusion?

Is the child able to verbally explain her dances? In particular, can she describe the types of jumps utilized and what the jumps are intended to express?

Do the jumps incorporated in the dance appear to express the qualities intended?

Are the jumping operations technically efficient?

Does take-off propel body high enough to fulfill objective of jump?

Is landing balanced and stable, or does the child frequently stumble or fall to the ground?

Does the child bend knees and hold arms backward in preparation for jump?

Do the eyes focus on the ball?

Does the child use a two-foot take-off, thrusting arms upward?

As the body extends upward, does the child reach for the ball with one hand while forceably pushing the other hand downward?

Challenge the children to jump to grab a rebound or tap a ball against a target on a wall.

When jumping to grab a rebound, does the child extend both hands upward to grasp the ball?

Have the children jump to mount or dismount apparatus and try to turn their bodies while airborne—clockwise, counterclockwise, one-fourth, one-half, three-fourths, and whole turns.

When preparing to dismount, does the child turn body counterclockwise in preparation for clockwise rotating turn?

Does the child vigorously propel himself upward while thrusting the arms, hips, and legs in the turning direction?

Does the child lose his orientation in turning and thus lose balance on contacting the floor mat?

Does the child remain in control, bending his knees and stretching his arms sideward to maintain balance?

In games, children use the ability to jump while catching a rebounding ball

Have children use a springboard to increase the height or distance of their jumps. For example, run, jump to a two-foot landing, and spring up high, landing on two feet on a mat.

Does the child push down forceably with his legs and feet as he contacts the springboard?

Does he spring upward from the springboard, greatly increasing the height of the jumps?

When landing, does he bend his knees and spread his arms sideward in order to maintain balance?

When landing, does he keep the body mass slightly behind the base of support, or is he leaning too far forward?

Provide opportunities for children to hurdle a series of barriers.

Does the child's lead leg forcefully extend upward and forward as she approaches the obstacles?

Does the child run through the hurdles rather than jumping up and down as she goes over them?

We have found it valuable to use *low* barriers at first. This allows youngsters to focus on proper technique without worrying about clearing the obstacles. Once children begin to exhibit quality hurdling actions, the height of the barriers can be gradually increased. Milk crates spread apart with bamboo poles supported between them make satisfactory barriers.

Children at the proficiency level often enjoy testing their hurdling skills against the clock. Stopwatches can be made available for those youngsters who wish to do so.

Provide experiences for youngsters to *vault* apparatus—to run and jump over an obstacle so that the hands give momentary support to the body. It is of value to have children utilize a springboard to enhance the height possibilities of their jumps. See Box.

Does the child approach the jumping board with a light run, with weight on the balls of the feet?

As the child reaches the board, does he utilize a two-foot buoyant take-off to propel the body over the obstacle?

Does the child firmly place his hands on the apparatus, shoulder width apart?

As the body travels over the obstacle, does the child push off with his hands to an erect, balanced landing on two feet?

VAULTING POSSIBILITIES

Vaulting with a Tight Body Shape

As children take off, they place their hands on the apparatus, shoulder width apart. They then bring their legs up between their arms in a squatting position and jump forward to the mat.

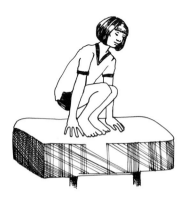

Vaulting with Legs Extended Outward

As children propel themselves upward from the take-off board, they place both hands on the apparatus, shoulder width apart. They quickly shift weight to one hand. They lift the other hand from the apparatus, bring feet together horizontally, and move the body over the obstacle under the nonsupporting hand. Then the children push off from the apparatus with the supporting hand and land on two feet with their backs to the apparatus.

Vaulting with a Wide Body Shape

As children reach the take-off board, they spring high and put both hands on the apparatus. At the same time they spread their legs far apart, landing in a standing position.

Vaulting with the Body in an Inverted Position

This is recommended only for those students who can perform a handspring along the floor. Children spring from the take-off board and come to a handstand position, keeping arms straight and locked. They tuck in their heads and fully extend their bodies over the apparatus to land on the mat.

A vaulting box, a horse without pommels, or a sturdy table can serve as vaulting apparatus.

Safety considerations: Mats need to be placed adjacent to any vaulting apparatus. And we highly recommend the placement of *trained spotters* (students or teacher) at vaulting locations.

CHAPTER 20
ROLLING

The sensations of rolling—dizziness, loss of perception, and not knowing where or how you will finish a roll—are fascinating to children. The feeling of not knowing where you are or where you will end up that is characteristic of a child's first attempts at rolling is both intriguing and perplexing. And so a child loves to roll. As a child becomes adept at rolling, the fascination of traveling upside down is augmented by pleasure in being able to roll in different directions and at various speeds while doing different rolls.

Rolling is the act of transferring weight to adjacent body parts around a central axis. In physical education classes, rolling is generally dealt with in a gymnastic sense, as a transference of weight. In gymnastics, safety through rolling is a skill introduced early to help children avoid crashing to the floor when they lose their balance. In the dance and games areas, rolling is dealt with briefly, to increase the children's range of movement and to enhance expressive abilities (see Figure 20.1).

Rolling is a skill that fascinates children

Figure 20.1   Sequence for developing the skill theme of rolling

PROFICIENCY LEVEL

Rolling to recover and maintain
an action
Striking and rolling
Rolling as an expressive movement
Diving over high obstacles and rolling
Arriving by rolling

UTILIZATION LEVEL

Rolling off apparatus
Rolling onto apparatus
Rolling along low apparatus
Diving over obstacles to roll
Rolling, balancing, rolling
Rolling with something in hand
Diving roll

CONTROL LEVEL

Jumping over objects, landing, and rolling
Jumping off objects, landing, and rolling
Rolling at different speeds
Rolling from different positions
Rolling in different directions
(sideways, backward)

PRECONTROL LEVEL

Rolling (squatting position)
Somersaulting (accidental rolling)
Log roll
Rocking

DEVELOPMENTAL STAGES OF A FORWARD ROLL

STAGE 1   The hands are of little use at this stage. They do not support the body weight evenly, and the body collapses to one side. Or the hands push unevenly and the body rolls to one side. The hands usually remain on the mat next to the head until the forward motion of the body pulls them off. As the knees extend to lift the hips forward and upward, the weight is taken onto the head. The head and upper back then lag behind as the lower back makes contact. One leg usually pushes off first, and the toes leave the floor only when the body reaches an off-balance position. The knees stay extended and the body is uncurled throughout the roll. The child usually ends up sitting or lying.

STAGE 2   In the second stage, the arms and hands begin to take the body weight at the beginning of the roll and serve to steady the body. The arms come off the mat when the back touches. The trunk and head are off the mat as the lower back touches. Early in the roll the body is curled, but it uncurls as the middle of the back touches. Now the knees tuck under as the legs uncurl, rather than completely extending. The roll may end with the body extended in a sitting position, or the body may curl up again as the trunk catches up with the legs, still in a sitting position.

MATURE STAGE   In the third stage, when the child has acquired a mature forward roll pattern, the arms and hands receive the body weight at the beginning of the roll. The head slides through as the weight goes from the hands to the upper back. The arms come off the mat as soon as the shoulders touch.

The arms assist the forward momentum by coming forward. The head leaves the mat as soon as the shoulders touch. The trunk and head continue moving upward and forward throughout the roll. The body stays curled and the roll ends on the feet.

SOURCE: Adapted from Mary Ann Roberton & Lolas Halverson, ''The Developing Child—Changing Movement,'' in B. J. Logsdon et al., *Physical Education for Children: A Focus on the Teaching Process* (Philadelphia: Lea & Febiger, 1977).

LEVELS OF SKILL PROFICIENCY

The precontrol level of rolling is characterized by rocking actions from head to feet on the back and stomach. At this level children are challenged when asked to perform actions such as rocking back and forth like a rocking chair or rolling in a stretched position like a log. Rolling, initially in a forward direction rather than from side to side, is also studied at the precontrol level. When a child first begins to roll, the hands and arms may be of little use. This child does "get over," but his whole body usually uncurls in the middle of the roll and he lands sitting down.

At the control level, the child is able to execute rolls that go over the head (as opposed to over the shoulder), using his arms and hands to push while staying curled. Tasks such as these can be presented to children:

1. Changing the direction of the rolls—backward, sideways, forward.
2. Changing the speed of the rolls—fast or slow.
3. Rolling from different positions—starting from low or standing positions and different balances (on one foot, two feet, three body parts).
4. Combining jumping, landing, and rolling.
5. Traveling and rolling.

Children discover the difficulty of rocking when not in a round shape

Rolling along equipment presents a more demanding challenge than rolling on the floor

At the utilization level children are able to roll in different directions while staying curled; the arms are a functional part of the roll and the child can end the roll on his feet. Children at this level begin to combine several different concepts along with the task of rolling. Some of these are:

1. Rolling with something in the hands.
2. Rolling after catching an object.
3. Diving and rolling.
4. Rolling on or over low equipment.
5. Combining rolling with other locomotor forms as an expressive movement.

By the time children can roll fluidly from any position and rolling has become an almost natural reaction to a fall, a child can function at the proficiency level. At this level appropriate tasks would be:

1. Rolling after flight from a high object so that the entire action is fluid.
2. Rolling along high and/or narrow equipment (such as a regulation balance beam).
3. Striking or catching in an off-balance position and rolling to recover and maintain the action (for example, a save in volleyball).

The child who masters the skill of rolling is able to comfortably and safely participate in activities that involve the risk of being off-balance and falling, because this child possesses sufficient recovery techniques. This skill also provides a child with a fluid way to connect different balancing actions and to change direction and/or speed in a dynamic, unpredictable situation.

When introducing the skill of rolling, we prefer to have one mat for each child. When we do not have a mat for each child, we try to use as many mats as possible. We have found that a good ground rule for any rolling situation is to have only one child on the mat at a time. This does not mean that the other children must stand in line and wait. They can stand around the mat and roll, in turn, as soon as the mat is empty. Sometimes we set up learning centers to prevent long waits in line.

Grassy areas or carpeting can also serve as appropriate areas on which to practice rolling.

The activities that follow include a range of tasks that focus on the skill of rolling at all four skill levels. They are stated in direct terms, and you are encouraged to modify the tasks as suggested in Chapter Four.

Precontrol Level

Overview   The ability to create arched or rounded body surfaces is an important prerequisite to rolling. Once children are able to curve their bodies, they learn that rocking and rolling actions can be used for traveling and transferring weight.

IDEAS FOR DEVELOPMENT

IDEAS FOR OBSERVATIONAL FOCUS

Ask the children to rock like a rocking horse or rocking chair, on their backs, on their sides, on their stomachs.

Does the child rock smoothly?

Is the body arched?

Can the child rock from any position and still maintain the body arch? Can the child rock in different directions?

Challenge them to rock as fast as they can and then as slow as they can. Ask them if they can rock to their feet from any position. Then encourage them to try touching their feet to the mat over their heads.

Is the child using her hands to help her rock?

Are the hands placed on the mat at the sides, palms down? Are fingers toward feet when on back? Toward head when on the stomach?

Have the children practice rocking so that their rock is continuous—almost as if they start rocking and can't stop. Ask them what needs to happen so that they can do this.

Is the child pushing with the hands and arms?

Ask the children to try rolling sideways like a log, going smoothly—sometimes fast like going down hill, or sometimes slow.

Are the hands placed above the head to facilitate the roll, or by the side so that it is bumpy?

Is the body stretched to its maximum?

Ask the children to roll forward and over their heads. Challenge them to do it smoothly, so that their heads don't bump and they don't land like a flat tire. Have them try to come to their feet when they finish (see Figure 20.2).

Do the arms and hands evenly support the weight? Or does the child roll over sideways?

Do the arms and hands push off as the knees extend? Or do they leave earlier or later?

Do the shoulders contact the mat first, or does the head hit first?

Do the knees stay tucked close to the chest, or does the body uncurl through the roll?

Figure 20.2   Hand positions on forward roll

Does the child end on her feet, or sitting, or lying?

Have the children try rolling forward from different positions:

1. Sometimes start from a low position.
2. Sometimes start from a high position.
3. Sometimes start from a balance on five, two (and so forth) body parts.

Can the child roll smoothly from different positions?

Have the children try rolling sideways in a curled position.

Is the body actually curled?

Does the body stay curled?

If children keep their chins close to their knees as they roll, they will be able to stay in a round shape

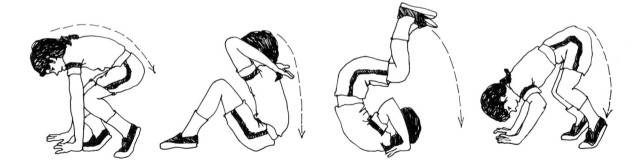

Hand positions on backward roll

Does the child use her hands to help complete the rolls? (Are the hands in position to help push off from the surface, or are they tucked in or wrapped around, holding onto the legs?)

Does the child end on her feet?

Control Level

Overview   Children must be able to roll in different directions and from different positions if they are to perform other movements safely. Rolling is studied as an automatic response to a fall. In addition, children learn that rolls are useful for connecting various balances.

IDEAS FOR DEVELOPMENT

Have the children try rolling in different directions:

1. Backward—with their backs going first.
2. Sideways—with the side of their bodies leading.
3. Forward—with their heads going first.

Challenge them to end on their feet from any direction.

IDEAS FOR OBSERVATIONAL FOCUS

Is the child able to change the direction of the rolls?

Is the child able to keep a curled body shape in any direction?

Is the child using his hands to help keep the rolls going?

Does he use his hands in the appropriate way for the direction? Are fingers pointed back to shoulder on back roll? Are fingers facing forward for forward roll? Are fingers facing head for sideward roll?

When trying to roll backward, children often get stuck and can roll no further. When this happens, typically two errors are occurring:

1. The child is making a flat rather than a round shape (knees move away from the chin) and finds it virtually impossible to roll.
2. The child fails to place his or her hands in the proper position and as a result is unable to push with the force needed to roll completely over.

Usually practicing these two critical aspects will enable the child to roll backward.

Can the child come to her feet at the end of the rolls, not sitting, lying, or on her knees?

Have the children roll from different starting positions:

1. Sometimes kneeling
2. Sometimes squatting
3. Sometimes standing.

Can the child roll smoothly with a curled body, no matter what position she starts from?

Is the child able to receive the weight of her body to roll from a standing position?

Smaller size mats are adequate for introducing children to rolling; larger mats can be used for rolling in sequences and in relation to apparatus

Have the children roll from different starting positions in different directions:

1. Forward from standing position
2. Backward from squatting position

Ask the children to change the speed of their rolls, so that some are fast and some are slow.

Have the children roll in different directions and at different speeds. Ask them in which direction it is easiest to go slow and in which direction it is easiest to go fast.

Have the children make up a sequence of three rolls in which they change direction and speed at least twice.

Is the initial contact with the surface a controlled, gentle one that allows smooth progression into the rest of the roll?

Is the child able to visibly change the speed of her work?

Is the child able to vary the speed of her rolls in all directions, particularly backward?

Can the child roll in a sequence?

While rolling in a sequence, can the child change the direction and speed of her work?

Milk crates can be obtained from the local dairy. Low boxes can be made by filling soft drink cartons with flat newspaper and taping heavily over the outside.

Encourage the children to jump off milk crates or low boxes, land, and roll.

1. Have the children change the direction of the jump and of the roll. For example, jump backward and roll backward, jump forward and roll sideways, and so forth.
2. Challenge the children to see how high they can get when they jump off the box, land on their feet, and roll.
3. Have different stations set up around the room with boxes and benches of different heights (see Figure 20.3). Have the children land and roll in different directions.

Is the child landing on his feet before he rolls?

Is the child able to control his body as he lands, so that he rolls, or does he fall down?

Does he achieve a tight curl as he rolls?

Is the child changing the direction of the jump and the roll?

Can the child control his jumps from any direction?

Can the child still roll after jumping to a greater height, or does he lose control of his body?

Can the child land and roll when jumping from slightly higher boxes, or does he fall?

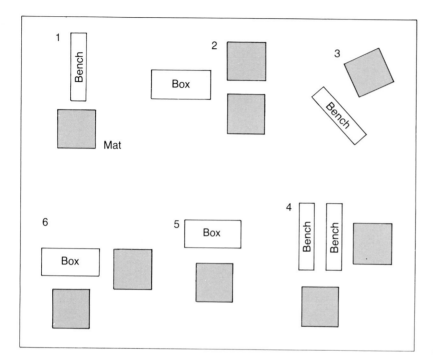

Figure 20.3   Stations to facilitate jumping, landing, and rolling

Jumping backward from the equipment is difficult for some children, as well as scary. It is helpful to have them first step backward if they are hesitant or fearful.

Provide each child with a block and cane at his or her mat. Have the children jump the block and cane, land, and roll.

Challenge the children, as they jump the block and cane, to try to change the direction of their jump and roll—for example, jump backward/roll backward; jump forward/roll sideways.

Is the child landing on her feet before she starts to roll?

Can the child return to her feet following each roll?

Can the child change the direction of his jumps and still clear the block and cane?

Is the child changing the direction of both the jump and the roll, or does he change the direction of the jump but always roll forward?

Ask the children to try to vary the speed of the jump and the roll:

1. Jump quickly, roll quickly
2. Jump slowly, roll quickly.

Ask the children to jump and land on their mats, then roll. Have them:

1. Try rolling in different directions after they jump—backward, sideways, and forward.
2. Change the jump that they use over the corners, land, and roll.
3. Try adding twists and turns to jumps over the corners, then land and roll.

Is the child able to vary the speed of the roll after the jump?

Is the child in control of his body, or does he fall after jumping and then roll from the position that results from the fall?

Can the child roll from a moving position, or does he jump, stop, and then roll?

Is the child able to travel, jump, and still roll in different directions, or does he begin to roll in the same direction every time?

Are the children actually using different jumps—one foot to two feet, two feet to one foot, and so on, or do they use the same jump every time?

Are the twists and turns in the air or on the ground?

Can the children control their bodies upon landing, so that they are able to roll, or do they fall?

Utilization Level

Overview   Children at the utilization level can develop the ability to incorporate rolling actions into other activities, such as rolling to connect locomotor movements or catching and rolling. They can also learn to precede a roll with a dive and to perform a roll with varying degrees of the effort qualities (quickly or slowly; with much tension and control or with little).

IDEAS FOR DEVELOPMENT

IDEAS FOR OBSERVATIONAL FOCUS

Have the children play follow-the-leader on a big mat—jumping the corners, landing and rolling; after three leads, have them change places.

Are the children staying far enough apart so that they can follow each other safely?

Are the children able to copy the leader?

The leader must be sensitive to the followers' capabilities and not ask them to do tasks that are beyond their skill levels.

Challenge the children to try to keep the mat busy. Someone should always be rolling on the mat, while the others are traveling and jumping around the outside. As soon as one person finishes rolling, another should start. The timing should be split second.

Encourage children to transfer their weight *smoothly* after they land from a jump and go into a roll. Suggest that they try not to hesitate.

1. Roll in different directions.
2. Land, facing different directions.

Have the children travel, roll, and then continue traveling. They can:

1. Gradually increase the speed of their travel.
2. Try to change to a different direction as they come out of their rolls, so that they do not make a straight pathway.
3. Roll without hesitation and continue traveling.

At stations around the room, set up different pieces of low equipment (low boxes, benches, beams, blocks and canes) with mats (see Figure 20.4). Have the children try rolling over the equipment.

Challenge the children to try to cross an object by rolling in different directions.

Can the children cooperate with each other, reading each others' actions so that they do not collide?

Are the children on the outside moving or are they just standing and waiting?

Are the children able to bend their knees and transfer weight from hands to shoulders without hesitation? Are there obvious pauses?

Is each roll actually from an off-balance position, or do the children catch themselves and then roll?

Is the child transferring weight from feet to hands and shoulders without hesitation? Without slowing down?

Can the child vary the direction of the roll (pushing unevenly with hands, rolling over a shoulder) to change the direction of travel after the roll?

Is the child pushing with her hands to regain her feet?

Is the child actually diving over equipment to roll, or are the feet still on the ground when the hands touch on the other side?

Is the child absorbing the force of her body as she hits the mat? Do the arms give when they contact the mat? Is she absorbing the weight on her hands and shoulders, tucking in her head?

Is the child rolling forward and sideways (from both left and right sides), or does she approach in a different direction and cross forward.

> At this stage in their development it is extremely difficult for children to roll backward over an object, and so we do not stress this movement.

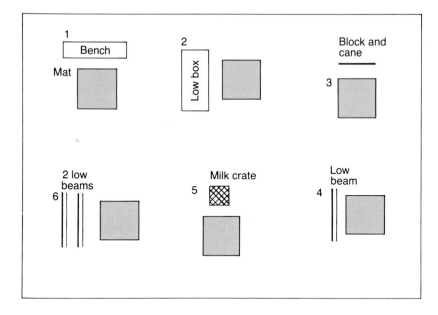

Figure 20.4   Equipment setups

Using boxes, benches, beams, and tables, have children mount the equipment in any way, roll along the top of it, and then dismount as they like:

1. Ask the children to try to change the direction of the roll on the equipment—backward, forward, sideways.

2. Have the youngsters try to change the shape of their bodies as they roll. Ask them to be aware of what their legs do in the air. Have them try extending them as they finish.

3. Challenge the children to roll along equipment. Have them try a different roll (either by changing direction or body shape) to

Is the child able to roll along the top of the equipment without falling off? Does he need wider equipment?

Is he able to keep his rolls smooth and curled?

Is he able to complete the roll while on the equipment, or does he roll off the end?

Is the child able to roll smoothly in all directions?

Can the child control his rolls enough to alter the leg action during the roll?

Is the child actually doing something different with his legs?

Is the child able to connect the parts of a sequence fluidly?

get off. Ask them to practice until they are able to repeat a sequence that they like, and then write their sequence down (see Figure 20.5).

Can he put in the appropriate moves when called for?

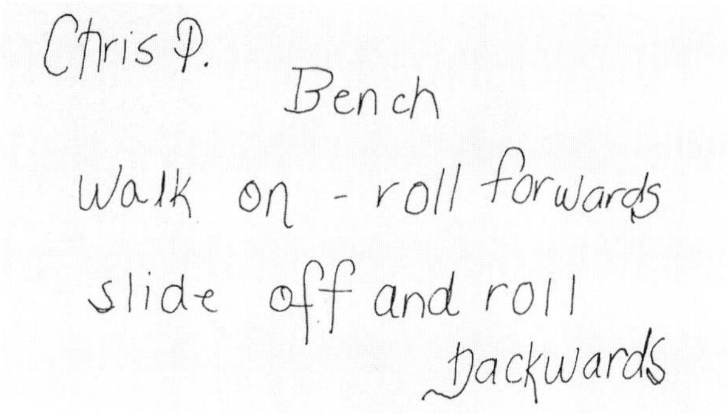

Chris P.
Bench
Walk on - roll forwards
slide off and roll
backwards

Figure 20.5   Child's rolling sequence

4. Place two pieces of equipment together (box and bench, or beam and table). Have the children roll one way to the end of the first piece of equipment; without touching the floor, travel to the second piece and roll a different way on that piece; jump to get off and roll. Have them make up a sequence that they like and repeat it until it is fluid and smooth.

Is the child rolling in different ways on the two pieces of equipment?

Can the child connect his movements?

Does he land on his feet before the final roll?

Roll to express an idea:

1. Work with a partner, one child scares the other one. The scared one falls and rolls in retreat. Ask the children if they are using their whole bodies to show fear?

Is the child using her rolls and her body to show fear, or does she simply roll without emotion? For example, is tenseness expressed through fingers, hands, leg positioning?

2. Have the children roll as if they are seeds being blown across the ground by the wind. Suddenly the wind stops and they move as if they are sending out roots and starting to grow.

Can the child roll slightly and freely, as if the wind is blowing her?

Does she maintain a balanced position?

Can she use the ideas of rising and spreading to show growth?

3. Ask the children to roll as if they are tumbleweed being blown across the desert.

Can she roll to show the lightness and bounciness of an object being moved by the wind?

4. Have the children roll as if they are a rock rolling down the side of a hill.

Is the child gaining speed as she rolls, to show the increased movement of going downhill?

Have children throw and catch a beanbag or a ball so that they have to stretch to catch. Have them roll after they have caught the object.

Is the child able to roll with an object in her hands, or does she let go of the object as she rolls?

Can the child concentrate on the total movement, or does she focus on the catch and forget the roll or focus on the roll and miss the object?

Have each child throw the object to himself so that he has to jump to catch the object in an off-balance position, and roll to break his fall from the off-balance position.

Is the child able to force himself into off-balance positions to catch?

Is the child rolling from an off-balance position, or does he catch his balance in some way and then roll?

Is the child returning to his feet after the roll with the objects in his hands?

Ask the children to throw to a partner so that they make the partner off-balance when he catches and he has to roll to recover his balance.

Is the child catching in an off-balance position and rolling, or does he catch and roll because that was the task given to him?

When throwing and catching with partners, success depends on the thrower's ability to throw so that he is actually forcing the catcher to be off-balance or to move to catch. Children should be at the utilization level of throwing and catching before dealing with these ideas.

---

1. Have half of the children jump off boxes to catch an object that their partner throws to them while they are in the air; they roll when they hit the mat. As they feel they are getting better, instruct them to have their partner put the object further away from them as they jump.

Is the child able to judge his jumps in order to catch the object and still be in control of his body to roll when he lands? Or does he catch the object and crash to the mat, or miss the object and roll?

2. Have the children throw a frisbee with a partner so that each has to stretch to catch it at many places around his body. Each catcher should roll in the direction that he is falling.

Is the child rolling in the direction that he was falling? Or does he roll in a way that is comfortable but not necessarily the direction that his force is taking him?

Have the children roll on a mat and then balance immediately after the roll, trying to roll right into their balance:

1. Have them change the balance each time they roll—make it on a different number of body parts (two, four, five, and so forth).
2. Have them try rolling into a balance from different directions.
3. Have them roll, balance, then roll out of their balance.

Is the child rolling into the balance, or does she stop after the roll and then balance?

Can the child balance on unstable parts after the roll—for example, on one foot, on elbows?

Is the child able to hold a balance from backward and sideways rolls?

Does she balance in the middle, or does she just keep going and forget the balance?

Challenge the children to dive over medium height hurdles (about two to three feet high) and roll when their hands touch the mat.

Have them use mats rolled up and tied with rope as obstacles to roll over without touching.

Is the child able to absorb the weight (force) of her body onto her hands, so that she rolls smoothly without crashing her body to the mat? Is she "giving" when she lands?

Have the children roll onto low benches and beams. They can travel in any way that they like, and then roll off.

Is the child rolling to get onto the equipment, or does she get on and then roll?

Is the child rolling to leave the equipment, or does she roll after she gets off?

1. Children can make up a sequence that they like on the equipment. It should involve rolling onto the equipment, traveling, and rolling off. It must include at least one change of direction.
2. Children can roll onto their piece of equipment, and balance in any shape they like. Have them leave the balance by rolling, and roll a different way to exit the equipment.

Can the child include a change of direction in her work?

Does the sequence include rolling at the proper places?

Can the child roll out of balance on the equipment?

Can the child roll in different directions while on or exiting the equipment?

Proficiency Level

Overview At the proficiency level children can learn to perform a roll as a part of another action. They are also ready to learn to roll spontaneously when a situation occurs that calls for a roll (such as a recovery in volleyball, a fall from a high piece of equipment).

IDEAS FOR DEVELOPMENT

IDEAS FOR OBSERVATIONAL FOCUS

Challenge the children to use high equipment (high boxes, regulation beams, parallel bars, or tables):

Is the child able to control his momentum from the swing, so that he can roll and travel on the box?

1. They can roll onto the equipment, travel, and roll off, varying the ways they roll onto and off of the equipment each time.

2. They can vary the direction of the rolls onto and off of the equipment—move backward, sideways, and forward.

Can the child roll onto the equipment in all three directions?

Can he roll off in all three directions?

3. They can roll onto the equipment; connect two locomotor actions on the equipment with a roll; roll to dismount. At least two changes of direction must occur. Have the children try to make their sequence fluid, with no breaks in it.

Is the child connecting two different locomotor actions (for example, hopping and skipping, walking and crawling) with a roll?

Does the child change direction at least twice, or does he turn around and move in the same direction?

Is the child able to connect all movements fluidly on the chosen piece of equipment?

Ask the children to swing onto a piece of equipment (box, beam, table) from climbing ropes; roll; travel and roll off.

Is the child able to control his momentum from the swing, so that he can roll and travel on the box?

Does the child land on the box so that he can accomplish all of the tasks asked for? Or does he land in the middle of the box or at the end of the box?

Have the children use high equipment (for example, high boxes or a cane suspended between chairs), dive over the equipment and roll when they touch the mat:

1. Have them add distance to their dives by adding a double set of blocks and canes. They should dive and roll.
2. Keep increasing the height of dive and roll (only as long as it is safe). Have the children try to obtain a longer period in flight before their hands touch the mat.

3. Challenge the children to try crossing the equipment from different directions and with different body parts leading, and roll when they touch the mat.

Working with a partner, the children can use each other as obstacles to dive over and roll.

1. As soon as the diving partner clears the partner, he makes a shape for the other partner. The interchange of places is continuous and the movement does not cease.

2. Ask the children to try diving so that they must roll in different directions and from different positions.

3. Suggest that the children put together a routine, that can be repeated, in which each person in the group does at least five different rolls.

Use equipment such as horses, beams, tables, or boxes. Have the children mount the equipment, balance, roll out of the balance, and dismount.

Is the child able to clear the equipment she has chosen?

Is she able to roll smoothly after diving and to absorb weight on her hands and shoulders?

Does the child's body begin to curl while he or she is still in the air, or does it remain spread out?

Is it clear which body parts are leading the action?

Do the rolls follow naturally from the body parts that have led the action?

Is the child approaching from different directions?

Is the child able to recover from his rolls in time to form shapes for her partners?

Are the rolls smooth and fluid after the dives?

Do the changes in direction result from the way in which the child dove, or only from the teacher's instruction?

Are the changes in the positions from which the child rolls clear and natural?

Do the movements flow together, so that the routine is smooth and even?

Are the various rolls different and clear?

Are the rolls out of the balances natural for the balances that are made or does the child try to force rolls that are not natural and flowing?

They can change the rolls out of the balances so that they go in different directions.

Is the child able to roll on the equipment?

Are the changes in direction clear and appropriate?

At the proficiency level in rolling, the emphasis turns from the roll to the flow and smoothness of the movement. A high level of motor development should already exist in the rolls; refinement is now the goal.

With the idea of meeting and parting, the children come together by traveling on their feet. They make a shape of their choice, and then part by rolling. Limit groups to about five children:

1. Tell the children to try to time their work so that all of them arrive in a group shape. They hold it, and then leave by rolling on their own. They freeze in another shape after they roll.
2. Suggest that they tell their own story with their dance. They may want to write the story down.

Are the shapes clear in the center?

Do the children separate by rolling, or do they move only slightly without creating the effect of leaving?

Can the group put together a sequence or dance that is fluid and continuous, or does it seem to be broken into segments?

Have children strike a ball with any body part, so that they fall off-balance when they strike it and then roll in the direction that they are falling:

Is the child able to roll in the same direction that she is falling?

Is she able to strike the ball before she rolls?

Do the strike and the roll seem to be one fluid movement?

1. Have them strike the ball so that they have to roll in all directions—backward, sideways, forward.

Can the child strike the ball and roll in any direction? Or does she only strike and roll in a forward direction?

2. Ask them to have a partner throw the ball to them. They try to strike the ball back to the partner and roll afterward—ready to receive the next throw. The partner should throw the ball so that the striker really has to reach for it.

Can the child strike the ball back to the partner?

Can the child roll to recover her movement and strike the next ball, or does she hesitate after one strike?

Have the children throw a ball to a partner so that he has to catch off-balance and roll; the catcher should see if she can get rid of the object back to her partner as she rolls.

Have the children play a teacher-designed game similar to Hot Potato. The children throw and catch in a well-defined area with a line across the middle. Groups play with two on a side. One child throws the ball to the other team, trying to make them catch off-balance. The child who receives the ball must roll as he catches it, but then must get rid of it to his partner or to the other team before he finishes his roll, again trying to make them catch off-balance. Each group works to see how long it can keep the ball going before someone misses.

Is the child able to throw the object accurately back to her partner as she rolls, or do the throws go wildly across the space?

Is the child throwing as she rolls, or does she throw after she has finished the roll?

Are the children forcing each other to catch off-balance?

Are the children getting rid of the ball accurately to the other team or to their partners as they roll?

Can the children recover from their rolls fast enough to play the next throw?

CHAPTER 21
BALANCING

Webster's dictionary defines balance as "stability produced by even distribution of weight on each side of the vertical axis" which is also "an aesthetically pleasing integration of elements." There is no extraneous motion, no flagrant waving of arms to maintain position, no near topple or wobble from side to side. The center of gravity is clearly over the base of support.

STATIC AND DYNAMIC BALANCE
The elementary school child attempting to do a headstand, walk a beam, or ride a skateboard encounters different types of static and dynamic balance challenges. Key teaching concepts in providing balance experiences include these:

1. A wide base of support is easier to balance over than a narrow base.
2. The center of gravity should be aligned over the base of support for stationary balance (see Figure 21.1).
3. Extensions to one side of the body beyond the base of support necessitate extensions in the opposite direction for counterbalance.

Static balance involves maintaining a desired shape in a stationary position. Gymnastics balances, headstands, and handstands are examples. Dynamic balance involves maintaining an on-balance position while moving, starting, or stopping. Dynamic balance occurs in weight transference, jumping, throwing, catching, and all forms of travel. Bal-

Figure 21.1   Center of gravity over base of support

Children can be challenged to balance on a variety of body parts

ance as a concept is found in Chapters Seventeen, Nineteen, Twenty-Two, and Twenty-Four as it applies to learning specific skills.

LEVELS OF SKILL PROFICIENCY

For the child at the precontrol level, achievement of balance is sporadic and is often more coincidental than intentional. Activities at this level are designed to introduce weight-bearing and stillness as prerequisites to balance. Appropriate tasks include using different body parts as bases of support, using wide bases to balance, and maintaining stationary balances.

The child at the control level is ready to focus on holding stationary supports for several seconds, balancing on smaller bases, and maintaining inverted balances. Appropriate tasks include:

Supporting weight on combinations of body parts (for example, head or hands).

Momentarily supporting weight on hands alone.

Balancing on narrow bases or in inverted positions.

Holding stationary balances on various types of large apparatus.

Balancing on four body parts

The child at the utilization level is ready to study balancing on equipment and in dynamic situations, combining balance with locomotion and weight transference. Appropriate tasks include:

Stationary balances combined with actions on benches, tables, and beams.

Nonsymmetrical balances.

Locomotion into handstands and back extensions.

Moving from an on-balance position to an off-balance position.

A nonsymmetrical balance

Balance as studied at the proficiency level is characterized by tasks that focus on maintaining inverted and narrow base balances. Children practice moving rapidly into and out of stationary balances; dynamic balances on high, narrow equipment; and contrasting balance time factors on the floor and on apparatus. Appropriate experiences include:

Extensions away from the body when balanced on a narrow base.

Partner and group balances.

Rapid turns, twists into balanced position.

Mounts on apparatus into an inverted balance.

Dismounts (from apparatus) that conclude with landings in balanced, stationary positions.

The sequence for developing the skill theme of balancing at the precontrol, control, utilization, and proficiency levels is shown in Figure 21.2.

Balancing on a narrow base while extending arms outward

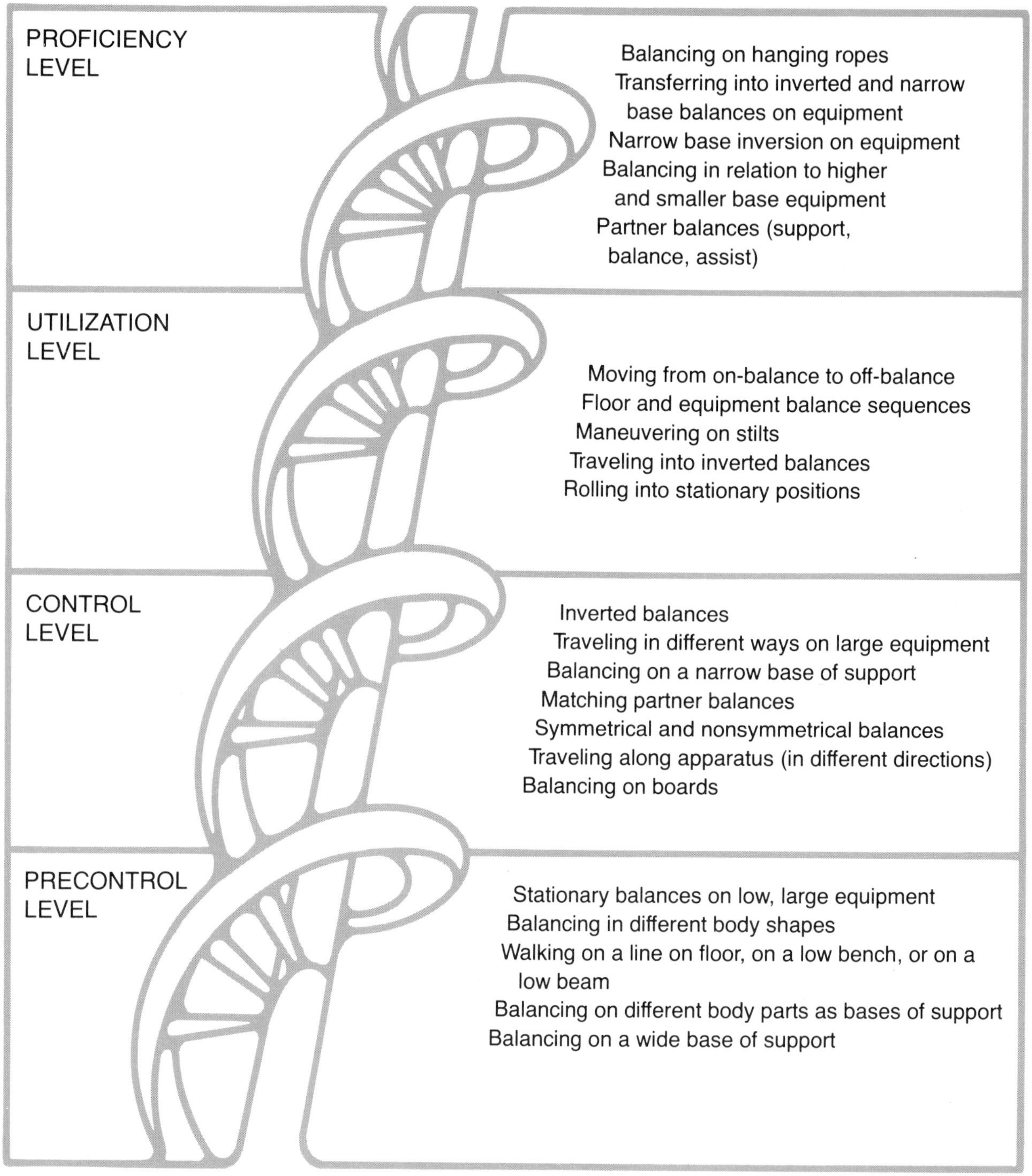

PROFICIENCY LEVEL

Balancing on hanging ropes
Transferring into inverted and narrow
base balances on equipment
Narrow base inversion on equipment
Balancing in relation to higher
and smaller base equipment
Partner balances (support,
balance, assist)

UTILIZATION LEVEL

Moving from on-balance to off-balance
Floor and equipment balance sequences
Maneuvering on stilts
Traveling into inverted balances
Rolling into stationary positions

CONTROL LEVEL

Inverted balances
Traveling in different ways on large equipment
Balancing on a narrow base of support
Matching partner balances
Symmetrical and nonsymmetrical balances
Traveling along apparatus (in different directions)
Balancing on boards

PRECONTROL LEVEL

Stationary balances on low, large equipment
Balancing in different body shapes
Walking on a line on floor, on a low bench, or on a
low beam
Balancing on different body parts as bases of support
Balancing on a wide base of support

Precontrol Level

Overview   Tasks at the precontrol level are designed to provide children with experiences in supporting weight on different body parts, establishing steady bases of support, and maintaining static balances. Children should move from balances that seem coincidental toward being able to choose and maintain simple balance positions on appropriate body parts.

IDEAS FOR DEVELOPMENT

IDEAS FOR OBSERVATIONAL FOCUS

Have children balance on various bases of support—for example, feet and hands, knees and elbows, one hand and one foot.

Do only those parts named as a base touch the floor?

Ask children to think of other body parts that are good bases. Challenge them to hold their balance for "X" seconds.

Can the child hold the balance without waving free body parts in space?

Does the child exhibit appropriate muscular tension to adequately hold the stillness?

Young children enjoy listing all the body parts that can serve as bases of support and labeling them on a large stick figure.

Have children travel through general space, stopping on signal balanced on three body parts.

Is the balance stationary, not tottering between on/off balance?

Challenge children to discover what combinations of three body parts they can balance on as a base.

Is the base sufficient in area to support body weight?

Have them try four, five, two, one.

Are the body parts appropriate for holding weight?

Ask children if their balance is different from the balances of other children who are near them.

Figure 21.2   Sequence for developing the skill theme of balancing

> Sometimes the image "long enough to take a picture of it" helps children know how long to hold a balance.

Ask children to balance on a chosen base of support.

Challenge them to move from a wide body shape to a narrower shape while still balanced on that base of support. For example, they can try to:

1. Move from a round to a twisted shape.
2. Balance on another base of support.
3. Create different body shapes on this base.

Have children travel on the following equipment without losing their balance (see Figure 21.3):

1. Tape line on floor
2. Jump ropes laid in various patterns
3. Length of two-by-four inch plank

Does the child remain on the same body part base for each shape?

Does the child demonstrate an understanding of "base of support"? Of "wide" and "narrow"?

Is stillness maintained for "X" seconds when the shape is created?

Does the child use arms for balance, if needed, without extraneous waving ("flapping wings")?

Does the child travel slowly as opposed to moving across fast?

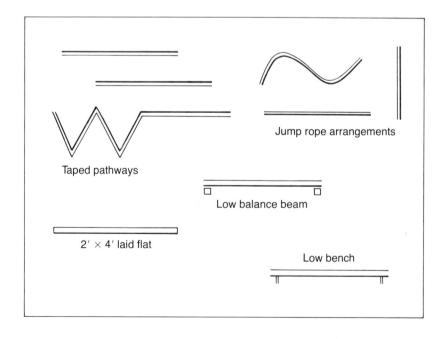

Taped pathways

Jump rope arrangements

Low balance beam

2' × 4' laid flat

Low bench

Figure 21.3   Equipment arrangement for traveling

4. Low balance beam
5. Narrow bench.

Sample tasks include:

1. Travel forward the length without falling off.
2. Travel backward.
3. Walk with arms above head.
4. Walk with beanbag on head.
5. Catch a ball tossed by teacher or older pupil.
6. Toss a ball to someone.

Have children balance on different body parts in relation to various large pieces of apparatus, such as boxes, tables, climbing frames, low balance beams (Figure 21.4), benches (Figure 21.5), and sawhorses (Figure 21.6).

Have children balance on feet, feet and hands, one foot and one knee, et cetera.

Does the child maintain erect posture—shoulders and head up?

Does the child concentrate on the opposite end of the equipment during travel?

Can the child maintain a stationary balance momentarily?

Are different body part combinations used as bases of support?

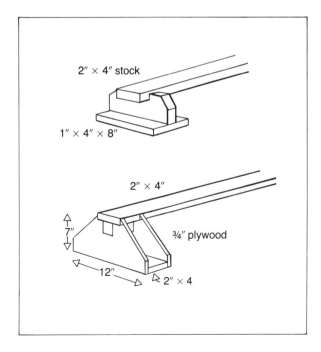

Figure 21.4   Construction of a balance beam

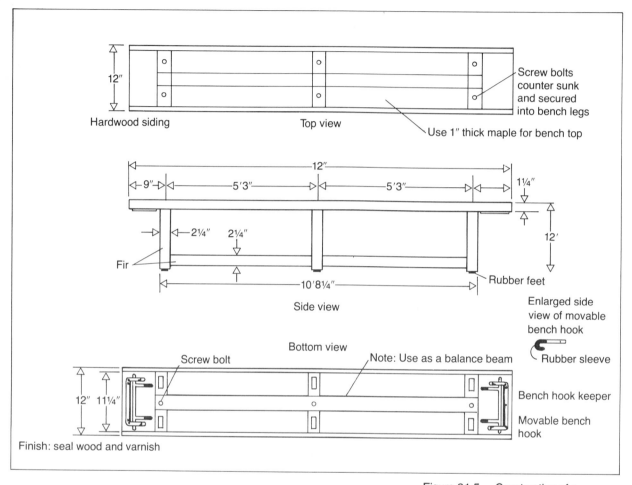

Hardwood siding   Top view

12"

Screw bolts counter sunk and secured into bench legs

Use 1" thick maple for bench top

12"
9"   5'3"   5'3"   1¼"
2¼"   2¼"
Fir
10'8¼"
Rubber feet
12'

Side view

Enlarged side view of movable bench hook

Rubber sleeve

Bottom view
Screw bolt   Note: Use as a balance beam

12" 11¼"

Bench hook keeper

Movable bench hook

Finish: seal wood and varnish

Figure 21.5   Construction of a balance bench

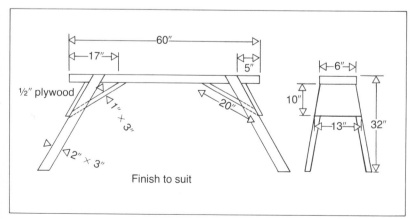

60"
17"
5"
½" plywood
1" × 3"
20"
2" × 3"
10"
6"
13"   32"
Finish to suit

Figure 21.6   Construction of a wooden sawhorse

Control Level

Overview   Experiences at the control level focus on balancing on increasingly smaller bases of support, holding the body in inverted positions, and learning to maintain the stillness and control of a balance. These experiences begin to provide ingredients for a movement repertoire of balances that may be included in sequences involving traveling and other balances.

IDEAS FOR DEVELOPMENT

IDEAS FOR OBSERVATIONAL FOCUS

Challenge children to balance on a balance board (Figure 21.7) without falling off:

1. Have them move their arms high above their heads.
2. Have them slowly move from standing position to low curl.
3. Have them catch and toss a ball while balanced on the board.

Is the center of gravity over the base of support?

Does center remain over the base?

Ask children to travel in different directions on various large pieces of apparatus—benches, tables, or low beams:

Does the center of gravity remain over base when the child is traveling?

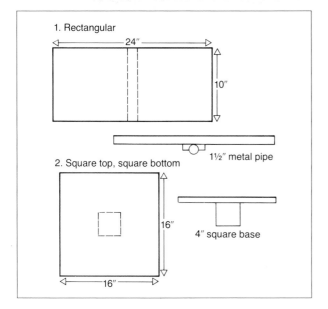

Figure 21.7   Construction of a balance board

1. They can travel forward.
2. They can change from high to low level as they travel.
3. They can travel backward.
4. They can travel, turn, continue travel.

Challenge children to try to travel on stilts. Tin cans and rope can be utilized to build an inexpensive form of stilts (see Figure 21.8). At first, it is a good idea for children to work with a partner. They can help one another get on the stilts and begin to travel.

1. Two holes are cut in the top sides of the cans.

2. Rope is strung through the two holes and tied together.

3. Children put each foot on a can and pull on rope with hands.

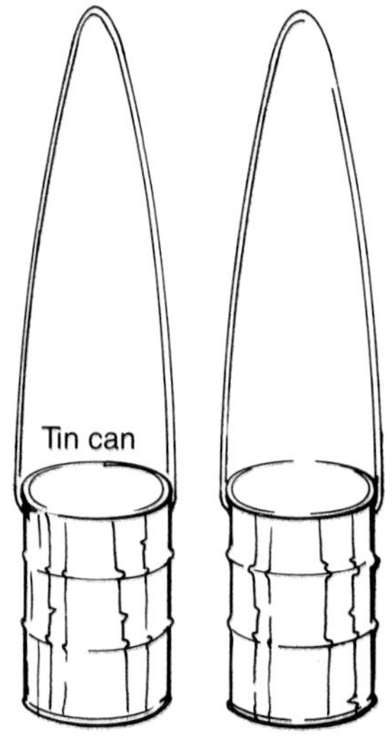

Tin can

Figure 21.8 Construction of tin can stilts

Have children move in relation to various large pieces of equipment. They can try to travel in different ways while maintaining dynamic balance:

1. Travel on four body parts.
2. Roll forward.
3. Hop, gallop, and leap as they travel.
4. Change levels and execute turns.

Can the child maintain balance when alternately traveling and stopping?

Are the arms used to aid balance, or do they cause extraneous movement or extensions into off-balance?

Is the center of gravity lowered when necessary to maintain balance?

Do the youngsters keep their center of gravity above the narrow base of support?

Do they hold their heads erect or look at their feet?

Do they pull the stilts upward with the arm and hand while pressing the foot firmly against the stilts when stepping?

Does the child travel safely (at an appropriate speed to maintain balance) on equipment?

Can child execute travel on floor or mat before attempting action on equipment?

Ask children to balance on a base of support. They slowly begin lifting as much of their body as possible away from the floor, gradually decreasing the size of the base.

Can the child remain stable over the base as it decreases in size?

Is the center of gravity maintained over the base of support?

Ask children how narrow a base they can use and still maintain balance.

Having children use their heads in combination with other body parts, ask them to try to balance on:

1. Head, feet, one hand.
2. Head and knees.
3. Head and hands.
4. Head and forearms.

Does child move slowly into a balanced, still position?

Does child support weight equally on body parts serving as base, as opposed to resting on head?

Are hips centered above shoulders when child is inverted?

Does neck remain tense during balance, as opposed to collapse of muscular tension?

Can the child move safely out of the balance position, particularly if balance is lost?

Challenge children to see how long they can hold their balance in an inverted position (Figure 21.9), on various bases of support:

1. Head/hands.
2. Shoulders and arms.
3. Hands alone.
4. Forearms alone.
5. Feet/hands.

Are the body parts sufficiently strong to support weight?

Has the child demonstrated the ability to curl the spine, tuck in the chin, and roll out of the inversion?

Are hips centered over base of support during inversions?

Is body stretched upward to aid balance and stability?

Balancing on their base of support, children create a symmetrical shape with the total body. Ask them if both sides of the body are exactly the same. Have them change to a nonsymmetrical shape while balanced on that base.

Does the child demonstrate understanding of the difference between symmetrical and nonsymmetrical?

Can the position of the free body parts be changed from symmetrical to nonsymmetrical without changing the base of support?

Ask children to create a sequence by changing from symmetrical to nonsymmetrical shapes while on a base.

Is the balance stable while the child is changing shapes?

Figure 21.9   Inverted balances

Challenge them to balance on different bases of support while creating symmetrical and nonsymmetrical shapes.

Have them create symmetrical and nonsymmetrical shapes while in an inverted balance.

Have them create nonsymmetrical shapes on a narrow base.

Utilization Level

Overview   Experiences at the utilization level include balancing in dynamic environments and transferring weight into stationary, still balances on various bases of support. Tasks that involve sequences of movement, on the floor and on apparatus, are particularly important and valuable. It is important for children to be able to make decisions about the combination of movements and to be able to select and invent ways for one movement to move smoothly into another.

IDEAS FOR DEVELOPMENT

IDEAS FOR OBSERVATIONAL FOCUS

Have children travel into an inverted balance; maintain stationary position for a few seconds; travel out of balance. For example:

1. Roll, balance on hands, roll out of balance.
2. Headstand, roll out.
3. Travel by transferring weight from feet and hands, pause in a handstand, then make a one-quarter turn to transfer weight back to their feet.

Is speed of travel into balance controlled so child does not move center of gravity beyond base in the stationary position?

Does the child have sufficient arm and shoulder strength to take lower body from inverted position to curled spine for rolling?

Using floor mats and low equipment (Figure 21.10), children can try to move into and out of stationary balances. For example:

1. Rock backward into shoulder stand, roll backward

Can the child distinguish between motion and balance? That is, does total body move into balance that is stationary?

Does child move safely out of balance with control, as opposed to collapse?

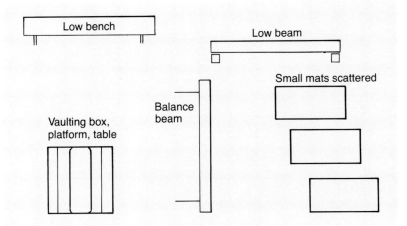

Figure 21.10   Large equipment for balancing

2. Roll backward into a handstand, transfer
   weight to feet
3. Roll on a table or bench into a stationary
   balance

Can child control speed into balance throughout
action?

Have children mount stilts (Figure 21.11) by
stepping down from an elevated position (a step or
chair). Or they can hold a stilt in each hand,
place one foot on one stilt, and hop up with the
other foot.

Have children walk forward, backward, and sideways with the stilts.

Are the children able to walk in a way that
counteracts the tendency to fall forward when
mounting the stilts?

Are the children pulling up with their arms on the
stilts as they walk?

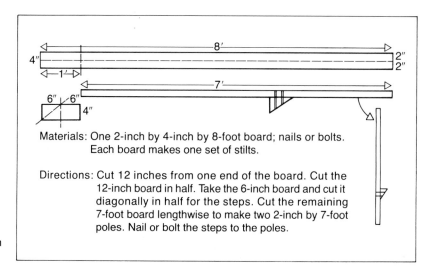

Materials: One 2-inch by 4-inch by 8-foot board; nails or bolts.
Each board makes one set of stilts.

Directions: Cut 12 inches from one end of the board. Cut the
12-inch board in half. Take the 6-inch board and cut it
diagonally in half for the steps. Cut the remaining
7-foot board lengthwise to make two 2-inch by 7-foot
poles. Nail or bolt the steps to the poles.

Figure 21.11   Construction of wooden
stilts

Ask children to combine stationary balances and
weight transfers to travel the length of their mats.
For example:

1. Place weight on hands.
2. Roll in a forward direction.
3. Roll backward, into a headstand or handstand.

Are balances held for at least ＿＿ seconds?

Are muscles firm and taut for balance over base?

Are movements smooth? Are balances controlled by the performer?

Challenge children to create a sequence to show
contrasts in time (fast and slow movements) and
weight (expressing power, delicacy/grace in balances). They can combine the following elements
as they choose:

Can the child distinguish between a balance
and a transfer?

Do balances vary in level?

1. Balances.
2. Weight transfer—hands, head, back, feet to feet.
3. Actions—turning, twisting.

Children can add excitement to their sequence with the following:

1. Changes in levels and directions, and inversion (head at low level and feet at high level, for example).
2. Bases of support using different body parts.
3. Bases of support of different sizes.
4. Extensions away from the center of gravity by arms and legs.

Balancing on equipment in an inverted position

Does the child balance on different bases of support?

Is the child stable on the base of support?

Is child capable of supporting weight on base on floor before attempting balance on equipment?

Is base firmly on equipment?

Can the child make any needed adjustments in

Children can balance in a stable position on each of various pieces of large equipment, such as tables and benches. They can:

1. Balance on different body parts.
2. Gradually decrease the size of their base of support.
3. Balance in an inverted position.

Balancing on a narrow apparatus

4. Balance with their body and free parts forming shapes that are wide, narrow, and twisted.
5. Balance with extensions at different levels, to the side, and high in the air.

Using large apparatus (bars, balance beam, platforms, climbing frames, and vaulting boxes), children can create a sequence of travel. They can include movement onto apparatus, stationary balances, movement between transfers, and a dismount ending in a stationary, balanced position.

base or position if a balance becomes unstable?

Does the child maintain stillness, creating an observable difference between balance and travel on equipment?

Are free body parts used to aid balance by counterbalancing weight in a given direction?

Are a variety of body parts used in the transfers and balances?

This sequence work is for the student who is proficient in balance and weight transference. Previous work in developing sequences, plus experiences with levels, directions, inverted balances, are essential for success.

Proficiency Level

Overview   At the proficiency level, balance is studied in combination with time and weight factors to express contrast in power, stillness, and excitement in sequences. This is done on the floor and on various pieces of apparatus. Children are encouraged to perfect the flow of their movements from one position to another and to develop their use of focus and full extension.

IDEAS FOR DEVELOPMENT

IDEAS FOR OBSERVATIONAL FOCUS

Working with a partner, children can create a stationary balance in which they are partially supporting each other's weight. They can:

1. Change from wide, to narrow, to twisted shapes while supporting each other.
2. Support their partner's weight entirely, and demonstrate matching shapes.
3. Support their partner's weight entirely, so she or he is in an inverted balance.
4. They can explore how many body part combinations can serve as bases of support for the partner. (See Appendix 2.)

Are the children using good mechanics for supporting the additional weight of their partners?

Are they working safely, particularly as they move into and out of the balance positions?

Are changes in the base made without loss of support of either partner?

Do the shapes match?

Do the children use a variety of body parts to support the partner's weight?

Are the chosen supports sturdy and stable?

Working in groups of four, children can create a balance statue in which each person partially supports another. They can:

1. Choose one wide, one narrow, one twisted, and one curled shape.
2. Travel as a moveable monster, maintaining their supporting role and chosen shape.

Does each shape exist clearly within the group?

Is the statue adapted safely for traveling—can the children travel without the shape collapsing dangerously?

Create an obstacle course from hoops, blocks and canes, and cones for the children to travel around and/or over while walking on stilts.

Is the child able to intentionally change the direction of travel by leaning in the appropriate direction?

Have children try to jump while on the stilts.

Is the child able to accurately time a pulling movement of the arms with a straightening of the legs to achieve elevation or flight?

Ask children to stand on one stilt, lift the other leg up, and swing it around.

Is the child able to lean at an appropriate angle to counteract the weight shift from one leg to another?

Have children dismount from large apparatus (beam or table or parallel bars) after maintaining an inverted balance on hands.

Is body stationary for desired balance?

Does the child have control of stationary inversion before beginning turn for transfer to feet?

Does the child keep head up, posture erect for landing on-balance when contacting floor?

In relation to a bench or beam, children can combine travel (turns, rolls) with stationary balances:

1. Using narrow bases.
2. Using inverted balances.

Can the child combine movement and stationary poses on the beam (bench) without losing balance?

Children will benefit from practicing actions
and balances on a tape line, bench, and low beam
before attempting skills on a beam.

Have children approach the vaulting box, use a spring take-off while a body length away, and balance on hands momentarily before continuing over box to feet.

Does the child wait for the center of gravity (usually hips) to move beyond the hands before pushing off with hands for landing on feet?

Have children approach a table, bench, or beam and use a spring take-off to transfer to an inversion, balanced in a handstand.

Does the child have sufficient arm and shoulder strength to support body weight?

Does body bend at beginning of transfer, then stretch to full inverted position?

Is the spring sufficiently controlled to prevent over-balancing while on hands?

While supporting weight with hands, hand and leg, or one hand, children can create balances on a hanging rope (either stationary or swinging; see Figure 21.12).

Does child have secure enough grip and wrap to maintain position on rope?

Is an extension from center of gravity counterbalanced on opposite side?

Creating a balance on a hanging rope

Figure 21.12   Balances on hanging ropes

Although often not readily available, such activities as unicycling, skating, skiing, and surfing
offer children at the proficiency level challenging dynamic balancing experiences. Sometimes
these experiences can be provided during field
trips or after school programs.

CHAPTER 22
WEIGHT TRANSFER

To travel is to transfer weight—walking, running, leaping, rolling, stepping, springing, sliding—on hands, on feet, on different body parts. The infant creeping on trunk and elbows is transferring weight. So is the toddler shifting weight from side to side as he begins to walk unassisted, the gymnast performing a walkover, the Russian dancer executing a series of rapid mule kicks, the athlete poised to shift weight to fake an opponent, and the dancer collapsing to the floor in an expression of grace and control. Locomotion is transfer of weight.

Probably the most common form of weight transfer is that from foot to foot. In its simplest form this is walking. At an advanced level—and when combined with the stretching, curling, twisting actions of flips, layouts, and full body twists—the transfer of weight from foot to foot demands extraordinary kinesthetic awareness, muscular strength, and control.

LEVELS OF SKILL PROFICIENCY
The child at the precontrol level is still trying to achieve control of his body when he transfers weight to different parts. He enjoys traveling on body parts other than feet, and he enjoys exploring apparatus. Activities at the precontrol level include:

1. Traveling on specific body parts (such as feet and seat, or hands and feet).
2. Transferring weight by sliding, slithering, or creeping.

Children at an advanced level can transfer weight using various body parts

The child at the control level is ready to transfer weight onto specific body parts, such as the back for rolling actions, and the hands for inverted balances and travel. Activities at the control level focus on:

1. Transfer as a result of on–off balance.
2. Transfer following steplike and spring take-offs.
3. Transfer of weight onto and off of equipment using different body parts.

The child at the utilization level is ready to transfer weight onto hands for travel and balances, for spring take-offs, and for neck springs and hand springs. At this level, weight is also transferred by rolling. At the utilization level, the child tries movements that combine the transfers onto specific body parts with stretching and twisting. Challenging activities include:

1. Dismounting apparatus with a stretching or twisting action (for example, a cartwheel from a balance beam).
2. A stretched layout prior to mounting apparatus (onto vaulting box).
3. Traveling over apparatus with curling actions.

Transferring weight onto and off equipment using different body parts

Youngsters can travel over, under, and through apparatus, transferring weight to a variety of body parts

The child who is proficient in transferring weight enjoys the transfer from foot to foot with aerial actions between the contacts. He combines stretching, curling, and twisting with flight onto, off of, and over apparatus. Tasks appropriate for children at the proficiency level include:

1. Aerial flip in free floor exercise.
2. Piking (bending while in the air) and twists off apparatus.
3. Transference of body weight to another person.

The full spectrum of weight transfer, from the precontrol level through the proficiency level, is presented in Figure 22–1. The Ideas for Development are stated to imply a direct approach. Alternative ways of developing the ideas beyond the direct end of the spectrum, are discussed in Chapter Four.

Figure 22.1   Sequence for developing the skill theme of transferring weight

PROFICIENCY LEVEL

Transferring weight through sequences on apparatus

Increasing vertical and horizontal distances of weight transfer

Dismounting apparatus, from hands to feet

Transferring weight over high obstacles

UTILIZATION LEVEL

Transferring weight to a partner

Transferring weight on bars

Transferring weight along apparatus

CONTROL LEVEL

Stretching, curling, and twisting between points of contact

Transferring weight from feet to hands

Transferring weight over low obstacles

PRECONTROL LEVEL

Transferring weight across mats or carpet squares

Transferring weight from feet to other body parts without traveling

Traveling on various body parts

Precontrol Level

Overview   Tasks at the precontrol level are designed to provide experiences traveling on various body parts, transferring weight onto and off of small apparatus, and developing an awareness of the body parts best suited for weight transfer.

IDEAS FOR DEVELOPMENT

IDEAS FOR OBSERVATIONAL FOCUS

Have the children travel on body parts other than their feet—for example, feet and seat, hands and feet, and total body log rolls.

Does the child travel on body parts other than feet?

Does the child use different combinations of body parts?

Very young children and those with learning difficulties enjoy (and benefit from) naming the body parts they are using for travel.

Remaining in self-space, the children transfer their weight from feet to other body parts (Figure 22.2), returning each time to their feet:

1. Feet to back to feet.
2. Feet to hands to feet.
3. Feet to head and hands to feet.
4. Feet to other combinations of body parts.

Does the child begin to momentarily take weight on body parts other than feet?

Is the transfer one fluid movement, from feet to other body part to feet, as opposed to feet to stationary balance to return to feet?

Using small mats (or carpet squares) and stretched ropes, the children transfer weight from feet to other body parts as they travel across the obstacle:

1. From feet to hands.
2. From feet rolling forward, then backward.
3. From feet to head and hands, then roll to backward.

Can the child take weight momentarily on parts other than feet?

Does the child use body parts in different combinations?

Does the transfer take the child across the mat or rope?

This task is very important in helping children to learn which body parts can be used to transfer weight.

Figure 22.2   Transfer from feet to
other body parts

Using boxes, crates, blocks and canes, hoops, and milk jugs (Figure 22.3), the children transfer weight from feet to other body parts as they travel over, under, around, through, onto, and off of these objects.

Does the child use body parts other than feet for transfer onto and off of boxes and crates?

Are feet and hands, backs, stomachs, knees, and other body parts used when traveling in relation to equipment?

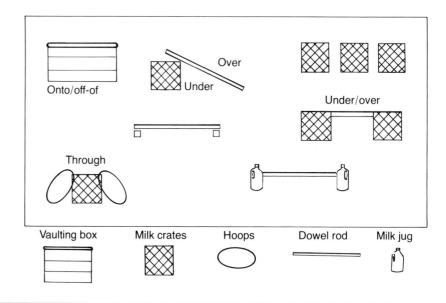

Figure 22.3   Equipment setups for transfer of weight in relation to small equipment

---

Control Level

Overview   Tasks at the control level are designed to help child transfer weight to specific body parts—for example, from feet to back, to hands, to head and hands—in order to travel or balance.

IDEAS FOR DEVELOPMENT

IDEAS FOR OBSERVATIONAL FOCUS

Have the children transfer their weight from feet to hands, then return to feet. Sometimes they can bring their feet down in a new place, sometimes in their original place. Have children try taking off on both feet, on one foot.

Are arms and shoulders strong enough to support the total body weight?

Are the feet going higher than the hips?

Are the hips in line with and over the hands?

Is the transfer to hands downward, not forward from the feet?

Is the head tilted backward for balance?

With the feet stationary, children can twist their bodies in different directions until the off-balance forces a transfer to a new base of support.

Do the feet remain fixed as the trunk rotates?

Is the twist to off-balance sudden or sustained? Can the child do it both ways?

Using different bases of support, children can twist the body in different directions until a transfer is made to a new base. For example, have the children begin on knees and hands, and transfer to a head stand.

Is the twist gradual showing control as the transfer of weight is made? Are a variety of different bases used?

Have the children transfer weight from feet to hands, bringing the feet together in the air; twist the trunk to bring feet down in new place in relation to hands.

Do feet come down with control?

Do feet come down to either side of hands? Beyond them?

Ask the children to transfer weight from feet to hands in combinations:

1. Alternate hands and land on two feet, as in a round-off.
2. Alternate from one hand to another by walking on hands; from two hands to alternate feet as in a cartwheel.

Is there sufficient arm and shoulder strength for support without collapse?

Is there sufficient balance for feet and hands to follow desired path throughout transfer?

Have the children transfer weight from feet to hands, stretching the body while inverted; slowly lower the weight to neck and spine, curling the body to roll to the feet.

Is the head lifted during the stretching action for momentary balance on hands?

Is the chin tucked in toward chest for transfer from hands to rolling action?

Utilization Level

Overview Tasks at the utilization level are designed to teach children to transfer weight onto, over, and from large apparatus. Transfer is now combined with stretching, curling, and twisting with increased periods of time in aerial moves. Emphasis is also placed on the development of more complex sequences involving weight transference.

IDEAS FOR DEVELOPMENT

IDEAS FOR OBSERVATIONAL FOCUS

Using a spring take-off, children can mount various large apparatus by transferring weight

Does the child bend at the knees and push off from the floor?

from feet to feet or to other body parts. For example, they can spring onto bench (beam) and land on feet; spring onto table (vaulting box) and land on lower legs; spring up to high bar and hang by arms.

Do the arms have sufficient strength to pull the body upward or to hold the weight momentarily after the spring?

Do the hands touch the vaulting box before the feet leave the floor?

Does the child keep head and shoulders up to aid balance when transferring?

Is there forward/upward arm swing to assist the spring?

Working in pairs, children can transfer part or all of their weight to a partner.

Are the children placing their weight over the arms and legs of the support person, rather than in the middle of the back?

Are the children being gentle with one another as they mount and dismount?

Dismounting apparatus with a stretching or twisting action

*Children discover many
ways to transfer weight
across large apparatus*

Children should be encouraged to invent new
mounts and to use many body parts for transfers
onto large apparatus.

Using large gymnastics apparatus (such as stationary bars, tables or benches of various heights, a stage, or vaulting boxes), children can travel along the apparatus by transferring weight to various body parts:

1. Feet to back for rolling.
2. Feet to hands (cartwheels, walkovers).

Has the child demonstrated sufficient arm strength to hold body in balance throughout transfer?

Has child repeatedly demonstrated proficiency in this skill on the floor or on apparatus?

Is timing of skill controlled?

The progression in gymnastics is from mats on
floor, to apparatus of large surface and low height,
to increased height and narrow surface.

Ask the children to transfer weight on bars by twisting, curling, and stretching as they move from one bar to another and circle the bars.

Does the child have a firm grip before beginning transfer?

Is thumb curled around bar, or is it lying next to index fingers?

In any curling action, is thumb curled around bar in direction body is to travel?

Proficiency Level

Overview   Tasks at the proficiency level are designed so that children focus on increasing the horizontal and/or vertical distance of the weight transfer. The activities can include intricate maneuvers (twists, curls) of the body and its parts as weight is transferred from and received by different body parts. Appendix 2 describes a Partner Stunt Learning center in which children can work on weight transfer.

IDEAS FOR DEVELOPMENT

IDEAS FOR OBSERVATIONAL FOCUS

Instruct children to approach their mats with a series of quick running steps, spring off two feet and land safely on two feet, very close to the take-off spot. Using this approach and spring take-off, children can transfer their weight from two feet to two hands, returning to two feet (for example, mule kick, handspring).

Does the child bend the legs for power and upward thrust in take-off?

Does the child push with the arms for power and return to feet?

Have children approach their mats with a series of quick steps. After a spring take-off, they can stretch their bodies momentarily in the air before transferring weight to hands.

1. Have the children curl the body in preparation for a rolling action.
2. Have the children gradually increase the distance of transfer from feet to hands either vertically or horizontally.

Does the child demonstrate sufficient arm and shoulder strength for momentary suspension in balance on hands, prior to addition of force that results in increased height or distance?

Challenge children to dismount large apparatus by transferring weight to hands; stretch or twist before landing on feet near apparatus.

Does the child have sufficient shoulder and upper arm strength to support body weight during inversion and transfer?

Does the child adjust to increased height from apparatus to floor by bending knees to absorb impact upon landing?

Try to challenge children to create a sequence of weight transference in relation to their favorite piece of apparatus. This sequence should include approach, weight transfer onto, travel on, and transfer off equipment.

Can the child combine the actions of stretching, twisting, and curling with transfer in relation to apparatus for a sequence that is exciting to view, challenging to perform, and illustrates the transfer potential?

Videotape each sequence and then have children evaluate it. Suggest that children make their stretches fully extended, their curls tightly coiled.

Have children use both fast and slow movements, not the same speed throughout.

CHAPTER 23
KICKING AND PUNTING

Children need many opportunities to practice kicking

A young boy kicking a stone along the sidewalk as he walks home from school, a neighborhood game of kick-the-can, kickball on the school playground at recess, an aspiring athlete practicing the soccer dribble, and the professional punter—all are executing a similar movement, the kick. This movement requires accuracy, body control, point of contact, force, and direction. Some children seem to perform the kick with intense concentration, others effortlessly.

We try to provide children with a variety of opportunities to practice kicking, so that they will develop a foundation of kicking skills that can be used in different situations. We emphasize the development of mature kicking patterns by focusing on experiences designed to elicit mature patterns. Kicking for distance leads to the development of a mature kicking pattern. This is not true of kicking for accuracy.

LEVELS OF KICKING SKILL PROFICIENCY

The child at the precontrol level of kicking is challenged by the task of making contact with a stationary ball. Once the child begins to consistently make contact with a stationary ball, we challenge him to kick the ball for distance. Appropriate precontrol tasks include:

1. Running to kick a stationary ball.
2. Kicking a ball rolled by the teacher (or an older child).
3. Tapping a ball along the ground while moving behind it.

DEVELOPMENTAL STAGES OF KICKING

STAGE 1   The child is usually stationary. There is slight flexion at the knee prior to striking. The slight flexion results in a kick that is a pushing action. There is little follow-through of the kicking foot.

STAGE 2   The body is stationary during initiation of the action. There is increased flexion of the knee of the kicking leg, and this results in a preparatory backward lift of the leg. Opposition of the upper and lower extremities occurs during the motion.

STAGE 3   The preparatory phase involves a deliberate step or steps toward the ball. The striking foot remains near the surface. The trunk is upright. The follow-through may result in child mov-ing beyond point of contact or remaining near point of contact, depending on whether the approach was rapid or cautious.

MATURE KICKING PATTERN   The approach to the ball involves one or more steps, with the distance just prior to the kick covered with a leap. The kicker is airborne in the approach. The knee of the kicking leg is slightly flexed due to the leap just prior to kicking. The trunk is inclined backward prior to and during contact. The momentum of the kick is dispersed by hopping on the support leg and stepping in the direction of the object that was struck.

SOURCES: Adapted from V. Seefeldt & J. Haubenstricker, ''Developmental Sequence of Kicking.'' Mimeographed materials. Presented at the University of Georgia, Athens, Georgia, June 1978.
R. L. Wickstrom, *Fundamental Motor Patterns*, 2nd. ed. (Philadelphia: Lea & Febiger, 1977).

At the control level children are introduced to contacting a ball with different parts of the foot—inside, outside, back, and front. They are also given challenges that involve dribbling with either foot, at various speeds, and in different directions. Appropriate control level activities include:

1. Sending a ball along the ground or through the air to a partner.
2. Kicking toward a target.
3. Making quick kicks.

One youngster tries to keep the ball away from his partner using only the feet—no touching

The child who is at the utilization level of kicking is able to kick for both distance and accuracy. He enjoys and learns from the challenge of one-on-one keep-away situations (trying to prevent another child from getting the ball) that combine the skills of tapping a ball along the ground with the skills needed to dodge an opponent. Dynamic game situations enjoyed at the utilization level can involve:

1. Kicking a ball to a target while on the run.
2. Kicking for accuracy while trying to maneuver around an opponent.
3. Differentiating between high kicks and low kicks.

The child who has reached the proficiency level in kicking enjoys group participation with more players, more complex relationships, and the excitement of strategy development. Sample tasks include:

1. Kicking for a target against defense.
2. Gamelike situations.
3. Kicking at moving targets.

The entire spectrum of kicking experiences, from precontrol through proficiency, is represented in Figure 23.1. This progression has been used as a guideline for developing the tasks that follow. The tasks are stated in terms that imply a direct approach (Chapter Four). Teachers are encouraged to vary the approach, however, according to the purpose of the lesson and the characteristics of the class.

Precontrol Level

Overview   At the precontrol level we want children to be able to make consistent contact with a stationary ball. When they are able to do this, we progress gradually to kicking a ball rolled by a skilled roller and tapping a ball gently along the ground.

IDEAS FOR DEVELOPMENT

IDEAS FOR OBSERVATIONAL FOCUS

Balls are placed around the play area, as shown in Figure 23.2. Children kick a large stationary ball so that it travels far away.

Where on the ball is contact made?

With what part of the foot was contact made?

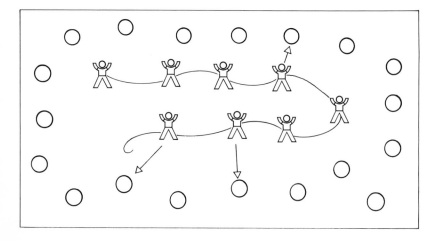

Figure 23.1   Sequence for developing the skill theme of kicking

Figure 23.2   Room arrangement for the approach and kick of a stationary ball

Ball   Pathway of child's travel
◯   ────────────────

Pathway of kicked ball   Children
────────▷   👤

PROFICIENCY LEVEL

Aerial kicking
Mini-games involving kicking
(for example, soccer and speedball)
Kicking for offensive maneuvers
combining pathway, force, relationship
Gamelike situations—one-on-one,
two-on-one, two-on-two, etcetera
Kicking for target against defense
Kicking for small, moving target

UTILIZATION LEVEL

Tap-kicking to self from low to
high level—foot to head
Tapping against defense—one-on-one
Combinations of tapping, traveling, and
kicking for accuracy
Kicking in expressive dance (as in
shadow karate or mime)
Kicking moving ball with moving partner,
both sending and receiving

CONTROL LEVEL

Kicking with stationary partner—sending/
receiving on the ground and in the air
Kicking a ball to different levels
Kicking balls received from different directions
Kicking in different directions in relation to body
Kicking with different parts of the foot
for distance or accuracy
Kicking at a target
Tapping a ball around obstacles
and along pathways

PRECONTROL LEVEL

Kicking a rolling ball from a stationary position
Tapping a ball along the ground and moving with it
Kicking for distance
Approaching a stationary ball and executing a kick
Kicking a stationary ball from a stationary position

Children stand behind the ball and kick it to the far wall or across the play area.

Can the child balance on the support foot long enough to execute the kick? Does the child exhibit flexion of the knee prior to contact and a follow-through of the kicking leg?

Children tap the ball lightly so it travels a short distance—three or four feet.

Numbering the balls 1, 2, 3, 4, et cetera will eliminate confusion about which ball belongs to whom.

Have the children approach the ball from a distance and kick it as far as they can.

Is visual contact with the ball maintained throughout the approach and contact?

Challenge the children to travel through general space. On signal each child approaches the stationary ball nearest him and kicks it to the wall (outside or over a boundary). Each child retrieves his ball and places it, and gets ready to travel again.

Is contact made while the body is still behind the ball, not after the child is over the ball?

Children can tap the ball gently as they travel around the room, keeping it within three to four feet. Ask them to tap with either foot as they travel.

Does the child adjust speed and force to maintain proper distance from the ball?

Very young children enjoy eight-inch plastic balls. Playground and kickballs can be partially deflated for beginning practice and for use indoors.

Ask children to roll their ball to the wall; when it rolls back from the rebound, they kick it to the wall.

Does the child assume a ready position for kicking as the ball approaches, or does he wait until it reaches him?

Have children kick a ball that is slowly rolled to them by another person—a teacher, older student, or peer.

Do the eyes remain focused on the ball throughout the roll?

The purpose of this activity is to contact a rolling ball. Children in the precontrol level are concerned with contacting the ball, not with force or accuracy. They enjoy having the balls go all over.

Control Level

Overview At the control level we provide a variety of kicking experiences that include kicking for accuracy, kicking in different directions, and partner relationships. Use of different parts of each foot and greater control of speed and direction are encouraged.

IDEAS FOR DEVELOPMENT

IDEAS FOR OBSERVATIONAL FOCUS

Have children approach a stationary ball and kick it as hard as they can.

Is the child executing a leaping action, with trunk leaning backward, prior to and at contact?

Have the children kick the ball so it travels through the air.

Ask children to kick so that it travels far but remains on the ground.

Is the child contacting the ball slightly under the middle of the ball for aerial travel? Above the middle for surface travel?

Establish target areas at various distances. Have children kick the ball in the air so that the ball lands (initial ground contact) within that area.

Does the child demonstrate a mature kicking pattern (see Developmental Stages of Kicking) while varying the amount of force according to the distance?

Areas may be marked by tape, string, or weighted jugs. Some children enjoy the increased demand for accuracy that is created by a smaller target formed with cones or hula hoops.

Have the children kick the ball along the ground so that it travels between the goal markers. They can vary their distance from the goal— sometimes to the side of the goal, not always directly in front.

Does the child make contact below or above the midpoint of the ball?

Does the child increase the force of the kick with distance from the goal?

The force required to kick a ball for accuracy is initially different from that required to kick for distance

Dribbling a ball around obstacles requires intense concentration

---

Weighted jugs, cones, or tape marks on the wall can serve as goals. The width of the goal is varied according to the individuals' abilities.

Challenge children to tap the ball with either foot as they travel through general space, increasing and decreasing their rate of speed.

Is control maintained when speed increases?

Is the child able to tap the ball lightly and also travel?

As they travel, children can try to contact the ball with either foot and also with both the inside and outside of the feet to send it in different directions.

Encourage children to travel and tap at their own rate of speed. On signal, they can run beyond the ball to tap gently with the heel, quickly turn and continue travel with controlled dribble.

Does the child use the nonpreferred foot as often as the preferred foot? Is the distance and direction controlled by the child, or does the child follow the ball wherever it leads?

Can the child control the force and direction of the heel tap? Can he turn quickly without losing the ball?

This is a favorite of children who have control of the dribble. Its application to games and strategy need to be emphasized.

Ask the children to travel and tap along curved, zigzag, and straight pathways, as though dodging opponents, angling in for a shot, or going directly toward the target.

Does the child maintain control regardless of the pathway traveled?

Is the child able to make the ball travel in curved and zigzag pathways?

Have children travel and tap at the speed and in the pathway needed to avoid contacting any obstacles—scattered plastic jugs, hula hoops, or cones.

Tell the children that you will give each of them 100 points. On signal they begin traveling. Each time the ball contacts an obstacle, they are to subtract 25 points. Challenge them to try to keep 100 points until the stop signal is given.

Does the child alternate so that he or she uses both the left foot and the right foot?

Can the child control the ball with his feet, yet increase his speed as he practices?

Have the children kick a stationary ball to a facing partner so the partner can stop the ball with his foot or catch the ball with his hand. Vary the distance between the partners.

Does the ball travel to the partner, not haphazardly through space?

Is the child kicking the ball along the ground and also varying the distance of the kicks?

Utilization Level

Overview   The focus at the utilization level is on providing experiences for applying kicking skills in unpredictable situations of increasing complexity. Performing skills on the move and in relation to an opponent are important challenges. A great degree of accuracy and control are desired at this level.

IDEAS FOR DEVELOPMENT

IDEAS FOR OBSERVATIONAL FOCUS

Suggest that the children kick the ball to a partner who is standing to the left, to the right, and at various angles from the kicker.

Does the child use both the right foot and the left foot for passing as well as both the inside and outside of each foot? Does he or she use sufficient force? Can the child control direction of the ball?

Have the children kick the ball along the ground to a partner as the partner is traveling.

Does the child anticipate the movement (speed) of the partner, so the ball does not go behind the receiver?

This activity of passing, traveling, and avoiding others is a favorite of children. The activity is continuous, so the time between rest signals should be short.

Tell the children to travel at their own speed, tapping the ball while avoiding the obstacles (see Figure 23.3). When they reach open space, have them kick for the goal. They get one kick for the goal, then they retrieve the ball.

Can the child combine gentle tapping and increased force for kicking?

Can the child convert quickly from tapping (dribbling) to kicking?

1. Suggest that the children vary their travel by tapping and kicking when they choose.
2. The children begin by tapping gently; on teacher's signal, they tap quickly to open space and then kick.

Figure 23.3   Room arrangement for combination dribble and kick with varying degrees of force

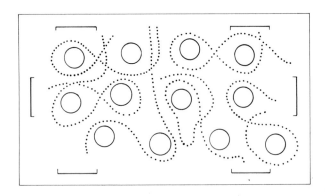

◯ Hoops, jugs, canes [Goals taped on floor or painted on grass with spray paint

Children are encouraged to travel while tapping around obstacles, moving continuously. They should not stand and wait for the signal to kick for the goal.

Have the children travel while tapping a ball and kicking to a partner. They should vary the speed of their travel and adjust the force of the kick to the distance of the partner. There are two objectives:

1. To kick *to* the partner whether he is to the left or right, in front of or in back.
2. To avoid bumping another person or letting the ball bump another ball. Control is the key.

Challenge the children to travel while maintaining control of the tap, so the partner cannot gain possession of the ball by using her feet.

Alternatively, challenge the children to gain possession of the ball the partner is tapping, by gently kicking it away. They must do so without touching the person; contact only the ball.

Working with a partner, the children can kick the ball gently (tap, dribble) until within scoring range, then kick for the goal. They could first cooperate with the partner, passing and scoring. Later they may choose to let one partner become the defense, trying to gain possession of the ball and/or prevent the scoring.

Have the children maintain control of the ball by tapping within fixed boundaries:

1. Children must keep traveling when in possession of the ball.
2. Opponent gains possession of the ball by taking it away with feet.
3. If ball travels outside boundaries, the person who kicked it out loses possession.

Boundaries: Use tape marks on floor, cones, or jugs to designate a square or rectangular area.

Have the children play one-on-one games involving tapping, kicking for goal using jugs, hula hoops, cones, and tape marks on wall.

Does the child maintain control of the ball, keep on balance during the activity?

Can the child combine the isolated skills—kicking in different directions and using the force, speed, and pathways needed to avoid others in an activity situation? Or are the skills forgotten in the activity?

Does the child combine tapping with travel or just kick the ball far away?

Is the force strong enough to move the ball away but not out of range of control?

Does the child use the skills appropriately when involved in the activity? Does he utilize a mature kicking pattern? (See Developmental Stages of Kicking.)

Is the child able to tap (dribble) the ball gently and still maintain control?

Does she keep her body between the ball and the opponent?

Is the child able to gain and maintain control of the ball?

Does he need additional practice in noncompetitive kicking situations?

Each child working alone gently taps the ball from low to high level, contacting it first with the foot, then with the head. Children can practice in self-space, then while traveling.

Is the child able to combine accuracy (contacting ball below midpoint) with light force to keep the ball close to the body while changing levels?

Proficiency Level

Overview   We provide children at the proficiency level with opportunities for using the skill of kicking in group games and for learning the strategy of offensive/defensive participation. Children play games they make up or games the teacher chooses. These games involve relationships that are made increasingly complex by the number of players and the types of strategies required.

IDEAS FOR DEVELOPMENT

IDEAS FOR OBSERVATIONAL FOCUS

Have the children begin kicking at a target that is approximately six feet wide. They record their scores for ten trials. After each series of kicks, reduce the width of the target by one foot until the target is only two feet wide. They record ten trials for each target size. Challenge them to try to make their scores for a two-foot wide target as good as for the six-foot target.

Is the mature kicking pattern evident as the size of the target is decreased?

Suspend a hula hoop from a rope; either hang the target from a frame or have a partner hold the rope. Swing the rope so the target is moving from left to right. Have the children kick for the target as the suspended circle is moving.

Does the child initiate the kick and adjust the force to correctly time the arrival of the ball to the target?

In small groups of four or six (two or three on offense and two or three on defense), children can take turns being on offense and defense. Set up a goal using cones, jugs, or hoops, and decide on boundaries. Each child on offense must kick the ball before a kick for the goal can be made. Children change from offense to defense after a goal is made or after a specified amount of time. Tell them to keep score only if they want to.

Are there any specific kicking skills in which the child is not proficient?

Teach Soccer Keep-Away.

Objective: To keep the ball away from the opponents.

Is the child able to pass the ball to a teammate? Can the child control the ball by dribbling away from an opponent?

Rules:
1. There are two teams, with three to six children on each team.
2. The game is begun by throwing the ball out into the playing area.
3. The team with the ball taps or passes the ball to keep it away from the other team.

Is the game simply a matter of kicking the ball hard and chasing after it? Or are the children actually controlling the ball?

Teach Alley Soccer (see Figure 23.4).

Objective: To score goals by kicking the ball into a goal area.

Are the children using the kicking skills as taught? Or are they simply running and kicking without passing to a teammate?

Rules:
1. There are twelve players, six on each team, including the goalie.
2. Players may not cross their alley lines, but may move the length of their alley.
3. The size of the field is determined by the available playing field.
4. Players rotate from alley to alley periodically.

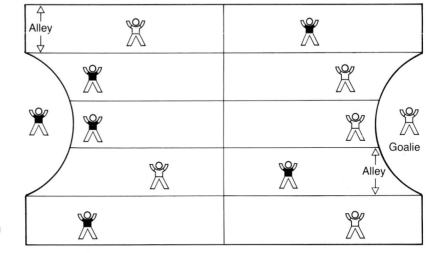

Figure 23.4   Alley soccer

🌟 Players on one team

🌟 Players on other team

You may want to have some children play a game like Alley Soccer (proficiency level) while other children practice different types of kicking. Rarely are all the children in a class ready for a game of this type at the same time (see Chapter Eleven).

Teach Cone Soccer (see Figure 23.5).

Objective: To kick a ball in order to hit the other team's cone or knock it over.

Rules:
1. Two cones (one to be defended by each team) are placed at opposite ends of the playing area and surrounded by a circle that is ten feet in diameter.
2. Team size can range from two to six.
3. Children may not touch each other or use their hands to stop the ball.
4. Infractions result in a free kick from the spot of the infraction. Everyone must be three yards away.
5. No one is allowed inside the circle.

Strategy is important in this game. How well are the children able to figure out a workable approach to defending their own cone and attacking the other team's cone?

Dimensions of the playing area are adjusted to the size of the available area and the number of players.

Figure 23.5   Cone soccer

Teach Aerial Soccer (may be cooperative or competitive).

Objective: To keep the small ball in the air by using the soccer skills of heading, instep and toe kicking, and foot to head taps.

Equipment: 6-inch woven bamboo ball or one of similar size, weight, and texture.

This game was observed at Regents Park in London, England. It is exciting for observers and challenging for highly skilled soccer players.

LEVELS OF PUNTING SKILL PROFICIENCY

Punting is a form of kicking; a ball is released from the hands and kicked while it is in the air. This is a difficult skill for children to master. The punt involves a complex coordination of body movements—moving the body forward, dropping the ball accurately, and kicking it before it reaches the ground. For this reason we have found it best to introduce the punt after children have practiced other types of kicking.

Punting is a difficult skill for children to master

DEVELOPMENTAL STAGES OF PUNTING

STAGE 1   The child is in a stationary position. There is flexion at the hip and knee of the punting leg. The ball is held at waist height or above and may be manipulated by (a) tossing it upward and forward, (b) holding it in both hands, or (c) bouncing it and attempting contact as it rebounds.

STAGE 2   The child is stationary during the preparatory phase. The ball is held in both hands and either dropped or tossed forward or upward in preparation for contact. The punting leg is flexed at the knee. As the punting leg moves forward, its momentum may carry the child forward a step. But usually the force is upward, causing the punter to step backward after contact with the ball.

STAGE 3   The child moves forward deliberately one or more steps in preparation for punting the ball. The ball is usually released in a forward and downward direction. The knee is flexed 90° or less. The follow-through of the kicking leg usually carries the punter forward.

MATURE PUNTING PATTERN   The child makes a rapid approach of one or more steps that culminates in a leap just before contact. If a leap does not precede contact, the forward momentum may be enhanced by a large step. The ball is contacted at or below knee level as a result of the ball having been released in a forward and downward direction. The momentum of the swinging leg carries the punter upward off the surface and forward after contact.

SOURCES: Adapted from V. Seefeldt & J. Haubenstricker, "Developmental Sequence of Punting." Mimeographed materials. Presented at the University of Georgia, Athens, Georgia, June 1978. R. L. Wickstrom, *Fundamental Motor Patterns,* 2nd ed. (Philadelphia: Lea & Febiger, 1977)

When children first try to punt, they toss the ball upward and then kick it with the knee or leg rather than the foot. Often the novice punter may try to contact the ball after it bounces. Children at the precontrol level are provided with round, lightweight balls and challenged to contact them with the foot before they touch the ground. At this level we emphasize dropping the ball rather than tossing it, and moving forward to make contact rather than standing in one place.

When a child continually contacts the ball with his foot before it hits the ground, we begin to provide control level experiences to expand the basic skill. These include:

1. Punting for distance.
2. Punting for height.
3. Punting different types of balls.
4. Punting for accuracy.

At the utilization level, experiences are designed to combine punting with other factors. Appropriate activities include:

1. Punting to a partner.
2. Catching and punting within a limited time.

At the proficiency level children are able to punt in relation to unpredictable, dynamic situations, such as might occur in a football or a rugby game.

Ideas for varying the contexts in which the skill of punting can be practiced are presented in the pages that follow (see also Figure 23.6). As in previous chapters, you are encouraged to alter the method of organization, as suggested in Chapter Four.

Precontrol Level

Overview   At the precontrol level we focus on providing children with repeated opportunities for dropping a ball, contacting it before it touches the ground, and sending the ball in the intended direction. The goal is for the child to consistently contact the ball with his foot before the ball hits the ground.

IDEAS FOR DEVELOPMENT

IDEAS FOR OBSERVATIONAL FOCUS

Have the children drop the ball to the surface and contact it with the foot as it rebounds. Use round plastic balls or slightly deflated round rubber balls.

Does the child drop the ball, rather than tossing it?

Is visual contact with the ball maintained from the moment of drop to contact with foot?

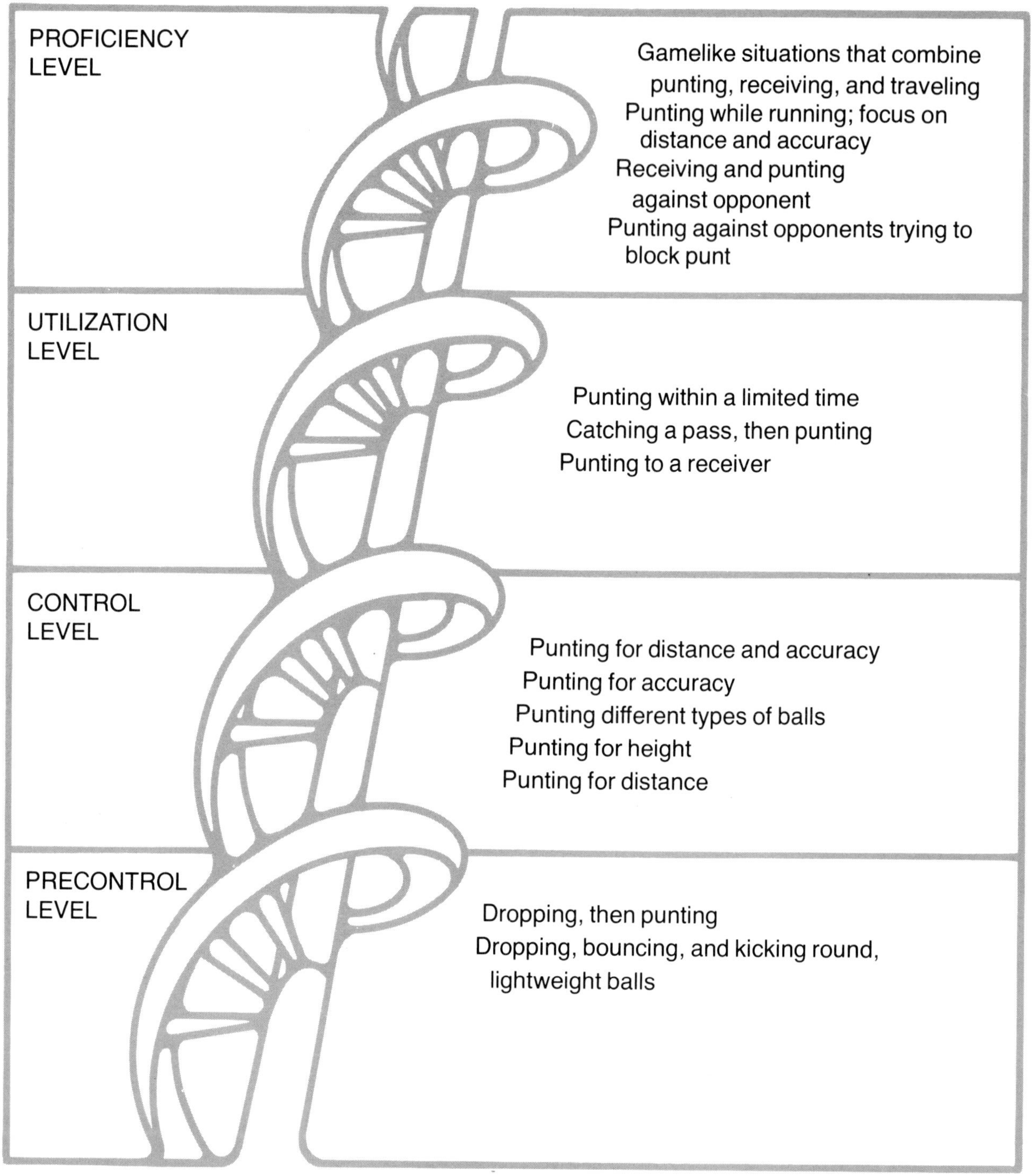

PROFICIENCY LEVEL

Gamelike situations that combine
punting, receiving, and traveling
Punting while running; focus on
distance and accuracy
Receiving and punting
against opponent
Punting against opponents trying to
block punt

UTILIZATION LEVEL

Punting within a limited time
Catching a pass, then punting
Punting to a receiver

CONTROL LEVEL

Punting for distance and accuracy
Punting for accuracy
Punting different types of balls
Punting for height
Punting for distance

PRECONTROL LEVEL

Dropping, then punting
Dropping, bouncing, and kicking round,
lightweight balls

The purpose of this task is to allow the teacher to observe the drop and also to ascertain the child's ability to visually track a ball. At this time we are not concerned about where the ball travels or how much force is used.

Challenge the children to drop and contact the ball with the part of the foot covered by shoelaces before the ball reaches the ground.

Holding the ball between both hands, the children try to take a series of steps, drop the ball, and punt it far away.

Is the ball released in a forward and downward direction?

Is contact made below waist level?

Does the nonsupporting leg swing with enough force to send the object through space?

Is the swing of the nonsupporting leg of sufficient force to carry the child upward and forward after contact?

Control Level

Overview   At the control level children need opportunities to punt different types of balls to develop increasing distance and consistency. These factors are focused one at a time rather than in combination. Distance is emphasized, for example, and then accuracy is emphasized.

IDEAS FOR DEVELOPMENT

IDEAS FOR OBSERVATIONAL FOCUS

Have the children practice punting with a foam football, trying to contact the ball with their shoelaces. The point of the football should be facing the direction they want the ball to travel.

Is the child able to drop the football so that it faces in the appropriate direction?

Is the contact made with the toe of the foot? The lower shin? The instep?

When working with children in elementary schools we use only foam footballs. They have all the advantages of rubber or leather footballs, but children are less afraid to catch them because they do not hurt. And foam footballs are less expensive, so we can make more practice opportunities.

Figure 23.6   Sequence for developing the skill theme of punting

Challenge the children to punt the ball as far as possible. Mark the spot with a colored streamer or brightly painted jug. Suggest that they find out how many times they can punt that distance.

Does the ball travel through the air at approximately a 45° angle for distance, as opposed to a maximum height with little forward direction?

When a new factor (distance) is added, children may modify their kicking patterns. Verbal clues (for example, "drop the ball," or "move forward for contact") may be needed by some individuals.

When children can consistently (eight or ten times in a row) punt a particular distance, have them increase the distance they are attempting to achieve.

Does the child take a series of steps prior to contact?

Is the kicking foot at the appropriate angle when contact is made?

Is contact made when the kicking leg is at an angle for 45° flight (not too soon, resulting in a high punt, or too late, resulting in a low punt)?

Using colored tape, spray paint, or cones, mark lines of varying distances. Be sure that the nearest is within punting distance of the poorly skilled, the farthest is just out of range for the most skilled. Areas may be color coded or numbered.

Does the child use a series of steps plus a leap in the approach?

Is the ball dropped, not tossed?

Have children approach the kicking line and punt the ball for maximum distance. Each child can keep track of her progress.

Is visual contact with the ball maintained until physical contact is made?

Does the force carry the child forward and upward after contact?

Challenge children to punt the ball as high as they can. Have them see if they can punt it so high that they can catch the ball before it hits the ground.

Is the child contacting the ball above waist level?

Is the point of contact on the bottom of the ball?

Because of the hazards of running to catch while looking upward, this needs to be done in a large outdoor field space. If such a space is unavailable, some children can practice punting for height while others practice punting for distance.

Ask the children to punt the ball so that it lands (not stops) consistently in the intended accuracy zone five out of ten times, eight out of ten times, ten out of ten times. Increased accuracy may be attained by adapting the accuracy zone areas outlined for distance punting (Figure 23.7).

1. Have children punt for consistency into broad zone, full width of area.
2. Have children punt for accuracy into left or right portion of zone.
3. Have children punt for accuracy into left-right-farthest distance.

Does the child increase or decrease force according to desired distance?

Does the child use a mature punting pattern whether accuracy target is near to or far from point of contact?

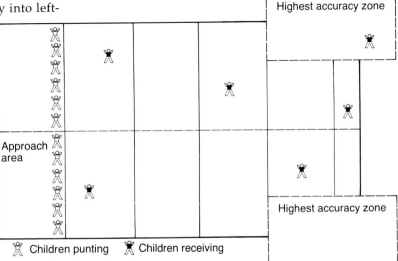

Figure 23.7   Accuracy zones for punting

Utilization Level

Overview   At the utilization level we provide punting experiences in dynamic situations. This encourages children to use punting skills in combination with other factors, such as time and accuracy. Relationships with a partner may be stressed by focusing on punting so that a partner can catch the ball or punt shortly after receiving a throw from a partner.

IDEAS FOR DEVELOPMENT

IDEAS FOR OBSERVATIONAL FOCUS

Have the children punt the ball to a partner so that he or she can catch it. They should choose a distance over which they can successfully punt and catch.

Does the child use a mature punting pattern when a partner is involved?

Is force adjusted appropriately to the distance from partner?

During this task, the teacher's observational focus is on the punter, not on the catcher.

Challenge children to try to punt *to* the partner—not beyond him, to the right, or left—so that the partner can catch the ball.

Does punt contact consistently come off top of foot rather than off the side?

Have children choose a partner. Ask them to receive a pass from their partner, then punt the ball, seeing if they can make their punt less than "X" seconds after the catch.

Is there a leap before contact is made?

Is there an approach before contact?

Is the ball dropped, not tossed, when the punt is hurried?

Challenge children to receive a pass that travels fifteen to twenty feet from the partner; then punt before the partner can cross the punter's approach circle (see Figure 23.8).

Does the child execute a mature punt—approach, drop, follow-through—when under pressure of a time limit?

Does the ball travel in the desired direction when the punt is executed quickly?

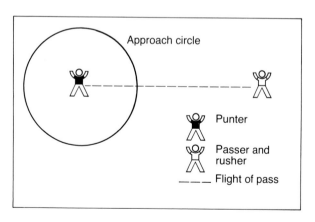

Figure 23.8   Partner pass and rush punting

Some children will enjoy developing point systems and mini-games for each task. Others will be content to practice the skill in the changing situation.

Proficiency Level

Overview   Punting experiences at the proficiency level will lead to the ability to punt accurately and for distance in dynamic and unpredictable situations. The relationships will be more complex. Emphasis is on punting while traveling and on working with others in game situations.

IDEAS FOR DEVELOPMENT

IDEAS FOR OBSERVATIONAL FOCUS

In a small group (for example, two on two), half the children receive a pass from a partner and punt before the opponents (from a distance of fifteen to twenty feet) can rush to tag them or block the kick. Opponents cannot rush until punter receives pass.

Does the punt include approach steps, leap, drop, and follow-through when others are rushing to block?

Have the children punt while running.

1. Ask them to try to increase their distance.
2. Ask them to try to increase their accuracy.
3. Suggest that they practice with a partner who tries to prevent the punt without touching them—he can only touch the ball. (This can be made into a game if desired. Score can be kept and a system of rotation devised.)

Are the children able to drop the ball to account for their speed of travel, so they still make contact with their instep rather than on the side of the foot or the shin?

Have children play Punt Over (see Figure 23.9)

Objective: To punt the ball into or over the opponents' end zone

Rules: 1. There are two or three players on each team.
2. Children take turns punting, using a foam football.
3. When the other team punts, opponents try to catch the ball. If they catch the ball, they take three giant steps toward the opponents' end zone before the next punt.
4. If the ball is missed, it is punted from wherever it is recovered.

Are the end zones adjusted so that they are appropriate for the children playing the game—not so far apart that there are no scores, or so close that there is a score every time?

5. The game *can* be scored as follows:
   One point if the ball is punted over
   the opponents' end zone. No points if
   the ball is caught in the end zone.
   One point if it is missed in the end
   zone.

Figure 23.9   Punt over

CHAPTER 24
THROWING AND CATCHING

Throwing and catching go together just as nicely as soup and sandwich. The two skills, however, are opposite in movement focus and unusually difficult for young children to master.

Although throwing and catching are complementary, we have learned that children have limited success in combining throwing and catching in game situations, unless each skill has been given specific attention and developed in appropriate practice situations. It is important for the teacher to be certain that children can throw *and* catch with relative success before progressing to the utilization and proficiency levels. Activities at those levels—throwing to a running partner, or trying to prevent an opponent from catching a ball—require mature throwing and catching skills.

LEVELS OF THROWING SKILL PROFICIENCY

Throwing is a basic movement pattern performed to propel an object away from the body. Although the style (overhand, underhand, sidearm) and purpose may vary, the basic pattern remains consistent:

1. An object to be sent away is grasped with one or both hands.
2. In a preparatory phase, momentum builds for the throw.
3. The actual propulsive phase—the release of the object—is performed.
4. In a follow-through phase, the body maintains control and balance while using up the momentum of the throw.

Throwing and catching complement each other and are taught together

The teacher can assess catching abilties by observing the youngsters while they toss and catch yarn balls

The catching abilities of young children vary

The physical educator in an elementary school setting observes a wide range of throwing abilities among a class of twenty-five children. Initially, the teacher focuses on ascertaining the skill level of each child. When the youngsters manipulate objects such as beanbags or yarn balls, the teacher can observe individual children for significant developmental characteristics.

DEVELOPMENTAL STAGES OF THROWING

STAGE 1   The throwing motion is essentially in a forward direction. The feet usually remain stationary. The force to propel the object is produced almost exclusively by arm movement—primarily forearm extension. There is little or no trunk rotation.

STAGE 2   The hips, spine, and shoulders rotate as one unit. During the preparatory phase, the hand grasping the object is placed behind the head. The child may step forward with either leg, and the throwing arm is brought forward across the body. The arm is continually held in an extended position, giving the appearance of a sling motion.

STAGE 3   The arm and leg on the same side of the body provide the action. The object to be thrown is placed in a position above the shoulder as the leg steps forward. Little or no rotation of the spine or hips occurs in preparation for the throw. The follow-through phase includes flexion of the hip, and the trunk rotates toward the opposite side.

STAGE 4   The leg opposite the throwing arm moves forward as the arm is moved above the shoulder (windup). There is little or no rotation of the hips and spine during the windup phase. The motion of the trunk and arm resemble those of stages one and three. The stride forward of the leg opposite the throwing arm provides a wide base of support and greater stability during the force production phase of the throw.

MATURE THROWING PATTERN: The windup phase begins with the throwing hand moving in a downward arc and then backward as the opposite leg moves forward. The hips and spine rotate into a position for forceful derotation. As the foot opposite the throwing arm strikes the floor, the hips, spine, and shoulders begin derotating in sequence. The leg opposite the throwing arm begins to extend at the knee, providing an equal and opposite reaction to the throwing arm. The arm opposite the throwing limb also moves forceably toward the body to assist in equal and opposite reaction.

SOURCES: Adapted from V. Seefeldt & J. Haubenstricker, "Developmental Sequence of Throwing." Mimeographed materials. University of Georgia, Athens, Georgia, June 1978.
R. L. Wickstrom, *Fundamental Motor Patterns,* 2nd ed. (Philadelphia: Lea & Febiger, 1977).

Throwing at a target

After making a gross assessment of each child's development in throwing, the teacher has a basis for structuring appropriate instructional tasks (Figure 24.1).

For children at the precontrol level, the first tasks are designed to provide a multitude of throwing experiences. Many of these experiences are designed to elicit distance throws, in which children use more mature throwing patterns.

We expose children at the control level to various contexts, so that they use throwing actions in different but relatively static situations:

1. Throwing fast/throwing slow.
2. Varying the distance of throws.
3. Throwing under/throwing over (a net or other obstacle).
4. Tossing a bean bag at a target.
5. Throwing a yarn ball through a hoop.
6. Throwing a foam ball into a basket.

When children begin to focus primarily on hitting a target, they sometimes regress and use inefficient throwing patterns. Generally, longer throws elicit mature throwing patterns. Thus, it is a good idea to vary distance, sometimes fostering success at hitting the target, other times enhancing the development of a mature throwing pattern.

Once the children are able to perform smooth throwing actions in a variety of static contexts, they are ready for utilization level experiences. At this level, children are provided with tasks that encourage refinement of skills and an increase in the breadth of throwing abilities. Appropriate activities include:

1. Throwing accurately while running.
2. Throwing at a dodging target (for example, a partner).
3. Throwing at a goal while off the ground.
4. Throwing a frisbee accurately.

Children are at the proficiency level of throwing when they are able to effectively throw in the unpredictable contexts of gamelike situations and are ready to study throwing as it is used in the relatively complex and changing environments that characterize sports. Appropriate tasks include:

1. Throwing a ball at a target (for example, basketball goal) as an opponent attempts to block and deflect the throw.
2. Throwing a ball to a partner so that it can be caught without being intercepted by an opposing player.
3. Making several accurate throws in a row (as in bowling and basketball free throw shooting).

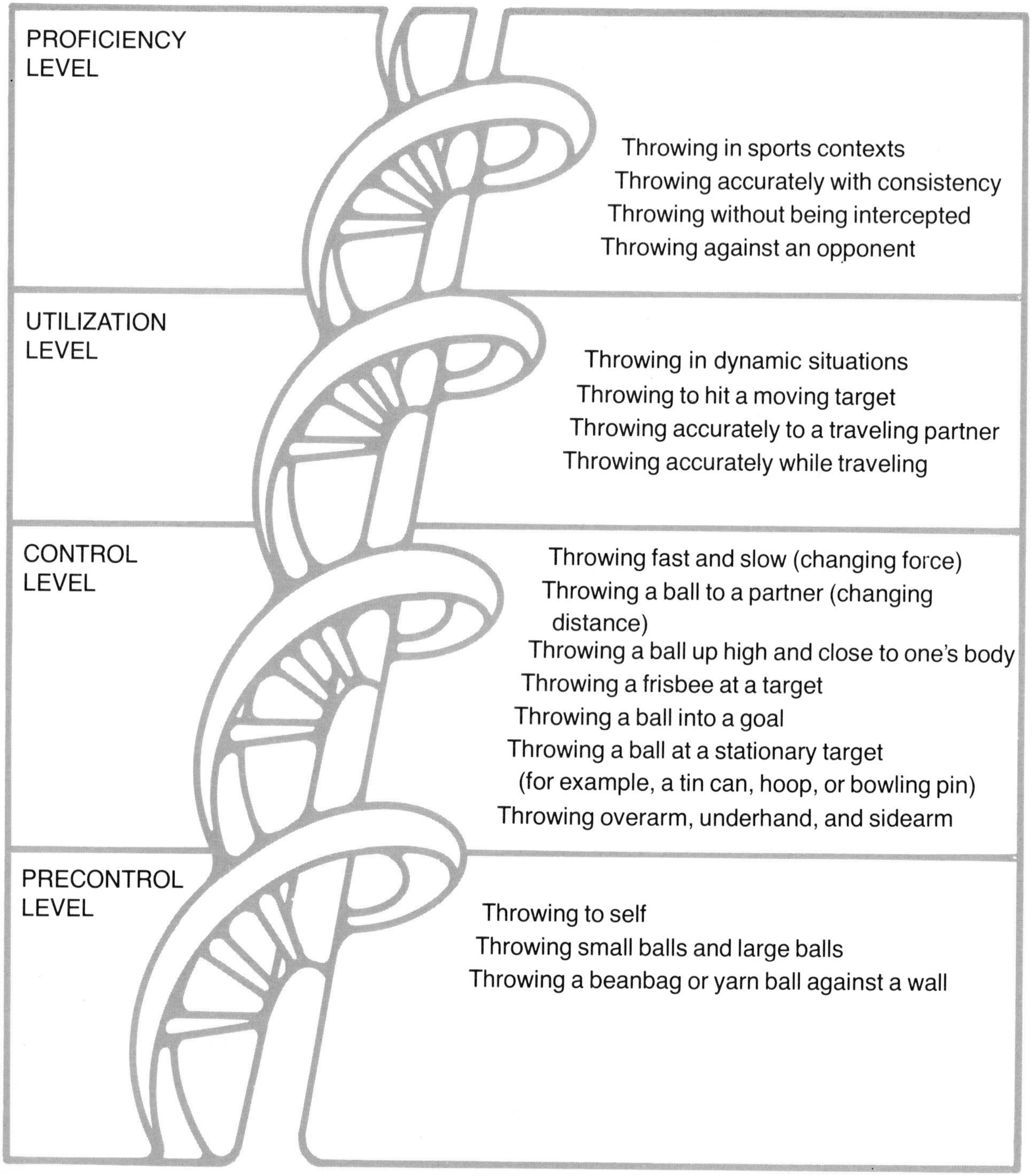

PROFICIENCY LEVEL

Throwing in sports contexts
Throwing accurately with consistency
Throwing without being intercepted
Throwing against an opponent

UTILIZATION LEVEL

Throwing in dynamic situations
Throwing to hit a moving target
Throwing accurately to a traveling partner
Throwing accurately while traveling

CONTROL LEVEL

Throwing fast and slow (changing force)
Throwing a ball to a partner (changing distance)
Throwing a ball up high and close to one's body
Throwing a frisbee at a target
Throwing a ball into a goal
Throwing a ball at a stationary target (for example, a tin can, hoop, or bowling pin)
Throwing overarm, underhand, and sidearm

PRECONTROL LEVEL

Throwing to self
Throwing small balls and large balls
Throwing a beanbag or yarn ball against a wall

CONSTRUCTION OF A YARN BALL

Materials

Yarn
Cardboard
Nylon string
Scissors

Instructions

1. Cut two "doughnuts"—rings made from cardboard—with a diameter that is one inch larger than you want the diameter of the yarn ball to be. Each doughnut should have a center hole that is about one inch in diameter.

2. Cut several ten-foot lengths of yarn. Rug yarn is excellent, but any heavy yarn will do. A one-ounce skein will make two three-inch balls.

3. Place one doughnut on top of the other. Wind yarn around them (through the hole and around the circle) until the cardboard is covered and the hole is full of yarn.

4. Slip the scissors between the doughnuts at the outer edge and cut the yarn all the way around.

5. Slip the nylon string between the doughnuts, making a circle around the yarn in the middle. Pull tight, and then make a strong knot.

6. Pull the doughnuts off and fluff the ball. You can trim any longer strands of yarn to make a smoother, rounder ball.

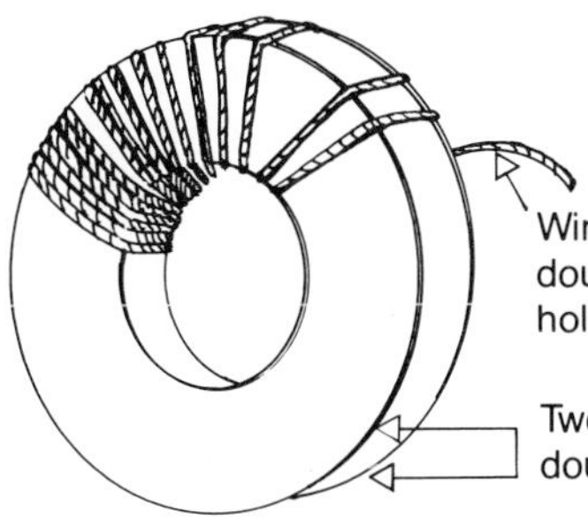

Wind yarn around doughnuts until center hole is filled

Two cardboard doughnuts

Figure 24.1   Sequence for developing the skill theme of throwing

LEVELS OF CATCHING SKILL PROFICIENCY

Catching is the receiving and controlling of an object by the body or its parts. Initially, a young child's reaction to an oncoming object is to fend it off, to protect himself—often by using the whole body rather than the arms and hands. Typically, a ball bounces against the young child's chest as the remainder of the body scrambles to surround it and still maintain equilibrium.

The catching abilities of children, like their throwing skills, vary immensely. The teacher who plans learning sessions in which young children manipulate soft, textured objects (such as beanbags, foam balls, or yarn balls) can observe for the developmental characteristics of catching.

This youngster moves one step to her right—ready to catch

The catching spiral (Figure 24.2) suggests a progression of activities on which the teacher can expand while leading children from the precontrol level to the proficiency level.

Initially, children need experiences that repeatedly challenge them to accurately manipulate their arms and hands into position to receive an object. When focusing on catching performances of children at the precontrol level, we find that many of these youngsters have difficulty throwing an object accurately to themselves or a partner; and an inaccurate throw is difficult to catch. We have found it helpful to teach the skill of throwing before teaching the skill of catching. Older, more skilled children serving as teacher aides can gently and accurately throw a ball to children who are at the precontrol level. And children can work with partners. For example, one child stands on a chair with a ball held in an outstretched hand. This child drops the ball to the partner, who is positioned directly below, ready to catch.

Children at the precontrol level experience greater success when soft, textured, relatively large balls are used. The primary task is for the child to catch a ball thrown directly to him.

Children at the control level need opportunities to develop the skills used when catching with the right and left hands, at either side of the body, and at various levels. Appropriate tasks for children at this level include:

1. Catching down low.
2. Turning and catching.
3. Jumping to catch.
4. Moving one step in any direction to catch.
5. Catching with the right hand and the left hand.
6. Clapping hands and then catching.

When children are consistently able to catch a variety of objects with one or both hands, they are at the utilization level and can begin to use their catching skills in dynamic, unpredictable situations. Appropriate tasks include:

1. Catching a passed football while traveling.
2. Catching a kicked soccer ball.
3. Catching a rebounding ball.
4. Catching a frisbee.

Figure 24.2   Sequence for developing the skill theme of catching

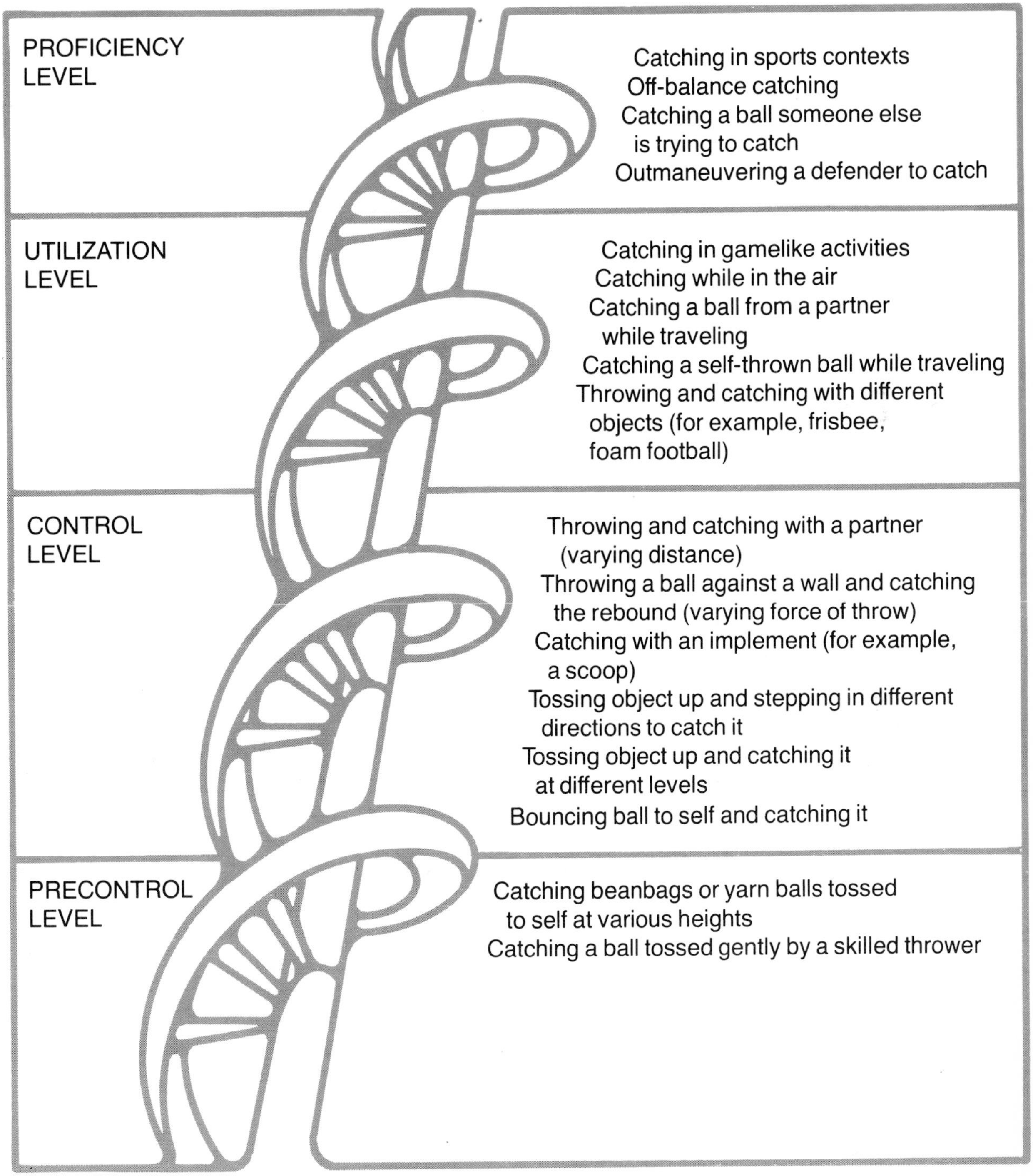

PROFICIENCY
LEVEL

Catching in sports contexts
Off-balance catching
Catching a ball someone else
  is trying to catch
Outmaneuvering a defender to catch

UTILIZATION
LEVEL

Catching in gamelike activities
Catching while in the air
Catching a ball from a partner
  while traveling
Catching a self-thrown ball while traveling
Throwing and catching with different
  objects (for example, frisbee,
  foam football)

CONTROL
LEVEL

Throwing and catching with a partner
  (varying distance)
Throwing a ball against a wall and catching
  the rebound (varying force of throw)
Catching with an implement (for example,
  a scoop)
Tossing object up and stepping in different
  directions to catch it
Tossing object up and catching it
  at different levels
Bouncing ball to self and catching it

PRECONTROL
LEVEL

Catching beanbags or yarn balls tossed
  to self at various heights
Catching a ball tossed gently by a skilled thrower

DEVELOPMENTAL STAGES OF CATCHING

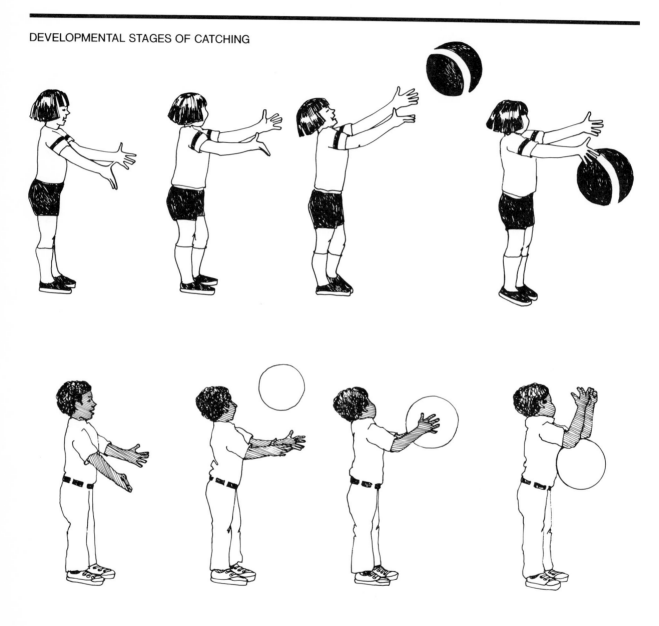

STAGE 1   The child places his arms directly in front of his body with the elbows extended and the palms facing upward or inward. As the ball contacts the hands or arms, the elbows are flexed as the arms and hands attempt to secure the ball by holding it against the chest.

STAGE 2   The child prepares to receive the object with the arms in front of the body, the elbows extended or slightly flexed. As the ball reaches the child, his arms begin an encircling motion that culminates by securing the ball against the chest. The receiver initiates the arm action prior to ball-arm contact.

STAGE 3   The child prepares to receive the ball with arms slightly flexed and extended forward at the shoulder. Many children also receive the ball with arms flexed at the elbows, with the elbows out in front of the body.

Substage a: The child uses his chest as the first contact point with the ball and attempts to secure the ball by holding it to his chest with the arms and hands.

Substage b: The child attempts to catch the ball with his hands. Upon failure to hold it securely, he maneuvers it to his chest, where it is controlled by his arms and hands.

STAGE 4   The child prepares to receive the ball by flexing the elbows and placing the arms in front of the body. Skillful performers may keep the elbows at the sides and flex the arms simul-

taneously as they bring them forward to meet the ball. The ball is caught with the hands, without making contact with any other body parts.

MATURE CATCHING PATTERN   The action of the arms and hands is identical to Stage 4. In addition, the child is required to change his stationary base in order to receive the ball.

Stage 5 is included because of the difficulty many children encounter when they are required to move in relation to an approaching object.

SOURCE: Adapted from R. L. Wickstrom, *Fundamental Motor Patterns*, 2nd ed. (Philadelphia: Lea & Febiger, 1977).

Children at the proficiency level are ready to learn to catch in changing environments. Experiences provided for children at the proficiency level challenge them to catch an object while traveling in relationship to other players. Appropriate activities include:

1. Losing a defender to catch a ball.
2. Catching a rapidly thrown or hit ball that bounces against the ground.
3. Catching a ball with one hand while off balance or in the air.
4. Catching a ball that someone else is trying to catch.

Precontrol Level

Overview   Instructional tasks at the precontrol level provide children with opportunities to repeatedly throw and catch. Emphasis is placed on throws made directly to the children, enabling them to experience success in catching.

IDEAS FOR DEVELOPMENT

Have children stand six to ten feet away from a wall. Challenge them to throw a bean bag or yarn ball forcefully against the wall. Gradually increase the distance from the wall.

IDEAS FOR OBSERVATIONAL FOCUS

How does the child grasp the object that is to be thrown?

Is the elbow away from the side and elevated?

Do the arms and legs move in opposition?

Is the weight transferred from the back foot to the front?

Is balance maintained when the object is released?

For children at the precontrol level, the emphasis is on providing many throwing experiences. Varying the context too early (for example, placing children in game-like situations) seems to cause children to use immature throwing patterns in an attempt to achieve the results called for in the game.

Ask a skilled thrower to throw a yarn ball or foam ball so that the precontrol level child can catch it.

Have children toss up a beanbag or yarn ball. Challenge them to catch it without moving more than one step away from their starting locations.

Do the eyes track the object into the hands?

Does the child seem to protect herself instead of trying to catch the object?

Do the hands give as the object is caught?

Do the elbows and wrists bend?

Is the object caught without being trapped against the chest?

Are the arms and hands primarily used?

Is balance maintained as the object is caught?

Control Level

Overview   Children at the control level are ready to focus on catching at different levels, catching at different places around their bodies, and using either hand to catch. Throwing experiences are designed to help the children learn to throw for accuracy and with varied degrees of force, and to throw a variety of objects.

IDEAS FOR DEVELOPMENT

IDEAS FOR OBSERVATIONAL FOCUS

Have children throw a beanbag through a target (a hoop or a tire).

Have children throw a yarn ball to hit a target on the wall.

Do the eyes focus upon the object to be hit?

Is the throwing motion fluent, or is it hesitant and jerky?

Is the child accurately timing the release of the object toward the target? (If the object is held too long, the object usually sails too low.)

Does the child exhibit mature patterns, or does he lapse into inefficient throwing actions?

Youngsters often become so enthralled with hitting the target that they rush their throws and move closer and closer to the target. You can tape lines on the floor (or spray paint on grass) to designate a minimum throwing distance from the target. Encourage the children to slow down and be accurate.

Challenge children to throw a ball to a goal, such as a basketball hoop.

Is the child able to effectively judge whether a throw to a particular goal requires a soft touch or a strong, firm quality?

Ask children to throw a plastic ring around a stick (similar to horseshoes).

Rather than using the same throwing pattern he would use with a ball, does the child perform this throwing operation using a flick of the wrist— away from the body, toward the stick?

Challenge children to try to throw a frisbee so that it travels in a desired direction (for example, across a line) without hitting the wall.

Is the frisbee thrown so that it is horizontal while in flight?

When several children are aiming for one target area (cans on a bench, for example), we always try to have enough target areas so that each child or group or pair of partners has a separate target area. This maximizes the number of throwing opportunities.

Have children throw a yarn ball to knock over a stack of cans.

Is the child using mature throwing patterns to generate forceful throws?

Challenge children to throw a ball "different ways" to hit a target—for example, behind their backs, under their legs.

Is the child releasing the ball too soon (high throws)? Too late (low throws)?

Is she putting too much emphasis on aiming and too little on throwing?

Is the child taking her time or rushing her throws?

Is the child using the same throwing pattern each time?

Reed and Sophie (who were five years old) were playing a game in which they threw a ball under their legs to knock over a pile of tin cans. Reed placed her head a bit too far under her legs and inadvertently fell into a forward roll as she released the ball. With an expression of sheer excitement, Reed announced that she had discovered the "flip throw."

Have children try to catch an object using an implement:

1. They can toss up a beanbag and try to catch it with a plastic scoop.
2. They can throw and catch a yarn ball over a net with a partner. Use a plastic scoop to catch it.
3. They can try to catch a ball with a plastic scoop while running.

Are the eyes tracking the object to be caught?

Does the hand have a firm grip on the implement?

Do the arms and hands move the implement into an accurate position to receive the object?

Is the open end of the implement facing the oncoming object?

Do the arms and hands give as the object arrives?

A baseball glove is an implement that can be used to catch an object. Generally, however, we prefer not to use baseball gloves in our program. When children bring their own gloves to school, there are problems. Many children prefer not to share their gloves with children who do not have gloves. We also have a hard time justifying the expense of purchasing gloves for a physical education program. In the schools we have taught in, it seems that we always want other equipment that needs to be purchased and is more important than baseball gloves.

Throwing a ball against a wall and catching the rebound

Have children throw a ball against a wall and try to catch it on the rebound.

Does the child throw the ball against the wall with various degrees of force?

Does the child anticipate where the rebound is going and position her body appropriately?

Does the child frequently miss the ball (for example, does it roll away or past her)? Or is she consistently able to position her body so she can stop and/or catch the ball?

Have children throw and catch with a partner. Neither partner moves more than a step away from the starting location. Have them try increasing the distance between partners.

Are the throws accurate? Does the receiver only move one step to catch?

Does the child securely grasp the ball or does he frequently make contact with the ball but then drop it? Does he maintain eye contact with the ball? Rather than stepping to catch, does he reach?

Are catches performed using primarily the hands and arms?

If children are relatively close to one another, mature throwing patterns should not be expected. However, as the distance between partners increases, mature patterns should be observed.

Have children throw and catch a ball over a rope or net with a partner. The height of the rope or net will vary depending on the size and ability of the children; if the rope is slanted, children can select the level at which they would like to practice.

Is the child able to throw over the rope or net so that the partner does not travel more than one step to catch?

Does the child throw the ball in arched pathways?

Is the child catching with hands and arms?

Can the child keep the ball going, throwing and catching in relatively fast succession?

Is the child controlling the ball, keeping it more or less in the designated area?

With a partner, children can bounce or throw their ball over a bench. A playground ball, beach ball, or volleyball works well with this activity.

Is the child able to throw or bounce a ball over the bench so that a partner does not travel more than one step to catch or collect it?

Can the child keep the ball going, throwing and catching in relatively fast succession?

Are the children controlling their balls, keeping them more or less in the designated area?

Utilization Level

Overview   Throwing tasks at the utilization level are designed to help children learn to throw while traveling, to throw accurately at moving targets, and to jump to throw. Catching experiences include catching while traveling, while in the air, and in gamelike activities that require the ability to catch while moving in relationship to various objects and/or people.

Jumping high to throw or catch

Throwing and catching on the run

IDEAS FOR DEVELOPMENT	IDEAS FOR OBSERVATIONAL FOCUS
Challenge children to toss a ball up high and make their catches close to the floor. Ask them to see how close to the floor they can make their catches without touching the floor?	Do the eyes track the ball into the hands? Does the child catch the ball close to the floor? Is the ball caught primarily with the hands? Does the child follow the ball all the way into the hands?
Have children toss a ball up high and move one or two steps to catch it—backward, forward, or to the side.	Is the child able to travel and still catch? Is the child traveling in different directions to catch?
Have children toss a beanbag up high and catch it with just one hand, then with just the other hand.	Does the child track the beanbag with her eyes? Is the child successful in catching with one hand? Is she throwing the beanbag too high? Too far away? Can the child travel and still catch with one hand?

Many of the Ideas for Development of throwing and catching skills at the utilization level can be transformed into gamelike situations for children. Some children at this level enjoy practicing in nongame contexts, while others seem only to be interested in practicing if the skill is used in a gamelike situation. Generally, these are the children who continually want to know, "When do we get to play the game?" See Chapter Eleven for specific information about teaching games.

Challenge children to toss a yarn ball high in the air and catch it as they travel. **1.** Have them do this while jogging, skipping.	Is the child able to decide where he wants the yarn ball to land and throw it to that area? Or is he surprising himself by throwing with little thought about where the ball might land?

2. Have them do this while moving forward, backward.

3. Have them catch with two hands; catch with one hand.

Is the child able to travel and still catch the yarn ball?

Does he track the path of the ball and still watch out for other children?

Have children travel and toss a yarn ball up in the air. Challenge them to travel in one direction to catch, and then swiftly change the direction of travel when they catch the ball.

1. Have them run forward, and then as they catch the ball begin moving backward.

2. Have them run sideways, and then as they catch the ball begin moving forward.

Is the child able to focus on more than one task at a time? Can he travel and catch? Can he change direction as he catches?

Does the child change direction quickly as he catches the ball?

Does the child continue to successfully catch the ball when he begins thinking about changing the direction of travel?

Partners bounce or roll a ball back and forth, trying to make each other move sideways to catch.

Does the receiver place his body in front of the ball before making contact with it?

Is the child able to travel in unpredictable directions and still catch?

Does the child maintain balance and control? Or does he frequently stumble and/or fall and miss the ball?

Have the children throw a ball to a partner so that he has to run, stretch, jump, or reach to make the catch.

Does the receiver track the flight of the ball? Does he keep an eye on the thrower while traveling?

Does the receiver stop to catch or continue traveling while catching?

Does the receiver reach his arms and hands toward the oncoming object and on contact pull it toward the body center?

Does the receiver get a good jump on the ball, or is he slow to react?

Does the receiver accurately anticipate the path the ball will travel?

Teach Frisbee Golf. This is a form of golf in which a frisbee is used instead of a club and ball.

Objective: To throw a frisbee for distance and often around obstacles, eventually placing it through a target hoop. Use as few throws as possible.

Rules:
1. Players make the first throw from behind a starting line.
2. Players make the second throw and any subsequent throws from the landing location of the previous throw. Players are allowed one step in throwing.
3. Players count how many throws were needed to place the frisbee through the hoop.

In building momentum for the first throw, is a running start used? Is a step-hop performed as the frisbee is released?

Do the children snap their wrists in releasing the frisbee (as they would in snapping a towel)?

Do the children release the frisbee smoothly? Does the release result in a flight toward the target?

A hula hoop tied between two chairs or a hoop suspended from a tree can serve as a target. The distance and angle of the target from the starting line can vary, depending on the amount of space available. We use a range of 50 to 150 yards. Trees, playground apparatus, fences, or back-stops can be used as obstacles to throw over or around. For a detailed analysis of Frisbee skills write for *Frisbee: Flying Disc Manual for Students and Teachers*, International Frisbee Disc Association, P.O. Box 970, San Gabriel, California 91776.

Have children work with a partner, who tries to block a ball from reaching a target or goal. One partner tries to throw or kick a ball into a goal area. The other partner tries to catch the ball to prevent it from reaching the goal. A beachball or light volleyball works well with this task.

Does the receiver maintain a balanced stance, ready to move in any direction (low level, arms spread sideward, feet shoulder-width apart, with weight equally distributed)?

Does the receiver continually track the movement of the ball and the travel of his partner?

When the ball is thrown or kicked toward the goal, does the receiver react quickly or slowly? Does the receiver continually remain alert?

Ask the children to throw fast to their partner. Start with a yarn ball and progress to a tennis ball, foam football, or small rubber ball.

When the ball is thrown, does the receiver consistently position his body into a blocking location to collect or catch the ball? Or does he frequently misjudge the path or speed of the ball and position himself where collecting or catching the ball is difficult?

Does the child use a wind-up phase to generate maximal speed?

Do the child's throws remain accurate when he throws fast?

Does the receiver appropriately reach to meet the oncoming ball, and then give with the ball by bending the arm and pulling it in toward the body?

Children should warm up before throwing fast, and they should not throw fast for extended periods of time.

Have children throw to a running partner. One partner remains stationary, the other partner runs a predetermined pathway. The stationary partner throws the ball to the traveling partner at a predetermined point along the pathway.

Does the receiver run slowly, at moderate speed, or at full speed?

Does the thrower accurately lead the receiver? Does the thrower know where the receiver is going? For example, does the receiver have to stop and reach back to catch?

Does the receiver catch the ball on the run or does he stop to catch?

Does the receiver track the ball all the way into his hands? Or does he frequently make contact with the ball but then drop it?

Challenge the children to throw accurately to a target from far away. A target is placed on the backstop of a softball field. From the outfield, students try to accurately throw a softball to the target.

Is a wind-up phase used to generate force for the throw?

Are the throws relatively accurate? Do they land in the backstop area or close to a partner?

Does the child aim the ball too much? Is he so concerned with accuracy that the force of the throws is weak?

Two players stand as far apart as appropriate for them. They try to throw a ball to one another so that neither of them has to travel to catch the ball.

Is the child accurately timing the release of the ball? Does it sail too high or land too close?

Have the children run to catch a ball thrown or hit to a high level, and then throw it accurately to a partner. Challenge the children to release the ball quickly.

Does the receiver react quickly as the ball is thrown or hit?

Does the receiver accurately judge the flight of the ball? Or does she run in as ball sails overhead?

Does the receiver position her body so that, as the ball is received, it can be quickly thrown to the intended person? That is, is the ball caught while traveling in the direction of subsequent throw?

Is the throw forceful and accurate?

Ask the children to pitch a ball accurately across a box or hoop to a catcher; use an underhand throw and an overhand throw. Have children see how many times in a row they can throw the ball across the target.

Do the hips and trunk rotate?

Is the throwing motion fluent? That is, do the preparatory, main, and follow-through phases of the throwing operation occur in a quick, smooth succession? Or is there a hesitant flow with an overemphasis on aiming?

Is the ball released in a forward direction with force?

Does the ball cross the target and reach the catcher?

Have children throw at a stationary target while running. For example, they can run sideways and throw a football forward, through a hoop hanging from a basket, a tire hanging from a tree, or at a target placed on a backstop.

Is the momentum of the run transferred to the throwing action? Is it a jerky transition, so that the run seems to hinder throwing action? Or is it smooth, providing momentum for the throw?

Is the object thrown in a direct, straight pathway, or in an arched, lobbed pathway?

Challenge children to try to throw accurately past a defender to a running receiver.

Do the thrower and receiver plan a predetermined route?

Does the thrower allow for the travel of the receiver? Does the thrower lead the receiver?

Does the thrower release the ball in an arched pathway or in a straight, forceful pathway?

Does the receiver attempt to fake out the defender (make quick changes in direction and/or speed)?

Does the receiver keep his eyes on the object to be caught?

Is the run timed so that the child meets the object in stride and continues traveling?

Does the receiver try to travel away from the object before he has control of it?

Ask children to jump and, while airborne, throw to a target.

1. They can jump and shoot a basketball into a goal.
2. Have them jump and throw a foam football through a hoop.

Is the child facing the target when airborne?

Does he jump off the balls of both feet? Are the feet about shoulder width apart?

Do both hands bring the ball to a throwing position?

Is the elbow of the throwing arm held perpendicular to the floor?

When the ball is released, does the arm fully extend as the fingers complete the follow-through?

Challenge children to make catches that lead into swift releases.

1. Working with a partner, they can catch a ball and release it back to the partner as quickly as possible. (Stress successful catches coupled with accurate throws. The distance between partners can be varied.)
2. Have them receive a ball from a partner and quickly release it toward a goal or target (a basketball goal or a tire).

Is the body moving in the direction of the upcoming throw as the catching action occurs?

Is the momentum of the body in the direction toward which the throw is headed?

Is the transition from the catching action to the throwing action swift and fluent, or is it awkward and sluggish?

3. Have them catch and throw quickly using just one hand.

Teach a game focusing on throwing and catching, such as Hit the Pin (see Figure 24.3).

Objective: To knock over the opposing team's pin.

Rules: **1.** Two or three players on each side.

2. Players can only take two steps when they have the ball. Then they must pass to a teammate or shoot at the pin.

3. No players are allowed in the goal area.

4. If the ball touches the ground, the last team to touch the ball loses possession. The other team begins play at that location.

Is the ball thrown accurately and forcefully or wildly with little speed?

Watch children's abilities to throw and catch in a game situation. Try to pinpoint weaknesses that can be focused on in subsequent lessons. Are children having difficulty throwing and catching while traveling? Are children having difficulty throwing around a defender to hit a target?

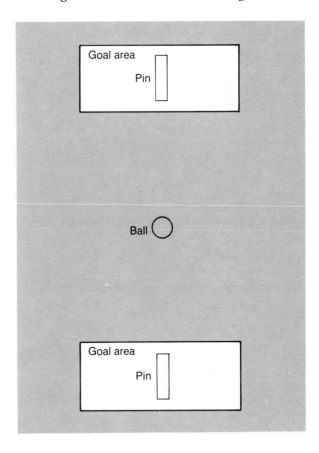

Figure 24.3   Hit the pin

Teach Blanket Volleyball.

Objective: To have two teams successfully throw and catch a volleyball over a net using a blanket as a throwing implement.

This is a novel activity that children really enjoy. We plan game experiences such as this one just for fun.

Rules: 1. Four to five players on each side.

2. A net separates the teams. No boundaries are required.

3. Each team has a blanket. The players support the blanket by holding it along its perimeter.

4. The volleyball is placed on one blanket. The two teams try to throw and catch the ball over the net without missing.

Possible Variations:

The two teams count how many successful catches they can perform before any misses occur.

The two teams count how many successful catches they can perform in sixty seconds or in two minutes.

Proficiency Level

Overview   Experiences at the proficiency level include throwing and catching in relation to an opponent who attempts to prevent the throw or the catch. These tasks foster development of consistent degrees of accuracy and distance in throwing. Children learn to catch a variety of objects while traveling at rapid speeds and making sudden changes of direction and level.

IDEAS FOR DEVELOPMENT

IDEAS FOR OBSERVATIONAL FOCUS

Teach Frisbee Stretch.

Are the players stretching high, low, and to the sides?

Objective: To stretch to catch a frisbee.

Rules: 1. Children work in pairs.

2. One partner throws the frisbee to the other:

a. If the frisbee is caught, that counts as one point.

b. If the player's body is stretched while reaching for the frisbee, that counts as three points.

Can players stretch to catch while remaining in the same location? Can they stretch to catch while traveling?

Teach Frisbee Football (see Figure 24.4).

Objective: To successfully catch the object (ball, beanbag, frisbee) in the opposing team's goal area.

Rules:
1. Two to four players on each team.
2. When a player has the object, she can take no more than three steps before passing it to a teammate.
3. A point is scored when a player catches the object in the opposing team's goal area.
4. If the object touches the ground, the team that touched the object last loses possession. The opposing team puts the object in play from that location. There is no out of bounds.

Figure 24.4   Frisbee football

Watch each child's ability to throw and catch the frisbee in a fast-moving game.

What strategies are most successful?

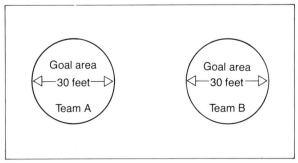

There are no boundaries other than the two goal areas, each of which has a diameter of thirty feet. Generally the farther apart the goal areas can be placed, the more interesting the game.

We allow children to play this exciting game without interruption. We observe the youngsters' abilities to throw and catch accurately in a pressure situation. Subsequent learning activities can be based on children's success in playing the game.

Teach Run the Bases.

Objective: For a team of fielders to throw a ball around the bases twice before runners circle the bases once.

Rules:
1. Four players to a team.
2. The fielding team places a player at each base—first, second, third, and home plate.
3. The player at home plate (the catcher) begins with the ball. On signal, two runners try to run the bases before the fielders throw the ball to each base twice.
4. If the runners travel the bases before the fielders throw and catch the ball twice, they score a run. If all the fielders throw and catch twice before the runners circle the bases, it is an out.
5. After three outs *or* when all runners have had a chance to run the bases twice, the teams switch roles.

Teach Passball (see Figure 24.5).

Objective: The offensive team tries to run pass patterns that result in successful catches. The defensive team tries to travel, staying with the receivers, to prevent them from catching the ball. The children can use teacher-suggested travel patterns or diagram their own.

Rules:
1. Three players on a side.
2. A line is spray-painted across the middle of the field. The quarterback must remain behind this line, and no defensive player may cross the line.
3. The offensive team has three plays or attempts to have successful pass completions. Then the teams switch roles.
4. A point is scored each time a receiver catches the ball. Two points are scored when a receiver catches the ball in the end zone.
5. After each play, the ball is again placed at midfield.
6. No player may purposely bump or block another.
7. All players rotate to different positions after each play.

Are the children running along predetermined travel patterns, or are they running randomly?

Are the receivers running at full speed?

Do the receivers change the direction of travel sharply and quickly?

Do they fake one way and go another?

Does the quarterback lead her receivers?

Does she throw to an open receiver?

Do the defensive backs begin about five yards from the receiver?

Do they keep one eye on the quarterback? (They should not turn their back to the quarterback.)

Do they watch the hips of the receiver and react quickly to her changes in direction?

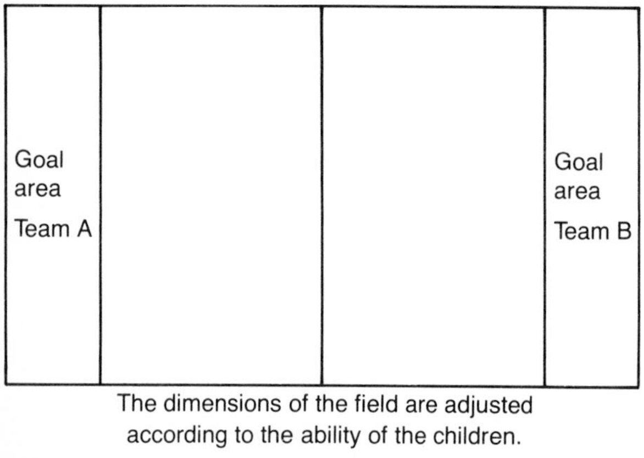

The dimensions of the field are adjusted according to the ability of the children.

Figure 24.5   Passball

Teach a modified game of European Handball (see Figure 24.6).

Objective: To throw the ball through the opposing team's goal.

Rules:
1. Three or four players on a team.
2. Players must stay out of semicircle.
3. Goalie must stay in semicircle. He tries to collect the ball to prevent it from going through the goal.
4. A player who has a ball can bounce it, pass it to a teammate, or throw it toward the goal. Once a player stops bouncing the ball, he must pass or shoot it. He can no longer dribble it.

Watch for the children's catching and throwing abilities in a dynamic game. Try to pinpoint weaknesses that can be focused on in subsequent lessons. Can the children find the open teammate to pass to, catch on the run, catch and then quickly release the ball?

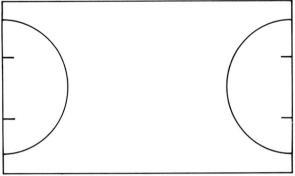

Figure 24.6 Modified game of European handball

Goals can be made of stacked tires.
Semicircle can be spray painted on ground.

Teach Four-Person Football. Use foam footballs or footballs that are smaller than regulation size balls.

Objective: To successfully catch the football in the opposing team's goal area.

Rules:
1. Two players on a team.
2. Each team is given four chances to throw and catch the ball in an attempt to move the ball from their goal line to the opposing team's goal area.
3. When on offense, one player is the thrower. She may not move forward. The thrower tries to accurately throw the ball downfield to her teammate, the receiver.
4. When on defense, one player tries to stay with the receiver to block or intercept the ball. The other player remains at the location where the play starts. That player counts aloud,

Observe the children's abilities to throw and catch while traveling and to avoid defensive players.

"1001, 1002" and so on, and then tries to touch the thrower or block her pass.

5. A play is over when the ball touches the ground or when a defensive player touches the offensive player who has possession of the ball.

Design a Frisbee Circuit. Each child has a frisbee and rotates from one station to another, as outlined in Chapter Four.

Activities at stations include:

1. Throw a frisbee to knock over tin cans. Cans are set up on chairs, milk crates, or benches.
2. Throw a frisbee through a hula hoop. Hoop hangs from basketball goal or is tied between two chairs.
3. Throw a frisbee to hit a bull's-eye on a target. Target is on a wall or attached to baseball backstop or to a tree.
4. Throw a frisbee into a designated goal area from a distance (from a line taped on floor or painted on ground).
5. Throw a frisbee through a hanging tire. Hang tire from basketball goal or from a tree.

Kids really get excited and have fun with this activity, and we enjoy playing it with them.

Teach a modified game of Half-Court Basketball.

Objective: To make a basket against opposition.

Rules: 1. Three players on each side.
2. When a player has the ball, he must shoot it to the basket or pass it to a teammate. (No dribbling or steps are allowed.)

Do the children cluster together or spread out?

Are the children who do not have the ball moving (trying to get open) or standing still?

Are the passes quick and accurate?

Do the potential receivers remain alert—ready for the ball?

Is the person with the ball holding it too long or getting rid of it quickly?

Have the children focus on traveling, with changes in direction, when they don't have the ball. When they receive the ball, have them focus on getting rid of it quickly—either to a teammate or toward the goal.

Teach Keep It Up.

Objective: To keep the ball from touching the floor.

Rules:
1. Three to four players on each side. A net separates the two teams.
2. One team begins play by throwing the ball over the net.
3. One player on the receiving side catches the ball and quickly passes it to a teammate, who catches it and quickly passes to the other teammate. That player throws the ball back over the net (all players must catch the ball before it goes back over the net).
4. Tally how many times the ball touches the floor in one minute. Try to beat the record.

Observe the abilities of children to throw and catch carefully when working with others.

Is the number of errors (ball touches the floor) high or low?

What causes the errors?

Teach Run Down.

Objective: To tag-out a base runner.

Rules:
1. Two players stand on bases spread apart (distance will depend on the players). On signal, one player who begins in the middle attempts to reach either base without being tagged by a base person possessing the ball.
2. The base runner must run every third throw.

Watch the children's abilities to throw quickly when they catch a ball in a game situation.

CHAPTER 25
VOLLEYING AND DRIBBLING

Striking an object upward

Figure 25.1 Sequence for developing the skill theme of volleying

For our purposes volleying is defined as striking or giving impetus to an object. This can be done by using a variety of body parts—for example, hands, arms, head, or knees. Dribbling, a subdivision of volleying, involves striking downward, generally with the hands. The sequence for developing the skill theme of volleying, from the precontrol level to the proficiency level, is shown in Figure 25.1. The Ideas for Development have, for the sake of clarity, been separated in this chapter. When teaching, you can develop dribbling and volleying together. Volleying is almost exclusively a game skill, used in such sports as soccer, volleyball, handball, basketball, and speedball.

LEVELS OF VOLLEYING SKILL PROFICIENCY

Children who are at the precontrol level of volleying are still struggling to achieve the hand-eye coordination required to contact the ball. They are rarely able to intentionally direct the flight of a ball when contact is made. Appropriate activities for children at this level include:

1. Striking a balloon up once so that it comes back down to the child.
2. Striking a ball up and catching it.

Once a child can contact the ball with regularity, he can be asked to:

1. Strike the ball up with his dominant hand so that he keeps the ball going, letting it bounce between strikes.

PROFICIENCY LEVEL

Aerial volleying to outwit partners,
  groups
Striking a ball to a partner
  with different body parts while traveling
Striking a ball to a partner after
  bounce, to outwit partner
Jumping to strike a ball
Striking a ball with different body
  parts while traveling

UTILIZATION LEVEL

Striking a ball to a target (over a target)
Striking a ball with different body parts
  (continuous—no bounce)
Striking a ball to a partner
Striking a ball with different body parts,
  to a wall
Continuous striking with hands, no bounce

CONTROL LEVEL

Striking a ball in different directions
Striking a ball in different places around body
Striking a ball at different levels
Striking a ball to different levels
Striking with different body parts,
  letting ball bounce
Striking a ball with different body parts
  (noncontinuous)

PRECONTROL LEVEL

Striking different size balls
Continuous aerial striking up with either hand,
  letting ball bounce
Continuous striking upward with both hands,
  letting ball bounce
Striking a ball upward with both hands and catching it

2. Strike the ball up with either hand to keep it going, but letting it bounce between strikes.

3. Strike different-sized balls.

At the control level a child is able to strike a ball continuously (letting it bounce) in his own space. He is able to control the amount of force that he puts into the volley, so that he can control the ball in his own space. Tasks such as these are appropriate:

1. Striking a ball with body parts other than the hands.

2. Striking a ball to different levels.

3. Striking a ball in different places around the body (for example, sides).

4. Striking a ball in different directions.

5. Striking a ball at different levels.

6. Continuous striking with hands and not letting the ball bounce.

At the utilization level children can also control the direction as well as the force of their strikes. They are able, with a variety of body parts, to produce a level surface with which to strike the ball. The child can also combine several different concepts with the skill of striking. Appropriate tasks include:

1. Striking a ball with different body parts without letting the ball bounce.

2. Striking a ball with different body parts while traveling.

3. Striking a ball to a target.

4. Jumping to strike a ball.

5. Striking a ball to outwit an opponent in a relatively stable situation.

When children are able to strike an object and simultaneously focus on the activity around them, they are able to function at the proficiency level. Appropriate tasks include:

1. Striking among a group to keep an object going.

2. Striking a ball to a partner while traveling.

3. Striking a ball among a group to outwit another group.

4. Striking a ball with a partner or group while traveling to outwit another group.

We focus on volleying as a major skill in many of our game situations.

Efficient striking patterns are generally the last of the fundamental manipulative patterns to develop. This is because of the fine perceptual

Striking an object upward while traveling

and motor adjustments that must be made by the child. Once the child does begin to be able to strike an object, the range of possible activities is enormous. The ideas that follow include suggestions for children at the different levels, and a range of activities within each level. They are stated rather directly. Remember, though, that you are encouraged to modify the suggested organizational structure to satisfy your objectives (Chapter Four).

Precontrol Level

Overview It is important for each child to be able to strike a ball with his or her hands so that the ball stays within a particular space. At the precontrol level we work toward control, so that children do not have to run after the ball to retrieve it after each strike.

IDEAS FOR DEVELOPMENT

IDEAS FOR OBSERVATIONAL FOCUS

Have the children strike balloons up into the air, trying to keep them off the floor.

Does the child actually strike the balloon, or does he catch it and throw it?

Is the child able to stay in his own space, or does he let the balloon lead him all over the playing area?

This is a great task for young children. They are usually able to keep the balloons up because balloons are so light. The balloons do tend to float, so the children will wander with their eyes on the balloons. Caution them to be aware of others.

Challenge children to strike a ball up with both hands so that it comes back to them. They can also try doing this with one hand.

Is the child striking up? Does he know what direction up is?

Is the child striking with a level surface, so that the ball goes straight up? Or does he use unsmooth surfaces that cause the ball to go in any direction?

Is the child contacting the ball in the middle of the bottom, or does he hit it from the side?

Is the child actually striking the ball, or does he

throw it? Can he momentarily release the ball before the hit?

Have children strike a ball up and try to keep it going; they can let the ball bounce on the floor between strikes to help them control it.

Is the child able to continually strike the ball, or does he rush the movement?

In a striking situation many young children get excited about their actions and don't wait for the ball to return, so they lose control of it. Advise them to wait until the ball returns to a level that they are able to strike at successfully.

Is the child striking the ball too high, so that she is unable to control it when it comes down?

Is the child striking the ball too softly, so that it does not bounce high enough for her to strike a second time?

Is the child actually striking continuously, or does she catch the ball between strikes and start again?

Is the child contacting the ball at a medium level, or does she end up contacting it at a high level?

Challenge the children to begin to use their other hand to strike the ball as well as the dominant hand.

Can the child perform the same movements with the nondominant hand as with the dominant hand?

Does the child use the nondominant hand when appropriate (for example, when the ball is on that side of the body) or does she force the use of it on the dominant hand?

The Ideas for Development at the precontrol level should be explored with a variety of balls— beachballs, plastic balls, and rubber playground balls (small and large). The size as well as the weight should be changed.

Control Level

Overview   At the control level, children learn to volley a ball in various directions and at various levels. They use different body parts, and relationships to other people and to objects begin to be important.

IDEAS FOR DEVELOPMENT

IDEAS FOR OBSERVATIONAL FOCUS

Have children strike a ball up with a variety of body parts—feet, elbow, heads, shoulders, knees, and legs.

Is the child striking the ball in the middle of the bottom of the ball, so it goes straight up?

> Children at the control level still find that it helps to let the ball bounce between strikes or to use the hands between strikes, so that they gain control over their volleying.

Is the child striking the ball with a level body part that is meeting the ball at a right angle?

Is the child striking the ball too high, or can he control it when it comes down?

Have the children keep the ball going between different body parts—head, floor, elbow, floor, knee, floor, and hands—letting it bounce in between.

Can the child continually strike with a flat level surface, or does he lose it after a couple of strikes?

Ask children to try to develop a repeatable sequence of striking with different body parts. They can use at least three different parts other than their hands.

Can the child control the striking well enough to put together a repeatable sequence, or are strikes in sequence accidental?

Does the child keep the ball close enough to the body to strike, or does it constantly drift away?

Have the children strike a ball up with their hands, keeping it off the floor as much as possible.

Does the child contact the ball with hands flat and level?

Does he contact the ball at an appropriate level (chest high)? Or, as the striking progresses, does contact occur at a higher level?

Does the child use both hands or only one?

Does he strike the ball to an appropriate level? Or does he hit it so hard and/or high that he can't control it when it comes down?

Does the child keep the ball close to the body? Or does he end up moving or reaching for it constantly?

Is the contact made in the middle or the bottom of the ball?

Children enjoy seeing how many times they can keep a ball in the air before it hits the floor.

Striking to different levels using different body parts

Have children strike the ball to different levels—high, medium, and low. They can:

Are the differences between the levels clear?

Can the child tell you the level at which he intends to hit and then strike to that same level?

It may be necessary at this point for children to start letting the ball bounce again, because of lack of control. We have found that when children are ready, they often eliminate the bounce themselves.

---

1. First strike low, then medium, then very high, then low. Have them try to control the ball after each strike without using the floor and keep the striking going.
2. Strike to different levels using different body parts—knees, heads, and feet.
3. Try to keep the ball going to different levels while using hands and other body parts.

Are the different levels clear?

Do the child's hands and arms give when receiving the ball from the previous hit?

Can the child control the ball between strikes, so that she can make a drastic change in levels? Or are the changes only very slight?

Is the child striking to different levels? Or is she concentrating more on keeping the ball going?

When using different body parts, is the child able to impart the necessary force and to give with those parts when necessary?

There are always some children who take great delight in seeing how many times they can hit the ceiling with the ball. We have found that one solution to this is to ask them "to come as close to the ceiling as possible, but never touch it." Usually it works!

With the body at different levels, children can try to strike the ball while:

1. Lying on the floor.
2. Kneeling.
3. Sitting.
4. Keeping one knee on the floor.

Is the child putting her body at different levels to strike? Can she tell you which level she is using?

Can she still strike with flat surfaces?

Children need to be reminded that their bodies need to be at different levels but the ball does not necessarily have to go to different levels.

Use different parts of the body to strike at different levels, children can:

1. Use their heads, from a kneeling position.
2. Use their feet while lying down.

Can the child keep the ball off the floor by using the hands to control it, rather than letting it bounce?

Have the children try to change their bodies from one level to another while keeping the ball going.

Is the child changing the body level used to keep the ball off the floor? Or does he focus only on the body levels and lose the striking ability?

Have children strike with different places around their bodies—the side, back, and front. They can:

1. Move the ball from one place around the body to another (for example, from side to back to front).

Is the child able to use the appropriate parts at different places around his body (for example, foot behind, elbow to side)?

Are the surfaces still flat when they make contact with the ball?

Can the child move a ball from one part of his body to another without letting it hit the floor?

2. Try to strike the ball so that it is further away from the body. Ask them to make themselves reach for the ball.

Can the child strike the ball so that it goes straight up while he is reaching away from his body?

Does he use the whole limb as a striking implement?

Can he move to get under the ball when necessary?

Children can strike a ball against a wall from:

1. Behind the ball.
2. On top of the ball.
3. Under the ball.

Can the child determine the direction in which she wants to strike the ball?

Ask children to strike the ball in different directions, with hands, and then with different body parts, so that it goes forward, sideways, and backward.

Can the child control the direction she chooses to strike the ball in? Does it go where she wants it to?

To strike the ball above a certain place on a wall, children can use:

1. An underhand striking pattern.
2. An overhand striking pattern.
3. A sidearm pattern.

Have children use each of the three patterns to strike the ball hard against the wall.

Have children strike a plastic ball against a wall so that it:

1. Travels in a high arched pathway.
2. Travels a relatively straight pathway.
3. Moves in a hard shot down (see Figure 25.2).

Is the child able to contact the ball using an underhand pattern? An overhand pattern? A sidearm pattern?

Is the ball contacted in the lower center, so that it travels directly to the desired location on the wall?

Can the child strike hard and still contact the ball directly?

Does the child step and transfer her weight as she attempts to strike the ball hard?

Is the child following through with her strikes?

Is the pathway of the ball clear? Can the child verbalize what pathway it is traveling in?

Does the child strike the ball in the appropriate place to accomplish the desired pathway?

Figure 25.2   Point of contact on ball: location of hit determines the direction of travel

Utilization Level

Overview   For continuing skill development, it is important that children develop consistency and accuracy. They should be able to use various body parts and to move in relationship to other people and objects. Strategic skills of placement in a relatively stable situation are developed at the utilization level.

IDEAS FOR DEVELOPMENT	IDEAS FOR OBSERVATIONAL FOCUS
Have children strike the ball to a target marked on the wall. They can: 1. Vary the sizes and heights of the targets. 2. Vary the distance they stand from the wall.	Does the child contact the ball so that it goes to the wall, not up in the air? Does the child use flat body parts to strike with? Can the child contact the ball in the appropriate place to send it to different heights? Does the child strike the ball with enough force to get it to the wall? Does the child simply strike to the wall or to a target on the wall?
Ask the children to throw a ball to a partner so that he can volley it back. Partners can decide when to change from throwing to volleying. Have the children: 1. Vary the body parts used to strike the ball. 2. Throw the ball to different levels, from different distances. 3. Throw the ball so that the partner has to travel—forward, to the side, and backward— to strike it.	Is the child adjusting his body so that he is in an appropriate position to strike the ball? Or is he reaching or off-balance? Can the child use different body parts to meet the ball so that it travels back to his partner?
Have the children try to keep the ball going and see how many times they can hit the target.	Is the child still aiming for the target, or does he simply concentrate on keeping the ball going?
Ask the children to strike the ball into a hoop or other target (for example, a circle made from a rope, or a square on the floor).	Can the child give the ball the right amount of impetus to get it to the target?
Have children use different body parts to strike the ball to the wall. They can:	Can the child give the ball enough force with each strike so that it returns to him each time?

1. Keep the ball going and always return it with a different part.
2. Try a new part each time, seeing how many parts they can use before using the same part again.

Cooperating with a partner, children strike a ball back and forth in a well-defined space using both hands (one hand, other body parts). They can:

1. See if they can keep it going. How many times can they send it back and forth?
2. Send the ball to different levels around the partner.
3. Send it to different places around the partner—back, sides, and front.

4. Change the pathway the ball travels to the partner—make it relatively straight, or arched. Remind them that it should always be a shot the partner can return.

5. Strike a ball over a rope to a partner.

6. Play the hoop game—striking to a partner with a hoop on the floor. The ball must bounce in the hoop each time before the partner hits it.

Is the child using all the parts he can to strike the ball to the wall?

Is the child using different body parts?

Does the child keep the ball going, or does he catch it and start again when he feels he can't strike it?

Is the child still using flat parts of his body to strike the ball?

Is the child aware of where his partner is or does he simply worry about striking the ball?

Is the child using appropriate amounts of force?

Is the child contacting the ball in the proper place for the desired pathway?

Is the child using body parts appropriate to where the ball lands? Or does she generally use her hands?

Can the child give the ball the necessary height on a bounce, so that it goes over the rope?

Is the child using an overhanded or underhanded striking pattern?

Is the child aware of where the hoop is and where the partner is?

A group of fourth graders added a new dimension to the hoop game. They spun the hoop and then tried to see how many times they could strike the ball through it before it stopped spinning.

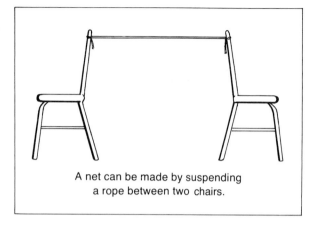

A net can be made by suspending
a rope between two chairs.

Figure 25.3   Construction of a net

With a partner, children strike a ball over a medium rope or net (see Figure 25.3). They can:

1. Try to keep the ball going in the air without letting it hit the floor.
2. Raise the height of the net.

Does the child contact the bottom of the ball so that it will go over the net?

Does he move behind the ball and under it to strike?

Does the child use appropriate parts to strike the ball? Does he use head, hands, and shoulders, if it is high, and legs, knees, and feet if it has dropped low?

3. With a small group, cooperate to keep the ball going over the net.

Can children on each side recover the ball on their side to keep it going?

Do they move where the ball is to help play it?

Working with a partner in a well-defined space, children strike the ball back and forth and try to make the partner miss it. Have them strike to open spaces. Ask them to try to incorporate other factors into their striking—changing the force behind the hit, the distance, the speed of the ball, and the height of the hit.

Is the child striking the ball to open space, or does she still strike to the partners?

Is the child able to vary her shots to outwit her partners?

Does the child travel to reach the ball?

Proficiency Level

Overview   Children at the proficiency level should be able to move consistently and accurately in relation to others. They should also be able to react effectively to increasingly dynamic and unpredictable situations. They can simultaneously focus on volleying and on the activity around them.

IDEAS FOR DEVELOPMENT

Working with a partner, children travel around the space while striking a ball back and forth with different body parts. Both partners should always be moving.

Working with two on each side of a net (or rope), children strike the ball to keep it going. Challenge them to never let it hit the floor and to try to make the other team miss.

Have children strike the ball back and forth with their heads.

Ask them how long they can keep it going.

Ask them to try to move around the space and still keep the ball going.

Have them change the amount of space between partners.

Teach Infinity Volleyball.

Objective: To keep the ball going as long as possible without a miss.

Rules: 1. There are four to six on each team.
2. There is no limit to the number of hits that can occur on each side of the net.

IDEAS FOR OBSERVATIONAL FOCUS

Can the child strike while moving or does he stop and then strike?

Is the child moving even when he does not have the ball?

Can the child strike to another moving person, or does he strike to behind other children?

Are the children actually setting each other up, or do they simply return the ball?

Is the child able to use different parts when appropriate?

Is the child striking to an open space? Is he aware of where the partner is and where the other team is?

Is the child able to vary his shots to throw the other team off? Or does he simply concentrate on keeping the ball going?

Is the child actually using her forehead to contact the ball or does it bounce off the top of her head?

Does the child get low under the ball when it is low or does she simply bend over and try to hit it straight on?

Are the children able to keep the ball high for each other?

Do the children move to get behind the ball?

Do the children stay spread out or close together?

Do the children strike the ball to cause it to go up in the air? Or do they throw it?

Volleying a ball with the head

Teach a game that uses striking and rotating.

Objective: To keep the ball in play as long as possible.

Rules: 1. There are four children in a line.
2. The first child strikes the ball against the wall and runs to the end of the line.
3. The second child returns the first person's strike with another strike to the wall.

Children practice serving over a net to target areas on the other side:

1. Using an underhand serve.
2. Using an overhand serve.
3. Using a side-arm serve.

Do the children strike the ball high enough and hard enough so that allows the person behind them time to get there to strike the ball?

Do the children move out of the way as soon as they strike the ball?

Is the child contacting the ball so that it goes to the chosen target?

After the child serves, does he follow through in the direction that he wants the ball to go?

Hoops, ropes or masking tape can be used to draw appropriate targets.

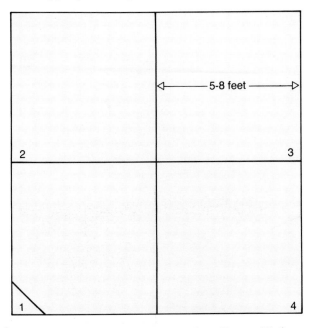

Teach Cooperative Four-Square (see Figure 25.4).

Objective: To keep the ball going as long as possible without a miss.

Rules: 1. The ball must bounce in each square.

2. The receiver must hit it to a different square.

3. The ball may bounce only once in each square.

4. Initially players are allowed to step into the square. As the skill increases, the players must stand outside the square.

With a small group, children work together to strike a ball and always keep it in the air. They must always be off the floor as they strike it.

When the child uses the underhand serve, does he throw the ball up and try to contact it? Or does he simply drop it from his extended hand and hit it?

On the overhand serve, does he throw the ball up so high that it is hard to control?

Does he use opposition as he serves?

Figure 25.4   Four-square court

Are the children contacting the ball so that it goes into another square and another player can hit it?

Can the children place the ball in the other children's squares, so that it is difficult for them to get to it?

Are the players constantly moving in relation to where the ball is coming?

Are the children striking the ball in the air? Or do they jump, land, and then strike the ball?

Can the children control the ball while they are in the air? Or does the ball go wildly across the space?

When you dribble, you strike or bounce a ball downward. Dribbling is included in this chapter because it is a unique form of striking with the hands. Basketball and speedball are the only traditional sports in which dribbling is used.

The rhythm of a bounding ball fascinates children

Dribbling a ball on the floor or ground, as in soccer, could have been included in this chapter. But it is also a kicking skill, and so it is included in the discussion of kicking (Chapter Twenty-Three).

Figure 25.5   Sequence for developing the skill theme of dribbling

LEVELS OF DRIBBLING SKILL PROFICIENCY

The sequence for developing the skill theme of dribbling, from the precontrol to the proficiency level, is shown in Figure 25.5.

At the precontrol level of dribbling, the child strikes the ball down once with the whole palm of his hand, which is kept rigid rather than flexed. After one bounce the child typically cannot control the ball when it rises again, because his hand and arm move in opposition to the ball rather than in unison with it. Tasks that are appropriate at this level include:

1. Bouncing the ball and keeping it going.
2. Bouncing the ball with one hand (rather than with two hands).
3. Bouncing a ball in self-space and trying to keep it going.
4. Dribbling with the other hand, keeping the ball going, and staying in self-space.

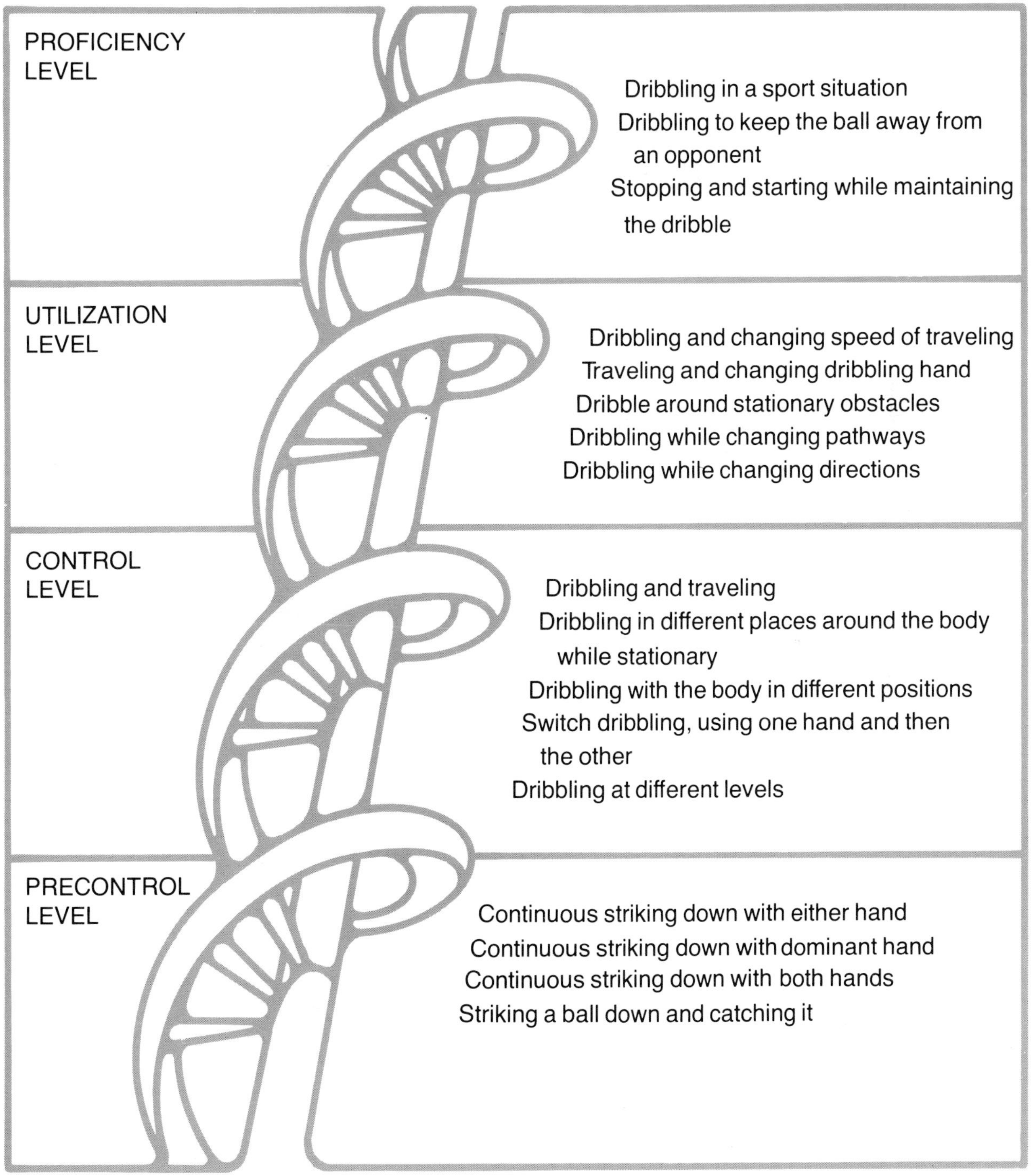

PROFICIENCY
LEVEL

Dribbling in a sport situation
Dribbling to keep the ball away from
an opponent
Stopping and starting while maintaining
the dribble

UTILIZATION
LEVEL

Dribbling and changing speed of traveling
Traveling and changing dribbling hand
Dribble around stationary obstacles
Dribbling while changing pathways
Dribbling while changing directions

CONTROL
LEVEL

Dribbling and traveling
Dribbling in different places around the body
while stationary
Dribbling with the body in different positions
Switch dribbling, using one hand and then
the other
Dribbling at different levels

PRECONTROL
LEVEL

Continuous striking down with either hand
Continuous striking down with dominant hand
Continuous striking down with both hands
Striking a ball down and catching it

When a child can repeatedly bounce the ball with either hand and remain in self-space, he is functioning at the control level. Appropriate tasks include:

1. Dribbling and traveling.
2. Dribbling and changing direction.
3. Dribbling in different places around the body.
4. Dribbling while changing speed.
5. Dribbling while changing pathway.

At the utilization level, children can successfully dribble with either hand and no longer have to look at the ball. They dribble with their fingers, and the wrist is relaxed. Appropriate tasks include:

1. Dribbling around obstacles.
2. Dribbling while changing the force of the bounce.

Children need a variety of dribbling activities so that they will be able to control a ball in different situations

You need advanced skills to dribble while successfully avoiding an opponent

When children reach the proficiency level, dribbling seems to be almost automatic. They are able to focus on the strategy of a particular situation that involves dribbling. Appropriate tasks at this level include:

1. Dribbling in different places around the body while traveling.
2. Dribbling to keep the ball away from an opponent (one-on-one).
3. Dribbling in a sport situation.

Dribbling is a skill that is normally developed for a basketball situation. We focus on it as one aspect of striking, rather than as a basketball skill. Children enjoy working with bouncing balls. Remember, though, that dribbling—like striking upward—is one of the last fundamental skills to develop because it requires fine hand-eye coordination.

Precontrol Level

Overview   At the precontrol level we provide opportunities for children to strike a ball down repeatedly without losing the ball from self-space. The children should use their fingers and a flexed wrist action rather than holding the whole hand rigidly.

IDEAS FOR DEVELOPMENT

IDEAS FOR OBSERVATIONAL FOCUS

Have children strike the ball down and try to make it come back to them.

Does the child keep his hands rigid when striking the ball? Or does he use his fingers and relax the wrists?

Is the child striking the center of the ball, so that it goes straight down? Or does he strike it on the back or side?

Does the child give the ball enough force so that it comes back up to him, so much that it bounces high over his head? Or does he give it just enough force so that the ball returns to him at waist level?

Does the child strike the ball far enough away from his body so the ball doesn't bounce off his feet?

Relatively light balls that bounce true (for example, they are not lopsided) are best for introducing children to dribbling. Eight-inch diameter playground balls are fine at this level.

Figure 25.6   Dribbling a ball

Have the children try to strike the ball down with one hand and make it come back to them. Then they try to do the same thing with the other hand.

Is the child's hand relaxed and flexible at the wrist (see Figure 25.6)? Or does he keep his whole hand flat and stiff?

Is the child able to coordinate his hand with the bounce of the ball, so that he is striking it down when he should?

Is he able to track the ball with his eyes?

Challenge the children to bounce a ball down in their own space and try to keep it going. How many times can they keep it going with one hand? The other? Can they beat their own record?

Does the child push the ball just as it stops its upward flight? Or does she rush her actions and strike the ball when it is already moving downward?

Does the child strike the ball so that it comes back to about her waist level? Or does it bounce too low or too high for control?

Is the child bouncing the ball so that it stays relatively close to her? Or does the ball move her all over the space?

Control Level

Overview   At the control level, children learn to dribble and travel at the same time. They will also be able to dribble in different places around their bodies and vary both direction and pathway.

IDEAS FOR DEVELOPMENT

IDEAS FOR OBSERVATIONAL FOCUS

Ask children to try to dribble the ball so that it does not go above:

1. The chin.
2. The waist.
3. The knees.

Children can use either hand to keep the ball below their knees.

Is the child able to repeatedly bounce a ball and simultaneously vary the force of the bounce?

Does he slap at the ball? Or is he able to push the ball with his fingers so that it returns to an appropriate level?

Challenge children to try to keep the ball going while switching from one hand to the other.

Does the child make contact with the ball on one side, so that the ball will travel toward the opposite hand (see Figure 25.7).

Ask children to try dribbling under their legs, around their legs, and around and under both legs.

Is the child able to appropriately vary the force of the bounce to keep the ball under a leg?

Is the child able to maneuver the ball to the appropriate side? Or is he bouncing the ball straight up and down and hopping over the ball?

In their self-space, children dribble in as many places as possible around the body—right side, left side, front, and back.

Is the child exploring every possible place around her body? Or does she stick to the easy ones?

Figure 25.7   Dribbling changing hands

Dribbling the ball at a low level

1. Each time that they dribble, children try to find a new place around the body to bounce the ball.

    Is the ball away from the body?

    Is the child able to control the ball in different places around her? Or does it cause her to roam all over the area?

    Does the child use the fingers and a flexed wrist or her whole flat hand?

2. Have children put their bodies in different positions (balance on different parts) while kneeling on one knee, and try to dribble.

    Is the child exploring a variety of positions?

    Can the child keep the ball going while in different positions?

3. Have children change the position they are in to another one and try to keep dribbling as they change.

    Is the child dribbling while she changes positions? Or does she catch the ball and start to dribble again?

    When in different positions, is the child bouncing the ball so that it comes back to her at an appropriate level or does she bounce it too hard or too gently?

Challenge children to dribble and walk around the room. (Remind children to watch out for each other!) Ask them to keep the ball close to them and travel at a safe speed. Have them stop on signal.

Is the child bouncing the ball ahead of her so that the ball does not bounce off her feet?

Is the child able to watch where she is going? Or does she look down at the ball all the time?

Is the child able to stop moving and maintain control of the ball?

Utilization Level

Overview   At the utilization level we provide situations in which children must dribble with either hand, without looking at the ball. Obstacles may be provided, and the children should learn to vary the force of the bounce.

IDEAS FOR DEVELOPMENT

IDEAS FOR OBSERVATIONAL FOCUS

Have the children change the speed at which they travel as they dribble around the space.

Can the child intentionally change the speed at which he is traveling?

Can the child push the ball ahead enough, while traveling fast, to maintain control of the ball?

On different signals—one beat for fast, two beats for slow, three beats for medium—have the children change the speed at which they travel.

Can the child listen to the signal and change speed accordingly?

Ask children to dribble around the space, changing their direction as they dribble—moving backward, sideways, forward.

Does the child move in different directions? Or does he simply change pathways?

Traveling backward and dribbling is not easy, because the ball must move toward the body and often hits the feet. Children will develop this direction last and should be made aware of the difficulty of dribbling backward.

1. On your signal, have children change the direction they are moving to another direc-

Can the child change direction and still control the ball as quickly as he hears the signal? Or does

tion. Challenge them to see if they can change each time a signal is given.

he hesitate or stop before changing directions?

Does the child have enough control of the ball to make it go with him? Or does he lose the ball as he concentrates on changing directions?

2. Ask children to change direction every time they get to a line on the floor.

Does the child change directions when she reaches a line? Or does she simply change pathways?

3. Have children change direction every time they approach another person.

Can the child change to an appropriate direction when confronted with another moving object?

Does she read the other person so that she does not run into her?

As they travel and dribble, have the children change the pathway they travel. They can move along a curved pathway, then along a zigzag pathway, then a straight pathway.

Is the child dribbling with her fingers?

Is she looking up as she travels?

Is the child actually traveling in different pathways? Can she tell you which pathway she is using?

1. Have children follow the lines on the gym floor (or playground) while dribbling the ball.

Does the ball go with her as she varies her pathway? Or does the child lose control of the ball?

2. As they travel and dribble, have children first dribble in a straight pathway, then in smooth curves, and finally in a sharp zigzag.

Can the child combine all three of the pathways without stopping between them?

3. Ask the children to try not to stop as they switch from one pathway to another.

Can the child dribble the ball while changing the pathways so that she does not stop traveling?

4. Challenge children to follow a partner's pathway while dribbling a ball.

Can the follower look up to see where the leader is going and still maintain control of the ball?

With obstacles (cones or milk jugs) set up around the area, children dribble around the obstacles. Have them always keep their bodies between the ball and the obstacles. They can pretend the obstacle is a person.

Is the child able to keep the ball away from the cone?

Does the child change hands as he approaches a cone in a different place, so that his body is between the ball and the cone?

Using people as stationary obstacles, children can dribble around them. The obstacles may try to take the ball if the children dribble next to them. But the obstacles may not touch the children and they may not move their feet.

Have children play one-on-one with a partner in a well-defined space. Each has a ball and tries to take the ball away from the other.

Have children play the dribbling game. They dribble through a field of four or five others, trying to get to the other side without having the ball stolen. The other children may reach but may not move their feet.

As children travel around the space, have them change their dribble from hand to hand as they travel. They change hands when they hear the signal (the faster the signal, the more difficult the challenge).

Challenge children to make up a sequence of changing pathways and speeds, including at least one change of speed and two different pathways.

Ask the children to make a map of directions and pathways (Figure 25.8) with a partner and try to follow it.

Have children dribble to a cone (cones should be spread out around the room). When they approach the cone, they plant one foot and reverse pivot around the cone so that their backs face the cone as they go around it. As they pivot, they must change hands with the ball; then keep going.

Can he change hands and places around the body quickly enough when he sees an obstacle? Or does he wait until he gets there?

Does the child change the places he dribbles as he moves? Or does he stop and then change?

In a dynamic situation can the child vary where he dribbles the ball in relation to the opponent?

Can the child change where he dribbles quickly enough to dodge the other children?

Can he choose uncrowded pathways to get through?

Is he looking up to see where to go?

Is the child moving the ball back and forth by placing a hand on the middle-top of the ball and pushing it to the other hand?

Can the child watch for others and simultaneously switch-dribble?

Is the child able to combine the ideas of pathways and speeds at the same time?

Does the ball follow the pathway of the child?

Is it clear what pathways and speeds are being used when? Can the child verbalize his movements?

Are the children able to read the map and follow it?

Is the child changing hands during the pivot as she turns? Or does she do it before or after the turn?

Use other children as cones. They may steal the ball if dribblers pivot the wrong way.

Is the child planting one foot as she pivots? Or is the foot picked up in the middle of the turn?

Does the pivot turn toward the foot that is planted with the back leading? Or does it cross over in front of the body?

Is the pivot smooth, without a break in speed?

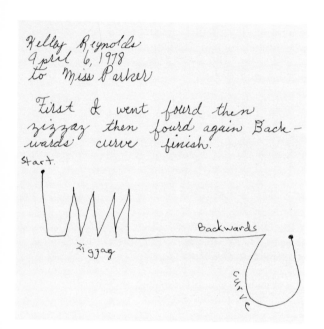

Kelley Reynolds
April 6, 1978
to Miss Parker

First I went fourd then zizzaz then fourd again Backwards curve finish.

Start.

Zigzag

Backwards

curve

Figure 25.8   A child's pathways map

Proficiency Level

Overview   Children at the proficiency level seem to dribble without thinking about it. They are able to change direction, speed, and pathway at will. They are challenged by situations that involve other children as partners or as opponents who make the situation increasingly unpredictable.

IDEAS FOR DEVELOPMENT

IDEAS FOR OBSERVATIONAL FOCUS

On signal, have the children stop traveling but continue to dribble the ball. Teacher gives signals to stop and start. This task becomes more difficult as the signals to stop and start come faster.

Is the child able to stop on signal? Or does he take a few extra steps after the signal?

Is the child able to keep dribbling when he stops? Or does he lose control of the ball?

Challenge the children to dribble a ball around the space while changing the speed of the bounce:

1. Sometimes high and slow.
2. Sometimes low and fast.
3. With either hand.

Teach Dribble Tag.

Objective: To keep from being caught by staying away from "it" and by maintaining control of the ball.

Rules:
1. Each child has a ball.
2. Two or three children are "it."
3. Children can only travel by dribbling a ball with one hand.
4. Children are caught if:
   a) they are tagged by an "it," or
   b) they lose control of the ball (the ball gets away from them) or they dribble with both hands.
5. If caught, children stand and hold the ball over their heads. They can be freed by another player tagging them on the back while she is dribbling the ball.
6. Have children change roles from time to time.

Challenge the children to jump over the ball as they bounce it and continue bouncing it after they cross it.

1. Have the children try to go under the ball as it bounces and keep bouncing it.

Can the child change the bounce of the ball so that the difference is apparent?

Is he able to control a low fast dribble as well as a medium-slow one?

Is the child looking up as he dribbles?

This game is appropriate initially in small groups and gradually in larger groups. Children need to be able to dribble successfully while traveling in relationship to others if they are to play the game with success.

Can the child time the jump so that he gets over the ball without hitting it?

Can he continue bouncing it after the jumps? Or does he lose complete awareness of where he is and the ball is?

Does he bounce the ball at a height that he can clear, yet high enough to control after he has crossed it?

Does he actually go under the ball?

Does the child actually bounce the ball high enough to get under, but not so high that he loses control of it?

2. Have the children try going over the ball on one bounce and under it on another, and keep bouncing the ball.

Can the child combine all these actions and tell you when he is performing each of them?

Is he able to continue dribbling the ball?

Have children receive a pass from a partner while moving. Without stopping, they start to dribble and keep moving. They dribble for a ways, and then pass the ball back to the partner. Have children keep doing this throughout their space.

Is the child receiving the ball on the run? Or does he stop to catch it and then dribble?

Is he starting to dribble as he receives the ball? Or does he catch and carry it for a few steps before starting to dribble?

Working in threes, two people dribble and pass while the third tries to steal the ball. The two pass as needed.

Do the children pass when the defender comes close to them or do they throw the ball away for no reason?

Are they able to make accurate passes to their partners?

Working two against two, have children play a game of keep-away that involves passing and dribbling.

Can the children apply their skills in a game situation?

Are they concentrating on dribbling and passing or do they end up throwing and catching?

Have children play a miniature basketball game, with only three or four players on a team and a small court. If necessary, use only one basket or target.

Do the children dribble the ball as they move? Or do they stand still and wait for someone to come help them?

Are the children able to look up as they dribble, to learn where the other players on their team are?

Are the children able to dodge their opponents as they move?

With two or three others, have children make up their own Harlem Globe Trotters routine. Challenge them to think of all the fancy dribbles they can use and try to master them—behind the back, under the legs, low dribbling, crazy passes, et cetera.

Are the children able to look up while they work, to look more professional?

Do they move around or stay in the same place?

CHAPTER 26
STRIKING WITH RACKETS AND PADDLES

The child who is learning to strike with a racket or paddle must coordinate many familiar skills into one new one. She must learn to accurately toss or drop the object to be contacted, visually track the object while she is traveling to an appropriate location, and contact the object at exactly the right moment. And simultaneously she must adjust to the weight and length of the implement. All of these variables must be coordinated by a successful striker.

Because striking with an implement is a complex skill, we teach this skill after children have been introduced to the skill of striking with body parts, specifically the hand (see Chapter Twenty-Five).

LEVELS OF SKILL PROFICIENCY

The difficulty of striking with an implement increases with the length of the implement. The child at the precontrol level benefits from practicing first with short-handled, lightweight implements. Balloons, which travel slowly, expedite visual tracking and eye–hand coordination. Appropriate tasks for the child at the precontrol level include:

1. Striking a balloon with a lightweight paddle or hose racket.
2. Striking a suspended ball.
3. Tossing a ball or object upward and hitting it.
4. Dropping an object and contacting it underhand.
5. Dropping a ball and contacting it after a bounce.

When a child is able to strike a ball consistently in these contexts, he is ready for control level experiences. These include contacting a re-

How many times can you strike an object before it touches the ground?

429

bounding ball a number of times in succession, sending the object in a desired direction, and varying the force of the contact. Other appropriate control level activities include:

1. Sending an object in straight or curved aerial pathways.
2. Sending a ball high enough to travel over a net.

The child at the utilization level is able to contact a ball repeatedly without a miss (bouncing it up or down with a paddle or racket) and is able to send a ball or other object various distances and in different directions. He is now ready to apply these skills in dynamic situations. These might involve moving into various positions to contact an object at different places around the body and returning shots to a partner. The skill of striking is now used in activities such as:

1. Striking with a variety of rackets and objects.
2. Continuously hitting to a rebound wall.
3. Striking cooperatively with a partner for high scores.
4. Striking with overhand, forearm, backhand, and underhand strokes.

Striking the ball at different places around your body

DEVELOPMENTAL STAGES OF STRIKING WITH RACKETS AND PADDLES

STAGE 1   Legs are usually stationary. Ball is given impetus, either by an overarm throwing action without any indication of a hit or by a pushing action. The trunk does not rotate.

STAGES 2 AND 3   A forward step is made with the same arm–leg pattern. Most of the action is still made by the arm. The trunk bends forward slightly. Limited spinal and pelvic rotation is exhibited.

The pelvis and trunk rotate as a unit. The rotation appears to result from rather than contribute to the swing (sidearm rather than overhand).

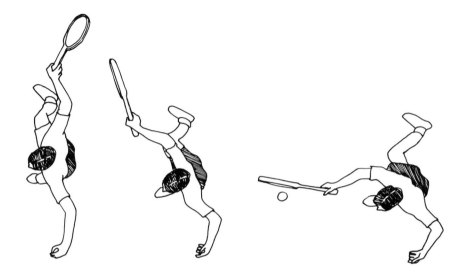

MATURE STRIKING PATTERN

In the preparatory phase, weight is shifted to the back foot, the trunk rotates 45° to 90°, the hip and trunk are cocked, and the racket is drawn back. This is followed by movements that occur in such quick succession that they seem almost simultaneous: the weight is shifted, the body rotates forward, and the racket is swung forward along a full arc (an arc around the body).

SOURCE: Adapted from R. L. Wickstrom, *Fundamental Motor Patterns*, 2nd ed. (Philadelphia: Lea & Febiger, 1977).

When the child has attained the proficiency level, she demonstrates a mature pattern of striking. She demonstrates both body and implement control while traveling and is able to select the most effective type of striking when responding to a partner. Experiences at the proficiency level center around game situations. Fast-moving, quick-reacting patterns of striking are required in both cooperative and competitive games. Appropriate activities include:

1. Playing cooperative or competitive games.
2. Offensive–defensive movements involving others.

Figure 26.1 presents ideas for developing the skill of striking with rackets, from the precontrol level through the proficiency level.

Figure 26.1   Sequence for developing the skill theme of striking with rackets and paddles

PROFICIENCY
LEVEL

Playing cooperative or
competitive games
Performing offensive–defensive
movements involving other players
Playing gamelike activities—against
a wall, over a net, in aerial
games, in ground games

UTILIZATION
LEVEL

Striking in various aerial pathways
in gamelike situations
Striking at different positions in relation
to the body
Cooperative and continuous hitting
with a partner
Striking with a partner, with minimum
traveling

CONTROL
LEVEL

Striking with various rackets, paddles,
and objects
Striking a ball rebounding from a wall
Striking an object to send it over a net
Striking an object to travel in desired aerial
pathway, straight or curved
Varying the force of the hit
Sending an object in a desired direction
Striking a ball upward or downward for more
than one contact

PRECONTROL
LEVEL

Striking a self-tossed object or dropped ball
Striking a suspended ball
Striking a balloon with a lightweight paddle

Precontrol Level

Overview   At the precontrol level we provide experiences for the children to use lightweight paddles to contact balls, shuttlecocks, and other objects. These objects are often suspended from ropes at various heights to make the task easier.

IDEAS FOR DEVELOPMENT	IDEAS FOR OBSERVATIONAL FOCUS
Have the children use a lightweight hose racket to strike a balloon up in the air.	Does the child focus on the object until contact is made?
1. Ask the children to see how many times they can hit it before it touches the floor?	
2. Have the children try to keep it up without moving from their self-space.	Does the child begin to adjust the angle of contact so the balloon travels upward, not back over the head?
3. Have the children try to keep it in the air in front of them as they travel slowly forward.	Does the child strike in a forward direction when traveling forward?

CONSTRUCTION OF NYLON HOSE RACKETS

Lightweight rackets can be made from old coat hangers, nylon hose (stockings), and tape.

1. Grasp the handle of the coat hanger and the bottom.

2. Pull in opposite directions until the coat hanger is the desired shape.

3. Pull one stocking over the coat hanger from bottom to handle.

4. Wrap the excess stocking around the handle after bending the sharp edge down.

5. Tape or tie the end of the stocking around the handle.

Youngsters at the precontrol level benefit from practice with short-handled, lightweight rackets

Striking a suspended ball is an effective form of practice for many children

Balloons are suggested at the precontrol level. The flight of a balloon is longer and slower than that of a ball, and so the child has more time for visual tracking. Heavier balloons, although a bit more expensive, are more durable than are inexpensive, lightweight balloons. They also tend to be less erratic during flight and consequently are easier for children to strike successfully.

Challenge the children to contact a suspended, swinging object (whiffle, tennis ball, or yarn ball) so it travels straight ahead.

Is contact made with face of racket for forward travel?

Young children enjoy the auditory feedback from a jingle bell or a metal bong when contact is made. This can be provided by attaching a small bell to a ball. Or a metal gong, loose plastic jugs, or similar sound-producing objects can be placed on a wall as targets.

A tennis ball can be attached to a rope with small squares of velcro so it will detach and travel when contacted.

Have children stand on the carpet square behind the ball to strike. (Balls are above shoulder height.)

Have children stand on the carpet square beside the ball to strike. (Balls are at waist height.)

Does the trunk rotate prior to contact?

Is weight shifted from back foot (in preparatory stage) to forward (contact) foot?

Is there arm–foot opposition?

Is follow-through in desired direction?

At this point the child should be striking on his preferred side. When the child begins to strike consistently, challenge the child to strike on the opposite side of the body (for example, backhand).

IDEAS FOR SUSPENDING BALLS ON STRINGS

Balls can be suspended from climbing

apparatus, [⌒●●⌒],

traveling rings [♀ ♀],   and between

volleyball game standards [[▮●▮]] ,

and they can be attached to walls in

corners of the gym [▷●].

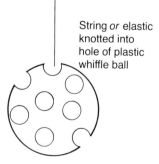

Velcro square glued onto string and tennis ball

(allows ball to release from string when struck)

String *or* elastic knotted into hole of plastic whiffle ball

Control Level

Overview Experiences at the control level are designed to help children go beyond just contacting the ball. At this level children learn to control the direction, force, and aerial pathway of an object.

IDEAS FOR DEVELOPMENT

IDEAS FOR OBSERVATIONAL FOCUS

Have children hold the ball at shoulder height and racket at waist or below. They release the ball and contact it with their hose racket before it drops to the floor.

Is ball or object released? Or is it tossed?

Does timing of the swing correspond with release of the object to be hit?

Have children contact a shuttlecock with a short-handled racket (wood or Plexiglas) in the same way.

Does child maintain visual contact with object to be hit until it touches paddle?

Is there a follow-through after contact? Is it in desired direction?

Using a paddle or racket, children can strike a tennis ball downward in a continuous dribble.

Is arm extended away from the body, so that the downward hit does not bounce on the feet?

1. Have them keep the ball below waist height.
2. Have them see how many times they can dribble in one minute.
3. Have them try an upside down dribble, striking the ball upward from the racket.

Is the face of the racket held flat, not at an angle, so that the ball travels straight down and rebounds straight?

Is the ball actually hit, not just touched or followed by the paddle?

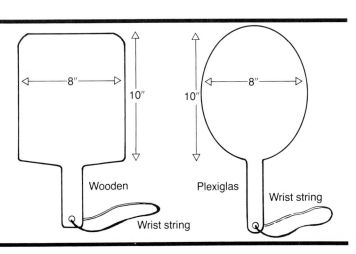

CONSTRUCTION OF SHORT-HANDLED PADDLES
Short-handled paddles can be cut with a jigsaw from half-inch finished plywood or from quarter-inch Plexiglas. Plywood edges need to be sanded until they are smooth, and the handles can be wrapped with fiberglass tape. Each paddle should have a wrist string for safety.

Ask children to see how many times they can strike the ball upward before losing control. Have them try to remain in self-space as they continually strike the ball.

Have the children strike a ball or shuttlecock at midlevel, so it travels straight ahead.

Have children initiate a strike at midlevel, so the ball travels upward as well as forward. Suggest that they try to send it to the left or to the right of where they are standing. Encourage them to continue working until they can send the ball where they want it to go.

Is the ball contacted with the proper amount of force? (Too little force makes it die flat; and too much makes it rebound out of control.)

Is contact with the ball or shuttlecock made before the paddle travels above waist height?

Is the swing of the paddle arm back to front, brushing the hip?

Is the face of the paddle at the appropriate angle so that the ball will rebound in the direction intended? Is the paddle facing forward (square face)? Upward (open face)?

Does the preparatory swing of the paddle travel in the direction in which the object is to travel?

Remind the children to step into the ball, so it is contacted at a point slightly in front of the forward foot. The angle of the swing can be suggested by the verbal clue of "drawing a line"—straight, left, right—with the swing.

Have the children strike the ball or object so it travels as far as they can send it. Mark the target spot. Now they can try to make contact that will send the object half that distance.

Challenge the children to vary the force to send the ball the desired distance from them.

Have the children strike an object so that it lands on a designated target (for example, markings on playground or on gymnasium floor).

Have the children strike the ball or object so it travels over a net. A low net is about three feet from the floor. A higher net would be five, six, or at most seven feet from the floor.

Ask the children to use various striking patterns (sidearm, overhead, and underhand).

Does the child use a proper swing and follow-through regardless of the force of the swing?

Can the child vary the amount of force for the contact, as opposed to (1) just hitting, or (2) hitting as hard as she can each time?

Does the child adjust (1) the force and (2) the angle of the racket to send the object to the target?

Does the child contact the object so it has sufficient height to cross the net? Does she use a sidearm hit or an overhead hit?

Does the child begin to control direction and force for placement in desired area?

Have the children use a short implement to strike a ball that rebounds from the wall.

Does the child move to be in proper position to hit the ball—slightly behind and to the side, about an arm's length from the ball?

Challenge children to see how many continuous hits they can achieve, allowing the ball to bounce only once?

Does the child bend her knees if ball is low, so that she swings at waist height?

Have the children strike the ball at waist height each time, using a sidearm swing on their right or left side.

If the ball is high, does the child wait for the ball to drop?

Have children experiment with striking from different angles in relation to the wall.

Is the child in a ready position before the moment of contact, with racket drawn back and weight on back foot?

Challenge the children to see how many successive hits they can make striking a tennis ball to the wall above a three-foot boundary (tape on wall).

Does the child adjust for proper grip on the implement when contacting on nonpreferred side?

Children may hit the ball as hard as they wish,

Does the child adjust body position for striking

Children at the control level benefit from repeatedly striking a ball against a wall

but it must rebound at least five feet from the wall. Remind them—only one bounce between hits.

on nonpreferred side, as opposed to reaching across the body?

At the control level we introduce children to a variety of striking implements and to objects with various surfaces, lengths, and types and degrees of bounce. These include:

> ping pong paddles
> racket ball paddles
> paddle ball paddles
> badminton rackets
> tennis rackets
> paddle balls
> tennis balls
> racket balls
> rubber balls
> shuttlecocks
> ping pong balls

At the utilization and proficiency levels we continue to provide a variety of striking implements and objects.

Utilization Level

Overview   Experiences at the utilization level enable children to strike with an implement—not as an invariant skill, but in dynamic environments that involve partners and striking from different positions in relation to the body.

IDEAS FOR DEVELOPMENT

IDEAS FOR OBSERVATIONAL FOCUS

Have children see how many times they and a partner can keep the ball going without a miss. They may choose cooperative striking:

1. Against the wall.
2. Over a net.
3. Over a line on floor.
4. Across a table or a bench.

Does the child attain ready position?

Does the child step into the hit?

Does the angle of the swing go in the desired direction?

Does the child use force and direction to hit so the partner can successfully return the hit?

Does the child hit the ball on either side? Or does he run around the ball, so that he can always hit on his preferred side?

Ask children to toss the ball higher than the maximum reach of their implement; stretch to contact the ball at the highest point. Send it in a straight, downward pathway over a net, line, or bench.

Have the children contact the ball or shuttlecock with an underhand swing to produce a lifted, curved, aerial pathway.

Working with a partner, children contact the ball with either a forehand or a backhand hit as needed; they send the ball alternately to the partner's preferred side and to his nonpreferred side.

Working with a partner and a short paddle or racket, children strike a ball that is bounced or tossed to them, adjusting the body to send the ball straight ahead regardless of the height of the ball. They are looking for a successful strike by only one partner. And so it is beneficial for partner A, who tosses the ball, to collect the ball after partner B hits it, and *not* attempt to strike it back.

Are the toss of the ball and the preparatory swing timed correctly for contact at the highest point?

Is the racket face at the proper angle to send the ball downward?

Does the child adjust force so that the ball does not travel beyond boundaries?

Does the child execute an equally strong and mature pattern (see Developmental Stages) on either side?

Does the child travel into an appropriate position to hit the ball?

Does the child anticipate the direction and force of the oncoming ball?

Does the child place hits? Or does he just return the ball?

Does the child maintain visual contact with the ball until she hits it?

Is the body an arm-extension distance from the ball?

Does the child use a mature striking pattern? (See Developmental Stages.)

In the beginning stages of striking a ball sent by a partner, children may benefit from the ball being tossed consistently to the preferred or non-preferred side. Then they can progress to adjusting the preparatory stage according to the direction of the oncoming ball.

Have children strike a ball that is sent to them by a partner striking.

Does the child move her body into position for the hit?

Does she react as soon as her partner hits, or does she wait until the ball is there before preparing?

> At this point we often observe a regression to an immature striking pattern, and frustration, because a successful hit depends a great deal on the hit of the other child. Remember: Children are individuals. Rarely will an entire class be ready for this task at the same time!

Proficiency Level

Overview   Experiences at the proficiency level encourage children to enjoy the challenge of striking with short-handled implements in game situations. These activities involve partner or opponent relationships, spatial strategy, and the varied use of effort qualities.

IDEAS FOR DEVELOPMENT

IDEAS FOR OBSERVATIONAL FOCUS

In relation to a partner, children create a game of striking and receiving. They decide on boundaries. Have them work to be able to strike from any direction in relation to the body, trying to cooperate with their partner by sending the ball to his preferred side. This activity can be changed to a competitive game by those children who choose to do so.

At this level the observational focus of the teacher is on defects in the mature pattern of execution and on the child's ability to implement and control the effort qualities as intended.

Teach Wall Ball (see Figure 26.2).

Objective: To hit the ball against the wall so the opponent will not be able to return hit after a bounce.

Rules: 1. Use racket ball paddles and rubber balls, or wooden paddles and tennis balls.
2. You score only when you serve.
3. The ball may be hit after one bounce or before the bounce.

Teach Corner Ball (see Figure 26.3). Same as Wall Ball except that either wall in a corner may be used.

Both Corner Ball and Wall Ball can be played cooperatively. That is, children may prefer to see how many hits they can make without a miss.

Does the child use both long and short strikes in his play?

Does he move into position quickly?

Does he swing through each strike?

Does he use wrist action as well as a draw-the-line swing (a swing that travels along an imaginary line to the target)?

Is there any deviation from a mature striking pattern?

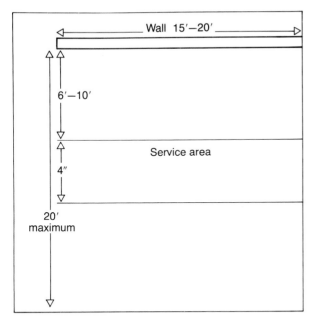

Figure 26.2   Wall ball

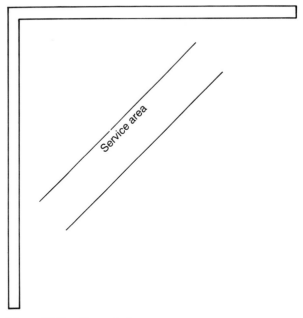

Figure 26.3   Corner ball

Teach aerial net games

Equipment: Solid paddles, badminton rackets, or shuttlecocks.

Net height: Between shoulder and head height of children.

Objective: To send an object over a net so that the opponent can return the hit before it touches ground.

Rules: **1.** Play begins with underhand strike (serve) behind designated line.

        2. Aerial strikes continue until object touches ground or goes out of bounds.

Is the underhand service at the proper angle for object to travel over net? Is swing for service front to back and close to body?

Does child use striking skills overhead and on either side of body?

Does she vary force and direction? Or does she just hit?

Does she use wrist action for added skill?

Aerial net games using a shuttlecock can be played with regular tambourines, with old ones that are discarded from rhythm band because the jingles have been lost, or with purchased tambourines with rubberized heads. Children enjoy the sound made when the shuttlecock strikes the tambourine.

Teach ground net games

Equipment: Short paddles, short-handled tennis rackets, regulation tennis rackets, or tennis balls.

The main difference in the short implement striking of tennis, as compared to those previously described, is the absence of wrist action.

Net height: A low net and a surface that permits the ball to bounce.

Objective: To send the ball over the net so it bounces within the court and the opponent is able to return the hit before it bounces twice.

(Can be changed to a competitive game by those children who prefer to do so.)

Does the child swing through the striking pattern with the swinging arm as a unit? The wrist does *not* bend at any point in the stroke.

Rules: 1. Play begins with an overhead strike (serve) behind the end line.
2. The ball can bounce no more than one time on either side of the net.
3. It may be contacted before the bounce (volley).

Children should decide on a scoring system and any other playing rules before beginning the game. Many will choose to play the game with few rules and no score—to just enjoy the activity.

Is the ball tossed high enough?

Does preparatory swing begin with the toss of the ball?

Does the child strike the ball at arm-plus-racket distance from the body on either side?

Does the child turn his body into position for a backhand, as opposed to reaching across the body?

Proficiency-level striking with rackets and paddles involves a complex of movement components—aerial pathways, force, direction, placement, and partner/opponent interactions. The teacher becomes a coach, looking for any deficiency in skill and helping each child to develop game strategies.

CHAPTER 27
STRIKING WITH LONG-HANDLED IMPLEMENTS

The skill of striking is used in many games. In this book, striking is divided into various categories: kicking and punting, volleying and dribbling, striking with rackets, and striking with long-handled implements. This makes it possible to cover in some detail the gamut of striking activities. The basic action in all striking is the same—giving impetus to an object with a hit, punch, or tap—though often the purpose and the equipment differ.

In this chapter we focus on striking with long-handled implements—golf clubs, hockey sticks, and bats. These implements are swung in horizontal or vertical planes, although the underlying challenge, of coordinating hands and eyes when striking with a long-handled implement, remains constant. Each of the swings has distinctive characteristics. And so we have chosen to subdivide this chapter and discuss the three types of implements separately in the Ideas for Development sections. Each swing involves striking away from the body. But the motor skills differ in relation to the purpose of the task.

Generally, striking is the last fundamental motor pattern that is learned, because of the complexity of the hand–eye coordination involved. A child may possess a mature striking pattern before he is able to consistently make contact with the ball.

A sidearm pattern is used when striking a ball with a bat. Generally a sidearm swing is made in an effort to keep the bat at the same distance from the ground and in a horizontal plane throughout the swing. In contrast, a swing with a hockey stick or golf club uses a more vertical arc. This is referred to as an underhand swinging pattern because in many ways it resembles the movement used to throw a ball underhand.

DEVELOPMENTAL STAGES OF SIDEARM STRIKING PATTERN

STAGE 1   The child tends to use a vertical pattern. He turns to face the object squarely and then swings the bat by extending the forearms and uncocking the wrists. The bend in the trunk is the counterpart of rotation.

STAGE 2   The child now swings in an oblique plane. The arm action initiates the movement and is followed by limited spinal and pelvic rotation. The pelvis and trunk rotate as a unit, as a result of the swing.

STAGE 3   At this stage there is more weight shift to the forward foot and a greater range of joint actions. The separation of rotatory elements becomes clearer.

STAGE 4   The child now swings the bat in a horizontal plane. He rotates his body around the long axis of the body and moves the bat to meet the trajectory of the ball.

MATURE SIDEARM STRIKING — A forward step is taken and is followed quickly by hip, trunk, and arm rotation. The forward movement of the trunk stops before contact, but the whipping rotation from the shoulders and arms continues. The pushing motion of the right arm and uncocking of the wrists are the final significant forces.

SOURCE: Adapted from R. L. Wickstrom, *Fundamental Motor Patterns,* 2nd ed. (Philadelphia: Lea & Febiger, 1977).

DEVELOPMENTAL STAGES OF UNDERHAND STRIKING PATTERN (USED WITH HOCKEY STICK AND GOLF CLUB)

STAGE 1   The child uses an overhead chop-
ping action, striking the top of the ball.

STAGE 2   A sidearm swing is now used. A step is taken, the implement swings downward, and it is then pushed forward. The child usually bends at the knees or the waist to lower his trunk toward the object.

STAGE 3   There is now an initial sideward and   of the trunk. The weight shifts forward,
           downward swing of the implement, ac-   the trunk rotates, the wrists uncock,
           companied by a slight forward bend   and there is a sweeping follow-through.

MATURE UNDERHAND STRIKING   The joints are cocked—weight is shifted to the back foot, the hips and trunk rotate away from the ball, the implement is raised up and behind the back shoulder, and the wrists are cocked. The body weight is then shifted to the forward foot. There is a forward rotation of the hips and spine, a downward swing of the forearm, and uncocking of the back arm and wrists. The forward arm stays straight throughout the swing.

SOURCE: R. L. Wickstrom, *Fundamental Motor Patterns,* 2nd ed. (Philadelphia: Lea & Febiger, 1977).

We do not introduce children to striking with long-handled implements so that they will become experts at golf or tennis or hockey. Rather, we provide children with opportunities to practice striking patterns they are likely to use in a variety of contexts throughout their lives. This rationale can be fully appreciated when watching an adult trying to strike with a long-handled implement. If that individual has had no previous experience with a particular striking pattern, the results can be disastrous. Frustration will result and ultimately the sport may be abandoned. Our emphasis is on providing children with a variety of movement opportunities, rather than on perfecting the technical aspects of a particular swing. Specific opportunities to refine and perfect different swings will be provided at the secondary level or in private instruction.

Most long-handled implements are designed for adults. Because children are not "regulation size," they find it difficult to manipulate implements of official size, length, and weight. For this reason we use lightweight, plastic implements in our programs. Or we make implements that match the sizes of the children. This eliminates the learning of poor habits that develop when children try to use equipment that is too heavy or too long.

LEVELS OF SKILL PROFICIENCY

Initial striking tasks at the precontrol level include:

1. Striking a stationary object with a hockey stick or golf club.
2. Striking a ball off a batting tee with a plastic bat.
3. Striking a ball (or puck) on the floor in different places around the body with a hockey stick.
4. Traveling slowly while striking an object with a hockey stick.
5. Striking a suspended object.

When the child is able to consistently make contact with an object (control level), he then becomes able to succeed at more difficult tasks, such as:

1. Traveling while striking an object (beanbag, puck, ball) and changing direction.
2. Traveling with an object and changing speed while using a hockey stick.
3. Striking a pitched ball.

4. Using a hockey stick to propel an object while traveling along different pathways.
5. Traveling, stopping, and controlling the ball (or puck).
6. Throwing a ball up to self and striking it.
7. Striking to a stationary partner.
8. Striking a ball for distance with a golf club.

At the control level the tasks typically include only one variable besides striking.

When a child can control a ball in the space around him (whether he is stationary or traveling) and his striking pattern is in the appropriate phase, he is functioning at the utilization level. Appropriate tasks include:

1. Propelling an object while traveling and dodging stationary objects.
2. Striking a ball consistently for distance and accuracy, at targets of different sizes, with a golf club.
3. Directing the pathway of a pitched or rolled ball using a bat or hockey stick.
4. Striking for distance.
5. Passing to a traveling partner.

When children reach the proficiency level, many possess mature striking patterns, and striking becomes a skill that can be used in dynamic situations. At this point children are able to incorporate previous experiences into situations that involve strategy and split-second decisions. Appropriate tasks include:

1. Traveling while propelling an object and dodging other children.
2. Positioning the body to strike an oncoming object to an open space, while traveling and while stationary.
3. Striking with a golf club to targets in a strategic situation.
4. Passing and receiving an object while moving and dodging other children.

Striking skills may be the last to develop. But once children have developed the ability to consistently strike objects with long-handled implements, they can participate in many fascinating activities.

The sequence for developing the skill theme of striking with long-handled implements from the precontrol to the proficiency level, is shown in Figure 27.1.

PROFICIENCY LEVEL

Striking with a group against
  another group to achieve a mutual goal
Striking to a teammate to avoid
  others in a dynamic situation
Directing the pathway, distance, and
  speed of an object
Passing and receiving on the move
Striking to dodge an opponent

UTILIZATION LEVEL

Passing from a stationary position to
  a moving target
Directing the air pathway of the
  object struck
Striking to distant targets of various sizes
Striking and dodging stationary objects
Striking a pitched object, varying
  the distance
Directing the placement of the object struck

CONTROL LEVEL

Throwing a ball in the air and striking it
Striking a pitched ball
Striking an object at various heights
Striking a stationary object,
  varying the distance and force
Striking to a stationary partner
Striking to a stationary large target
Traveling while changing speeds, pathways,
  and/or direction
Traveling, stopping, and controlling the ball

PRECONTROL LEVEL

Traveling slowly while striking a ball on the floor
  with an implement
Striking a suspended object
Striking in different places around the body
Striking off a batting tee
Striking a stationary ball on the floor

Precontrol Level

Overview   Children at the precontrol level are provided with experiences that help them adjust to the additional length of the implements and the greater demands on hand–eye coordination. They learn to strike a stationary object with a bat, hockey stick, and golf club, and they begin to be able to control a ball with a hockey stick while traveling.

HOW TO MAKE A GOLF CLUB OR HOCKEY STICK (DESIGN BY TOM TRIMBLE, UNIVERSITY OF GEORGIA)

Materials

Hardwood dowel rod, ⅝″ X 3′

Garden hose or rubber tubing, ⅝″ (inside diameter)

Roll of electrical or adhesive tape (one roll will be sufficient for at least 12 sticks)

Two flat headed nails, ⅝″

Coat hanger

Directions

1. Cut an 18″ length of the garden hose and slip it approximately 3½″ onto the dowel.

2. Insert a piece of coat hanger wire into the hose so that it butts up against the bottom of the dowel and extends almost to the end of the hose.

3. Bend the hose so that the ends meet on the dowel rod. The hose can be formed at whatever angle is desired.

4. Use two nails to secure hose to dowel. One of the two nails can be used to attach the bottom portion of the hose bent in half to the top portion.

5. Tape should be used to give further support to the hose or the dowel.

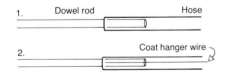

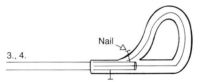

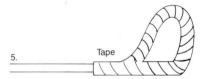

IDEAS FOR DEVELOPMENT

Have children use a golf club to hit a whiffle ball straight ahead. Have them see how far they can hit it.

Figure 27.1   Sequence for developing the skill theme of striking with long-handled implements

IDEAS FOR OBSERVATIONAL FOCUS

Is the club held appropriately? (See Figure 27.2.)

Does the child face the ball from the side or from behind it?

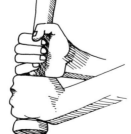

How far can you hit the ball?

Is his entire body used in the swing? Or does he use just his arms?

Does the club fully contact the ball? Or does it skim across the top?

Is the swing full from behind the head? Or is it cut short?

Does the child move away from the ball to get a full swing? Or does he stand on top of it?

Do the child's feet remain stationary? Or does he step, as in a baseball swing.

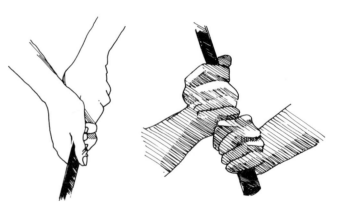

Figure 27.2   Golf club grip

Have children hit a ball from a batting tee with a bat.

Figure 27.3   Batting grip

Is the bat held appropriately? (See Figure 27.3.)

Is the swing level?

Is the child standing far enough away from the ball to get a full swing?

Does the whole side of the bat contact the ball?

Do the eyes remain on the ball? Or do they follow the bat to the ball?

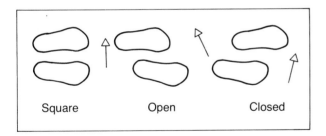

Square   Open   Closed

Figure 27.4   Stance position

Does the child use a mature striking pattern when hitting the ball? Is the entire body involved?

Does the child change the placement of her feet to direct where the ball is going? (See Figure 27.4.)

Suspend balls on string around the space. Have children practice striking at them with plastic bats. Be sure to remind the children to watch for others.

Do the child's eyes remain on the ball?

Do the wrists break as the ball is struck? Or are the arms stiff?

HOW TO MAKE A BATTING TEE
The easiest way to make a batting tee is to use a large (36″) traffic cone. For young children this is high enough. You can increase the height by placing the traffic cone on a cardboard box.

A batting tee can also be made out of a tin can and a plastic tube.

Materials

large tin can (available from the school cafeteria)

plastic golf club tube (obtained from sporting goods store)

sack of ready mixed concrete (¹/₁₀ to ⅛)

Directions

1. Place the golf club tube into the tin can.
2. Add water to the concrete mix and fill the tin can approximately one-half full.
3. After a few minutes, when the concrete begins to harden, make sure that the golf club tube is not leaning to the side. Once the concrete dries, the batting tee is ready to use.

The heights of the batting tees can be varied by shortening the plastic golf club tubes before inserting them in the cans. We try to have batting tees of three different heights.

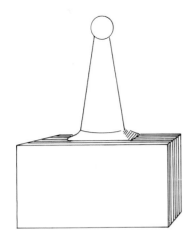

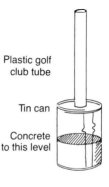

Plastic golf club tube

Tin can

Concrete to this level

Batting tees are helpful for children at the precontrol level who are unable to strike a moving ball

Learning to swing level by practicing with a ball suspended on a string

Traveling while manipulating a ball with an implement

Is the swing level?

Does the bat contact the ball at the midpoint, on the top, or on the bottom?

Are the arms away from the body? Or do the elbows stay close to the sides?

Are the hands crossed on the bat? Or are they natural, to provide a full swing? (See Figure 27.3.)

Have children hit a ball suspended from a basketball backboard or a rope.

Do the trunk and hips rotate with the swing and the feet remain stationary? Or does the child spin around as he swings?

Does the ball contact the bat on the far end of the bat or close to the hands?

Challenge children to see how many times in a row they can hit the ball without a miss.

Is the swing full, starting from behind the shoulders and coming across the body? Or is it short from inside the shoulders to the point of contact?

Striking practice can be enhanced by tying plastic balls onto heavy string and then tying the suspended balls to a rope stretched across the practice area.

Ask children to stay in their own space, or inside a hoop, and with a ball and a hockey stick move a ball around as much as possible. They must try to keep it moving.

1. Have them use both sides of the stick.
2. Have them use both sides of their bodies.

Is the child holding the hockey stick appropriately? (See Figure 27.5.)

Is the blade of the hockey stick striking the ball?

Do the child's eyes follow the contact?

Figure 27.5   Hockey stick grip

3. Ask them to make it go backward and forward, and from side to side.

Is it clear that the child is striking in different places around the body?

Is the child maintaining the same hand grip on both sides of the body?

Can the child move her feet out of the way when necessary to keep the ball going?

Does the child strike the ball away from her feet or is she falling over the ball?

Challenge children to strike a ball against a wall with a ball and a hockey stick.

Do the child's eyes follow the ball and the stick as she strikes it?

Does the child use two hands on the stick?

Are the child's arms away from her body as she strikes? Or are her elbows close to the body?

Does the child contact the ball from behind? Or does the stick hit the top of the ball or miss completely?

Is there a step into the action or is the child stationary?

Do the trunk and hips rotate with the swing?

Is the ball contacted away from the feet or close to them?

Is the swing an underarm pattern?

Does the child stand erect? Or does he bend his knees so he is sure it hit the ball?

Ask children to walk around the space slowly while dribbling a ball or puck with a hockey stick.

Is the child actually dribbling the ball? Or is he pushing it?

Is the child able to look up and still dribble?

Is the ball close to the stick?

Is the child using the proper grip on the stick? (See Figure 27.5)

All the preceding activities need to be done with balls of various sizes. For beginners, yarn balls or large plastic balls are easier, as they are larger and/or do not roll as fast as other balls. For tasks that involve traveling, plastic pucks are easier to control initially, if the lesson is being taught on a smooth wood or tile floor. Until children become skilled and responsible, we recommend that plastic balls be used. The flight is not as true, but safety is an important consideration.

Control Level

Overview   At the control level children begin to develop mature striking patterns that are used in increasingly complex contexts. Traveling while striking or tapping an object along the ground is combined with a single variable, such as changing direction or speed. The children also practice striking a pitched ball and striking a golf ball for distance.

IDEAS FOR DEVELOPMENT	IDEAS FOR OBSERVATIONAL FOCUS

Bat

Children work with a partner. One child pitches a ball; the other strikes it with a bat.

Are the swings level?

Is a mature striking pattern used?

Do the eyes follow the ball through the point of contact?

Is the swing smooth? Or is it disjointed and broken?

Does the bat contact the ball clearly behind the ball? Or does it skim the top or bottom?

Use a plastic bat and ball. Children throw the ball into the air so that they can hit it.

1. Have them try to change the distance they hit the ball.
2. After they are able to contact the ball consistently, have them try to strike the ball to the same place each time.

Are the arms extended as the child swings? Or are the elbows close to the body?

Is the child's side to the ball or does she face it?

Do the shoulders and trunk rotate as she swings?

Is the swing level?

Is the contact with the ball directly behind it? Or does the child swing from underneath or on top of it?

Does the child follow through with the bat and her body after contact.

Are the hands placed properly or are they crossed? (See Figure 27.3.)

Do the eyes follow the ball through contact?

Working as partners—one child pitches a ball; the other strikes it with a bat

Hockey stick

With a hockey stick and puck (or ball) children travel around the area:

1. They can change direction—backward, sideways, and forward—every time that they hear the signal.
2. They can change direction when they come close to another person.
3. They can follow the direction that is called out by the teacher. (The teacher can vary the speed of the changes as the ability of the class changes. Children enjoy trying to make rapid changes in direction.)

Does the child strike the puck (or ball) about eighteen inches in front of his body, so that he has the maneuverability to change the direction?

Is one of the child's hands low on the stick, so he has more control of the object?

Is the child able to keep the puck with him as he changes directions?

Does the child actually strike the puck? Or does he push it along?

Is the stick in a vertical position? Or is it slanted back toward the body?

Does the child contact the entire puck with the blade of the stick? Or does the stick contact the top of the puck?

Is the stick held stiffly as it contacts the puck? Or do the wrists give and allow the stick to turn sideways?

When first working with this idea, some children may have to be reminded to slow down. The purpose is to travel with the object, not to hit and then chase it.

4. They can try to cross the area, watching what pathways they need to use so that they don't run into anyone.

Is the child using the appropriate pathways to get across the room? Or does she change only when asked to?

5. They can develop a sequence that involves at least two changes of pathway and two changes of direction.

Is the child changing pathway and direction at the same time? Or does she do them separately?

Can she verbalize both the pathway and the direction?

6. They can work with a partner and play follow-the-leader copying the partner's pathway as they go.

Does the child contact the ball with both sides of the stick to keep the pathway true?

With a hockey stick and a puck (or ball), children try to strike the puck:

1. Into a milk crate on its side.
2. To an X on the wall
3. Between two cones.
4. To a goal cage.

Are the child's arms away from her body?

Is the puck about eighteen inches in front of the body? Or is it too close or too far to hit?

Is the puck in front of the foot on the same side as the stick?

Is the child cleanly contacting the puck? Or does she slap at it?

Is the puck contacted with the full blade of the stick?

Is there enough force in the hit to get the puck to the target?

Is the follow-through in the intended direction of the hit?

Children work with a partner and strike a ball back and forth with a hockey stick. Both of them should be standing still.

Are the arms away from the body as the child strikes and receives the ball?

Have children ask for the ball by placing their stick in certain places around their bodies and see if their partner can hit it there.

Does the child contact the ball with the whole blade of the stick vertical?

Is the follow-through in the direction of the intended hit?

Is the ball struck on the same side of the body as the stick is?

Do the arms and stick give as the ball is received?

Is the child able to send the ball straight to the partner?

Tell the children that they can sometimes have their partner stand further away.

Does the child put the right amount of force behind the ball to get it to the partner but not so much force that the partner cannot control the ball?

Golf club

With a golf club, children see if they can hit balls to different distances.

Does the child use a full swing? With proper form?

Is the entire club face contacting the ball?

Is the ball placed far enough away from the body to allow a full swing?

Can the child choose the distance he would like to hit the ball to and then do it? Or are the variations in distance accidental?

As with batting, children enjoy having a field marked off at different distances, so it is very clear where they are aiming.

Utilization Level

Overview At the utilization level, situations are provided in which children learn to consistently strike objects with long-handled implements. A variety of contexts are planned, particularly ones that involve more than one variable in an unpredictable or changing environment.

IDEAS FOR DEVELOPMENT

IDEAS FOR OBSERVATIONAL FOCUS

Golf club

With a golf club, children see if they can gently lift the plastic ball off the ground in an arched pathway:

1. Over a block and cane.
2. Over a cone.
3. Over a box.

Is the club striking the ball so that the ball is entirely on the club face and so rises into the air?

Is the child pulling away or looking up, causing the club to hit the ball in the middle or on top?

Is the child keeping his knees bent as he shifts his weight?

Try to strike the ball into the hoop using as few strokes as possible

Spread hoops around the field. With a golf club, children try to strike a ball between the hoops, using as few strokes as possible. Place the hoops different distances apart.

Does the child use a mature striking pattern involving the total body?

Does he transfer his weight to the forward foot as he swings?

Does the child vary the length of his swings to adjust for different distances?

Bat

Children have a partner pitch easy balls to them, and hit the balls with their bats.

1. Have children try to hit the ball to different places in the field—right, left, straight.
2. Have children try to hit the ball different distances—sometimes short, sometimes long.

Does the child decide on the distance and then hit the ball? Or are the variances accidental?

Does the child alter the speed and amount of force behind the swing, depending on the distance that she wants the ball to go?

Does she use her entire body to swing the bat, or only her arms and shoulders?

Does the child step into the swing?

3. Challenge children to see how many times in a row they can strike the ball without a miss.

Does the whole bat contact the ball?

Children can hit a ball from a batting tee. With three or four players scattered around an area, they try to hit the ball where the players aren't, so nobody can catch the ball before it hits the ground.

Is the child changing her stance to hit where the fielders aren't? Or does she try to do it by using her arms?

Have children hit a pitched ball. With three or four players scattered around an area, they try to hit the ball where the players aren't.

Is the child changing her stance to hit where the fielders aren't? Or does she try to do it by using her arms?

Hockey stick

With a hockey stick and a ball, children strike back and forth to a partner.

1. Have children see how long they can keep going without missing.
2. Have children send the ball to both sides of the partner as well as in front of him.

Is the child striking the ball? Or does he slap at it or push it?

Does the child stop the ball before he sends it back?

Is one hand farther down the stick to stop the ball when receiving it?

Does the child give with the stick when receiving the ball?

Does he receive the ball in front of his body? Or does he let it get under his feet?

Does the child travel to get behind the ball?

3. Have children vary the distance between themselves and their partners.

Does the child use enough force to get the ball to his partner?

Does the child still hit the ball with the stick held vertically, so that the ball does not leave the ground?

Does the child hit the ball away from the body?

With cones and hoops (or other equipment) develop an obstacle course. Children travel through the course striking a ball with a hockey stick.

Is the child looking up as he travels?

Is the child keeping the ball close to the stick?

Can the child change direction and pathway as needed?

Using a hockey stick, children send the ball to a partner who is running.

Does the partner receive the ball on the run? Or does she stop, collect it, and then start running again?

Does the child relax her grip on the stick when receiving the ball?

Does the child receive the ball with the whole flat blade of the stick?

Does the sender strike the ball in front of the receiver?

Does the child receive the ball away from her body or close to it?

Is the stick vertical?

Are the hands separated on the stick as the child receives the ball.

Proficiency Level

Overview   At the proficiency level, children are provided with situations that facilitate development of the ability to strike with implements while focusing on the strategy and outcome of the action as well as on the skill. The attainment of consistency and accuracy, while standing still or moving, is the focus at this level.

IDEAS FOR DEVELOPMENT

IDEAS FOR OBSERVATIONAL FOCUS

Golf club

Teach Whiffle Ball Golf (see Figure 27.6). This game is played like golf.

Objective: To get the ball to land in the hoop using as few shots as possible.

Rules: Developed as needed.

A golf course can be created on an available field to enable the children to learn the fundamen-

Are the children playing quickly and in the proper order?

Are the children careful not to swing their clubs when others are close by?

Do the children understand how to score? Do they understand the hazards of this game?

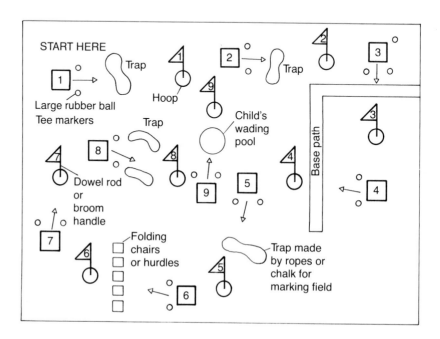

Figure 27.6   Whiffle ball golf course

tals of golf. Plastic golf balls and short golf clubs or teacher-made golf clubs are used. The holes are made from hoops and dowel rods or broomsticks. Larger rubber balls can be used for tees. Traps and hazards can be created by using jump ropes. Chalk can be used to mark a field. Or existing features, such as a fence or baseball diamond, can be used.

During the class we focus on each child's individual improvements, rather than on class or individual competition. Voluntary tournaments, after school or at lunch time, are enjoyed by many children. And faculty!

Bat

Teach Six-Player Tee Ball.
This game is similar to softball and involves the skills of striking, throwing, and catching.

Objectives: To place a batted ball, catch and throw, and run bases.

Rules:
1. Three players on each of two teams.
2. The batter strikes the ball from the tee and tries to run the bases.
3. The fielders try to catch or collect the ball and throw it to one another, so that all three players catch the ball before the batter completes running the bases.
4. Each player on a team bats, and then the teams switch places.

Observe the children's abilities to catch and throw quickly under intense game conditions.

Children have a partner pitch the ball to them. With three or four others scattered in the field, they try to hit the ball:

1. To open spaces
2. On the ground
3. High, long, and arched

Does the child change her batting stance to direct the ball?

Does the child hit pitches that facilitate what she is trying to do?

Is the direction in which the child is trying to hit the ball clear?

Teach a one-base baseball game (see Figure 27.7).

Objective: To get to the base and back before the pitcher gets the ball.

Rules: 1. Three or four people on each of two teams.

2. Each person bats, and then the teams trade places.

Do the children hit the ball to open spaces, so that they have more time to run?

Are they hitting the ball far enough away?

Are their swings smooth and level?

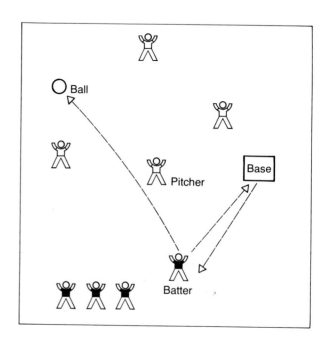

Figure 27.7   One-base baseball

Teach Half Rubber.

Objective: To score runs, as in baseball.

Rules: 1. Three or four players on each side.

2. Use a 3″ to 4″ solid rubber ball, cut in half, and a broom handle as a bat.

3. Follow baseball rules.

Do the children's eyes follow the ball?

Do they use mature striking patterns?

This activity is fun, although extremely difficult. For years we played it on the beach, and it is a challenge to master. It can be done! Kids love to try it!

Hockey stick

Children play with a partner. Both traveling in the same direction, passing a ball back and forth with a hockey stick. Both of them should always be traveling.

Does each child pass the ball so that it leads the partner? Or does the passed ball end up behind the partner?

Is the partner receiving the ball by giving with his stick and then controlling it?

Try to keep the ball away from a partner

Are the arms away from the body when the ball is passed and received?

Have the children play a game with four in a circle. They continuously pass the ball to the person across. Challenge them to always keep the circle moving and the ball moving.

Are the children controlling the ball before returning it?

Is the ball received in front of the feet?

A group of children made up this game and enjoy trying to do it. But the game does not last for very long because it is so fast and intense.

Some of the children use a hockey stick and puck or ball. Other children are obstacles (see Figure 27.8). Those with sticks travel around the space, trying to keep the ball away from the obstacles. The obstacles may take the ball away if it comes too close.

Are the children looking up to see where the obstacles are? Or are they watching the ball or puck?

Do they keep the ball close to the stick?

Do they place their bodies between the ball and the obstacles?

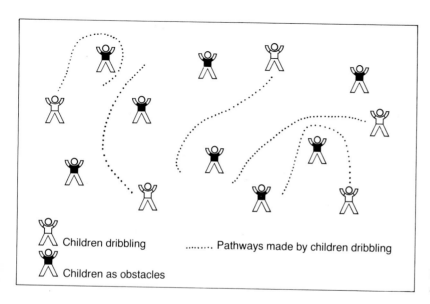

Children dribbling .... Pathways made by children dribbling

Children as obstacles

Figure 27.8   Arrangement for dribbling and dodging activity

Do they dribble out in front and to the side of their bodies, with the ball far enough away so that it does not get under their feet, but close enough to control?

Are children using changes in pathway, speed, and direction to avoid their opponents?

Children play in groups of three. Two of them pass the ball, both moving in the same direction. The third player tries to intercept the ball.

Are the two children who are passing waiting until the third makes a move to intercept? Or are they randomly passing?

Do they pass to open space near their partner, or straight to them?

Do the children use just enough force to get the ball to the partner? Or do they take a full swing?

Does the stealer try to take the ball when it is off the others' sticks or while his stick is on the ball?

Teach Mini-Hockey.

Objective: To hit the ball or puck into the opponent's goal

Rules:
1. Two or three on each side
2. Cones, milk jugs, or boxes used as goals
3. Players decide boundaries and width of goal

Are the children able to incorporate all the previous skills into the game, so that it flows smoothly? Or is the game constantly broken?

Are passes made to open spaces around the receiving player?

SECTION 5
DREAMS

T his final section has only one chapter, but it is an important section. We want to end the book by focusing on the future. Chapter Twenty-Eight, Physical Education for Tomorrow's Children, presents some of our thoughts about the future. We hope it will encourage you to dream, too.

CHAPTER 28
PHYSICAL EDUCATION FOR TOMORROW'S CHILDREN

Some men see things as they are and say why. I dream things that never were and say why not.
ROBERT F. KENNEDY

All teachers have ideas about "the way things might be," and so do we. Some of our dreams are already reality in some schools for some teachers and some children. Some of our dreams may never become reality. We believe that it is as important to continue to dream as it is to see our dreams realized. Perhaps our hopes for the future will stimulate you to think and dream about the way things could be. The paragraphs that follow describe the world of the physical education teacher as it would be if we had our way.

Every child would have quality instruction in physical education every day.

Physical education, in both elementary and secondary schools, would receive as much emphasis as high school athletics. Communities would understand that an appropriate program of physical education for every child is at least as important as athletic programs for the gifted. And so all schools would have appropriate equipment, facilities, and budgets for physical education programs.

All school districts would recognize the importance of providing children with quality physical education programs. None would overlook the most important years of learning and wait until junior or senior high school to provide adequate instruction, equipment, and facilities.

All school districts would understand the differences between teaching children and teaching adolescents, and would refuse to hire individuals whose primary interest and expertise is in coaching or teaching at a high school. Instead, school districts would hire, as elementary instructors, only teachers who are professionally qualified and dedicated

to a career of teaching physical education to children.

Teacher education institutions would offer programs of professional preparation for elementary school physical education specialists that would be different from the programs for secondary school physical education teachers.

Administrators and others who schedule classes would understand that physical education is intended to be an instructional experience, not a loosely organized recess. This understanding would be reflected by scheduling only one class rather than two or three classes with sixty or even ninety children at a time.

Teachers would have adequate time between lessons to jot down a few notes about the progress made by the last class, rearrange equipment, review lesson plans, and shift their thoughts to the next class.

There would be time during the day to sit down with individual children and cooperatively plan a personalized curriculum for each. This would help children to learn to make significant decisions about what they want to learn and how they want to learn it.

Assistance would be readily available for those children who require special remedial attention. This program would include instruction for parents, so that they could help their children at home.

Parents would become involved in their children's education. The concepts and skills introduced at school would be enhanced and embellished at home, through parent–child activity nights, after school programs for parents, and parent volunteer programs.

There would be times during each school day, beyond scheduled physical education classes, when children could choose to come to the gymnasium to practice something in which they were interested.

Classes would be scheduled to facilitate tutorial teaching—fifth graders working with first graders, or proficiency level children working with precontrol children, for example.

Classes would be scheduled so that beginnings and endings were determined by the children's interest and involvement in a lesson, rather than by an impersonal and insensitive time schedule.

Children could be grouped—by interest in a specific activity, by ability, by experience—to accomplish the specific goals of a series of lessons, then regrouped when the teacher decides to move on to a new movement theme. For example, some upper-grade children might be interested in putting on a dance performance for lower-grade children. Those upper-grade children could be grouped to meet together for two weeks, to prepare their dance and perform it. When that goal is accomplished, they could be regrouped as appropriate for another activity.

Teachers would have access to audiovisual equipment that would facilitate valuable projects. They would be able to make continuous videotapes of classes without having to reuse tapes. Teachers could do graph-check sequence filming of complex skills to help children develop the ability to analyze their own movements. Children would be able to make their own super-8 film strips and loop films.

Portable environments would be made available to schools throughout the year. Children would have opportunities to use portable swimming pools for swimming lessons, portable ski slopes for skiing lessons, and portable antigravity chambers to experience moving in a weightless atmosphere.

It would be common practice for individuals from the community to share their expertise and experiences with children. Children would learn about mountain climbing, hang gliding, hiking, centering, human spatial ecology, and weightless gymnastics.

Teachers would be able to make arrangements to switch teaching assignments with other teachers for a day or a week. Then all teachers would have more experiences working in different environments and with children from various backgrounds.

Teachers would cooperate and would organize curriculum into organic, natural contexts (consistent with the way children view the world), rather than artificially separating learning into compartmentalized subjects like reading, mathematics, art, and physical education. For example, building a house involves reading, mathematics, climbing, balancing, and working with others.

All classroom teachers would understand that a quality program of physical education can make a significant contribution to the total development of children. No one would prevent children from going to physical education class because they had not finished their work or because they had misbehaved.

All colleagues, parents, and administrators would be vitally interested in our teaching and physical education programs. They would demonstrate this interest by visiting our classes regularly, not only at the first PTA meeting of the year or during school lunch week.

All colleagues, parents, and administrators would understand the important contribution that a well-designed and effectively taught program of physical education can make in the quality of each individual's entire life.

Schools would become community centers that could involve parents and children in educational projects of mutual interest and benefit. These would include child–parent designed and constructed playscapes, child–parent designed and implemented field days for preschool children or underprivileged children, and child–parent programs designed for senior citizens.

Adequate funds would be made available for resource centers operated by teachers for teachers. Such centers would offer assistance in making materials or equipment, opportunities to hear visiting lecturers, in-service courses, discussion and sharing sessions, and up-to-date professional libraries.

All physical education programs, recreation programs, and youth serving agencies would cooperate to enhance the lives of children. No longer would they exist as independent agencies who serve the same children but rarely communicate or coordinate their efforts.

Teachers would be able to easily arrange frequent visits to other schools and teachers.

Elementary school teachers and college teachers would work together to discover better ways to enhance the learning experiences of children.

Elementary school teachers and college teachers would work together to discover better ways to enhance the learning experiences of preservice and in-service teachers.

Preservice teachers would work in elementary schools for several years before going to college so that they could learn the right questions to ask about children and teaching. Then as students they would ask the kinds of questions that real world teachers ask.

College teachers would regularly trade teaching assignments with public school teachers. This would allow the public school teachers to study current theories and practices at a college and would provide the college teachers with realistic opportunities to translate their theories into practice.

Nonthreatening, nonevaluative professional assistance would be available to teachers who want to improve their teaching effectiveness.

Ways would be found to continually inform teachers about current educational thinking, to keep them from feeling isolated and out of touch.

Teachers would be involved in conceptualizing and conducting research. The resulting studies would have the potential to find answers to the questions that teachers want answered.

Research results would be disseminated in forms that teachers of children would find useful, practical, and interesting—e.g., in weekly pamphlets or newsletters or monthly television programs that would use the language of the layman, not professional jargon or advanced concepts related to experimental design or statistics.

We continue to dream about and search for better ways of teaching children. And we would like to hear your dreams and ideas about children, teaching, and physical education. If you would like to communicate with us, please write to us in care of the publisher.

One other dream emerged as we were writing this book. Wouldn't it be great if the ideas from our book help you to become a more effective teacher of children! We've done our part—now it's up to you.

APPENDICES

APPENDIX 1

APPROACHING DANCE THROUGH MUSIC: A LIST OF SOURCES

SUGGESTED MOVEMENT

Slow, smooth, delicate, or flowing music

"Chapter Two"—Roberta Flack
Atlantic Recording Corporation
SD 1569

Smooth, flowing turns, gentle
leaps

"Morning Has Broken"—Cat
Stevens (from "Teaser & the Fire-
cat") Motown Record Corporation
8555-S

Dance study of the "Life Cycle of
a Flower"

"Carole King Tapestry"
A & M Records SP 77009

Sustained rising and sinking

"James Taylor's Greatest Hits"
Warner Brothers Records BS 2979

Fluent leaps with turns in flight;
relaxed abdominal breathing
after strenuous work

Gay, lively, locomotor

"Earl Scrugg's Nashville Rock"
Columbia Records CS 1007

"Loraderojosp III Breakdown"—
Children vigorously move one
body part to music (elbow, finger, tongue)

"Country Boy"—Lester Flatt
RCA Records APL1-0131

"Feudin' Banjos"—Dance study based on the concept of question/answer

"Dueling Banjos/Reuben's Train"
Eric Weissberg & Marshall Brinkman
Warner Brothers Records GWB0309

"Dueling Banjos"—Partners contrast or match movements

"Reuben's Train"—Exciting locomotor patterns (slide, skip, gallop)

Rhythm and blues (simple underlying beat; a range of qualities)

"Roots/Soul Sounds of a Proud People" Kent Records KST-700

Change of direction or body shape on the accented beat

"Turn On Your Love Light"
London Records SHL 32044

"Bright Lights, Big City"—Creative dance study based on the theme of "cool members of a street gang"

Jazz (exciting, vibrant, moody)

"Honey in the Horn"—Al Hirt
RCA Records LPM-2733

"Java"—Ideal for exciting locomotor movements with quick stops or changes in level or direction

"Feels So Good/Maui-Waui"
—Chuck Mangione
A & M Records SP-6700

Exciting, high leaps with turns in flight—sudden, fluent pivot turns concluding in dramatic body shapes

Television themes (a range of qualities)

"TV Hits Volume II"
Pickwick International SPC-3566

"Nadia's Theme"—Smooth, fluent sequencing of travel skills and balances

"Hit TV Shows, Volume II"
Peter Pan Records 8197

"Hawaii Five-O"—Vibrant exciting locomotor combinations

"Little House on the Prairie"—Light, gentle gallop, skip, leap

Music from the movies (a range of qualities)

"West Side Story" Columbia Records OL 5670	"The Rumble"—Two groups use fighting gestures (punch, kick, slash, jab) in creating a dance; music is also appropriate for a creative dance based on "The Bull Fight"
"Original Soundtracks and Music from the Great Motion Pictures" United Artists Records UAS 3303	"How the West Was Won"—Exciting locomotor patterns, combining jumps with other travel skills
	"Lawrence of Arabia—Heavy, hot, tired, lethargic movement; creative dance, crossing the desert
"The Big Gun Down" United Artists Records UAS 5190	Creative dance based on idea of battle—two primitive tribes, the bull fight, crossing the desert
"The Graduate" Columbia Records OS 3180	"Sounds of Silence"—Lends itself to sustained, light or gentle movements
"Born Free" MGM Records SE-4368	Creative dance based upon theme of freedom—Exciting, joyful movements, free use of space, free to meet and part with others
"Roots Medley/Many Rains Ago" Quincy Jones & Orchestra A & M Records SP-4626 (from "Roots" album, SP-4626)	Creative dance based on the theme of black history—slavery, arrival of freedom, continued struggle, strength and pride, family strength, unity as a people
"Theme from Summer of 42" and "Brian's Song"—Peter Nero & Orchestra Columbia Records ZSP 156095	Smooth, fluent, delicate movements. By changing speed to 78 rpm, abstract dance creations become possible—e.g., PinBall Mania
"For A Few Dollars More"— Hugo Montenegro & Orchestra RCA Records 447-0799	Mystery, intrigue, imminent danger

"Star Wars" 20th Century Fox 2T-541	Abstract floor and air patterns, "Robots!"
"Godspell" Arista Records SP 3300	"Day By Day"—Joyous, vibrant movements—for example, turning with eyes focused upward and arms spread outward

Electronic music

"The In Sound From Way Out"— Perrey-Kingsley Vanguard Recording Society VSD-79222-B	"Jungle Blues from Jupiter"— Stop and go, change direction or level "Visa to the Stars"—Study of slow motion or loss of gravity
"Switched On Bach" Columbia Records MS 7194	Lends itself nicely to study of sudden, jerky gestures; creative dance based on idea of electrocution

Halloween Sound Effects

"Chilling, Thrilling Sounds of the Haunted House" Disney Records 1257	Creative Movement: Alone in a haunted house—scared expressions, hesitant, nervous travel, jumping in reaction to a creak or howl
"The Sounds of Halloween" A & M Records SP 3300	Creative Movement: Lost in a mob, or caught in the midst of a hurricane

Other Sources

A variety of physical education records—square dance albums, ethnic dance records, tininkling activities, basic rhythms, and music from around the world—are available from educational companies. Two popular companies are:

Kimbo Educational Records Box 246 Deal, N.J. 07723	Educational Records, Inc. Freeport, N.Y. 11520

APPENDIX 2
PARTNER STUNTS

Many children enjoy Partner Stunts. Rather than teaching weight transfer with a partner to an entire class, we prefer to provide a Partner Stunts Learning Center that allows those children who are interested to work at their own rate. Additional information about the organization of learning centers is provided in Chapter Five.

PARTNER STUNTS LEARNING CENTER

Equipment: Mats, carpeted or grassy area.

Note to Teacher: For the children's safety it is important that they proceed in order when working on these challenges. Children should be approximately the same height and weight. Stunts marked with a dagger (†) should only be attempted with a spotter.

Name_____

Teacher_____

Date accomplished	Verification initials	Challenges
_____	_____	WRING THE DISHRAG. Two children face each other and join hands. Each raises one arm (right for one and left for the other). Grasp hands and turn under that pair of arms, continuing a full turn until back to original position—without letting go of one another's hands. Care must be taken to avoid bumping heads.
_____	_____	TOE TOUCH TRANSFER. Partners lie on backs with heads near each other and feet in opposite directions. Grasp each other, using a hand–wrist grip, and bring up legs (both partners) so the toes touch. One partner carries a beanbag between his feet and transfers it to the feet of the other partner, who lowers it to the ground.

_____ _____

PARTNER PULL-UPS. **Partners** sit down facing each other in a bent-knee position with the heels on the floor and the toes touching. Pulling cooperatively, both come to a standing position. Return to the floor.

_____ _____

BACK RISER. Two children sit back to back and lock arms. From this position both try to stand by pushing against each other's backs. Sit down again. If the feet are sliding, do the stunt on a mat.

_____ _____

DROMEDARY WALK. The first (support) child gets down on hands and knees. The second (top) child sits on him, facing to the rear, and fixes his legs around the chest of support. The top child leans forward (for him) so he can grasp the back of the support's ankles. Arms are reasonably extended. The support takes the weight off his knees (up on toes) and walks forward (minimum of ten feet) with the top child's help.

_____ _____

CENTIPEDE. The support player should be the stronger and larger individual. He gets down on his hands and knees. The top player faces the same direction, placing his hands about two feet in front of those of the support player. Now he places his legs and body on top of the support.

The knees should be spread

apart and the heels locked together.

The centipede walks with the top player using hands only, and the support player using both hands and feet. The support child should gather his legs well under him while walking and so should be off his knees.

†TABLE. Bottom performer assumes crab position (base). Top performer straddles base, facing to the rear, and positions his hands on base's shoulders, fingers pointing toward the feet. His feet are now placed on top of the base's knees, forming one crab position on top of another. As the final touch the heads are positioned so the eyes look up toward the ceiling and the seats are lifted so the backs are straight.

†LIGHTHOUSE. Support is down on hands and knees. Top child completes the figure by standing on the *shoulders* of the support, facing the same direction. He stands erect with hands out to the sides.

†FLYING DUTCH MAN. The under (support) person takes a position flat on his back. The top person takes a position facing the support, grasping his hands, and at the same time bending over his feet. The top person now is raised from the floor by extending his knees, arching his

back, and resting on the feet of the support person. He can release his grip and put his arms out level to the side in a flying position. A little experimentation will determine the best spot for the foot support. *Spot as needed to get into position and for safety.* Hold for five seconds.

†SIDE STAND. **Support gets down on hands and knees to form a rigid base. Top performer stands to the side, hooks his hands, palms up, well underneath the chest and waist. He leans across, steadying with his hands, kicking up to an inverted stand.** *Spotters are needed on the far side.*

†ANGEL. **The top performer stands erect on the support's knees with his arms level out to the side. The bottom performer takes hold of the top's thighs and leans back to place the figure in balance. Hold for five seconds.**

To get into this position, the top performer stands in front of the support partner. Support squats down and places his head between the legs of the top performer. Support raises up, so that top is sitting on his shoulders. As the top performer takes his position on support's knees, support must lean well back for balance, removing his head from between the top performer's legs. Children will need to experiment with each other to determine the best way to achieve the final position.

INDEX

A

Activity time, 54, 58; recording of, 98, 99, 100
Aerial net games, 443
Aerial Soccer, 356
Age, skill level in relation to, 110, 111
Ali, Muhammed, 272
Allen, Dwight, 5n
Alley Soccer, 355
"Alone in a mass" relationship, 201–202
Apparatus. *See* Equipment
Arend, S., 71
Assessment. *See* Evaluation, of student progress; Evaluation, of teaching performance
Attitudes: of students, 54, 79, 87; of teachers, 53
Audiovisual aids, 480

B

Balance beam, construction of, 317
Balance bench, construction of, 318
Balance board, construction of, 319
Balancing, 15, 16, 17, 45, 126, 161, 189, 196; control level of, 142–143, 267, 274, 275, 291, 311, 314, 319–322, 337; defined, 309; and **ideas for development and observational focus,** 315–328; inverted, 146, 181, 309, 312, 313, 314, 321–328 passim, 337, 339, 340; in jumping and landing, 267, 274, 275, 276, 277, 282, 283, 284; precontrol level of, 22, 223, 245, 311, 314, 315–317; proficiency level of, 282, 283, 284, 313, 314, 327–329; progression spiral for, 314; in rolling, 291, 302–308 passim, 314, 323–324; static and dynamic, 309–311; task sheet for, 47; in throwing and catching, 381; utilization level of, 143, 145, 276, 277, 302, 303, 312, 314, 323–326; in weight transfer, 314, 323–331 passim, 337, 490–493
Balls: plastic, 463; suspending, 436; yarn, 375, 463
Barth, Roland, 9
Baseball, one-base, 472
Baseball glove, disadvantages of, 384

Basketball, 244, 282, 399, 416, 419, 428; Half-Court, 398–399
Bat, 445; developmental stages of striking with, 446–449; **ideas for development and observational focus** for striking with, 458–460, 463, 468, 471–472
Batting tee, construction of, 459
Behavior: disruptive, 54, 59–68 passim; rules of, 57, 58, 59; of teacher, 59, 60, 61, 68. *See also* Discipline
Behavior games, 66, 67
Biddle, Bruce, 9
Blanket Volleyball, 393–394
Block and cane, construction of, 191
Body Part Tag, 251–252
Body parts, concept of relationships of, 15, 16, 17; and **ideas for development and observational focus,** 188–193; teaching, 186, 187–193
Body Parts (game), 56
Body shapes: in balancing, 310–326 passim; and concept of relationships, 187, 190–193, 197, 201, 206, 208, 209; in jumping,

270, 274; in rolling, 301–307
passim; symmetrical/
asymmetrical, 192, 201, 312, 314,
316, 321–322
Bombardment (game), 249
Boyd, Ellsworth, 220
Brophy, Jere, 9

C

Calisthenics, mass, 43, 44, 52
Cartwheel, 108, 109, 181, 280, 331,
337, 339
Catching, 15, 16, 35, 115, 116, 117,
119, 161, 169, 171, 309, 428;
combined with throwing, 367;
control level of, 319, 376, 377,
382–386; defined, 375; in games,
114, 115, 116, 119, 209, 373, 381,
387, 399; and **ideas for
development and
observational focus,** 381–399;
precontrol level of, 376, 377,
381–382; proficiency level of,
266, 292, 308, 377, 381, 394–399;
progression spiral for, 377;
utilization level of, 266, 277, 278,
303, 304, 376, 377, 386–394
Centering, 481
Chasing, fleeing, and dodging, 15,
17, 18, 208–209; control level of,
241, 242, 243, 246–249; defined,
239–240, 242; in games, 239, 244–
256, 425, 428; and **ideas for
development and
observational focus,** 244–256;
precontrol level of, 241, 242–243,
244–245; proficiency level of,
241, 244, 252–256; progression
spiral for, 241; utilization level
of, 241, 243, 250–252
Checklists, as evaluation technique,
80–81, 87, 88–89
Child-designed activities, 46, 52,
206, 324, 481; dances, 134–135,
220, 236–238, 307, 324; games,
120–121; 122, 220, 244, 282, 364,

411, 428, 442, 473; gymnastics,
280, 297, 304, 306, 321, 324–326,
341; travel patterns, 236–237
Circles (games), 56
Clacker, construction of, 129
Class as unit, instructing, 42–45, 52
Class discipline, 66–67, 68
Class meetings, frequency of, 26
Class organization: patterns of, 40–
50, 52, 480; selecting form of, 50–
51, 52
Class size, 6, 9, 26
Climbing, mountain, 481
Climbing apparatus, 143, 249, 329
Cohort instruction, 44–45, 51, 52
Collecting (manipulative skill), 15,
17
Comaneci, Nadia, 139
Combinations (game), 56
Community centers, schools as, 481
Competition, 116, 205
Cone Soccer, 356
Control level, 107, 108, 110, 111,
177; in dance, 128, 230; in games,
114, 246–249; in gymnastics, 142,
143, 249, 270, 271, 274, 275, 295–
299, 319–322. *See also under
specific skill theme*
Cooperation, in physical education
programs, 479, 480, 481, 482
Cooperative Four-Square, 415
Corner Ball, 442, 443
Corporal punishment, 67
Crawling. *See* Traveling
Creative experiences, 137; in dance,
128, 130–132, 138
Curling. *See* Stretching and curling

D

Dance, 13, 14, 19, 34, 105; balancing
in, 324–325, 327; at control level,
128, 130; and creative
experiences, 128, 130–132, 138;
designing of, 132–133; 135–136,
138, 220, 236–238; difficulty in
teaching, 123, 138; and effort

concepts, 131, 133, 174, 175–183;
expressive content of, 126–128,
138; forms of, 125–126, 138;
imagery in, 127–128, 219, 230–
231, 327; jumping and landing
in, 126, 258, 274, 276, 277, 280,
282; movement concepts in, 126–
128; music for, 128–130, 132, 134,
136, 226–227, 485–488;
nonmanipulative skills in, 126–
127, 136; at precontrol level, 128,
130; process of teaching, 133,
135–136, 138; at proficiency
level, 130, 132, 327; props for,
136, 138, 194, 196; purpose of
teaching, 123, 124–125; and
relationships, 131, 133, 188–192,
194, 196–201, 205–209; resistance
to studying, 133, 138; and
rhythmic experiences, 128, 130,
138, 221, 232, 233; rolling in, 286,
302–303, 307; space awareness in,
133, 159–160; traveling in, 126,
127, 131, 133, 219–238 passim;
turning in, 126–127, 136; at
utilization level, 128, 131, 302–
303, 307, 324–325
Decision-sharing, 52, 203; in
designing activities, 46, 119, 121,
122; in gymnastics, 147–149;
regarding practice, 40–41
Development and observational
focus, ideas for, 72, 151–152. *See
also under specific concept or skill
theme*
Directions, 15, 16, 17, 153, 157, 243;
in balancing, 317, 319, 320, 324,
325, 326; in chasing, fleeing, and
dodging, 245–253 passim;
defined, 153–154, 159; in
dribbling, 423–424, 425, 426;
**ideas for development and
observational focus** re concept
of, 160–161; in kicking, 347, 349,
351, 352; in punting, 361, 364; in
rolling, 293–307 passim; in
striking, 433–444 passim, 465;

teaching concept of, 159–161, 169–170; in throwing and catching, 383, 387, 388, 389, 392, 394; in volleying, 402, 403, 405, 408, 409

Discipline, 6, 10–11, 23, 54; of class, 54, 66–67; and corporal punishment, 67; guidelines for, 59–60; of individual, 54, 60–66; and teaching, 67–69

Dodgeball games, 208, 239, 240, 242, 243, 247–249

Dodging. *See* Chasing, fleeing, and dodging

Dribble Tag, 427

Dribbling, 15, 16, 17, 19, 35, 37, 116, 183; control level of, 345, 350, 351, 417, 418, 421–423, 437; defined, 400, 416; in games, 425, 426, 427, 428; and **ideas for development and observational focus,** 420–428; precontrol level of, 347, 348, 416, 417, 420–421, 463; proficiency level of, 417, 419, 426–428, 474; progression spiral for, 417; utilization level of, 109, 352, 353, 417, 418, 423, 426

Dribbling Tag, 427

Drum, construction of, 129

Duration recording, 96–100, 102

E

Effort concepts, 15, 16, 17; in dance, 131, 133; in games, 175, 180–181; in gymnastics, 174, 175, 181, 183; and **ideas for development and observational focus,** 173, 175–183 passim; imagery in, 173, 175–182 passim; teaching, 28, 151, 172–184. *See also* Flow; Force; Speed; Time; Weight

Electives, 46, 52

Equipment, 3, 6, 10, 26, 37; for balancing, 311–329 passim; dance, 129, 136, 138; future, 481,

482; for games, 245, 361; for kicking, 361; gymnastics, 143–149 passim, 197, 266, 280–282, 283, 285, 293, 297–306 passim, 311–329 passim; how to make (*see* Equipment, construction of); for jumping and landing, 266, 280–281; 283, 285; moving of, 147–148; for rolling, 292, 297–306 passim; for striking with long-handled implements, 445, 454, 457, 459, 460, 463, 470–471; for striking with rackets or paddles, 434, 436, 437, 443–444; for throwing, 384; for traveling tasks, 225, 230, 233, 316–317; for volleying, 404; for weight transfer, 331–332, 336–341 passim

Equipment, construction of: balance beam, 317; balance bench, 318; balance board, 319; batting tee, 459; block and cane, 191; clacker, 129; drum, 129; golf club, 457; hockey stick, 457; hoop, 194; net, 412; paddle, short-handled, 437; racket, nylon hose, 434; rope, 195; sawhorse, wooden, 318; shaker, 129; stilts, tin can, 321; stilts, wooden, 324; suspended balls on string, 436; vaulting box, 281

Equipment setups: for balancing, 316; for kicking, 352; for rolling, 301; for space awareness, 165; for striking, 470; for traveling, 225, 227, 231, 233, 316; for weight transfer, 336

European Handball, 397

Evaluation, of student progress, 23, 27, 50–51, 52, 133; techniques for, 80–86, 89, 341; types of, 79–80, 89; uses of, 81, 86–89

Evaluation, of teaching performance, 23, 61, 90–102; peer-assisted, 92, 95–100, 101–102; student-assisted, 92–94, 101;

and support group, 101, 102; unassisted, 91–92, 101

Extensions, 15, 16, 17, 153; in balancing, 309, 312, 313, 325, 326, 327; defined, 154, 168; **ideas for development and observational focus** re concept of, 168–169; in jumping and landing, 283, 284, 285; teaching concept of, 168–169, 170–171; in volleying, 408

F

Facilities, 3, 6, 10, 26–27, 49, 51, 52; future, 481, 482

Fear: in jumping, 279; in rolling, 298

Fight Dance, 282

Flag tag, 252–253

Fleeing. *See* Chasing, fleeing, and dodging

Flips, 330, 332

Flow, 15, 16, 17, 172; in balancing, 323, 327; in dance, 131, 133; examples of, 180–181; **ideas for development and observational focus** re concept of, 181–183; in rolling, 300, 302, 306, 307; in striking games, 475; teaching concept of, 180–183, 184; in throwing, 389, 391, 392

Follow-the-leader. *See* Leading and following

Football, 244, 266; Four-Person, 397–398; Frisbee, 395

Footballs, foam, 361

Force, 15, 16, 17; in dance, 131; in dribbling, 420; in jumping and landing, 267, 283, 284; in kicking, 348–353 passim; in punting, 262, 263, 364; in striking, 437–444 passim, 465, 466, 468, 469, 475; in throwing, 382, 383, 385, 391, 393; in volleying, 407, 409, 410, 411

Four-Person Football, 397–398

Frisbee, 304, 389, 394, 395, 398
Frisbee Circuit, 398
Frisbee Football, 395
Frisbee Golf, 389
Frisbee Stretch, 394

G

Galloping, 15, 17, 126, 130, 158, 165, 183, 211; pattern of, 217. *See also* Traveling
Games, 13, 14, 34, 105, 120, 209, 229, 232, 445; behavior, 66, 67; chasing, fleeing, and dodging, 239, 244–256, 425, 428; child-designed, 120–121, 122, 220, 244, 411; dribbling in, 116, 244, 425, 426, 427; and effort concepts, 175, 180–181; jumping and landing in, 258, 278, 282–283; kicking, 116, 347, 353–356; lesson designs for, 117–121, 122; listening, 54–55, 56; objects in, 194; practice experiences for, 113–117, 121–122; punting, 365–366; and relationships, 188, 189, 194, 199, 207–209; rolling in, 286, 292, 308; and skill proficiency levels, 114–115; and space awareness, 157–164 passim, 169; vs. sports, 113n, 121; striking in, 118, 119, 342, 433, 442–444, 470–475; throwing and catching in, 114, 115, 116, 119, 209, 373, 381, 387, 393–399; traveling designs for, 220; volleying in, 115, 402, 411, 413–414, 415
General space, 153, 246; defined, 153, 156; **ideas for development and observational focus** re concept of, 157–159; teaching concept of, 156–159, 169
Golf, 454; Frisbee, 389; Whiffle Ball, 470–471
Golf club, 445; construction of, 457; developmental stages of striking with, 450–453; **ideas for development and**

observational focus for striking with, 457–458, 466–468, 470
Good, Thomas, 9
Grade levels, in relation to skill levels, 107, 111
Grades, 87, 89
Ground net games, 444
Group and intergroup relationships, 131, 201–210 passim
Group instruction, 41, 45–46, 51, 52, 148
Guarding the Dynamite, 255
Guided discovery, 45, 52, 202
Gymnasium, open, 49, 51, 52. *See also* Facilities
Gymnastics, 13, 14, 19, 26, 34, 105, 201, 209, 229, 232, 481; balancing in, 142–143; 145, 283, 315–329; in chasing, fleeing, and dodging, 245, 249; content of, 141–143, 145; at control level, 142, 143, 249, 270, 271, 274, 275, 295–299, 319–322; and effort concepts, 174, 175, 181, 183; equipment for, 143–149 passim, 197, 266, 280–282, 283, 285, 292, 297–306 passim, 311–329 passim; jumping and landing in, 143, 258, 267, 270, 271, 274, 275, 279–280, 283–285; notation for, 144; Olympic, 139, 143, 148, 149; popularity of, 139, 141, 148; at precontrol level, 142, 143, 245, 267, 293–294, 315–317; process of teaching, 146–148; at proficiency level, 143, 145, 283–285, 292, 304–307, 327–329; purpose of, 140–141; and relationships, 189, 190, 193–198 passim, 201; rolling in, 142, 292, 293–302, 304–307; self-testing nature of, 139, 148; safety in, 146, 147, 148, 149; and space awareness, 156–164 passim, 167, 168, 169; traveling in, 143, 145, 230, 231; at utilization level, 143, 145, 279–280, 299–302, 323–326; weight transfer in, 143, 145, 314, 323–329 passim, 490–493

H

Half-Court Basketball, 398–399
Half Rubber, 472
Handball, 400; European, 397
Handicapped students, mainstreaming, 49–50, 55, 57
Handstand, 146, 181, 309, 321, 323, 324, 325, 328, 337
Hang gliding, 481
Headstand, 309, 321, 323, 324, 325, 337
Hellison, Don, 68
Higgins, J. R., 71
Hiking, 481
Hit the Pin, 393
Hockey, 454; Mini-, 475
Hockey stick, 445; construction of, 457; developmental stages of striking with, 450–453; **ideas for development and observational focus** for striking with, 461–462, 464–466, 468, 473–475
Hoffman, S. J., 70
Hoop, construction of, 194
Hoop game, 411
Hopping, 15, 17, 126, 165, 183, 196, 211; pattern of, 215. *See also* Traveling
Hot Potato, 308
Human spatial ecology, 481
Humor, 232, 277
Hurdling. *See* Jumping and Landing

I

Imagery: in balancing, 316, 327; in dance, 127–128, 219, 230–231; and effort concepts, 173, 175–182 passim; in rolling, 302–303; in traveling, 219, 228, 230–231
Independent contracting, 48, 50, 52
Individual differences, 5, 12, 27, 51, 63, 87
Individualization, 87, 88–89; and discipline, 60–66; of instruction, 41–42, 47–49, 50, 51, 52, 480
Infinity Volleyball, 413

Information on physical education, dissemination of, 482

Instructional time, 100; recording of, 96, 98, 99

Instruments. *See* Rhythmic instruments

Intergroup relationships, 201, 204, 205, 210

Invariant teaching, 6; components of, 7

J

Jogging, 158, 175, 387

Jumping, 136, 182, 183, 245, 309, 393, 401; defined, 257; fundamental patterns of, 257–258; on stilts, 327; vertical and horizontal, 258

Jumping and landing, 14, 15, 17, 71, 126, 143, 193; control level of, 259, 265, 270–276, 291, 297, 298–299; in dance, 126, 258, 274, 276, 277, 280, 282; developmental stages of, 258, 260–266; in games, 269, 277–278, 283–284; in gymnastics, 143, 258, 267, 270, 271, 274, 275, 279–280, 283–285, 298–299; and **ideas for development and observational focus**, 267–280, 283–284; precontrol level of, 258, 259, 267–270; proficiency level of, 259, 266, 280, 282–284, 401, 415; progression spiral for, 259; sample sequence for, 30–31; utilization level of, 259, 266, 276–280, 303

Jumping rope, 267, 269, 272–273; skill progression in, 272

K

Keep-away game, 429

Keep It Up, 399

Kickball, 116

Kicking: characteristics of, 342; control level of, 345, 347, 349–351; developmental stages of, 343–344; games for, 116, 347, 353–356; and **ideas for development and observational focus**, 346, 348–356; precontrol level of, 342, 346, 347, 348–349; proficiency level of, 346, 347, 354–356; progression spiral for, 347; utilization level of, 345, 347, 351–354, 389. *See also* Punting

Killer (game), 249

Kinte, Kunta, 134

Korbut, Olga, 139

Kounin, Jacob, 68

L

Laban, Rudolf, 144

Leading and following, 203, 205, 208, 209, 229–230, 299

Leaping, 114, 130, 136, 158, 183, 211; pattern of, 215–216. *See also* Traveling

Learning centers (stations), 45, 52, 489; in gymnastics, 148, 292, 297–298

Learning environment, establishing, 23, 53–58

Lesson planning. *See* Planning

Levels (in space), 15, 16, 17, 27, 153, 248; in balancing, 325, 326; defined, 154, 161; **ideas for development and observational focus** re concept of, 161–164; in jumping and landing, 269, 279; in kicking, 347, 349; in rolling, 306; teaching concept of, 162–164, 169–170, 184; in throwing, 383, 391, 394; in volleying, 402–411 passim

Levels of motor ability. *See* Skill proficiency, generic levels of

Linear approach, 5–6

Listening games, 54–55; examples of, 56

Listening skill, 54–56, 58

Location, 15, 16, 17, 133

Locomotor skills, 15, 17, 126. *See also* Chasing, fleeing, and dodging; Traveling

M

McGee, Rosemary, 86

Mainstreaming, 49–50, 57

Magladry Ball, 119

Management time, 54, 57, 100; recording of, 97, 98, 99

Manipulative skills, 15, 17, 126, 157, 208, 209. *See also specific skill theme*

Mass calisthenics, 43, 44, 52

Matching, 203

Meeting and parting, 203, 206–207, 307

Mini-Hockey, 475

Mirroring, 203, 206

Moore, Kenny, 51

"Mork award," 64

Motor ability, *See* Skill proficiency, generic levels of

Mountain climbing, 481

Movement concepts, 3, 15–19, 21, 27, 124; in dance, 126–128; teaching of, 27–38. *See also* Effort concepts; Relationships; Space awareness

Movement experiences. *See* Skill themes

Music, 182; in dance, 128–130, 132, 136, 226–227, 282, 485–488; suggested records for, 485–488; in traveling, 223, 226–227, 230

N

Net, construction of, 412

Net games, 443–444

Nonmanipulative skills, 15, 17, 126. *See also specific skill theme*

Notation, gymnastics, 144

Numbers (game), 56

O

Objectives, writing, 36

Objects, concept of relationships with, 15, 16, 17, 280; in balancing, 317, 320; in dance, 131; and **ideas for development and observational focus**, 194–201; teaching, 185, 193–201, 209;

in traveling, 221, 245; in volleying, 405, 410

Observation, 23, 27, 70, 81; effective, learning of, 75–78, 83–84; process of, 71–75

Observational focus. *See* Development and observational focus, ideas for

Obstacle couuses, 143, 196, 197; for balancing, 327; for dribbling, 424, 425; for jumping and landing, 271, 275; for kicking, 350, 351, 352; for rolling, 298–306 passim; sets for, 225, 231, 298, 301, 350, 352; for striking, 469; for traveling, 225, 231

One-on-one game, 425

Opie, Iona, 243

Opie, Peter, 243

Organization. *See* Class organization

P

Paddle, construction of, 437

Parents, 5; conferences with, 88; involvement of, 480, 481; reports to, 64, 65, 68, 81, 87–88, 89

Partners, 115, 143, 161, 166; in balancing, 314, 320, 327; in chasing, fleeing, and dodging games, 243, 245, 246–247, 251; and concept of relationships, 185, 191, 197–201, 203, 205–207, 210; in dance, 131; in dribbling games, 425, 426, 428; in jumping and landing, 269, 270, 277, 278; in kicking, 347–353 passim; in punting, 359, 363–364, 365; in rolling, 306, 307–308; in striking, 432, 433, 440, 441, 442, 466, 468–469, 473; stunts with, 489–493; in throwing and catching, 374, 376, 377, 384, 385, 388–393 passim; in volleying, 401, 402, 410, 411, 412, 413, 428; in weight transfer, 332, 333, 338, 489–493

Pathways, 15, 16, 17, 18, 153, 157, 196, 199–200, 208; in chasing,

fleeing, and dodging, 248–249, 250, 253; in dance, 133, 282; defined, 154, 164; in dribbling, 417, 423, 424, 425; **ideas for development and observational focus** re concept of, 164–167; in jumping and landing, 282; in kicking, 346, 351; in rolling, 300; in striking, 433, 437, 441, 456, 465, 467; teaching concept of, 28, 164–167, 169–170, 171; in throwing, 385, 390, 391, 392; in traveling, 220, 229, 231; in volleying, 409, 411

People, concept of relationships with, 15, 16, 17, 280; in dance, 131, 133; **ideas for development and observational focus** re, 205–209; teaching, 185, 193, 201–210; in traveling, 221; in volleying, 405, 410

Performance: analysis of, 23, 74, 75, 76, 78; observation of, 23, 71–78; prescription to improve, 23, 75, 77–78, 88; solo, 201, 202–203; standards of, 57, 58

Person-to-person dialogue, 63–64, 69

Photographs, for analyzing motor skills, 100

Physical education: future possibilities for, 477–482; recess vs., 23, 46, 53–54, 57, 58

Piking, 332

Pirate's Treasure, 254

Planning, 23; effective, 27–36, 54; enjoyable, 37–38; and lesson design, 36–37; necessity of, 25; reflective, 25–27, 32–34

Portable environments, 481

Practice: decisions regarding, 40; and game skills, 113–117; opportunities for, 94, 95, 96, 101–102, 115–116, 342; value of, 37

Praise, 55, 57, 60, 158

Precontrol level, 19, 107, 108, 110, 111, 177, 210; in dance, 128, 130; in games, 114, 244–245, 381; in gymnastics, 142, 143, 245, 267,

293–294, 315–317. *See also under specific skill theme*

Principals, role in discipline, 66, 68

Problem-solving, 45, 52, 202

Proficiency level, 19, 107, 109, 110, 111, 172; in dance, 130, 132, 327; in games, 252–256, 282–283, 292, 308, 347, 354–356, 365–366, 373, 394–399, 402, 413–414, 415, 432, 433, 442–444, 470–475; in gymnastics, 143, 145, 283–285, 292, 304–307, 327–329. *See also under specific skill theme*

Progress record, 36, 80, 81–84

Progression spiral, 19–21. *See also under specific skill theme*

Punt Over, 365–366

Punting, 15, 17; characteristics of, 356; control level of, 359, 361–363; developmental stages of, 357–358; games for, 365–366; and **ideas for development and observational focus,** 359, 361–366; precontrol level of, 359, 361; proficiency level of, 359, 365–366; progression spiral for, 360; utilization level of, 359, 363–364. *See also* Kicking

R

Races, relay, 44, 52

Racket, construction of, 434

Recess, physical education vs., 23, 46, 53–54, 57, 58

Recordings, duration, 98–100, 102

Recordings, tape. *See* Tape recordings

Records of progress, 36, 80, 81–84

Recreation programs, 482

Reflective planning, 25–27; guide for, 32–35

Reflective teaching, 3; concept of, 6; components of, 7; implications of, 12

Relationships: of body parts, 15, 16, 17, 185, 186, 187–193; in dance, 131, 133; **ideas for development**

and observational focus re concept of, 188–201 passim, 205–209; with objects, 15, 16, 17, 131, 185, 193–201, 209, 221, 245, 280, 317, 320, 405, 410; with people, 15, 16, 17, 131, 133, 185, 193, 201–210, 221, 280, 405, 410; teaching concepts of, 28, 151, 185–210

Relays, 44, 52

Reports to parents, 54, 65, 68, 81, 87–88, 89

Research, future, 482

Resource centers, 481–482

Rewards: class, 66–67, 68; individual, 63–64, 68

Rhythm instruments, 128; construction of, 129

Rhythmic experiences: in dance, 128, 138, 139; in jumping, 266, 272, 274, 276; in traveling, 221, 223, 230, 232, 233

Rip-Flag, 255–256

Rocky (movie), 272

Rolling, 15, 16, 17, 19, 183, 184, 193; control level of, 142, 275, 287, 291, 295–299; in dance, 286, 302–303, 307; defined, 286; developmental stages of, 288–290; fascination of, 286; in games, 286, 292, 308; in gymnastics, 142, 286, 293–302, 304–307; and **ideas for development and observational focus,** 293–308; precontrol level of, 108, 287, 291, 293–295; proficiency level of, 287, 292, 305–308; progression spiral for, 287; utilization level of, 287, 292, 299–304, 314, 323–324

Roots (movie), dance based on, 134

Rope: balancing on, 314, 328–329; construction of, 195; jumping, 267, 269, 272–273

Run Down, 399

Run the Bases, 395

Running, 15, 17, 126, 136, 158, 182, 183, 196, 362, 391, 396; in concept development, 158, 182, 183, 196; pattern of, 213–214; precontrol level of, 211. *See also* Traveling

S

Safety, 55, 58, 72, 227, 279; in gymnastics, 146, 147, 148, 149, 285

Sanders, Steve, 144

Sawhorse, construction of, 318

Scheme theory, 14, 21

Schmidt, R. A., 15

Schools: as community centers, 481; differences in, 5–12 passim

Seidentop, Daryl, 67, 68

Self-space, 153; defined, 153; **ideas for development and observational focus** re concept of, 156; teaching concept of, 154–156, 169

Self-testing, in gymnastics, 139, 148

Sequence, in developing skill themes, 35; sample of, 31. *See also* Progression spiral

Sequences, development of: in balancing, 314, 321, 324–326; in dribbling, 425; effort concepts and, 179, 183; in jumping and landing, 275, 280; in rolling, 297, 302, 304, 305, 306; in traveling, 230; in volleying, 405; in weight transfer, 333, 341

Set induction, 33

Shaker, construction of, 129

Shapes. *See* Body shapes

Simon Says, 188

Six-Player Tee Ball, 471

Skating, 329

Skiing, 329

Skill proficiency, generic levels of, 107–109, 111; and games, 114–115; and motor development, 111; as task related, 110, 111; teacher's use of, 111. *See also levels* under specific skill theme

Skill progress. *See* Progression spiral

Skill themes, 3, 13–21, 27; characteristics of, 13–14; and movement concepts, 3, 15–19, 28, 151; sequence for developing (*see* Progression spiral); support for, 14–15; teaching by, 3, 13–21, 151–152

Skipping, 15, 17, 126, 130, 211, 387; in concept development, 158, 165, 183, 184, 196; pattern of, 216. *See also* Traveling

Sliding, 196, 211; pattern of, 217

Soccer, 244, 354–356, 400

Soccer Keep-Away, 354–355

Socioeconomic status (SES), learning styles and, 6, 7, 9

Softball, 118

Solo performance, 201, 202–203

Space, concept of, as quality of movement, 15n, 172n. *See also* General space; Self-Space

Space awareness, 15, 16, 17, 239; in dance, 133; **ideas for development and observational focus** re, 156–168 passim; teaching of, 28, 151, 153–171. *See also* Directions; Extensions; General Space; Levels; Location; Pathways; Self-space, concept of

Speed, 143, 157, 158, 200, 206, 207, 228; in chasing, fleeing and dodging, 244–253 passim; in dribbling, 423, 425, 426, 427; **ideas for development and observational focus** re concept of, 175–177; in kicking, 348–352 passim; in rolling, 297, 299, 300; in striking, 468; teaching concept of, 19, 172, 174–175, 183–184, 226; in throwing, 390, 393, 394, 396

Speedball, 400, 416

Sports, games vs., 113n, 121

Spotting, 147

Standards for performance, 57, 58

Stations. *See* Learning centers

Stilts: balancing on, 314, 320, 328; construction of, 321, 324

Stop and Go, 56

Stretching and curling, 15, 17, 126, 130, 156, 190–191; control level of, 333, 337; proficiency level of, 330, 332, 340, 341; utilization level of, 337, 340

Striking, 16, 171, 207, 292, 402–403, 445

Striking, with body part. *See* Dribbling; Volleying

Striking, with long-handled implements, 15, 17, 118–119; control level of, 454–455, 456; developmental stages of, 446–453; in games, 118, 119, 474–475; and **ideas for development and observational focus,** 457–475; pattern of, 445; precontrol level of, 108, 454, 456; proficiency level of, 455, 456; purpose of teaching, 454; progression spiral for, 456; utilization level of, 455, 456

Striking, with rackets and paddles, 15, 17; characteristics of, 429; control level of, 429–430, 437–440; developmental stages of, 430–432; in games, 432, 433, 442–444; and **ideas for development and observational focus,** 434–444; precontrol level of, 429, 434–436; proficiency level of, 430, 442–444; progression spiral for, 433; utilization level of, 432, 440–442

Student logs, 80, 84–86, 88, 89

Surfing, 329

Swinging, 156, 180, 305

Switch and Rotate, 56

T

Tag games, 239, 240, 242–243, 247–256, 428

Tape recordings: of lessons, 61, 92; of observations, 83–84. *See also* Videotapes

Tapping. *See* Dribbling

Task sheets, 47–48, 52

Tasks: related to skill proficiency, 110, 111; variation in, 35–36, 146

Teacher education institutions, 480

Teachers: assistance for, 482; attitude of, 53; experience of, 6, 9, 90–91, 479; future, 479–482; layman, 481; role of, 51

Teaching: future, 479–482; invariant, 6, 7; reflective, 6, 7, 12; by themes, 3, 13–21, 151–152; tutorial, 480; variables in, 6–11; variation, 6, 7, 35, 114–115. *See also* Class organization; Evaluation, of teaching performance

Tennis, 454

Tests, standardized, 80, 86, 89

Themes, teaching. *See* Skill themes

Thomas, Kurt, 139

Throwing, 15, 17, 35, 37, 169, 170–171, 199, 207, 309, 428; combined with catching, 367; control level of, 108, 247, 248, 319, 373, 374, 382–386; defined, 367; developmental stages of, 369–373; evaluating, 368, 373; in games, 114, 115, 116, 119, 209, 373, 381, 387, 393–399; and **ideas for development and observational focus,** 381–399; precontrol level of, 373, 374, 381–382; proficiency level of, 308, 372, 374, 394–399; progression spiral for, 374; utilization level of, 277, 278, 303, 304, 373, 374, 386–394

Time (movement concept), 15, 16, 17, 173, 183–184; in balancing, 324, 327; in dance, 131

Time-out, for disruptive behavior, 63, 68

Times, learning and nonlearning, 54, 57, 58; recording of, 96–100, 102

Tinikling, 221, 233, 234, 235

Token systems, 63–65, 68

Traveling, 15, 16, 17, 28, 126, 309; and concepts of relationships, 187–200, 203, 205, 207; control level of, 218, 220, 221, 224–228, 421, 423, 463; in dance, 126, 127, 131, 133, 219–238 passim; and effort concepts, 173–183 passim; in game designs, 220; in gymnastics, 142, 143, 145; and **ideas for development and observational focus,** 222–237; patterns of, 158, 211–217, 221, 231, 236–238, 245, 274, 275–276, 305; precontrol level of, 211, 218, 219, 221, 222–224, 333; proficiency level of, 220, 221, 232–237, 394, 402; progression spiral for, 221; and space awareness, 156–171 passim; utilization level of, 219, 220, 221, 229–232, 300, 302, 352, 386–392 passim, 402, 423–424, 425. *See also specific skill theme*

Traveling (game), 56

Trimble, Tom, 457

Turning, 15, 17, 37, 183; control level of, 299; in dance, 126–127, 136; utilization level of, 325

Twisting, 15, 17, 126, 156; control level of, 299, 333, 337; proficiency level of, 330, 332, 340, 341; utilization level of, 325, 337, 340

U

Unicycling, 329

Unison and contrast, 203

Utilization level, 19, 107, 109, 110, 111, 177; in dance, 128, 131, 302–303, 307, 324–325; in games, 115, 250–252, 278, 353–354, 387, 393, 411; gymnastics at, 143, 145, 279–280, 300–302, 323–326. *See also under specific skill theme*

V

Variation: in activities, 34–35; in tasks, 35–36, 38, 146; in teaching, 6, 7, 35, 114–115

Vaulting, 280–282, 284–285
Vaulting box, construction of, 281
Videotapes, 341, 480–481
Volleyball: Blanket, 393–394;
    Infinity, 413
Volleying, 15, 16, 17, 115; control
    level of, 275, 401, 402, 405–409;
    defined, 400; in games, 115, 402,
    411, 413–414, 415; precontrol
    level of, 400, 401, 402, 403–404;
    proficiency level of, 282, 307,
    401, 402–403, 412–415;
    progression spiral for, 401;
    utilization level of, 278, 401, 402,
    410–412

W
Waddling, 196
Waiting time, 54, 58, 100; recording
    of, 97, 98, 99

Walking, 15, 17, 126; in concept
    development, 157, 158, 159, 182,
    183, 196; pattern of, 211–212;
    precontrol level of, 211. *See also*
    Traveling
Wall Ball, 442–443
Weight, concept of, 172, 324; and
    **ideas for development and
    observational focus,** 178–180;
    teaching, 177–180, 183, 184
Weight support, 189, 197, 201;
    control level of, 108, 296;
    precontrol level of, 145;
    proficiency level of, 145; in
    rolling, 293, 296; utilization level
    of, 143, 145. *See also* Balancing
Weight transfer, 15–19 passim, 126,
    156, 190, 195; in balancing, 314,
    323–331 passim, 337; control
    level of, 108, 275, 331, 333; forms

of, 330; in gymnastics, 143, 145,
    314, 323–329 passim; and **ideas
    for development and
    observational focus,** 334–341; in
    jumping and landing, 275;
    precontrol level of, 293, 330, 333;
    proficiency level of, 327–328,
    330, 332, 333; progression spiral
    for, 333; in rolling, 286, 293, 300;
    in striking, 468; utilization level
    of, 143, 300, 323–326, 331, 333; in
    volleying, 409
Whiffle Ball Golf, 470–471
Wickstrom, Ralph L., 213, 257
Wilson, Nettie, 116

Y
Yarn ball, construction of, 375
Youth-serving agencies, 482